Cornwall
& the Isles of Scilly

The Complete Guide

Cornwall

& the Isles of Scilly

David Clegg

First edition 2003: ISBN 1 899293 83 3
Second (revised) edition 2005: ISBN: 1 904744 99 0

Matador
9 De Montfort Mews, Leicester LE1 7FW, UK
Tel: (+44) 1166 255 9312 / 255 9311   Email: matador@troubador.co.uk   Web: www.troubador.co.uk/matador

For Becca and Georgia

Front cover photograph: Pendeen Lighthouse, © David Clegg
Back cover photograph: Hayle Sands, © David Clegg

The publishers and author have made every effort to ensure the accuracy of information presented in this guide; however, they can accept no responsibility for any loss, injury or inconvenience sustained by any traveller as a result of advice contained in the Guide.

Considerable research has gone into making this Guide as accurate and up to date as possible, but inevitably things change. Please help us by telling us of anything that we have got wrong or if we've left something important out; suggestions, comments or corrections should be sent to the Publishers at the address above, and all such contributions will be acknowledged in future editions of this Guide.

Typesetting: Troubador Publishing Ltd, Leicester, UK
Printed and bound by The Cromwell Press Ltd, Trowbridge, Wilts, UK

Matador is an imprint of Troubador Publishing Ltd

Contents

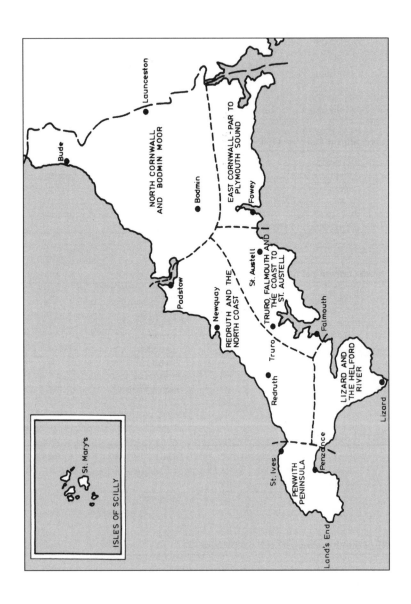

List of Maps

Cornwall
The Complete Guide

Introduction

Cornwall, the south-west extremity of England, is one of its most distinctive regions. It was the last bastion of the English Celts, who maintained their language and culture here long after it had been extinguished in the rest of the country. It is dominated by the presence of the sea, with nowhere being more than 30 minutes drive from the coast. The wind-lashed cliffs of Penwith and the north coast contrast with the sheltered estuaries of the southern coastline. Inland are the bleak granite moorlands of Penwith and Bodmin with more fertile, rolling hills occupying the lower land.

A surprise to many visitors is the legacy of the once strong industrial economy, particularly tin and copper mining, when in the C18 and C19 Cornwall was the world's largest producer. China clay mining continues around St Austell and granite and slate quarrying is centred on Delabole on the northern edge of Bodmin Moor. Today, the county is a depressed economy, officially classified as one of the poorer regions of Europe. Tourism is now the most flourishing industry and the main employer in the county.

There is much to attract the visitor. The superb cliff scenery and wonderful beaches rival any in Europe. The South West Coast Path follows the entire Cornish coast, providing some of the best walking in Britain, while the sheltered estuaries of the south coast, particularly the Helford and Fal rivers, provide beautiful scenery and marvellous sailing. The Isles of Scilly have a unique atmosphere of a long lost England with little if any commercial development and some of the best beaches, walks and wildlife in the country. The coast has the brash seaside resorts of Bude and Newquay, but also plenty of smaller, unspoilt fishing villages and resorts. Many of the best beaches are in relatively remote locations and few people ever visit. St Ives is a major resort that has managed to retain its character and integrity despite the number of visitors. It is also the site of the Tate Gallery and many other artist's studios and galleries. Indeed the whole of Cornwall, but particularly Penwith, has numerous artist's galleries and studios which are open to visitors.

South West Coast Path

Tate Gallery

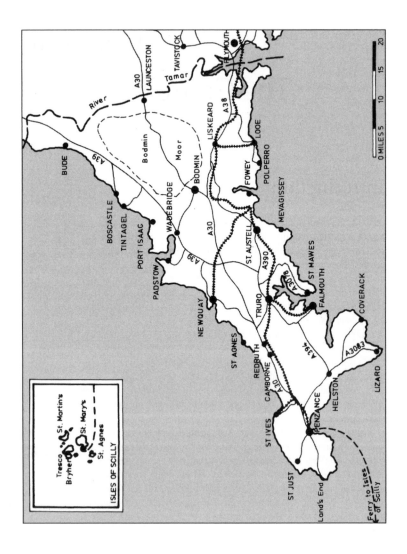

It is not a county particularly noted for its country houses, but those at Trerice, Lanhydrock, Antony and Cothele can hold their own with the best of their age. When it comes to gardens, the mild climate has led to the creation of an astonishing number of major importance – Heligan, Trebah and Glendurgan being just a few. The Eden Project, near St Austell, is one of the major tourist attractions in the country with its two huge biomes with their own micro climate. Cornwall is not an area of large towns, but Truro and Penzance have a certain metropolitan feel and good examples of Georgian and Regency architecture. Falmouth is the major port and a lively place in its own right. The new National Maritime Museum Cornwall is likely to draw even more visitors to the town, which is also to be home to the new University of Cornwall. There are a number of pleasant market towns, like Lostwithiel and Launceston, that have been all but untouched by tourism and many smaller villages and coastal settlements that have retained their traditional character.

The Eden Project

National Maritime Museum Cornwall

Most visitors come in the summer months, particularly the school holiday period, when it can get unpleasantly crowded. However, there are always areas that receive few visitors and more and more people are beginning to realize that Cornwall, out of peak season, has much to offer the visitor.

Getting There

The majority of visitors to Cornwall arrive by car and there are certain benefits in having a car to travel around, especially outside the summer when public transport within Cornwall is more limited. The main approaches are the M4 and M5 motorways from the east and north respectively and then the A30 from Exeter. The A30 is recently much improved and is largely dual carriageway. However, at peak times there can still be delays. An alternative route from London and the South East is the A303 from the M3 motorway at Basingstoke, joining the M5 at Exeter. This, again, is largely dual carriageway and is a more direct route from the south of London than the M4. The journey time from London to Penzance is around 5–6 hours.

Express buses ply the same routes and link Cornwall to all the major towns of Britain. National Express have the most comprehensive service. For example, they have seven daily buses between Penzance and London taking 8–9 hours. The bus normally stops at St Ives, Camborne, Redruth, Truro, St Austell, Bodmin, Liskeard and Plymouth, as well as many stops between these. The cheapest fares are £43.00 return, and these have to be booked at least seven days in advance. Services from other towns within Cornwall are conveniently timed to connect with these London buses. Full details and fares are available by telephoning **08705 01 01 04**.

Buses

Cornwall is well served by main line train services with 11 daily connections to London Paddington. The journey takes around 5–6 hours to Penzance and is probably the most relaxing way to travel. The part from Exeter to Penzance is particularly scenic. The train stops at all the main stations on the west coast line in Cornwall. Fares vary widely, but the cheapest is the Apex Return which costs

Train

£35.50, while the saver return is £65.90. The Apex fare needs to be booked at least seven days in advance and seats are limited. Sleeper compartments are also available on the overnight train and are good value at £20.00 per person for a double and £30.00 for a single. There are connections to all the major cities in Britain via Plymouth. Further information is available from any railway station or rail booking office or telephone **08457 484950**. Cycles can be carried on trains if a reservation is made in advance, £1.00 charge.

Air travel

Air travel is also a viable consideration with Ryan Air (www.ryanair.com tel. **0871 246 000**) flying between London Stansted and Newquay. There are two flights per day and fares start from an improbably low £0.99. Air Southwest (www.airsouthwest.com tel. **0870 241 6830**) have four flights per day from London Gatwick with fares starting at £20. Tickets can be purchased on-line or by telephone.

Ferry

The only direct international connection to Cornwall is via the Brittany Ferries service to Plymouth from Santander and Roscoff. There are two sailings a week from Santander (one only in winter) and between twelve a week in summer to six a week in mid-winter from Roscoff. The journey time is 24 hours from Santander and six hours from Roscoff. Further information and fares are available from Brittany Ferries, **08705 360 360**.

🚗 Getting Around

Cornwall is one of the largest counties in England at 350,000 hectares. It is dominated by its coastline with nowhere more than 15 miles from the sea – in the west the land mass is no more than 8–10 miles wide. The main arterial routes run through the centre with the A30 and the West Coast railway line providing the two transport spines off which other spurs radiate to feed into the coastal communities.

Car

The easiest and most convenient way to travel within Cornwall is by car. Whilst most places are connected by public transport, at least in the summer months, services are sometimes infrequent. By car, the more remote areas are opened up and there is no waiting for transport connections. The distances are small and traffic is light outside the peak summer months. However, many of the minor roads are very narrow and often incredibly steep as well. Drivers need to be confident and ensure their vehicles are in good condition. Those towing caravans and trailers need to be particularly aware of the steep gradients and should heed any warning signs. Some of the smaller, more picturesque villages were not designed for cars and you may need to leave vehicles on the outskirts and walk in. Also, in the more popular resorts such as St Ives, it can be difficult to park in the peak summer months.

Public Transport

Convenient as the car is, it is by no means impractical to tour Cornwall by public transport and there are some decided advantages. For a start it can be more relaxing, it can link in well with walking and cycling expeditions and you are not going to have any worries over car parking or negotiating the tortuous, winding and steep lanes. Often, you will find that you will be able to get further into the centre of towns by public transport than you will by car, where you may well end up parking on the outskirts of the more popular tourist destinations.

Train services within Cornwall are restricted to the main West Coast line which passes through the centre of the county and the branch lines to Gunnislake, Looe, Newquay, Falmouth and St Ives. This is more comprehensive than it sounds for there are regular services between Plymouth and Penzance stopping at all the stations between. Given the linear nature of the county you are never that far from your destination from any of these stations. If there is no branch line available, there is likely to be a connecting bus service. Even if this fails, distances are likely to be short enough to make a taxi connection perfectly affordable. Besides being the most relaxing and comfortable way to travel, the Cornish railways also have the considerable bonus of being some of the most scenic in the country. In particular, the branch lines to St Ives, Falmouth and Gunnislake are worth a trip in their own right for the marvellous views. Further information is available from any railway station or by telephoning **08457 484950**. Tourist Information Centres will also be able to provide you with train times. Rail Rover tickets are available which provide unlimited travel on railways in Cornwall for a set number of days, for example any 3 days in 7 in the summer months for £18.00, or 8 days in 15 for £33.00. These could be worthwhile if you were planning a lot of travel by rail. They can be purchased from any staffed railway station in Cornwall.

Train

Bus services in the County vary from summer to winter. In the summer, there are a number of additional services, particularly along the coast and to other tourist destinations. Many of these stop or are severely curtailed outside the summer months – normally from the end of May to the end of September. Bus deregulation has confused the picture with regard to timetabling with no less than 35 bus companies operating in Cornwall. However, the largest company is First and they provide a reasonably comprehensive service throughout the county. Their customer helpline is **0870 608 2608**. They can provide information on services, timetables and fares. There are Bus Explorer tickets available which allow unlimited travel for a set number of days and are good value if you are intending to do a lot of travelling by bus. They can be purchased on the bus or in advance. Bus services and frequency are mentioned in the relevant chapters, but it would be well worth purchasing a local timetable if you are intending to do a lot of travelling by bus.

Bus

Ferries form an essential part of the county's transportation system providing many links across the county's estuaries and rivers. Several of them take vehicles but there are also a number that will only take passengers and cycles. Details are provided in the relevant parts of the guide.

Ferry

Given the hilly nature of much of the terrain, it may be thought that cycle touring is only for the diehard enthusiast. However, there are areas of the county which are relatively flat and lend themselves to cycling. The Lizard, the area around the River Fal, Redruth and Camborne, inland from Padstow along the Camel Trail and the Penwith Peninsula all make wonderful areas for cycle touring with relatively easy going and plenty of narrow lanes to explore. Details on cycle hire are included in the guide.

Cycling

Walking   Walking is a surprisingly good way of getting around. The distances are relatively small and the South West Coast Path provides a continuous circuit from which detours can be made inland to sites of interest. There are plenty of towns and villages with overnight accommodation and it is easy to start and finish routes to coincide with the available public transport connections. Further information is given in the section on Outdoor Pursuits.

For onward travel to the Isles of Scilly, there is the option of ferry, helicopter and aeroplane. Full details are given in the relevant chapter.

Climate and When to Go

Cornwall is blessed with a temperate climate that rarely gets very hot in the summer or too cold in the winter. Temperatures are the mildest in England and, while westerly storms can bring cold spells and the occasional snowstorm in winter, prolonged cold weather is rare. The average January temperature for the south coast is 5°C (41 F) while the Isles of Scilly has an average of 8°C (46 F). Summer average temperatures are relatively low compared to the rest of the country. Rainfall is well distributed throughout the year, but within the county there are significant variations from around 35 inches on the coast to over 70 inches on the high moorland. Cornwall is also considerably sunnier than the rest of England with June and July being the sunniest months. Wind and, to a lesser extent fog, are common and more in evidence in the winter than the summer months.

When to go depends very much on what you want to do on your visit. If you want to sunbathe, then summer is the only time to go. However, the school holiday period from late July to early September is the busiest and the more popular places can become unpleasantly crowded. Any time outside this period should be fine and the weather is normally good between late May and the end of September. For walking, any time is good, although the winter months are more prone to storms and rain and protective clothing will be required. However, on a fine, crisp winter's day the coast path is at its best. The crowds have also vanished and you can virtually have the place to yourself. If you are sightseeing, however, you need to bear in mind that many of the historic houses and other sites of interest close down from the end of October to April or May. Some guest houses and restaurants also close, but there are always enough to meet demand. Probably the best months to visit are May/June and September/October when it is still pleasantly warm, but relatively uncrowded. All the sites and attractions will be open and the summer bus services running.

Information and Maps

Tourism is a mainstay of the Cornish economy and there are no shortage of Tourist Information Centres (TICs). There are 24, with virtually every town of any size having its own. They can all provide maps and information relating to the local area, as well as full lists of accommodation. Most will also book accommodation if required, although there may be a small charge for this service. Full details of local TICs are listed in the text. The main Cornwall Tourist Board can be contacted at Pydar House, Pydar Street, Truro, TR1 1EA (**01872 274057**).

**Cornwall
Tourist Board**

The TICs can provide you with, generally free, maps of the towns and area they serve and these are adequate for most uses. However, for more detailed information and particularly for walkers, the *Ordnance Survey* produce a series of maps of the County. The best for everyday use is probably the Landranger Series at 1:50,000 scale (2cm to 1 km). This scale allows most topographical features to be distinguished along with all footpaths. They can be purchased from any good bookshop and most TICs. They also produce a 1:25,000 Outdoor Leisure Map to the Scilly Isles which is in greater detail and highlights those items of interest to the visitor.

For walkers on the South West Coast Path, there is a series of four excellent Trail Guides published by *Aurum Press* in association with the *Countryside Commission* and *Ordnance Survey*, which cover the entire 600 miles from Minehead in Somerset to Poole in Dorset. Rather inconveniently, the Cornwall coast is covered by three of the guides. However, the main part from Padstow to Falmouth is covered in one volume. There are detailed route maps and descriptions of the flora, fauna and sites of interest along the path.

Accommodation

The price coding system that is used throughout this guide is on a scale of A to E and indicates the cost of the lowest priced double room in that establishment during the peak summer period. This is clearly marked by the telephone number of the listing for each establishment. It should be borne in mind that single rooms are likely to be considerably more than half the price of a double. In the off peak months, many establishments reduce their rates considerably and even where they do not you may be able to negotiate a discount.

**A –£44
B £45–£64
C £65–£80
D £81–£100
E £100+**

Cornwall has hundreds of places to stay ranging from luxury hotels to guest houses and hostels. The biggest concentrations are in the main tourist centres of Newquay, Falmouth, St Ives and Penzance, but there are places located throughout the county to cater for all tastes and pockets. The guide indicates a selection of places to stay in most locations, although full lists of accommodation are available from the local Tourist Information Centres. In most areas, outside the peak summer months, there will always be some accommodation available. However, if you want to stay in a specific hotel or guest house it is best to book in advance if possible. Where there is a particular shortage of accommodation in an area it is noted in the guide. In the peak summer months, late July to early September, it is advisable to reserve accommodation in advance. Telephone numbers of listed accommodation are provided in the guide, but if necessary Tourist Information Centres can book accommodation for you.

Hotel prices vary widely with the standard of the establishment. Some upmarket hotels will charge anything up to £200 for a double room per night, although many will have cheaper rooms and special rates for longer stays. The mid-range hotels will charge around £60–£80 for a double room. For this price you will get a

Hotels

comfortable en-suite room in a medium-sized hotel, but probably lacking any significant social or sporting facilities. The cheaper hotels will be more basic and often difficult to distinguish from the grander bed and breakfast places. Double rooms here will go for around £40–£60. In this sense, Cornwall is no different to the rest of Britain and hotel prices are woefully expensive compared to the Continent.

Guest Houses and Bed & Breakfast

Guest houses or bed and breakfast provide the bulk of the accommodation recommended in this book. They provide the only reasonably-priced accommodation in many areas and the best can provide a wonderfully warm and welcoming environment for the independent traveller. Many of them are also located in historic buildings and the guide indicates where this is so. They will all provide a substantial cooked breakfast and some provide evening meals on request. You can expect to pay between £40 and £60 for a double room. Pubs and inns often provide accommodation and this can also be reasonably priced. Many are also wonderful, historic buildings.

Pubs and Inns

Youth Hostels

The Youth Hostels Association, YHA (**0870 770 8868**) has a large number of hostels in Cornwall, many of them located in historic buildings and in beautiful locations. Accommodation is normally in dormitories, although some have smaller rooms that can be booked by groups. Entire hostels can also be booked by groups during the winter period when they would otherwise be closed. YHA hostels are only open to members of the Association and membership is restricted to residents of England and Wales. The fee is £14.00, under 18s £7.00 and you can join by contacting the YHA or at any youth hostel. Visitors who are members of a hostelling organization that is affiliated to Hostelling International have automatic membership of the YHA. Charges are around £10–£12 per night for a dormitory bed and they provide the only really cheap accommodation for the single traveller. For a couple, the difference in price between a hostel and the cheaper B&Bs is negligible. Most hostels provide meals, though they often have to be booked in advance. At peak times, and in particular, school holiday periods, hostels can become very busy and it is recommended to book ahead at these times. Hostel opening times vary and it is advised to check in advance by telephoning the number given in this guide. There are also several independent hostels in Cornwall who have no membership requirement but are run on similar, although less formal, lines than the YHA hostels.

Camping

Camping provides an alternative to all of the above and will probably represent the cheapest option. Realistically, a car will be required as many campsites are located some way outside towns and away from public transport routes. If you intend to camp, it is worth getting hold of one of the many comprehensive guides to campsites. Two of the best are the English Tourism Council's *Official Guide to Camping and Caravan Parks in Britain*, £5.99 and the AA's, *Caravan and Camping, Britain and Ireland*, £9.99. With the exception of the Isles of Scilly, this guide does not recommend any sites, although there are a large number throughout the county.

Self-catering

Self-catering is another option and there are many attractive properties for rent, often in beautiful locations. It can be good value for large groups or families who may want to base themselves in one particular area. There are a number of companies who provide such accommodation and the TIC's can also provide lists of self-catering properties in their area. The English Tourist Council's *Official Guide to Self Catering Holidays* £9.99 lists over 8000 properties throughout the country. Of the many firms specializing in renting properties you could try:

English Country Cottages Grove Farm Barns, Fakenham, Norfolk, NR21 9NB (**01328 864041**). Some 2000 cottages and other properties in the rural areas of England.

National Trust PO Box 536, Melksham, Wilts SN2 8SX (**01225 791199**) have about 200 cottages and other properties for rent. They are all historic buildings and are invariably well restored and furnished. Many of them are also set in beautiful surroundings. Highly recommended.

Landmark Trust Shottesbrooke, Maidenhead, Berks SL6 3SW (**01628 825925**) similarly specializes in the restoration and letting of historic buildings. The Egyptian House in Penzance is typical of the type of unusual building they tend to feature. Rooms are beautifully furnished, often with genuine antiques. Rates tend to be on the high side.

Food and Drink

The prices quoted in the guide are inevitably just an indication of costs and represent the price for a meal of two courses with a drink. In the listings, they are indicated by the letter I, M or E, immediately after the telephone number of the establishment.

Inexpensive under £15
Moderate £16 – £25
Expensive over £25

England is not particularly noted for its cuisine or the quality of its regional cooking. However, Cornwall is something of an exception with many establishments making a point of exploiting the county's abundance of high quality, fresh produce, particularly the fish and seafood. The large number of hotels, pubs and restaurants means that most areas will usually have at least one good place to eat. Not surprisingly, the major towns, with certain notable exceptions, provide the best choice when it comes to eating out. However, there are also some smaller towns, like Padstow and Porthleven, where a particular concentration of fine restaurants have created small centres of culinary excellence.

The speciality of the region is fish and seafood, which is landed at harbours around the coast, but particularly Newlyn, the busiest fishing port in the country. The other regional speciality is the Cornish pasty – an ubiquitous pastry case filled with a variety of fillings, but traditionally, meat and vegetables. It is known to date back at least 300 years and was, supposedly, first baked for miners who would hold the distinctive crimped edge to eat it, so that their dirty fingers would not soil the food. Such is the reverence with which the Cornish pasty is held that when a New York Times food critic recently declared it fit for use only as a doorstop, there was a local outcry with the Stars and Stripes being burnt. Other specialities are Saffron Cake and the ubiquitous Cream Tea, scones with clotted cream and jam.

While restaurants are usually the best bet for a decent meal, one should not forget that most pubs also serve food and that standards are often high. Prices are generally cheaper than eating at a restaurant and the atmosphere more informal.

Drink in Cornwall means beer. There are very few local wines, although obviously foreign wines are readily available. Cornwall used to be something of a desert for real ale, but recent years have seen a resurgence of pubs stocking the real thing. Many are guest beers that are brought in from elsewhere in England. Cornwall also has three breweries of its own – the largest, *St Austell*, has been trading for over 150 years, while *Sharp's* and *Skinner's* are more recent developments. All produce excellent ales with Sharp's being particularly highly regarded. There are also a number of micro breweries which produce beer, normally for their own premises – the Blue Anchor at Helston being the most notable and one of the best.

Outdoor Pursuits

Organized Sports

Cornwall is a large county with a small population. As such, its contribution to the sporting life of the nation is limited. There is no Football League team in the county for instance – the nearest being Plymouth, just over the boundary in Devon. Nor is the county represented in the County Cricket Leagues. Where the Cornishman is a force though is in the sport of Rugby Union, which is played avidly throughout the county. While none of the county's clubs can hold a place in the major English Leagues, the county side has been a formidable force in the County Championship.

Walking

South West Coast Path Cornwall has some of the best coastal walking in Britain with the South West Coast Path extending the whole length of the coastline. The north coast between Morwenstoe and Polzeath, the Penwith Peninsula and the Lizard have some of the most dramatic coastal cliff walking, while the south coast is characterised by lower hills surrounding more sheltered estuaries and coves. Guides are available to the Coast Path (see Information and Maps) and the South West Coast Path Association produce an Annual Guide Book and more detailed Path Descriptions covering short sections. Guides and membership enquiries should be directed to the Membership Secretary, South West Coast Path Association, Windlestraw, Penquit, Nr. Ivybridge, PL21 0LU. While the guides are useful, they are by no means essential as the Path is extremely well signposted.

Bodmin Moor Bodmin Moor also provides fine walking opportunities in good weather and has a wealth of pre-historic remains. In foul, wet weather it can be a bleak and inhospitable place. Other long distance paths have been established within **St Michael's Way** Cornwall, including St Michael's Way (Lelant to St Michael's Mount) and The **The Saints' Way** Saints' Way (Padstow to Fowey). Further details are provided in the guide. The **Camel Trail** Camel Trail, inland from Padstow along the River Camel, is also open to walkers, although it is primarily marketed at cyclists.

Elsewhere, there are endless opportunities for short walks along the many footpaths. The Ordnance Survey 1:50,000 Landranger maps are perfectly adequate as they show all the footpaths and tracks. There are also a number of books of local walks. For example, the Ordnance Survey, Pathfinder Guide, *Cornwall Walks* contains descriptions of 28 short walks. There are also free leaflets available in TICs describing walks in their local areas.

Cycling

Cycling in Cornwall is quite a viable proposition – distances are relatively low, the number of places to stay and take refreshment is high and the topography, with a few notable exceptions, not too demanding. The best areas are probably the Lizard, the Penwith Peninsula and parts of the south coast. The Camel Trail is an off road cycle route between Padstow and Bodmin Moor and a number of other cycle ways have been developed around Redruth as part of the Mineral Tramways Project. Cycle hire is available in most towns and details are included in the guide. There are a number of cycling guides, for example the Ordnance Survey's, *One Day Routes* series which includes a volume on Cornwall and Devon (£9.99). The Cycle Touring Club (**0870 8730060**) publishes maps for long distance routes and information sheets for members.

Cycle Touring Club

Beaches, surfing and sailing

Beaches

Cornwall's beaches are some of the finest in Britain and the main reason why many people holiday in the county. With over 250 miles of coastline, they range from the developed and crowded to the secluded and unspoilt. Water quality and the cleanliness of beaches is generally good by England's standards, although none of Cornwall's beaches qualified for the European Blue Flag Award in 2002. However, this is partly due to the level of infrastructure and services required to qualify for an award, as many of Cornwall's best beaches are in secluded locations and not in the developed resorts. The guide includes descriptions of all the beaches in Cornwall. It is worth bearing in mind that dogs are banned from many of Cornwall's beaches during the summer months. Details are available from any TIC or local Council.

Despite its northern latitude and cold water, Cornwall has established itself as a significant surfing centre. Newquay, in particular, is the premier surfing centre in the country. At peak times, it is astonishing the number of surfers that pack the town. Fistral beach is the main break and there are regular international contests here in the summer. Many surfers prefer to escape the hype and crowds of Newquay and explore some of the more secluded beaches. Sennen Cove, with its exposed west facing beach is popular, as are Constantine Bay and Polzeath on the north coast. There are many smaller coves which are even more secluded and have good surf in the right conditions. Tuition is available, with the main centres being Newquay and St Ives. Surf equipment can be hired at many places along the coast – these are listed in the guide.

Surfing

Sailing is a popular activity and there are many clubs dotted along the coast. The majority of these are on the more sheltered and heavily populated south coast. A number of places hire sailing craft. You are normally required to produce evidence of some form of competence. Alternatively, you could join a trip on a

Sailing

crewed yacht. *Golden Blade Sailing* (**01209 715757**) offer one-day, two-day and longer trips from their Falmouth base.

Gig racing   Gig racing is a particularly Cornish sport and regular races take place during the summer months. The gigs are long-oared sea going craft and they are raced between fixed points. The centre of gig racing is the Isles of Scilly, where the sport first developed. The origin is said to have come from the practice of racing pilots out to waiting ships so that they could guide them through the treacherous waters. First one there got the job!

Art in Cornwall

Artists began to be attracted to Cornwall towards the end of the C19 when the railways were first opening up this remote and inaccessible area. The quality of the light, the wealth of subject matter and the low cost of living all helped to attract young artists who had been taught in the "plein air" studios of Brittany and the Lowlands. Significant artistic communities established themselves at Newlyn, Lamorna and St Ives.

The Newlyn and Lamorna Schools were at their peak in the years before the First World War when a succession of talented artists used the local subjects of fishermen and villagers to produce a series of masterly pictures, now recognized as internationally important. A picture by *Stanhope Forbes* recently became the first of the Newlyn School to fetch over £1 million at auction. The heyday for the St Ives' artists was to start later and stretched from the 1920s through to the 1960s with many world famous artists taking up residence in the town. The influences here were different and abstraction was the recurring theme of the St Ives artists. The importance of Cornwall to the arts in England was recognized in 1993 with the opening of the Tate Gallery in St Ives. It is dedicated to showing works of art associated with Cornwall.

Many artists still live and continue to be attracted to the area and West Cornwall, in particular, has the highest concentration of resident, working artists outside London. They constitute a significant micro economy within the county and the number of commercial galleries continues to grow. It is one of the factors that distinguishes a visit to Cornwall from many other destinations. The guide includes a comprehensive list of galleries for each area.

Architecture

Cornwall has few buildings of the highest architectural merit. However, it has a rich, vernacular tradition and its prehistoric remains are of national significance. The prehistoric structures of Cornwall are some of the oldest standing architecture in the country and, as such, the cliff forts, rock tombs and ancient courtyard houses are of major archaeological importance.

More so than in most places, Cornwall's buildings and architecture are a reflection of its history and culture. The Celtic tradition of dispersed hamlets and farms did nothing to promote great civic architecture. Instead, the isolated vernacular cottage became the archetype of Cornwall's buildings and is to be found throughout the county. However, along the coast, the essential communality of fishing required the formation of small settlements and, today, these constitute some of the most beautiful showcases for the vernacular architecture of England. The relative absence of Lords of the Manor in medieval Cornwall precluded the development of many large manor houses and stifled the patronage that existed elsewhere in the country. Only with the wealth from mining in the C18 and C19 did the gentry begin to build substantial houses and provide the churches, schools and institutions that respectable society required.

With regard to its building materials, Cornwall is the most distinct of all English counties. Unlike the rest of England there was little timber, so the medieval tradition of timber-framed construction is virtually unknown. Brick was also a late arrival, the first known use dating from 1700, and, even then, it was only used sparingly. Remoteness and poverty led Cornwall to rely upon its local natural materials for longer than most other areas of the country. They were primarily granite, the hardest of stones, and slate. Neither lend themselves to fine detail and embellishment and it is the rugged uniformity of these materials which gives Cornish vernacular architecture its special identity.

Roman and Saxon architecture is unknown – the surviving remains of these **Roman** times are the stone crosses found all over the county. Christian missionaries began to arrive in the C5 and the crosses marked the sites of simple, Christian worship, long before the erection of any churches. There are over 300, Celtic influenced, almost certainly from Ireland, and dating from the C5 through to the C11. Many are from the latter part of this period and these have been interpreted by some as a final flourish of Celtic culture against the growing influence of Saxon rule.

The Norman occupation brought an explosion of church building and Norman **Norman** work is still evident in around 140 churches with about 110 Norman fonts also surviving. Church architecture is as important in Cornwall as elsewhere in the country. Often, the church will be the earliest building still standing, as well as the biggest and most architecturally accomplished. The fixtures, fittings, glass and memorials within them are one of the greatest repositories of medieval art and craft that the country possesses. For the medieval masons, churches provided the opportunity to push their skill and creativity to the limit. Perhaps due to the intractable nature of the local granite, Cornish craftsmen tended to display their skills in the carving of wooden roofs, screens, bench ends and other furnishings, which are collectively some of the finest in the country.

It is unusual for churches to be of any one period or style. Normally you will find that successive rebuilding has resulted in a happy co-existence of the prevailing architectural styles of the time. After the first burst of Norman building, the main periods of further development were in the C15 and C16 and in the C19, when many of Cornwall's churches were modernised and rebuilt, some sensitively and some badly. In many respects, it is this fusion of styles that makes church architecture so interesting and important.

With only the faintest remains of Saxon work surviving, the Norman or Romanesque style is the earliest to be commonly found in Cornwall's churches. It is **Romanesque** characterized by round arches, thick walls and small windows with a typical cruciform plan. Richly carved decoration with zigzag and naturalistic patterns of leaves and beasts were common. The best examples of Norman architecture in Cornwall are found at St Germans and Morwenstow, both in the east where the Norman control was strongest. Towards the end of the C12 the arrival of the pointed arch from **Gothic** France led to the development of what has become known as the Gothic style. This enabled wall thicknesses to be reduced and windows enlarged, freeing the medieval mason to construct the lofty and richly decorated edifices we now associate with true Gothic architecture. Between Norman and Gothic there was a Transitional style including elements of both while Gothic architecture, itself, developed through several stylistic phases identified as Early English (1150–1280), Decorated (1280–1380) and Perpendicular (1380–1550). Early English was the first phase of Gothic design and noted for the use of the pointed arch and lancet window. Decorated was a more ambitious stylistic development with masons using all their skills to enrich the churches with elaborate carving including ornate window tracery for which the period is most associated. Perpendicular saw a reduction in ornamentation and a concentration on regular and rectilinear designs with lofty proportions and wide aisles. Decoration was generally more restrained, but in Cornwall the latter part of the period saw a number of richly decorated churches with the best examples at Launceston, St Mary, Truro and St Neot. This seems to be peculiar to Cornwall and has been associated by some to a deep-seated link to its Celtic past.

Military   Military architecture is not particularly evident. The Norman military occupation resulted in the construction of a number of castles, Restormel and Launceston being the best preserved. Of more importance, however, are Henry VIII's castles at St Mawes and Pendennis, which were among the most advanced military architecture of their time. The Garrison on St Mary's in the Isles of Scilly is notable for being developed over several centuries and provides a good example of how military fortifications changed with the times.

Little secular architecture survives from pre-1700 period, although the great houses at Trerice and Cothele are an exception. Indeed, there was little building at all until the growth in the mining industry led to a rapid increase in wealth for the **Georgian** gentry owners and an equally rapid increase in population. Georgian architecture, however, is still relatively sparse with only Truro and Penzance having any significant amount. Several minor houses were built throughout the county but the only major Georgian houses are at Antony and Trewithen. The Georgian churches at Helston, Redruth and Penzance reflect their growing populations rather than any increase in Christian fervour. More common, by far, are the Wesleyan and Methodist chapels found all over Cornwall, but particularly in the mining areas.

Only during the C19, with the great wealth of the mines and the improved links to London, did the landed aristocracy and gentry begin to build houses on a large scale, Lanhydrock being perhaps the most notable example. The mines and industrial architecture of this period are some of Cornwall's most enduring landmarks and their crumbling remains can be found scattered throughout the landscape. Some have now been restored as museum pieces, most notably at Pool, near Redruth.. A number of large churches were built during the C19 to cater for the rapidly growing population, none more significant than Truro Cathedral.

The C20 has been unkind to Cornwall – its towns and villages have suffered at the hands of architects and town planners. There is little, good C20 architecture in the county, although the Tate Gallery and the Truro Law Courts established a benchmark of quality for other public buildings to follow. More recently, the Eden Project, the National Maritime Museum Cornwall and the University of Cornwall are landmark projects that offer a more promising future for C21 architecture in Cornwall.

History

The history of Cornwall is dominated by its location at the remote and isolated far west of England. It is extraordinarily rich in the evidence of its prehistory. It provided a haven for the Celtic culture, that was driven out of lowland England by the Romans and Saxons, and which continued in the far west, largely untouched, until the Norman occupation of the late C11. Throughout the Middle Ages, Cornwall was peripheral to the main events of British history, although that did not stop numerous uprisings and rebellions by the unruly populace. However, during the English Civil War, it was a major centre of activity with the staunchly Royalist Cornish proving a formidable force. The expansion of the mining industry during the C18 led to both economic and population growth and Cornwall began to play a more integrated part in the affairs of the nation. However, it was only with the coming of the railway towards the end of the C19 that Cornwall's isolation truly ended.

Early Days
The first residents of Cornwall are likely to have been from the Middle Stone Age (c7000BC) with some evidence of occupation having been found around the coastal areas. They would have arrived from the south, possibly south-west France. They were hunter/ gatherers and made little impact on the landscape of Cornwall. By 2500BC, Neolithic Man (New Stone Age) had arrived in England from the Middle East and brought with him the skills of cultivation. They settled mainly on the chalk uplands of Southern England but they also reached Cornwall – on the granite heights of Carn Brea near Camborne are the remains of one of their settlements. They were the first to start to mould the landscape to their needs creating tiny fields and communities. Around 1800BC settlers from the Aegean, probably in search of copper and tin, appeared in Cornwall. They buried their dead under tombs of gigantic slabs of rock, most often on ridges overlooking the sea. West Cornwall, and in particular the Scilly Isles, have the greatest concentration of these megalithic tombs in Britain.

The arrival of the Beaker people in southern England may well have pushed more neolithic farmers west into Cornwall, but there is little evidence of any Beaker inhabitation of the far west. However, their culture was advanced and some of their influence must have spread westwards. Tin and copper are the essential elements of bronze and a trade was soon established taking Irish gold and copper and Cornish tin to the Continent. The easiest route from Ireland was by sea to North

Middle Stone Age

Neolithic Man

Beaker people

Cornwall, then overland to the south coast and over the sea to France. The two main overland routes were from the Hayle Estuary to Mounts Bay and the Camel Estuary to the sheltered harbours around Fowey. A number of Bronze Age relics of this trade have been discovered in these areas. This seaborne trade meant that Cornwall was more likely influenced by the prevailing culture across the Channel and in Ireland than by that which lay beyond the Tamar to the east.

Middle Bronze Age

By the Middle Bronze Age, the development of new overland routes in Europe led to a reduction in this trade and Cornwall became isolated from the growing prosperity of the rest of the country.

Celts and Romans

By 900BC, the Celts had arrived from France and West Germany. They introduced their own language, that was to be preserved as Welsh and Cornish, along with a more advanced culture and better tools. Agriculture now became the basic occupation of man and Cornwall's prosperity increased with its mild climate and tin

Late Bronze Age

deposits. All the most important finds of this Late Bronze Age have come from the extreme west which was the most prosperous and highly populated part of Cornwall at this time.

By 500BC, more Celtic immigrants from France and the Netherlands had settled peacefully in their characteristic pattern of scattered hamlets and farms. The major difference was that their weapons and tools were now made of iron, a much harder and more durable material than bronze. In early 300BC, Central Europe's Celts burst out from their homelands, sacked Rome and pressed east into Macedonia. This opened up new trade routes, which brought earthenware and bronze cups from Greece, embellished with their distinctive stylised plant forms. Celtic craftsmen further developed them into the graceful curvilinear designs that are now considered typical of Celtic Art.

La Tene

In Cornwall, La Tene warriors from Western France, landed to look for the rich deposits of tin for which the area was now known. They quickly subdued the peaceful and ill-equipped Cornish Celts. Their most notable legacy is the large number of hill forts, including Chun Castle and Castle-an-Dinas. Around the same

Venetti

time the Venetti of Brittany were trading with Cornwall. They had an established practice of cliff-top forts, which undoubtedly influenced the Cornish Celts of the time. One of the first was Trevelgue Head, just north of Newquay – many more were to follow and are still evident throughout Cornwall.

By the end of 1BC, the whole of South West England was loosely bound together by the Celtic culture of the La Tene warriors and the seafaring Venetti. Much of the early Celtic settlement had been on higher ground, but as the climate worsened, the villages were moved down the slopes towards the sea. Up to this time, Cornwall had been at the forefront of contact with the Mediterranean, the most

Romans

sophisticated culture in the world. All this was to change when the Romans crossed the Channel and made eastern England the main point of entry. Cornwall became a backwater, isolated from the main cultural influences.

In 43AD, a large Roman invasion force landed in Kent and proceeded to push into southern England. It is likely that a large number of Celts were displaced and moved west into Cornwall. The Romans never occupied Cornwall, Exeter being their most westerly town. However, there is evidence to show that some Roman pioneers must have pushed west into Cornwall. By 250AD, the Roman Empire was in decline and the tin deposits in Spain were lost to the Barbarians. As a result, the Romans began to commercially exploit Cornish tin and a profitable trade was established with the native Celts. Thousands of Roman coins of 250–350AD have been found in Cornwall as evidence of this trade.

The Dark Ages

The Romans withdrew from Britain in 410, leaving it undefended against invaders. The Germanic Saxons soon took the opportunity, landed in eastern England and pushed west, despite fierce resistance from the native Britons. The decisive battle was at Dyrham in 577 where three British Kings were killed. As the Saxons pushed west they cut off the Celts of Cornwall from those of Wales and Scotland. King Arthur, a semi-mythical figure who fought against the Saxons is first mentioned in 685. The legend has Arthur as a Cornishman and the county is full of Arthurian connections, including his "castle" at Tintagel. The legend is almost certainly only that, but it is possible that there was an early C6 British leader of that name and he may well have hailed from the Celtic strongholds of the far west.

King Arthur

By the C6, Irish missionaries were arriving in Cornwall to convert the native Celts. Small baptistrys were set up by wells and springs and the earliest stone crosses date from this time. The far west, for so long the richest and most populous part of Cornwall, now declined. The focus shifted to the centre, where the major trade route between the Camel Estuary and Fowey became dominant. At the northern end of this route, the monastery of St Petroc, the patron saint of Cornwall, became the ecclesiastical capital of Cornwall – a role it was to hold until the Saxon conquest.

St Petroc

In 597, St Augustine landed in Kent and began the conversion of the Saxons to Roman Christianity. However, the Cornish Church remained separate, Celtic rather than Roman. The Saxons had little influence in Cornwall until 814 when Egbert invaded and subjugated the Cornish Celts. In 825, the Cornish rebelled and were crushed. Egbert was now the first King of all England. However, the Vikings were already raiding the coast and the Cornish Celts, seizing their opportunity, joined forces with the Vikings to expel the Saxons. Egbert defeated them at Hington Down, near Plymouth, in 838 and the Cornish were forced to repeat their oaths of allegiance, never to break them again.

Vikings

In 865, a substantial Danish Army landed in East Anglia and pushed west. By 878, the Danes had reached the borders of Devon and, the English King Alfred was trapped in the marshes of Somerset. Alfred proved a dogged resistance fighter and by the time he died in 900 he had pushed the Danes back from his Wessex kingdom, in the process saving Cornwall from any threat of Danish invasion. However, Alfred's grandson, Athelston, brought Cornwall under English rule and in 931 created a Diocese of Cornwall, with its see at the monastery of St Germans, conveniently located on the eastern borders of the county furthest from the strongholds of Celtic influence in the west. In 1040, St Germans lost its Cathedral status, which was combined with Devon and moved to Exeter, where it remained until 1876.

King Alfred

St Germans

The Early Middle Ages

William, Duke of Normandy In 1066, William, Duke of Normandy, landed at Hastings. By 1068, he was at Exeter, which surrendered after an 18 day siege. Cornwall submitted peacefully, apart from a minor rebellion in 1069 which was easily put down. William extended control via the feudal system, many thousands of freemen lost their lands which were given to William's tenants-in-chief for services rendered. Two-thirds of Cornwall was granted to his half-brother, Robert, Count of Mortain.

Domesday Book In 1086, The Domesday Book recorded that Cornwall was still thinly populated with around 20,000 people and most of these were in the east. The English were dispossessed. Only 15 small English sub-tenants remained in the county, while **The Normans** there were probably no more than 80 Norman Lords of the Manor. The Normans maintained their rule over the vastly more numerous English by military domination based on a series of fortified castles throughout the land. In Cornwall, Launceston, Trematon and Restmorel were the most important – all significantly in the east of the county. It is likely that the far west was still relatively untouched by Norman influence. Further rebellions occurred in 1090 and 1106, but were easily put down.

By the late C13 and early C14, England had started to forge an identity – a nation of English people. But, Cornwall retained its own nationalism. To the western Celts, the English were foreigners, their language a foreign language. They pursued their own way of life as much as possible, living in their hamlets and avoiding towns. The Cornish towns that there were, were not the result of spontaneous growth but the speculation of English Lords of the Manor. Some 30 Boroughs were founded in this period, but all were tiny. Even in 1377, when the population of the County must have been about 60,000, Helston, Penryn and Looe had less than 300 inhabitants each. Bodmin was the biggest and wealthiest town, while Launceston was the only walled town in the county. Remoteness was still the dominant factor and, while the southern estuaries were to grow in importance with the war with France, the journey to London still took 4 days, a journey that few Cornishmen would ever undertake..

Edward III In 1337, Edward III raised the Earldom of Cornwall to a Duchy and created the 7 **Duke of** year old Prince Edward, later to be immortalized as the Black Prince, the first Duke **Cornwall** of Cornwall. Ever since, the Duchy has been given to the eldest son of the sovereign, thereby saddling Cornwall with a series of absentee Lords and several periods where it reverted to the Crown for want of an eldest son.

Late Middle Ages

The Hundred Years War The Hundred Years War with France began in 1337. This was a time of relative prosperity for Cornwall as her sailors and ports were busy ferrying provisions and troops to France. The western ports offered 70 ships of 100 tons or more for the defence of the nation. However, within 10 years of the start of the war, disaster struck when the Black Death arrived from the Continent. It is estimated that the population of Cornwall, like England, may have fallen by a third from 60,000 to **The Black** 40,000. In 1354, the Black Prince visited Cornwall and ordered the rebuilding of **Prince** the castles, many of which had fallen into considerable disrepair. Even during the lulls in fighting, the seaman from France and England continued to harry and plunder each other's ships and ports. Fowey was attacked and burnt in 1378 and Looe in 1405. Impoverishment following the plague and the need to raise taxes to pay for the foreign war led to growing disgruntlement culminating in the unsuccessful Peasants Revolt of 1381. There was much support for the cause in Cornwall but little action other than local outrages, which were swiftly put down.

In 1413, Henry V acceded to the throne and renewed the Hundred Years War in which Cornish ships and men were to play a significant part. On the cessation of the war with France, the Wars of the Roses flared up, a 30 year Civil War over rival claims to the throne. Cornwall was far from the action, but had identified itself with the Lancastrian cause. Near anarchy spread throughout the land. The lawless seamen of Fowey needed no second invitation and proceeded to attack Norman, Breton, Spanish and even Plymouth ships. In retaliation, a Breton fleet attacked and burnt part of Fowey in 1457, after which the port defences were strengthened with two towers on either side, between which a great chain was strung. In 1473, the last, forlorn Lancastrian revolt against Edward VI resulted in the Earl of Oxford seizing St Michael's Mount, where he was besieged for 4 months before surrendering. Edward finally subdued the unruly seamen of Fowey by luring the leading burgesses to Lostwithiel where they were imprisoned and one executed. Goods were confiscated and their harbour chain given to Dartmouth. Fowey would soon be eclipsed by Plymouth and Falmouth.

Wars of the Roses

St Michael's Mount

By the end of the C15, relative prosperity had returned to Cornwall, despite the depression in tin mining, which saw production fall from 800 tons in 1400 to 400 tons in 1455. Most peasants were now freemen, not serfs. Agriculture was more efficient and there was no need to farm the higher ground which was now abandoned. The ports of the south coast were doing well with the foreign wars, piracy and trade. There were, however, few medieval houses of any consequence, but there was an explosion of church building and virtually every church in Cornwall has evidence of C15 rebuilding. By now, the upper and educated classes spoke English, while the, illiterate rest spoke Cornish. The conversion of the educated classes to English and the absence of a written Cornish heritage doomed the Cornish language to extinction.

The Tudors

When in 1485, Henry VII won the crown at Bosworth from Richard III, the fortunes of his western supporters were restored. Yet Cornwall was economically depressed and there was much discontent. When taxes were sought to pay for the war against the Scots, the collectors met sullen resistance which soon flamed into open rebellion. The rebels marched east picking up supporters on the way and by June they were south of London, where they were defeated at Blackheath on 16 June 1497, the leaders captured and condemned to death. This only increased Cornish outrage and when on 7 September, Perkin Warbeck, claiming to be the rightful King, landed at Whitesand Bay, near Sennen, he soon amassed a force of 6,000 men and crossed the Tamar into Devon. He was repulsed by the defenders of Exeter and moved towards Taunton where he was met by Henry's army, defeated and the leaders captured. Warbeck was spared and a huge levy of £600 imposed on the already impoverished region.

Henry VII

Perkin Warbeck

Henry VIII   In 1509, Henry VIII succeeded to the throne. While not himself a Protestant, he was to instigate the Church of England and its split from Rome. The Act of Supremacy of 1534 made him the supreme head of the Church of England. The monasteries were dissolved and their property confiscated.

Edward VI   When Henry died in 1546, he was succeeded by his son, Edward VI, a confirmed Protestant. Cornish was now banned from the Mass which had to be in English and all Popish idolatory, relics and images were removed from churches. The Cornish had by now become fanatically attached to the Roman Church and the imposed changes were pushing tempers to the edge. There was a minor revolt in Helston when the King's man was murdered. The ringleaders were caught and taken to London where they were executed. By 1549, Cornwall was in open rebellion. The gentry sought protection in their castles, while the mob, some 6,000 strong, crossed into Devon and besieged Exeter. They were defeated by the King's forces, with the significant aid of German and Italian mercenaries. The Cornish re-

Sampford
Courtenay   grouped and took up position at Sampford Courtenay, 15 miles north west of Exeter where they were finally beaten, the ringleaders caught and brutally executed. The Cornish were now suppressed and their churches stripped of all their lavish decoration.

Mary   In 1553, the Catholic Mary took to the throne, married Philip II of Spain and restored the Catholic doctrine. The Cornish plate and treasures were released from St Mawes castle, where they had been stored.

Elizabeth I   Elizabeth I followed her onto the throne. She was Protestant, but was astute enough to maintain good relations with the powerful Spain during the early years of her reign. When the Protestant Netherlands revolted against Spain, she could not intervene directly, but could hardly stop English privateers and pirates, many

Francis Drake   of them Cornish, attacking and plundering Spanish ships. Francis Drake was, perhaps, the most successful and Elizabeth, who shared in his profits, found it increasingly difficult to convince Spain that she was trying to restrain him. The Spanish used Elizabeth's anti-Catholic position to try and undermine her from within. All Catholics became suspect and the country was rife with rumours of plots and intrigue.

As tension with Spain mounted, efforts were made to strengthen the county's

Raleigh   defences and Raleigh was appointed Lord Lieutenant in 1585. When the war finally began, Cornwall became one of the front lines of any potential conflict. Any invasion fleet from Spain would have to sail past Cornwall. Earthworks were thrown up and beacons manned on hills and headlands. By 1587, Philip's invasion fleet was almost ready, when Drake slipped into Cadiz and burned some of the fleet. In

Armada   1588, however, the Armada was ready and on July 19 was sighted off the Scilly Isles. The English fleet attacked at Gravelines, off Calais and dispersed the Spanish ships, which fled up the north coast of England. In 1590, the Spanish occupied Brittany from where they had a base to attack Cornwall. In one such raid in 1595, Mousehole, Newlyn and Penzance were ransacked. The Spanish only withdrew once a sizeable force had been mustered on land and, more significantly, Drake had sailed from Plymouth with a naval force to intercept the Spanish raiders. In 1597, a bigger Armada sailed from Spain to attack England, but was struck by gales that dispersed the fleet. By now, Pendennis Castle had been strengthened with the

arrival of 200 regular soldiers and a more efficient training of the militia had been devised. Raleigh could now call upon 6,000 men for the defence of the county.

The Stuarts

In 1603, James IV of Scotland acceded to the throne upon the death of the childless Elizabeth. Henry, his eldest son, became the Duke of Cornwall. James made peace with Spain, although Cornwall remained at the prey of North African pirates. In one daring raid in 1625 they took 27 ships and 200 people. James died in 1625 and the reign of Charles I began.

Around this time, Puritanism, a form of extreme Protestantism, was a growing force in the county as elsewhere in England. Tension between Parliament and the King became intense with Charles insisting on the divine right of Kings, a notion that was becoming rapidly unacceptable to the people, and, in particular, the Puritans with their secular view of the world. Conflict was inevitable and when Parliament opposed the King's taxes, Charles had it dissolved. Between 1629–40, he ruled without Parliament. In 1640, the Scots rebelled and occupied the north of England. Charles was forced to recall Parliament to raise taxes for an army, but Parliament proved more interested in curbing the power of the King than supporting his military ambitions. Several Cornish gentry refused to pay the taxes and were imprisoned. Their leader in the House of Commons, Sir John Eliot of Port Eliot, was imprisoned in the tower where he eventually died. Parliament passed The Grand Remonstrance, declaring no confidence in the King and a Militia Bill depriving him of total control of the Army. On 10 January 1642, the King fled London and The Civil War had begun.

Despite much dissatisfaction with Charles' rule, most Cornishmen were inherently conservative and had a deep reverence for the ideal of kingship. Most of Cornwall was Royalist and followed Sir Basil Grenville, while the east of the County, along with Devon, Somerset and Dorset was more Puritan and supported the Parliamentarians. As such, the Cornish Royalists were isolated from the rest of England. However, they soon pushed the Parliamentarians out of Cornwall and the gentry set about organizing "The Cornish Army". Comprised chiefly of their own tenants, they were loyal, disciplined and brave. They were to prove some of the most reliable troops on the Royalist side. In January 1643, the Parliamentary forces invaded Cornwall and the first battle on Cornish soil was fought at Boconnoc, near Braddock, on 19 January. The Royalist army won easily. On 16 May at the Battle of Stratton, Cornwall was made secure for the King and the Cornish Army moved east into a larger sphere of action. Within three months they had fought several battles and had helped take Bristol, although at the cost of its four greatest leaders and almost half of its number. Grenville, himself, was fatally wounded at Bath and is buried in Kilkhampton.

In 1644, a Parliamentarian Army moved into Cornwall. They were soon surrounded by the Royalist Army on the Gribben peninsula, near Fowey. Trying to break out, they were caught at Castle Dore where they made their last stand. Only 1,000 out of 6,000 men returned to Devon. However, with the creation of the New Model Army under Cromwell, events moved rapidly away from the Royalist forces, who were decisevly defeated at Naseby and Marston Moor. The Parliamentarian

Army advanced into Cornwall and the Royalists signed the Treaty of Surrender on 12 March 1645. Sir John Arundell was besieged in Pendennis Castle for five months. He surrendered on 17 August and marched out with all colours flying. Many Royalist leaders chose exile rather than submit. Resentment continued to smoulder and by 1648, Cornwall was again ripe for rebellion, but when it came it was easily put down. In 1651, the Parliamentary forces took the Isles of Scilly and ended once and for all the prospect of any successful Royalist revolt in the west. In 1659, Cromwell died and there followed a period of confusion, only to be resolved by the succession of Charles II to the throne. The King duly rewarded the loyal Godolphins of Cornwall and allowed his Coat of Arms to be erected in the loyal parishes of Cornwall.

The Eighteenth Century

The end of the Civil War brought the independent political history of Cornwall to an end. The county was still remote and barely accessible, almost a foreign country to the majority of the English. The economy was still dominated by mining, fishing and agriculture. At the start of the C18, the export of pilchards to Roman Catholic countries was as important to the Cornish economy as the export of tin. However, for the next two centuries the history of Cornwall would be essentially the history of its mining industry.

Tin production

Tin production had shifted gradually westwards and until about 1700 the metal was still being obtained almost wholly from alluvial deposits. The first steam-powered pumping engine was installed in a tin mine near Helston in about 1715. As the industry grew so did the population and by 1760 Cornwall was home to 150,000 people. Great fortunes were to be made by the gentry owners, but little wealth filtered down to the miners. Indeed, as deep mining developed, conditions declined significantly. Hours were long, the work dangerous and the miner's homes little more than thatched hovels. Many sought solace in beer or smuggled spirits. Violence was commonplace and the grim business of wrecking proved irresistible to the impoverished community.

Wrecking

Cornwall had long been a graveyard for ships. Luring them onto the rocky shore by showing false lights added to the natural toll of this most savage of coastlines. Wrecking was a callous and brutal business, made more so by the law itself, which decreed a wreck of the sea as one from which no living creature reached the shore. If man or beast escaped, the wreck remained the property of the legal owners. This gave little incentive to help survivors, and dark tales tell of desperate survivors being "finished off" as they struggled ashore, exhausted.

Smuggling

Smuggling also flourished during these times. Between 1700 and 1850, it was one of England's major "trades" and Cornwall was at the forefront. The rugged coastline with remote coves and poor communications was perfect for smugglers. Some villages virtually lived from smuggling. It is estimated that by 1770, some 470,000 gallons of brandy and 350,000 pounds of tea were being smuggled into Cornwall at a cost to the Treasury of £150,000. All sections of the community supported the trade in one way or another and while the business was often violent and dangerous, it could never have flourished without the support of the gentry and merchant classes who could buy their luxuries at tax free prices. The Coast

Guard service was formed to specifically target the smugglers, but for all their hard work, it was the reduction in import taxes in the 1840s and the introduction of "free trade" that did more to end large scale smuggling. By the end of the 1850s it had all but ceased.

Into this wild and lawless place, in 1743, came John Wesley, the greatest **John Wesley** preacher of his age. By now, few working class Cornishmen attended church with any enthusiasm. The clergy themselves often held more than one trade to increase their salaries and there was little sense of religion being at the centre of people's lives. Wesley and his brothers visited Cornwall almost every year until 1789. At first, they met considerable opposition and even violence, much of it orchestrated by the clergy and gentry fearful of the threat to the status quo. He preached in the open air, as no church would let him enter, and his courage and evangelism struck a chord with the Cornish miners. At this time, the mining areas of Cornwall were among the most densely populated in the country, St Just was almost as big as Manchester, St Ives considerably larger than Liverpool. Wesley described the miners of St Just as "the chief of the whole country for hurling, fighting, drinking and all manner of wickedness." By the time of his last journey in 1789, Methodism had taken firm hold, drunkenness had declined and wrecking had been checked. Cornwall had become a less barbarous place.

Tin and copper production continued to grow and in the mid C18 china clay, **China clay** the key ingredient in porcelain, was discovered at St Austell. In 1777, James Watt came to Cornwall and oversaw the installation of one of his engines at Ting Tang mine in Gwennap, which proved to be a huge success. However, momentous events were taking place over the water with the French Revolution and the execution of the King. By 1793, Britain was again at war with France which was to continue through to 1815. Many Cornishmen served in the army and navy and the increased naval traffic brought greater prosperity to many of the county's southern ports.

The Nineteenth Century

In the first half of the C19, Cornwall was transformed by an age of invention and expansion. Watts patent came to an end, making his machines more economical to use. In 1800, there were 75 mines employing 16,000 people, by 1837, 200 mines employing 30,000 people. Cornwall now produced two thirds of the world's supply of copper. The county's population grew from 200,000 to 350,000. Many of the gentry and landowners made fortunes, much of which was spent on rebuilding their country seats. Truro became the centre of Cornish society, with the construction of new townhouses and a surprisingly elegant social season. Many towns, such as Penzance and Falmouth, formed their own learned Societies, cut off as they were from the centres of culture and learning.

However, the wealth was not shared and conditions for the miners and other workers worsened during this period. In St Cleer in 1830, before the mine opened, the average age of those buried in the Parish was 45. By 1860, it was under 22. Disasters were frequent – in 1847, it was estimated that 1 in 5 Gwennap miners died in an accident. Cornwall was remote from the other working class centres of England and the organized labour movement found it difficult to gain hold. The first strike in Cornwall was not recorded until 1857 in St Just.

After its peak in the 1850s, the output of copper collapsed with the discovery of new deposits in South Africa, Australia and the Americas. A period of depression settled on Cornwall and many miners emigrated to work overseas. A brief revival of tin mining in the 1870s helped to alleviate the full effects of the depression, but within 30 years these mines too were almost worked out. While the population of England and Wales rose steadily during this period, that of Cornwall fell 2% in the 1860s and 9% in the 1870s, when a third of the mining population left the county.

Some alternative employment existed in the growing china clay industry and in **The railways** the construction of the railways. In 1849, London was connected to Plymouth and a four horse omnibus left Camborne early in the morning to catch the evening train to London. By 1858, the line from Truro to Saltash was completed, a major construction project in itself with 34 viaducts on its 53 mile route, and in February 1859 the opening of Brunel's Saltash bridge connected Truro to London. By 1867, direct through traffic was possible between Penzance and London, the journey being cut from 40 hours by stagecoach to just 12 by train. By 1879, it was down to 9 hours and in 1904, the Cornish Riviera Express did the journey in 6 hours 35 minutes. No longer was Cornwall remote and inaccessible. For the convenience of railway timetabling, the clocks were brought into line with London for the first time. Before, there had always been 20 minutes difference.

The railways opened up new markets for Cornwall's farming and fishing communities, and just in time, for the huge shoals of pilchards that had sustained the Cornish fishing industry stopped appearing around the end of the C19, never to return again. The fast train connection to London meant that fresh fish could now be landed in Cornwall and in the London markets the same day. It also allowed farmers to exploit the mild climate and early spring to provide cut flowers and early vegetables for the huge London market.

The train also heralded the arrival of the first tourists, who would become the mainstay of the county's economy. In 1887, the Great Western Railway acquired Tregenna Castle in St Ives to establish a hotel. Artists also began to be drawn to the area and established significant communities in Newlyn, St Ives and Lamorna.

The Twentieth Century

Tin production recovered briefly during World War I, but slumped again in 1921. By 1939 only 5 mines remained, employing fewer than 1000 men. Fishing suffered a similar decline. Fortunately, agriculture flourished as did china clay, granite and slate quarrying, ship repairing (at Falmouth) and mining engineering (at Camborne). The new tourist industry, boosted by the arrival of paid annual leave, became an increasingly important part of the economy.

Second World War   During the Second World War, the population was boosted by evacuees and members of the armed forces – the civilian population between 1939-41 shot up by 20% from 308,000 to 370,000. Cornwall had a strategic location in the Battle of the Atlantic to keep England's vital trade routes with the New World open. Many members of the armed forces were stationed in Cornwall, and their numbers increased as Allied Forces built up for the invasion of Europe on D Day. Falmouth, in particular, was a key port of embarkation for the invasion fleet. German bombing was sporadic, but virtually all the south coast ports were bombed at some time during the war.

From the 1900s onwards, the improved transport links to the rest of England had started to dilute the traditional isolation of Cornwall, but it was not until the 1950s that Cornish culture came to be radically challenged by tourism and the mass media. As a response to this, the Cornish Revival of the 1920s, part of a wider Celtic Revival, grew stronger, leading to the formation in 1951 of the nationalist group, Mebyon Kernow (Sons of Cornwall). Its aims were economic and political, rather than separatist, and it fostered support for the Liberal Party.

Mebyon Kernow

During the 1950s the Cornish economy maintained its strength. Agriculture flourished and tin prices had quadrupled in 1951 when the Korean War broke out. By now, there was such a shortage of skilled workers, that miners had to be brought in from Italy and elsewhere. The unemployment rate stood at 2% but even then there was growing concern over how long it could last. Since the early 1960's the area has been eligible for regional assistance from the Government and these programmes have continued through to the present but have failed to stop the economic decline.

With the 1973 oil crisis and the general decline in the UK economy, firms no longer had to look to Cornwall for cheap labour and land. The rise in fuel prices made the long distance from the major markets of England significant. Manufacturing and mining collapsed and even tourism began to diminish as cheaper foreign holidays became available.

1973 oil crisis

In the 1980s, the late Thatcher years resulted in a developer-led boom in Cornwall, exploiting the improved transport links and the explosion in disposable income of residents in London and South East. Hotels, marinas, retail parks and theme parks were rapidly developed, the worst example being Peter de Savary's, Lands End Experience. Fortunately for Cornwall, the bubble burst with the worldwide recession of the late 1980s and a more considered development of its natural resources and tourist potential is hopefully underway.

Thatcher

Throughout the latter decades of the C20, Cornwall's population has exploded. Growth had been slow up to 1961 when the population stood at 339,000 – a rise of a mere 9000 since the end of the war. However, by 1991 there was an amazing 39% increase to a total of 473,000. This has since slowed to only a litttle over the national average – the population in 2002 being 505,000. The population increase is soley due to in-migration, as the outflow of young people looking for jobs continues unabated. Contrary to popular belief, the new residents are not elderly retirees but predominantly working age people with children, many taking early retirement or downscaling to enjoy a higher quality of life.

The economy, however, is still poor. In 2000, the whole of Cornwall was granted Objective 1 Status by the European Union, the category reserved for Europe's most deprived regions. Massive inward investment can be expected from this designation and the future looks better for the county than at any time in the recent past. The test will be to see whether this money is spent wisely in the long-term development of the region's economy without destroying the natural beauty of the area.

Objective 1 Status

North Cornwall
and Bodmin Moor

Introduction

An area of high moorland and rolling hills. Where the granite uplands reach the sea, the high, sheer cliffs create some of the most spectacular coastal scenery in the country. The coast path provides some of the best walking in the county and the area has an appealing remoteness, for the few natural harbours have restricted the scope for development along this wild coastline. On the whole, the area is little visited by tourists, although there are the hot spots of Bude, Tintagel and Boscastle. Inland, Bodmin Moor is the largest and highest area of upland in the county and the only area that can have any claim to a feeling of remoteness. Throughout the moor, there is evidence of prehistoric occupation with many stone circles, round houses and other remains. Launceston is a fine, country town, rarely visited but with a castle and one of the most important churches in the county. Bodmin has little to show for its historic past but it does boast the biggest church in Cornwall with some extraordinary furnishings to the interior. To the south, Lanhydrock is the finest Victorian country house in the county and nearby St Neot has some of the best medieval glass to be seen in any parish church.

Launceston

Launceston has long been the "gateway" to Cornwall. It owes its existence to its strategic position guarding one of the main approaches to the county. Today, it is a small town, bypassed by the more recent events of Cornwall's history. It has a useful range of shops and facilities and a pleasant town centre with many fine Medieval and Georgian buildings. It's two main sites of interest, the castle and the Church of St Mary Magdalene are worth visiting in their own right, and, while there is little else to detain the visitor, the town has a pleasant country town feel and is relatively untouched by tourism.

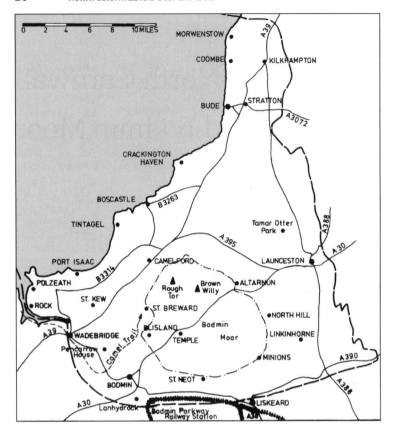

 ## Historic development

There was Celtic and Saxon occupation of the area around St Stephen's, a mile to the north, but the origins of Launceston itself date from the Norman invasion and the establishment of the castle by *Brian de Bretagne*, the first Norman Earl of Cornwall. It is likely that the first castle was built in 1067–68 to suppress a Saxon revolt. The first record is in the Domesday Survey of 1086. The castle controlled the land between Bodmin Moor and Dartmoor as well as the main crossing point of the River Tamar. Built on high ground overlooking the river and the approaches from the east, its strategic significance is clear. The earldom passed to *Robert, Count of Mortain*, the half brother of William the Conqueror, in 1076 and he soon established the town by transferring the existing market from St Stephen's to the vicinity of the new castle. Cornwall was by far the most important of Robert's extensive estates and he established his court and the administrative centre of his earldom at Launceston, easily defended and close to the Norman strongholds to the east. The town gradually developed under the shadow of the castle and derived much of its importance from the administrative functions of the earldom. Just outside the town, by the crossing of the River Kensey, an Augustinian Priory was founded in 1127. Its remains can still be seen by St Thomas's Church.

The high point of the castle's importance was due to *Richard of Cornwall*, younger brother of King Henry III, who held the earldom between 1227 and 1272. He was one of the wealthiest and most powerful men in the kingdom and his Cornish estates were particularly valuable due to the local tin industry. He remodelled and strengthened the castle's defences and added a stone wall around the town with three gateways, of which only the south gate survives. Launceston was to be the only walled town in Cornwall.

With Richard's death in 1272, the earldom's administration was moved to Lostwithiel to be nearer the centre of tin production. As a result, the castle and town lost some of their importance, though Launceston remained the centre for justice and manorial rights. The accession of *Edward, the Black Prince* as the first Duke of Cornwall in 1337 led to a certain amount of rebuilding and modernisation of the castle.

Between 1511–24, Launceston's status was reaffirmed with the building, by Sir Henry Trecarrel, of the most elaborate church west of Exeter. The priory was dissolved in 1536 but the town itself prospered throughout the C16 to C18 from its role as the county town and the centre of justice within the county. There are many fine houses from this period testifying to the wealth of the town. During the Civil War the town and castle, with their strategic importance, were held for the King except for two occasions when they were captured by the Parliamentarians in 1642 and 1644. They were finally captured by Fairfax's army in February 1646.

By the C19, the focus of development in the county had moved westwards to the fast developing tin and copper mining areas. Launceston's easterly location suddenly became an inconvenience and in 1838 the courts and the county seat were transferred to Bodmin. Launceston was bypassed by the major impact of the Industrial Revolution in Cornwall and even the later development of tourism has left the town largely untouched. Today, it remains a small market town catering for a large agricultural hinterland.

The Town

Launceston is clustered on the hillside around the foot of the castle. Bodmin Moor looms on the western edge of the town while Dartmoor is clearly visible to the east. The town is a pleasant jumble of buildings from the middle ages onwards. The Southgate Arch is one of the earliest surviving structures in the town. The main arch is part of the C13 town wall and is the only one of the three original gateways to remain. The two rooms above, now occupied by an art gallery, were added around 1550. The arch was further altered in the C19 with the addition of a battlemented parapet. The buildings on either side of the arch are some of the finest in the town. Elsewhere, within the town centre, there are many

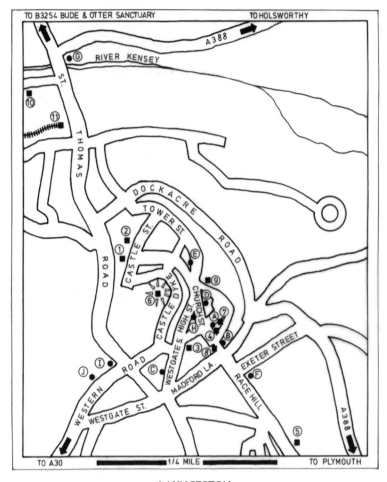

LAUNCESTON

ACCOMMODATION

1   Eagle House Hotel
2   No. 11 Castle Street
3   White Hart Hotel
4   Bakers Arms Hotel
5   Glencoe Villa

ESSENTIALS

6   Castle
7   Tourist Office
8   Southgate Arch
9   Church of St Mary Magdalene
10 Church of St Thomas the Apostle

11 Launceston Steam Railway

RESTAURANTS AND BARS

A   Roberto's
B   Café de L'Arche
C   Launceston Fryers
D   Harveys
E   Bell Inn
F   Newmarket Inn
G   White Horse
H   Mad Hatters
I   Dezigns
J   Sagar

interesting buildings. The buildings on the corner of the Square and High Street are some of the earliest and date from the C16. The White Hart Hotel on the Square is a substantial Georgian building with a sadly mutilated interior. The front door is reputed to be C12 and to have come from St Thomas's Priory.

Castle Street, to the north of the Castle, has some of the best C18 architecture in the town. The Eagle House Hotel was built in 1767 and is a grand, classical design. Lawrence House at no.9 is a more restrained Georgian composition with particularly fine brickwork and windows. It is owned by the National Trust and is now the *Town Museum* (**01566 773277**). The rest of the town is picturesque and a pleasant place to stroll. There are some fine C19 shopfronts. The one on the junction of Church Street and High Street is particularly elaborate.

Open April to Sept, Mon–Fri, 10.30am–4.30pm Admission free

Launceston Castle

The Castle dominates the town. The site is owned and managed by English Heritage. The grounds are maintained as a public park and are free to enter while the keep is open. In its day, the castle was one of the most important in the county, although now there is little of the original structure remaining. The south gatehouse is now the main entrance to the castle and would originally have led to the castle park and faced away from the town. All that remains now of the C13 and C14 structure is part of the front wall. The north gatehouse or Town Gate would have been the main entrance in the Middle Ages and led directly into the town. Little remains other than the gate passage and the ground floor room alongside it. This room may originally have been used by a porter but subsequently became a prison – the constable's chamber also being incorporated into the gatehouse. George Fox, the founder of the Quakers, was imprisoned here in 1656 for distributing religious pamphlets in the town. An earlier prisoner was the Catholic priest Cuthbert Mayne who was tried and executed at Launceston in November 1577. He was the first Roman Catholic priest sent into England to be executed during the reign of Elizabeth I. He was canonised in 1970.

Open every day, 10am–6pm (closing at dusk in the winter). Admission, £2.30, conc. £1.70, children £1.20

The courtyard or bailey was the site for the main buildings of the castle and is now the public park. In the C13 a stone wall with several towers was erected along the line of the ramparts. Little now remains. Excavations have revealed several buildings within the courtyard and this would have ben the centre of the castle's social and administrative life. The site of the Great Hall is marked out in the grass. This substantial building was used as the Assize Hall (courthouse) until the early C17. The county gaol was also located within the courtyard in the C18 and C19.

The Mound and High Tower were the strongest point of the castle's defences. The mound has a distinctive cone shape that has been added to and formed over the centuries of the castle's existence. The keep on top of the mound was reached via a walled approach that was almost certainly roofed. A small C13 tower, the base of which still survives, guarded the approach. There are good views over the town, immediately below the castle at this point. The line of the outer ditch still survives as a narrow lane known as Castle Dyke. The massive stone walls of the keep were built during the C12 and it was principally designed to be used as a fighting platform. The High Tower was added in the C13 and was built within the walls of the keep. The intervening space was roofed at the level of the wall walk and the holes for the joists are clearly visible in the tower wall. The tower contained rooms on two floors, although its residential use must have been limited. The tower leans about 1m out of the vertical, although it is difficult to perceive this from close up.

The castle had a fairly precarious existence with several rebuildings and intervening periods of decay. The Black Prince instigated major rebuilding work in the C14 and this continued through the C15. By the end of the Civil War, the defences were in a poor state and attempts were made to patch them up. However, a contemporary survey indicated that the only part remaining habitable was the north gatehouse. In the C18, the main prison was erected in the courtyard. It was a relatively small building with just seven cells. This use ceased when the Assizes moved to Bodmin in 1842 and the gaol was subsequently demolished. This removed the last vestige of the castle's medieval functions and it was subsequently turned into a public park for the people of the town.

St Mary Magdalene

The parish church of Launceston is found in the centre of the town. It is one of the biggest and most important ecclesiastical buildings in Cornwall. The church was built between 1511 and 1524 and replaced an earlier chapel on the site. The west tower is the only part of the earlier chapel to survive and dates from the late C14. The tower was only connected to the main body of the church by the addition of the vestry in the C19. The C16 church is entirely the work of Sir Henry Trecarrel and is unusual in being a complete C16 creation with no later additions and few alterations. The church is large, over 100 feet long and has a light and airy feel due to the large windows along the north and south walls.

The glory of the church lies outside with its elaborately carved external stonework. Granite has been carved in intricate panels to cover the complete exterior of the church. Pevsner cites it as "barbarous profusion, impressive more by their numbers than their quality." At the east end is a carved figure of Mary Magdalen, recumbent in a niche with four kneeling figures to either side. Tradition says that if you cast a pebble over your shoulder up into her back and it stays there, then you will have a new suit of clothes. At the top of the east gable is the royal arms of Henry VIII. The porch displays particularly elaborate decoration.

The interior is spacious and light with slim, graceful piers separating the aisles from the nave. The pulpit is a superb example of pre-Reformation carving, easily the best in the county. The carved screens to the sanctuary, either side of the high altar, display unusual art nouveau influences. There are a number of good monuments, including a grand, classical memorial of 1731 to Granville Piper and Richard Wise, mayors of the town. By the main door is a splendid carving of two figures kneeling, facing each other – a remnant of a much larger memorial dating from 1650.

Launceston Steam Railway   To the north of the town centre is the *Launceston Steam Railway* (**01566 775665**), a narrow gauge line that runs along the Kensey Valley. It is open daily, except Saturdays, July–September and Sundays to Wednesdays in June. There are seven trains a day starting at 11.00am with the last leaving Launceston at 4.30pm. Just beyond the railway, beside the river is the Church of St Thomas the Apostle. There are some wall paintings inside, but the main interest is the carved Norman font, reputedly the largest in Cornwall. The narrow footbridge over the Kensey, opposite the church, was built by the town in 1580 and has remained largely unaltered.

The town has a good range of shops that can satisfy most needs. The Tourist Information Centre (**01566 772321**) is in Market House Arcade, Market Street. Launceston is something of a hub for local buses and there are regular connections to Bude, Liskeard, Tavistock and Plymouth as well as other local towns and villages. By car, Launceston is just off the main A30.

Tourist Information Centre

Accommodation

There is relatively little accommodation in Launceston and what there is tends to be rather ordinary. One of the better options is is the **Eagle House Hotel**, Castle Street (**01566 772036**) *B* located right next to the castle in one of the nicest streets in town. The **White Hart Hotel**, Broad Street (**01566 772013**) *B* overlooks the main square and is a substantial Georgian building. However, the interiors leave much to be desired and show little trace of their Georgian origins. Near Southgate Arch, the **Bakers Arms Hotel**, Southgate Street (**01566 772510**) *B* is fairly basic. Just outside the town centre is **Glencoe Villa**, 13 Race Hill (**01566 775819**) *A*, a comfortable B&B in a large Victorian house. More central, **No.11 Castle Street** (**01566 773873**) *A* offers good value accommodation in a period Georgian house and is probably the nicest place to stay in the town.

Restaurants and bars

Launceston's nightlife is pretty low key and is unlikely to be one of the highlights of your stay. However, options have improved in the last few years with the opening of a number of new restaurants and bars. **Roberto's** in Southgate Street (**01566 777202**) *M* is long established and serves Italian food in its basement dining room with an amazing 'retro' ambience. Nearby, the **Café de l'Arche**, 1 Southgate Place (**01566 775748**) *M* is open for morning coffee through to evening meals. On the corner of Western Road, opposite the castle entrance, is the smart **Dezigns Restaurant** (**01566 779 888**) *M* with an interesting menu of fish and meat dishes and a very good value set menu. Next door is **Sager** (**01566 777 778**) *I* a good quality Indian restaurant. The **Launceston Fryers** in Westgate Street (**01566 773063**) *I* is an award-winning fish and chip take-away with a restaurantt attached. The **White Hart Hotel** on the main square and **Harveys** (see below) also serve food in the evenings. For tea, coffee and sandwiches during the day, the **Mad Hatter's Tea Shop** at 28 Church Street is recommended.

Nightlife in Launceston is limited to drinking in the many pubs dotted around the town. Nicest of the lot is probably **Harveys Bar and Bistro** in Churchgate which can get very busy. The **Bakers Arms**, Southgate Street, has a pleasant wood panelled lounge bar and a selection of real ales. Food is available at lunchtimes. The **Bell Inn**, off Church Street, is a basic locals pub. Just outside Southgate Arch, the **Newmarket Inn** caters for a younger crowd with pool tables and big screen TV. To the north of the town centre, over the river, is the **White Horse**, Newport Square, which has a range of real ales and a separate restaurant.

Around Launceston

To the north is *St Stephen*, the mother church of Launceston. It dates largely from the C13 and C14. There are good views back over Launceston from the church-
Tamar Otter yard and some nice rows of cottages, but little else to detain the visitor. The Tamar
Sanctuary   Otter Sanctuary (**01566 785 646**) is signposted off the B3254, some three miles north of Launceston. British otters are bred here for release into the wild so as to re-establish this previously common indigenous species into our countryside. In addition to the otters, there are also deer, wallabies, owl aviaries and other birds around the protected woodland and open areas. It is open from April (or Easter) to the end of October, 10.30am–6.00pm. Entry is a rather hefty £6, OAPs £5 and children £3.50.

The area around Launceston is one of gentle hills and wooded valleys dotted with a number of largely undistinguished villages. It is a pleasant area to travel around but there is little of great interest for the visitor. However, two of the nicest villages are Linkinhorne and North Hill which both have interesting church-es and good pubs.

Linkinhorne   The former is located about 6 miles south of Launceston and approached down narrow lanes off the B3257. The village is tiny, but lovely, with a big church in a rural churchyard setting. The tower is the second highest in Cornwall and its size is said to be due to the generosity of Sir Henry Trecarrel, also responsible for St Mary in Launceston. The interior has evidence of C15 wall paintings in the south aisle. The interlace carving on the entrance to the south porch shows some Celtic influence lingering on late into the day. There are good views towards Bodmin Moor from the churchyard. Opposite the church is the **Church House Inn** (**01579 363631**), a pleasant pub and restaurant with good food. Just outside the village is a well preserved *Holy Well* from the C15, one of many in this area. To the
Horsebridge east of Linkinhorne and approached down narrow lanes is Horsebridge where one of the finest of all Cornish medieval bridges crosses the Tamar. It is over 200 feet long and was erected in 1437. The fact that no major roads cross the Tamar here has led to its survival in such good condition.

North Hill   North Hill is an attractive granite and slate village tucked under some of the highest parts of Bodmin Moor by the River Lynher which defines the eastern edge of the moor. It is located just off the B3254, Launceston to Liskeard road. The *Church of St Torney* is a large church constructed of big, granite blocks. This, along with the battlemented aisles and porch, gives the building a rather bleak and menacing appearance. The church dates largely from the C15 and C16, although the chancel is earlier. The original wagon roofs survive within and there is a good, undecorated Norman font. The main interest, however, are the monuments, which are exceptional for Cornwall in their number and quality. There are several, good C17 slate memorials and an unusual slate altar tomb of 1606 to Thomas Vincent, wife and 15 children. The most elaborate, though, and one of the finest in

Cornwall is to Henry Spoure with sister and parents (1688). The father and mother kneeling opposite each other with the children standing in niches behind. All four figures are realistically coloured and set within a large wall monument with columns, entablature and pediment. The **Racehorse Inn** (**01566 782337**) serves real ales and food. From North Hill the B3254 provides a scenic drive as one approaches Minions and Bodmin Moor.

Bodmin Moor

Bodmin Moor is the biggest of the four granite uplands of Cornwall and yet covers an area little more than 10 miles by 10. Its apparent size is further diminished by the main A30 which divides the moor into north and south. The north is bleak and wind-swept, while the south is more inhabited, dotted with isolated sheep farms and criss crossed by narrow lanes. Nowhere is very far from roads and houses and while there are extensive views in fine weather, there is little scope for any extensive hill walking. In foul weather, the moor can be an inhospitable place and the boggy nature of the terrain can make walking during prolonged wet weather an unpleasant and trying experience. The main interest is in the wealth of prehistoric remains that litter the surface and testify to the more intensive habitation of the moor in the past.

At the centre of the moor is the hamlet of Bolventor and **Jamaica Inn** (**01566 86250**) **C**, dating from the mid C18. It was once a haunt for smugglers as well as a stop for coaches and travellers crossing the moor. Daphne du Maurier immortalised it in her book of the same name. Today, it is a tacky theme park with fibre glass smugglers and a tasteless museum of stuffed animals masquerading as little furry people having tea and other senseless pursuits. There is a restaurant and bar and if you want to spend a night by the A30 there is a hotel too.

Jamaica Inn

Bodmin Moor – North of the A30

The character of this part of the moor is of isolated moorland with few farms and little agriculture. The only settlement on the moor itself is Altarnun, a lovely village of granite and white-painted houses alongside a brook in a sheltered valley just off the main A30. The church, known as the "cathedral of the moors" has one of the highest towers in Cornwall at 109 feet but its scale is disguised by being located against the rising hill behind. The church and churchyard have a beautiful setting by the stream and ancient footbridge at the north end of the village. There is a light and airy feel to the interior with its thin piers widely spaced and the big Perpendicular windows with clear glazing. The piers, their capital and base, are all carved from individual pieces of moorstone, dragged down from the moors above and simply stood on end.. The church has some excellent furnishings with over 70 carved bench ends from the C16 including jesters, serpents and musicians, some of the best in the county, a good rood screen and altar rail (1684) running right across the width of the church and a magnificent Norman font, unusually large

Altarnun

and with bearded faces at the corners. There are barely discernible traces of medieval colouring still remaining on the font.

Altarnun would make a pleasant base for exploring Bodmin Moor but the choice of accommodation is rather limited. In the centre of the village is the pleasant, but pricey, **Penhallow Manor Country Hotel** (01566 86206) *D* located in the former vicarage and right next to the church. It is a handsome Georgian house in beautiful landscaped gardens. Just to the south of the village at a road junction known as Five Lanes is the **Kings Head** (01566 86241) *A*, a C16 coaching inn with stone flagged floors and good value accommodation. It has a restaurant and serves food at lunchtime and in the evenings. Inexpensive. A good range of real ales are also served. Penhallow Manor also has a nice restaurant which is open to non-residents. *M*

From Altarnun, it is a short walk along the lanes to the west or south to take you up onto the high open moorland of West Moor and East Moor – some of the best walking in the area. The area to the north is one of rolling hills, isolated farms

St Clether

and small villages on the very edge of the moors. St Clether boasts a church, heavily rebuilt in 1865, but with the most marvellous, crudely worked, granite Norman font. A clear example of the craftsmen grappling with this most difficult of materials. From the churchyard, a path leads for some 10 to 15 minutes walk to the *Holy Well*, the biggest in the county. It is in a lovely setting, totally isolated and consists of the well proper and an associated chapel with the well waters channelled through it.

Camelford

Apr–Sept, Mon–Fri. Admission £1.25, conc. £1.00, children £0.75

Camelford is the largest settlement on the northern edge of the moors. The town is grim and grey with a rather run-down appearance and a traffic-choked main street. There is little to detain the visitor, but there are a range of shops that can provide essential items and the **Camelford Gallery** (01840 213980) has some interesting paintings and exhibitions. There are also two small museums. The **North Cornwall Museum** (01840 212954) is located in the centre of town on The Clease. It houses a collection of items depicting aspects of north Cornish life over the last 200 years. There is also a changing exhibition of local arts and crafts. More stimulating, perhaps, is the **British Cycling Museum** (01840 212450), housed in the old Camelford railway station about a mile north of the town on the B3266, Boscastle road. It is open between 10.00am and 5.00pm (closed Friday and Saturday) and has over 400 cycles on display as well as other memorabilia. Admission £2.50, children £1.50. **The Darlington Inn** (01840 213314) *B* on the main street is a C16 coaching inn and post house with slate floors, beams and real fire. They serve real ales and bar food and also have accommodation.

Just to the north, at the evocatively named *Slaughterbridge*, is a nine foot long stone, covered in moss and lichen, and with an inscription in Latin and barely discernible Ogham script. It dates from the C6 or C7 and reads "Latinus lies here, son of Magarus." Due to a misreading, it was thought to commemorate the death of the legendary King Arthur. It is more likely to be for another Celtic chieftain slain in one of the many battles between the Cornish and the Saxons. If you want to visit the site, there is a car park signposted off the B3314, from where it is a pleasant 10 minute walk to the site. To the south east of Camelford and approached along a long, narrow straight road is *Rough Tor*, one of the highest points of the moor and with wonderful views over the surrounding contryside. There is a free car park from where it is an easy 20 minute walk to the summit capped with extravagantly wind-eroded granite boulders. From here, there is open access to all the high moorland with *Brown Willy*, the highest point in Cornwall (420m) a short way to the east. The area around here is rich in prehistoric remains with traces of many settlements and stone circles dotted around the moorland. To the south, and more conveniently reached from the lanes above St Breward, is *King Arthur's Hall*, 56 moss and lichen-covered stones forming an incomplete rectangle some 150 feet by 60 and set within an earth bank up to 20 feet wide. The purpose of this early Celtic monument remains a mystery, but there is certainly no connection with King Arthur. Nearby are two Bronze Age stone circles, and other hut circles and prehistoric field systems cover the top of King Arthur's Downs.

St Breward is a long straggling village of largely undistinguished buildings. The **St Breward** church, a solid granite edifice, is the highest in Cornwall. The big, circular Norman piers and arches that have ben retained inside lend comparison with the later, more slender south arcade of the C15. Some medieval painted bench ends have been re-used in the parclose screen to the north chancel chapel and in the front pews. The nearby **Old Inn** serves a good range of real ales and food at lunchtimes and in the evenings.

From here, there is a beautiful drive along the edge of the high moorland to Blisland, an attractive village of granite houses with a picturesque grouping **Blisland** around the large village green surrounded by mature trees. The *Church of St Protus and St Hyacinth* on the south side of the green is one of the most interesting and surprising in Cornwall. The church is essentially Norman with a C15 transformation and C19 remodelling. The C19 work has lent an extraordinary quality to the interior. It was carried out by F.C.Eden who also contributed the stunning, painted and gilded rood screen and the altar in the Italian Renaisance style. The shock of this gilded richness is almost overwhelming when entering an otherwise, apparently conventional Cornish parish church. John Betjeman considered the restoration could not be bettered, even as an improvement on a medieval church. The church has an unusual plan with the tower to the north transept and no west door. The big, high rood screen gives the interior an almost square plan, most unusual for medieval churches. The C15 pillars have a spectacular lean to the south which has thrown the well-carved wagon roof into all sorts of disarray. To the layman, it seems almost impossible that it remains standing. There are traces of medieval wall paintings, some good slate memorials and a fine, simply-carved Norman font. The **Blisland Inn** on the other side of the green serves excellent real ales and good quality bar food. It was voted CAMRA Cornwall Pub of the Year 2000. About a mile south of the village is **Trewardale** (**01208 821226**) *C*, a wonderful, secluded country house with excellent and good value accommodation.

Just to the west of Blisland is the *Camel Trail*, an off-road cycle path that links Bodmin Moor to Padstow on the coast. Mountain bikes are available to hire from the **Silverstream Restaurant and Tea Gardens** (**01208 74408**) *B* in the hamlet

Hellandbridge of Hellandbridge, two miles south west of Blisland. As well as morning coffee, lunches and afternoon teas, they also provide bed and breakfast accommodation in a beautiful granite cottage in a very quiet and secluded location. It is good value and probably one of the nicest places to stay in this part of the moor. Self-catering cottages are also available. The C15 bridge is one of the best in the county and one of the few to survive the great flood of 1847 which carried away most of the other bridges over the River Camel.

Bodmin Moor – South of the A30

Dominating the centre of the moor is Colliford Lake, encircled by a narrow lane from where are good views across the water. To the east and just south of Bolventor is *Dozmary Pool,* one of the many places on the moor linked to the legend of King Arthur. It is supposed to be the resting place for Excalibur, the sword that Arthur was given by the Lady of the Lake. After he was mortally wounded, he ordered Excalibur to be cast into Dozmary Pool whereupon a woman's hand appeared, caught it and held it aloft before drawing it under the waters. The area around here is populated with a number of isolated farms served by narrow lanes.

Temple   The tiny hamlet of Temple, just off the A30 to the west of Colliford Lake, is one of the few communities on the moor. It consists of no more than a few houses and the extraordinary church of *St Catherine*. The original church was built around 1120 by the Knights Templar, who owned the land hereabouts. These warrior knights were one of the influential forces in the Crusades of the early Middle Ages. Due to their growing power, they were suppressed in 1314 and the Knights Hospitaller took over their property. Their mission was to protect pilgrims and provide them with hospitality and Temple served this function for those pilgrims crossing the moor. By 1883, the church was in ruins when *Sylvanus Trevail* rebuilt it in an exemplary fashion retaining all the simplicity and strength of the early medieval church. The base of the tower, the tower arch and the bowl of the font are all that remain of the original church and yet, such is the quality of the rebuilding, that you would be hard pushed to tell that so little survived. The result today is a beautiful, contemplative space enhanced by its remote setting on the bleak moorland.

To the east of Colliford Lake is an area of high moorland around East Moor and Twelve Men's Moor which provides good walking and views west towards Devon and Dartmoor. The area can be approached from the east via the narrow lane from Bolventor to St Cleer from where a number of tracks and paths lead off or from the west where there are a large number of roads and lanes which provide access for walkers to the high ground. At the southern edge of this high moorland is the **Minions** small village of Minions and some of the best prehistoric remains on the moor. Just to the north of the village are the *Hurlers*, three stone circles in a line. The southern one is badly damaged and barely distinguishable but the other two are clearly visible. The significance of the three circles is unknown. To the north, on Stowe's Hill, are the remains of a large Bronze Age or Neolithic settlement with two stone enclosures, Bronze Age cairns and a large number of house platforms, where stone has been cleared to make way for the erection of wooden houuses. On the summit are some extraordinary weather-worn, natural granite tors – the two most famous being known as *The Cheesewring* and *The Devil's Chair*. From here, the view over the surrounding landscape reveals a vast number of prehistoric sites along with many chimneys and mine buildings. The nearby Rillaton Round Barrow is one of the largest on the moor. It contained the famous Rillaton Gold Bowl, which was "lost" for many years before being rediscovered in the dressing room of King George V. A copy is displayed in The Royal Cornwall Museum in Truro.

There is car parking in Minions village. On the northern edge of the village, in a converted engine house is the exhibition area for the *Minions Area Heritage Project*, which provides information about the moors, their geology, flora and fauna and their occupation by man over the last 6500 years. The village itself is little more than a scattering of buildings. There is a shop and tearoom and the **Hurlers Halt** (**01579 363056**) *B*, a tea room with attached accommodation, normally for weekly hire, but sometimes available on a bed and breakfast basis. The **Cheesewring** public house is nearby. Just to the west of the village, beside the road, is the *Longstone Cross*. A large, upright stone, it is most probably of prehistoric pagan origin. It would have been adopted by Celtic holy men who carved the round headed cross on it during the Dark Ages as a symbol of the new religion.

To the south of Minions is the large village of St Cleer with the attractive   **St Cleer**
Church of St Clarus. The tower is big while the main body of the church is comparatively low and small. The interior is well lit from the big windows to both aisles. The north arcade is the earlier of the two and has cruder octagonal piers and simpler arches than the south arcade which shows a more sophisticated hand at work with a more complex profile for the piers and a complex arch moulding. On the outskirts of the village is the C15 *Holy Well*, much restored in 1864, but still a good example of its type. The niches in the back wall are where bathers would store their valuables. Just outside the village is *Trethevy Quoit*, a Neolithic tomb (c3500 BC) consisting of six large stones supporting a massive capstone. Access to the inside would have been by a small rectangular hole in the front, the small hole in the capstone remains unexplained. The village has a number of useful shops and two good pubs. The **Market Inn** opposite the church serves food and real ales and the **Stag Inn** in Fore Street has a good range of real ales and cider and serves food, lunchtimes and evenings.

Heading west from St Cleer, after 1 mile on the right hand side of the road, one comes to *King Doniert's Stone*, the bases of two intricately carved C9 granite crosses. They are some of the best examples of Celtic carving in the county. The next right turn is signposted for *Golitha Falls*, a local beauty spot and National Nature Reserve. There is a car park and toilet facilities. There is a pleasant woodland walk along the tumbling River Fowey, little more than a stream here. The further you walk, the more scenic it becomes as the stream divides into a number of channels.

From here, a narrow lane leads on to St Neot, a large and attractive village   **St Neot**
spread over several hills on the edge of Bodmin Moor. It is a good base for exploring this part of the county – there are some excellent places to stay, a nice pub

serving good food and a magnificent church. The *Church of St Anietus* dominates the village from its raised position and is consciously designed to show its best side to those approaching up the valley. The plan form is typical Cornish but particular emphasis is placed on the exterior design of the south aisle and porch, both built of large, regular granite blocks. The south elevation, including the two storey porch, is embattled with pinnacles on the buttresses and was built around 1425. The tower is earlier, the north aisle about a hundred years later and much plainer. The porch has an intricately carved stone vaulted roof and the south aisle, its original wagon roof with shield bearing angels along the wall plate. The windows are all C15 and most unusually they contain a large proportion of their original stained glass. It is the finest collection of medieval stained glass in the county and one of the finest to be found in any parish church.

There are 15 windows in all and they contain about half their original glass, despite a good deal of renewal and restoration undertaken by John Hedgeland in 1830. How the windows came to survive the Reformation and the Puritans is something of a mystery. After the Battle of Braddock Down, Cromwell's defeated troops stabled their horses in the church and the story goes that they were too exhausted after their defeat to inflict the wanton destruction they meted out elsewhere to such ungodly flourishes. However, more recent research indicates that the parishioners petitioned for the windows to be saved, an act of some bravery in those times. The earliest of the windows, the finest and least restored, is the Creation Window at the east end of the south aisle. The panels tell the story of the Creation, ending with Noah doffing his cap to God as he receives his instructions. This leads on to the first window in the south aisle which presents the story of the Flood. The panels are wonderfully detailed and give realistic expression to the story with Noah's Ark being represented as a three masted ship of the time. In these windows we see the medieval tradition of storytelling via the medium of stained glass. The original intention was to provide a visual record of the Old Testament, but the project had to be abandoned, most likely due to lack of funds. Instead the vicar had to turn to the principal families of the parish for help and the following windows contain representations of their favourite saints, as well as the patrons themselves. These fill the rest of the south aisle and the Harys family window which is on the north aisle just to the west of the screen.

It would appear at this point that the number of wealthy sponsors had been exhausted and the remaining windows are provided by public subscription. The wives of the western part of the parish provided one and the young women another. Both carry depiction's of their donors kneeling at the bottom of the window. The remaining window on the north side is the most famous of all – the St Neot window, given by the young men of the parish. It shows 12 scenes from the life of the patron saint which are depicted with great detail and charm. The west window of the north aisle is the St George Window and is one of the best preserved. Again, it depicts 12 scenes from the legendary history of the saint. The window is of unique interest because some of the scenes depicted are not found anywhere else. The east window over the high altar is entirely Hedgeland's work and provides a useful comparison with the medieval glass in the other windows.

Outside the porch is a crowd of Celtic crosses, one from the C9 having the best example of interlace carving of any in Cornwall. It was re-erected in 1889 and placed on St Neot's stone. Tradition says that he was so small that he could not reach the church door keyhole, so he used to stand on this stone and throw the key into the keyhole. There are also several good slate memorials in the churchyard. The area was strongly Royalist during the Civil War and the church still sports an oak bough from the tower roof to commemorate Charles II's escape after the Battle of Worcester by hiding in an oak tree. It is renewed every Oak Apple Day on 29 May.

Open Mar–Oct daily, 10.00am– 5.00pm (8.00pm in Aug), closed Sundays. Admission £5.00, children £3.50, family £15.00.

The *Holy Well* is a short walk away, signposted up the lane opposite the village shop. It is an extraordinary, little building in which the dwarf-like St Neot would stand up to his neck in water while reciting the Book of Psalms. The **Carnglaze Slate Cavern** (01579 320251), just south of the village on the way to the A38, are three underground caverns created by local slate miners which now contain an underground lake with crystal clear blue-green water. There is a guided tour lasting 45 minutes.

Next door to the church is the **London Inn** (01579 320263) *B*, a warm and welcoming pub with real ales and good food, served lunchtimes and evenings. They also have en-suite accommodation. Just outside the village, on the road heading south, is **Lampen Mill** (01579 321119) *B*, a beautifully restored and extended mill in a tranquil setting. Accommodation is in large en-suite rooms and residents have their own lounge. **Lampen Farm** (01579 320284) *B* is a lovely C16 farmhouse just south of the village with good value accommodation.

To the west of St Neot and just to the east of Bodmin is the local beauty spot of Cardinham Woods, which is signposted from the A38. They extend to 650 acres and there are a number of waymarked walks and cycle routes, although cycles are permitted to use all the tracks in the forest. The terrain away from the valley bottom is quite steep and some of the routes are challengingly hilly. There is a pay and display car park and café which is open Sundays, school holidays and during the summer.

It would be an easy walk or cycle ride through the forest to the attractive village of Cardinham, just to the north. The church has some good memorials and medieval carved bench ends. Of more interest, though, are two exceptional crosses in the churchyard. The smaller, a wheel-headed cross was originally a gravestone. The larger has superb ornamentation carved onto the shaft and is one of the finest in the county. The powerful, medieval family, the Cardinhams, had their castle some 700 metres to the south.

Cardinham

Lanhydrock
National Trust: Open April–October, daily except Monday (open Bank Holidays), 11am–5.30pm. October 5pm. Gardens open all year. Tel. 01208 265950. Admission £7.90, children £3.95, under 5 free. Family £19.75. Garden and grounds only £4.40, children £2.20

Lanhydrock is one of the grandest houses in Cornwall. Its appearance at first seems to be wholly Tudor, but it was largely destroyed by fire in 1881. The building you see today is predominantly Victorian, albeit giving the outward appearance of a C17 creation. The internal planning is resolutely Victorian and one of the delights of the house is the picture it presents of Victorian Society and the small army of servants required to maintain standards. Some 49 rooms are open to the visitor and sufficient time should be allowed for the tour of the house. The gardens and park surrounding the house are also notable and provide excellent walks.

The original building dates from the acquisition of the manor of Lanhydrock by Sir Richard Robartes in the 1620's. The Robartes had established their wealth from servicing the tin mining industry and were to become one of the most influential families in C17 England. The original building was built around the four sides of a quadrangle in the then fashionable, but rapidly dating, Tudor style. The east range was demolished in the 1780's to leave the U shaped courtyard we see today. The only parts of the original house to escape the fire of 1881 are the gatehouse, the two storey porch and the north wing with its superb C17 gallery and plasterwork.

The house is approached across the park with the elaborate gatehouse visible from some distance. The gatehouse was begun in 1636 but not finished until 1651, sometime after the main house. It shows elements of Renaissance detailing which are absent in the much plainer north wing of the main house. The proliferation of arches and columns and the delicacy of detailing is probably explained by its later date and the new ideas coming from London where the classical references of the Renaissance were by then all the rage. The stumpy pinnacles on top reappear on the house, the lodges and in the gardens as a recurring motif. The low battlemented wall linking the gatehouse to the main house was added in 1857 by George Gilbert Scott, the most fashionable architect of the time.

One enters the house through the surviving C17 porch. The outer hall is pure Victorian with the exception of the granite fireplace which probably pre-dates the fire. The wood panelling, frieze and plasterwork are typical of the rich detail of the Victorian interiors. Its size indicates the importance of the house for entertaining and the numbers of guests who may be received. The inner hall has a wonderful mosaic floor and engraved glass double doors, not unlike those found in public houses of the period.

The Victorian rebuilding was undertaken by the architect *Richard Coad* and took no more than four years to complete. As such, it is an extraordinary example of the planned Victorian country house, free from all the constraints that earlier designs may have imposed on the internal planning. Coad was merely instructed to provide "a modest and unpretentious family home" and to retain the basic outward form of the original building. The plan of the house was based on the Victorian principle of segregation – of family from servants, male from female and young from old. A warren of corridors and stairs connected the various parts of the house and allowed circulation to be segregated as well. Rooms were designed to be private and serviced by corridors rather than the earlier concept of rooms as a succession of spaces through which one passed. To create the extra space required for this new plan, Coad cut back the hill behind the house and built a high retaining wall. He filled this space, which was not visible from the front, with the new servants quarters grouped around two internal courtyards. The house was built as fireproof as possible with wrought iron girders replacing timber joists, concrete floors and ceilings of a patent fireproof construction. A new reservoir was constructed behind the house from where it fed hydrants both inside and outside the building. A below ground boiler house supplied domestic hot water and operated a central heating system, still working today.

The tour leads on to the lavish dining room, one of the key rooms in the house for entertaining and then on to a series of servants rooms conveniently placed for servicing the dining room. Grandest of these is the kitchen with a high roof supported on wooden trusses and with clerestory windows, designed to remove smoke, heat and smells. The elaborate arrangement of roasting spits is an indication of the scale of entertaining that went on. The servery between the kitchen and dining room enabled food to be kept warm prior to serving and there is a large steel hot-cupboard that was fuelled by the central heating system. The kitchen was surrounded by a large number of subsidiary rooms for storing and preparing food. The number of servants required to run a kitchen of this size was considerable with up to 20 being involved at any one time.

In the south wing are the male preserves of the house, the billiard room and smoking room as well as the stewards room, where the business of the estate was conducted. On the wall are the architect's plans for the rebuilding of the house. Upstairs is the nursery wing where the young of the household would be looked after by the nannys. Through the nursery corridor, you come to the staircase for the male servants. The luggage lift by the stairs was for the many heavy trunks and boxes arriving by train from the station on the edge of the park. They would be carried up to the first floor for unpacking, then up to the second floor for storage. The staircase leads up to the servant's quarters on the upper floor.

Back on the first floor, the family bedrooms are found. One of the only two bathrooms in the house is located next to His Lordships Room. The lack of bathrooms does not reflect low standards of hygiene but rather the Victorian tradition of bathing in one's bedroom – there was no shortage of servants to fill hip baths. All the main reception rooms at Lanhydrock are on the first floor, presumably so that they could connect directly with the gallery. Here we find the drawing room and the morning room off to one side.

The entire first floor of the north wing is occupied by the great gallery, the major part of the original C17 house saved from the fire. The long gallery in Tudor houses was a room of state and parade, used for excercise in inclement weather. They were often highly decorated and this one is no exception with a marvellous plaster barrel-vaulted ceiling dating from just before the Civil War in 1642. The 24 panels show scenes from the Old Testament with smaller panels surrounding them depicting birds and beasts. The wood panelling is Victorian but the carved oak frieze is contemporary with the plaster ceiling.

Immediately behind the house is the Church of St Hydroc, dating from the C15 and of little interest, although typical of its period. The house is surrounded by a Victorian landscape of gardens and parkland superimposed on the earlier landscapes of the C17 and C18. The most obvious survival of the C17 planting is the avenue of sycamores running east from the house, planted in 1648 and since subsequently replaced with beech trees and now forming the principal feature of the park. There are extensive walks down to the River Fowey and in the surrounding

Lanhydrock is easy to reach by public transport with a direct connection to Bodmin Parkway station on the main West Coast line. t is a gentle 45 minute walk or an easy cycle ride through the park. Bus no.55 runs from Bodmin Parkway via Lanhydrock to Bodmin and on to Padstow. By car it is signposted off the A38

woodland. The Station Drive, the old carriage route, can be followed to Bodmin Parkway railway station.

Bodmin

Church of St Petroc

Located on the south western edge of the eponymous moor, Bodmin has little of interest for the visitor other than the Church of St Petroc. The town's history begins with the coming of St Petroc in C6 who ministered here and founded a monastic community. At the time of the Domesday Book, Bodmin was the only town in Cornwall recorded as having a market and indeed during the Middle Ages it was one of the most important towns in Cornwall, although little remains to bear testimony to those times. Of the monastery, with its famous shrine of St Petroc, nothing remains other than a few scattered remains in the Priory Grounds.

The only major medieval survival is the C15 *Church of St Petroc*. It is the largest in Cornwall and was rebuilt on the site of earlier structures in 1469-72. The tower is Norman up to the third storey and would have been much more impressive with its original spire, 150 feet high. This was destroyed by lightning in 1699 which also destroyed much of the original roof. The church is a standard Cornish design although the proportions of the interior are more generous than normal. The real interest lies in a small number of remarkable furnishings and memorials within the church. The font is C12 Norman and without doubt the finest in the county. It has a deep bowl on a central shaft supported by four slimmer shafts in the corners with the busts of angels as their capitals. The bowl is carved in a deep and intricate design of foliage and scroll ornament, with the tree of life and beasts below. Nearby are a series of excellent carved slate memorials, that to Peter Bolt (1633) being considered particularly fine. The battle flags of the Duke of Cornwall's Light Infantry hang in one of the aisles and date back to the Battle of Waterloo.

Beside the High Altar is the extravagant Tomb of Prior Vivian, the last but one Prior of Bodmin, dying in 1533. The monument was relocated from the Priory Church. It is of black Catacleuse stone and grey marble with the figure of the Prior lying on a decorated chest. The style was very up-to-date for Cornwall having close references to the tomb of Henry VII completed 14 years earlier. However, the churches' most treasured possession is the Reliquary of St Petroc, which is kept in a display cabinet in the south aisle. The reliquary is a rare ivory casket with gilt copper straps and has been identified as being made by Arabs in C12 Sicily. It is reputed to have contained the bones of St Petroc which vanished from the monastery in 1176, presumed to have been stolen. The remains were traced to Brittany and returned to Bodmin in 1177, the elaborate casket having probably been made in atonement for the theft. The casket was lost for centuries after the Dissolution of the monastery in the C16. It was returned, minus the relics, to the Church in 1957. It was subsequently stolen again in 1994, but later returned.

In the churchyard stands the now ruined *Chapel of St Thomas Becket*. Around Mount Folly, there are a group of early C19, neo-classical, granite buildings which bear witness to the transfer of the Assize Court from Launceston in 1835. The **Town Museum** is located here and tells the history of Bodmin up to the end of

World War II (Easter–September 10.30am–4.30pm, admission free.). **The Shire Hall** (01208 76616) itself has been converted into a museum recreating the Victorian courtroom and cells. Fore Street is the principal shopping street of the town and there are a number of C19 buildings and shopfronts but the whole has a rather tired appearance. To the south of the town centre is Bodmin Central Railway Station, unfortunately no longer a part of the regular rail network but the home of the **Bodmin and Wenford Railway** (01208 73666) which runs steam trains between Bodmin Parkway and Boscarne Junction. The former is handy for Lanhydrock House and the latter for the Camel Trail, a long distance cycle and footpath. Services vary throughout the year and it is advised to telephone for further information. Just beyond the station is Bodmin's **Military Museum** (01208 72810), housed in the old militia barracks built in 1859. It includes much military memorabilia and charts the history of the Duke of Cornwall's Light Infantry, including the valiant defence of Lucknow during the Indian Mutiny when no fewer than 4 Victoria Crosses were awarded to the regiment. The *Beacon*, a large area of parkland due south of the town is surmounted by the 144 foot high granite memorial to Sir Walter Gilbert. **Bodmin Gaol** (01208 76292) was built in 1778 and was the first to house prisoners in individual cells rather than communal dungeons. It has a curious "French chateau" appearance and was the site of the last public hanging in Britain in 1909.

10am–5pm (closed Sun). Admission £3, conc. £2, children £1.50, family £6.50

Mon–Fri, 9.00am–5pm. Also Sundays in July/Aug Admission, £2.50, £1.50 children

Easter–Oct, every day 10am (11am Sat)–6pm. Admission £4.50, children £2.50

Accommodation in Bodmin is a limited and not particularly attractive proposition. In the town centre is the rather grim-looking **Westbery Hotel**, Rhind Street (01208 72772) *C*. Nearby is **Priory Cottage**, 34 Rhind Street (01208 73064) *B*. To the south of the town centre, in St. Nicholas Street, is **Fernside** (01208 72168) *B*, a big Victorian granite house with car parking. The Tourist Information Centre, Shire Hall, Mount Folly (01208 76616) can provide other options if necessary.

The really limiting factor about staying in Bodmin is that the town has a generally run down appearance and there is little in the way of restaurants and pubs to make an enticing evening. **The Weavers Inn**, Honey Street, opposite the church, is one of the nicest with a comfortable, old interior. They serve real ale and food, lunchtimes and evenings. On the other side of the street is the **Providence Café** opening lunchtime and Friday and Saturday evenings. They have a good selection of organic and vegetarian dishes. **Nicals**, directly opposite, has an eclectic international menu. The **Hole in the Wall** in Crockwell Street, entrance from the town car park, used to be the town's Debtors Prison and provides an interesting ambience to consume their range of real ales. They serve lunchtime meals.

The North Coast – Morwenstow to Rock

Relatively unvisited, the North Cornwall coast is an area of high cliffs, backed by rolling countryside and interspersed with huge sand beaches with some of the best surfing in the country. This part of Cornwall has a rugged character and there are many opportunities for enjoying the magnificent scenery and landscape. With the exception of Bude, there are no towns of any size and most communities are based on the small fishing ports and trading harbours that grew up on the few sheltered parts of this most exposed coastline.

Morwenstow

Located at the northernmost point of Cornwall, Morwenstow has a dramatic setting in a wooded valley just back from a coastline of towering cliffs and jagged ofshore rocks. There is an excellent church, superb cliff views, fine walks and a nice tea shop and pub. The area is perhaps best known though for the eccentric vicar, *Stephen Hawker*, poet and sometime opium smoker who was vicar of the parish between 1834–75. Among his best known poems is "The Song of the Western Men," the unofficial anthem of Cornwall. He was one of the first to provide Christian burials for sailor's shipwrecked along this "iron bound coast." He was married twice, first to a woman twice his age and secondly to one 41 years his junior. He once persuaded the people of Bude that they possessed a mermaid by sitting out on the rocks beyond the breakwater dressed only with seaweed. Eccentric to the last, he was received into the Roman Catholic Church hours before his death in 1875.

The church is one of the most interesting in Cornwall and has a fine location on the south side of a steep valley. The nearby free car park is on higher ground and one descends through the well-treed churchyard to the church, which possesses some of the best Norman work in the county. The north arcade has three thick circular piers which are pure Norman. The aisle was subsequently extended with two Early English piers from the C13, also round but with pointed arches. The south aisle in contrast is Cornish medieval from the C16 with much thinner, more graceful piers. The interior provides as good example as there is of the stylistic transition from Norman Romanesque to Late Medieval Gothic. The south doorway and porch are also Norman with typical colonnetes and zig zag decoration to the arches. The best of the Norman work though are the many crude heads of beasts and animals on the porch and on the spandrels between the arches. The wagon roofs of both nave and aisle are original. The font is thought to be C10 and is a crude, uneven bowl shape with cable decoration typical of the Saxon period. There is a complete set of bench ends from 1575 and a good rood screen of the same date, re-assembled by Hawker in 1845 with cast iron tracery. There are the faint remains of a wall painting of St Morwenna on the north wall of the chancel.

From the churchyard, there are good views down the valley to the sea beyond. The churchyard contains the graves of over 40 sailors shipwrecked on the nearby cliffs and buried by Hawker. The figurehead of the Caledonia marks the grave of its captain and crew, wrecked in 1842. The adjacent vicarage was built by Hawker and its unusual chimneys are meant to be based on the towers of churches with which he was connected. Just across the nearby lane is St John's Well which still supplies clear spring water for baptisms and was known to be in use by 1296, although the well head you see today is probably C16.

From the church there is a fine walk down to the coast from either the lane and path from the top of the churchyard or the path that follows the little stream at the bottom of the valley below the church. The latter is steep in places and can be muddy but provides a wonderfully slow transition from the warm, sheltered environment of the valley bottom to the more open and harsher conditions near the coast. The coast here is fabulously dramatic with the 450 foot high Henna Cliff dropping sheer into the clear waters below. Out to sea there are the many exposed rock ledges that give this coast its most fearsome of reputations. A few hundred yards to the south is a small hut made out of driftwood and built by the Reverend Hawker. Here he would sit looking out to sea, smoking pipes of opium, writing poetry and keeping an open eye for ships in distress. The hut is now looked after by the National Trust and is signposted off the main coast path. There are several paths that return from the coast further to the south, the last of which follows the narrow Tidna Valley – these will all return you to the car park by the church.

Henna Cliff

The latter returns via the nearby, small hamlet of Crosstown where there is the wonderful **Bush Inn**, an unspoilt granite inn, once a chapel. There are three tiny bars, slate floors, exposed beams and a warm welcome. They serve real ales and food, lunchtimes and evenings. Opposite the church, there is the **Rectory Tea Rooms** which provides lunches and cream teas in beautiful surroundings – open summer only. Morwenstow is signposted off the A39 at Crimp and is easily reached by car. Public transport is very limited and largely impractical for the visitor. Regular buses ply the main A39 but from Crimp it would be a good two hour walk, although you may be able to hitch a lift. For those walking the coast path, it is only a short detour inland and one well worth taking.

Crosstown

The coast around Morwenstow is one of high, precipitous cliffs with steep sided valleys or coombes cutting through the cliffs at regular intervals. This results in a tortuous, switchback path that can be hard going. The benefit is that this part of the coast path is not heavily visited and the scenery is breathtaking. The views from *Higher Sharpnose Point* are particularly fine. Slightly further to the south is *Stanbury Mouth*, an isolated cove with sand and rocks. Swimming can be dangerous, but the beach makes a beautiful spot for sunbathing and picnics. On the hills above are the massive satellite-tracking aerials which dominate the views hereabouts.

At Coombe the cliffs start to reduce in height as they approach Bude, but the descent from *Steeple Point* to the valley bottom is vertiginous. There are superb views up the Coombe valley where almost every inch belonged to the Grenville family for over 450 years. The Grenvilles were one of the most important families in the land under the Tudors and Stuarts. Roger Grenville was the captain of the *Mary Rose* which went down off Portsmouth in 1545, Sir Richard died fighting the Spanish in *The Revenge* off the Azores in 1591 and Sir Bevil was one of the leading Royalist leaders in the Civil War. The Grenville house of Stowe was rebuilt in 1679 as one of the noblest in the west of England, a classical brick mansion, four storeys high and reputed to have 365 windows. When the last male heir died in 1711, the eldest daughter declined to live there and had the mansion demolished in 1739, just 60 years after it had first been erected. All that remains now is the stable block which forms part of Stowe Barton Farmhouse, a fine structure of 1793 built of reclaimed materials from the great house.

Coombe

The small hamlet of Coombe is very picturesque and maintained by the Landmark Trust – several of the cottages are let as holiday homes (**01628 825925**). The bridge over the river was built in 1836 after Reverend Hawker raised a subscription, the list being headed by the King himself who donated £20. The *Coombe Valley* is a lovely wooded place of narrow lanes and footpaths and there is a car park and woodland trail in Stowe Wood. The footpaths lead all the way up the

Kilkhampton valley to the old Saxon village of Kilkhampton from where there are regular bus connections to Bude and Barnstaple. The village is of no particular interest although the church has a very good Norman, south doorway. It is a big church with a high nave and aisles and dates largely from the C16. There is a good and complete set of 157 bench ends dating from the first half of the C16. There is also a good memorial of 1714 to Sir Bevil Grenville and an unusually complete set of stained glass, all Victorian or modern but nevertheless giving a good, overall effect. Just to the west of the village is the remnants of Kilkhampton Castle, probably erected during the civil war of the C12. The site is largely overgrown but it is still possible to discern the outline of the motte and bailey. Parking by the site is very limited but it is only a short walk from the village. The **New Inn** and **London Inn** in the village both serve real ales and food, lunchtimes and evenings.

Duckpool Duckpool at the mouth of the Coombe valley is a sandy cove surrounded by high cliffs. Swimming is not recommended as conditions are often dangerous. There is a small car park and toilet facilities. From here to Bude, there are sandy beaches at low tide. Extreme care needs to be taken when bathing and should be avoided at low tide when the rip tides that sweep along this coast can be very strong. At *Sandy Mouth* and *Northcott Mouth* there are car parks, toilets and cafes as well as a summer lifeguard service. Care should be taken not to get stranded on the beach by the incoming tide. It is an easy walk along the coast path from Bude to Sandy Mouth, but to the north the going gets much more arduous. These beaches provide a more secluded alternative to those nearer Bude.

Bude

Bude is the only sizeable town and resort on this part of the coast. It started life as an agricultural trading port serving the inland farming communities which were remote from any other port or major centre of population. In 1823 the Bude Canal was commenced with a view to linking the Bristol and English Channels via Launceston and the Tamar River. While this was never achieved, it was used to transport lime rich beach sand to fertilize the inland farms.. It fell into disuse towards the end of the C19 and now only a mile or so remains navigable for recreational purposes. The tramway for moving the sand to the quayside can still be seen near the lock gates in Bude. Nowadays, Bude is nothing more than a holiday resort for the many thousands who come to use the expansive beaches. The town, however, is a disappointment with a scruffy appearance, few amenities and a dearth of good places to stay and eat and drink. In 1899 it was described as "unpicturesque, uninteresting......nothing commendable in the place itself; the houses are as ugly as tasteless builders could contrive to erect." The 1939 Penguin Guide found it dificult to disagree with the opinion of 40 years before and today it would be an optimistic man who could offer an alternative verdict.

The **Bude-Stratton Museum**, Lower Wharf (**01288 353576**) provides some background information to the history of the area with paintings, photographs and salvage from shipwrecks. The nearest beaches are *Crooklets* and *Summerleaze*. Both are big and sandy and in the right conditions can have excellent surf and consequently are very popular with surfers. Both have full facilities including a summer lifeguard service. Swimming can be dangerous at certain states of the tide and care should be taken. There is a sea water bathing pool near the cliffs at the north end of Summerleaze Beach which provides safe swimming.

*Easter-
end Sept,
11am–5pm
every day.
Oct – Thurs &
Sun only.
Admission
£0.50, chil-
dren free.*

There is no shortage of places to stay in Bude and availability is not normally a problem. However, there is a shortage of accommodation with any real character. There are a number of guest houses in Summerleaze Crescent with views over a large car park to the main beach. They are all very much the same in quality and facilities. You could try the **Edgcumbe Hotel** (**01288 353846**) *B*, **Atlantic House** (**01288 352451**) *B* or the **Grosvenor** (**01288 352062**) *B*. There are also several slightly cheaper guest houses in Burn View overlooking the golf course, including **Tee-Side** (**01288 352351**) *B*, **Linkside** (**01288 352410**) *A* and **Sunrise** (**01288 353214**) *A*. The **Inn on the Green** (**01288 356013**) *C* is located close to the beach and overlooks the golf course and has slightly more character than most. The **Falcon Hotel**, Breakwater Road (**01288 352005**) *E* is more upmarket and located directly opposite the Bude Canal in the centre of town.

Finding a good place to eat or drink in Bude is significantly harder than finding a bed for the night. The restaurant at the **Falcon Hotel** (**01288 352005**) *M* is comfortable with good views and an interesting menu. **Summers Seafood Restaurant**, 16 The Strand (**01288 356050**) *M* overlooks the canal and has fresh fish and seafood dishes. The **Mirchi** (**01288 350300**) *I–M* in Lansdowne Road is open in the evenings only and is a good quality Indian restaurant with a smart interior. **Bellini's Pizza and Café Bar** (**01288 359550**) *I* in Queen Street has an Italian feel with marble floors and chrome furniture. Also in Queen Street is the **Taste of India** (**01288 356417**) *I*, a basic Indian restaurant and several fish and chip take-aways. Good places to drink are like gold dust. You could try the **Bencoolen**, Bencoolen Road by the roundabout to the south of the town centre or the **Carriers Inn** or **The Globe** on The Strand. All three serve real ales but have little atmosphere. Alternatively, you could have an early night – one of the best options in Bude.

Practicalities

The Tourist Information Centre is at The Crescent Car Park (**01288 354240**) by the canal to the south of the town centre. By car, Bude is easily found off the main A39. Parking in the town is generally no problem. There is no railway but it is well connected by bus to all the major towns in Cornwall and North Devon. The coast path passes right through the town. Towards the end of August every year, is the *Bude Jazz Festival* which lasts a week and hosts over 200 events. The style is New Orleans Revival and if this is your cup of tea then a visit at this time would be worthwhile.

**Tourist
Information
Centre**

Just to the north of Bude is the small, attractive village of Poughill. The *Church*

Poughill

of St Olaf, a Danish dedication, has an excellent, complete set of bench ends and two over-restored wall paintings. On the north wall, there is a watercolour of the original wall paintings from 1894 allowing comparison with the restored version. There is good tracery in the east window and some bright Victorian glass. The roofs are also very good with excellent carving and the part by the chancel decoratively painted. The nearby **Preston Gate Inn** is a lovely C16 inn with log fires in the winter. They serve real ales and food, lunchtimes and evenings, and make a good option for anyone staying in Bude and prepared to travel a few miles.

Stratton

A mile or so inland from Bude is Stratton, an ancient town clustered around the foot of the medieval church on its hill in the centre of the town. The town was a Royalist stronghold during the Civil War and the Battle of Stamford Hill took place just to the north of the town in 1643. A re-enactment takes place every year in May. *The Church of St Andrew*, once the mother church of Bude, dates from the C14 and has a big C16 tower that dominates the town. The door has been re-used from the old prison and there are good, original wagon roofs and a Royal Coat of Arms, as would be expected in this most loyal of parishes. There is an excellent rood screen of 1901 by *E. H. Sedding* and some good Victorian stained glass. The whole has a rather sombre, civic feel consistent with the status and history of the town. After the Battle of Stamford Hill, the dead of both sides were buried in unmarked graves in the churchyard. There is a lovely triangular square to the front of the church surrounded by handsome, vernacular buildings. Elsewhere, the town is a pleasant jumble of medieval and Georgian buildings, including the tiny *Tree View Cottage* opposite the Tree Inn with a frontage of no more than 8 feet to the street and a pretty slate-hung upper storey.

There are some good places to stay and some pleasant pubs which make it a good alternative to Bude for anybody who wants to explore the area. The **Stratton Gardens Hotel** (**01288 352500**) *B* on Cot Hill, behind the Methodist Chapel, is one of the nicest places to stay. It is a C16 house with a handsome Georgian front and a walled garden to the rear. There is a car park and restaurant with a good value set dinner. **The Tree Inn**, Spicer Street (**01288 352038**) *A* is a C13 inn that was the Royalist headquarters during the Battle of Stamford Hill. They have accommodation and a separate restaurant *I*. Just to the south of the town on Howard Lane is **Cann Orchard** (**01288 352098**) *B*, a lovely old farmhouse with very good value en-suite rooms. There are several pubs in the village that serve meals and bar food. The **Kings Ams** is particularly recommended for the range and quality of its real ales.

Launcells   Just to the east of Stratton is the isolated *Church of St Swithins* at Launcells. It is beautifully located on the side of a wooded valley and is signposted from the A3072. It can be easily walked from Stratton by taking the road east from the church and staying to the right until a footpath leads off to the right over the fields. It dates largely from the C15 and is rare in being relatively unaltered since. The proportions of the interior are light and airy with high arches on slim piers and big Perpendicular windows with clear glass – much of the glass is of considerable age. The south arcade is of polyphant, while the north of the more usual granite. The wagon roofs to the aisles are original while the nave has a white plastered ceiling which with the white walls further accentuates the unusually bright interior. Within the church there are some furnishings of exceptional interest. The C15 carved bench ends are some of the most important in the County with unusual and symbolic representations of the Biblical stories. Against the north wall can be seen some Georgian box pews while the pulpit is Georgian Gothic. Of particular interest are the C15 encaustic tiles from Barnstaple in the chancel. They depict fleur-de-lis, Tudor roses, lions, pelicans and other beasts. On the west wall is a large and fine wall painting showing Abraham in the act of sacrificing Isaac, both depicted in Tudor dress, contemporary to the time. It has recently been sensitively restored. There are further traces of wall painting on the south wall and of script on the north wall containing the words of the letter of thanks written by Charles I in 1643 to all his Cornish subjects. Part of this is still clearly visible. Behind the altar, there is an unusual C18 reredos in polished marble. By the bridge over the stream to the front of the church is the tiny *St Swithin's Holy Well.*

To the south of Stratton and a pleasant walk or drive along narrow lanes is **Marhamchurch**, a small village around a wide main street and set on high land overloking the countryside around. The church has an unusual floor of slate laid to form an elaborate pattern. The **Buller's Arms Hotel** (**01288 361277**) *B* is an excellent village pub with a good selection of real ales and good food either in the bar or the separate restaurant. Accommodation is also available.

The Coast, Bude to Boscastle

The coast south of Bude is one of dramatic cliffs and massive ranges of offshore rocks. At **Widemouth Bay** it widens out to allow for an extensive strip of sand and rocks, backed by an unattractive development of bungalows and with a big petrol station beside the beach. There are all facilities including a summer lifeguard service. It can get crowded in the summer months. The coast path now starts to climb as the cliffs rise up towards *Dizzard Point.* The coast from here to Bosacastle provides some marvellous cliff walking, albeit on high exposed sections that can be unpleasant, even dangerous, in high winds. Just inland from Millook and accessible by footpath from the coast path or by road from the A39 is the small hamlet of **Poundstock**. The church is beautifully situated in a little hollow surrounded by trees. Inside, there are traces of wall paintings while imediately adjacent is a rare C14 Guildhall, a long barn-like two storey structure in granite and slate.

Crackington Haven, one of the few coves that offers any shelter on this exposed coastline, served as an improbable harbour during the C19 when boats would simply run onto the beach as the tide dropped and offload limestone and coal and load slates for the return journey. It has a magnificent setting at the head of a narrow valley with 400 foot high cliffs crowding the small stony cove. Despite the lack of sand, the beach is very popular and the surfing is good in the right conditions. Swimming can be dangerous and a summer lifeguard service is in operation. There are two cafes, a beach shop and the **Coombe Barton Inn** (**01840 230345**) *B*, a big pub right on the seafront. They serve a good range of real ales and food lunchtime and evenings. They also have accommodation. A mile or so to the south is **Trevigue Farm (01840 230418)** *C*, a C16 farmhouse built around a cobbled courtyard. It is owned by the National Trust, is beautifully restored and furnished and located near the dramatic 700 foot high *High Cliff*. They have three rooms on a bed and breakfast or half board basis and the cooking is reputed to be very good. Slightly closer to the village and just south of Middle Crackington is the isolated, medieval farmhouse of **Hallagather (01840 230276)** *B* which has good value en-suite rooms on a bed and breakfast basis.

St Gennys   Just to the north is the small hamlet of St Gennys, well worth a visit to see the delightful church with its old rectory alongside. The only other buildings are a terrace of cottages. They are owned by the National Trust and the cottages are available for hire. The earliest parts of the church are Norman with the chancel, unusually, being built in greenstone from Tintagel rather than the more normal granite. From the churchyard to the rear there are wonderful views over the coast and rolling hills. **St. Gennys House (01840 230384)** *B*, the former rectory, is a beautiful historic building with gardens and provides excellent accommodation in this tranquil setting. Just to the north of here and approached down very narrow lanes is another remote farmhouse B&B in a building owned by the National Trust. **Lower Tresmorn (01840 230667)** *B* is a medieval farmhouse with oak beams and real fires. They also serve evening meals by arrangement.

By car, Crackington Haven, is approached along steep narrow lanes and signposted from the main A39. There is a large car park by the beach. The bus service is limited to 4 or 5 a day between Bude and Wadebridge. The coast path passes through the village and it is an excellent base for walking the surrounding area.

The coast from Crackington Haven to Boscastle is high, wild and dramatic. If walking, it is essential to stay on the higher cliff top path as many of the lower paths have fallen away and are dangerous. *High Cliff* at 731 feet is the highest in Cornwall. The coast along here has a fearsome reputation for shipwrecks, in just one year in the 1820s over 23 vessels foundered on or close to these rocks. Far below the cliffs are the sandy coves of *The Strangles* and *Rusey Beach* accessible by a steep and difficult path. They are consequently often deserted. Swimming is not recommended due to the strong currents. There are superb views all the way along this stretch of the coast.

Boscastle

With its spectacularly tortuous harbour, Boscastle has become a popular tourist destination on the north coast. However, it remains pleasantly unspoilt, largely it has to be said through the benign ownership of the National Trust, and is a wonderful spot to visit with many interesting sites in the immediate area. It is well worth staying for at least one night as many of the visitors are daytrippers and at night the village returns to a quiet and peaceful existence. The poet *Swinburne* rode here at night in September 1864 and described it "very queer, dark green swollen water, caught as it were in a trap, and heaving with rage against both sides at once..."

Two factors were primarily responsible for the Boscastle you see today. The narrow, winding inlet is the only possible place for a harbour in some 40 miles of coastline and the *de Botterell* family built Bottreaux Castle on a spur above the Jordan Valley in the C12. Consequently, Boscastle consists of two villages linked by the later development along the Jordan valley. While the upper village was the earliest, centred around the castle, the lower, harbour village was soon to become the commercial focus of the area and the raison d'etre for the village's existence. The first pier was erected in the C16 but soon fell foul of the sea. In 1588, *Sir Richard Grenville* ordered its rebuilding and this is the structure that largely exists today, having been extensively restored in 1740. A second breakwater projects into the narrow entrance from the north shore to help break the heavy seas which can rush into the ravine. Originally built in 1820, it was blown up by a floating mine in 1941 and rebuilt as recently as 1955. A substantial fleet of trading vessels was maintained by the port with 200 vessels calling in one year in the C19 when the port activity was at its peak. The railway did not reach north Cornwall until 1893 and before then all heavy goods to the area had to be shipped in and out. Coal, iron and limestone were brought in from South Wales and fertilizers, timber, wine, spirits and general merchandise from Bristol. The main exports were slate, china clay and manganese ore from a mine in the Valency Valley. The tortuous harbour entrance meant that it was never safe for ships to enter unaided. They were therefore towed in by small boats assisted by gangs of men onshore who took ropes to guide the boats in. Most of the buildings in the lower town were once associated with the harbour trade and used as warehouses, stables, forges and houses for the many workers. The railway arrived in Camelford in 1893 and the port trade rapidly declined. However, the railway did bring the first tourists and they have gradually helped to revive the economy of the area. The harbour is still used by pleasure craft and fishermen working the north coast shell-fishing grounds. The fish-shaped weather vane on Penally Hill to the north is to tell sailor's the wind direction in the open sea, as it is impossible to read from the sheltered harbour.

The upper town is gathered around the site of the castle. The main street runs downhill to the harbour along the side of the steep Jordan valley. There are many old and atractive buildings, none more so than the two small cottages, *Smugglers* and *Tinkers*, with their dipping roofs and leaning walls and chimneys. This steep, narrow lane used to be the only road down to the harbour from the village until New Road was built in 1886. The distinctive split-level brick houses on the steep slope between the two roads were built soon after and are a good response to the difficulties of building on such an incline. Three houses were built nearby in the same manner in the 1980s. On the hill to the west of the village is *Forrabury Church*. The short tower dates from the mid C18 while the church retains evidence of Norman work in the south wall and transept. The font is also Norman with simple decoration on the bowl. To the north are the *Forrabury Stitches*, narrow strips of cultivation and the survivial of a rare form of Celtic land tenure known as "stitchmeal." The tenants may crop their stitches individually during the summer growing season but thereafter the land must be grazed in common. This is one of only three surviving examples of stitches being farmed in Britain today and the practice is maintained by the National Trust who own the common. The best view of the stitches is from *Willapark*, the high promontory to the west with the white painted

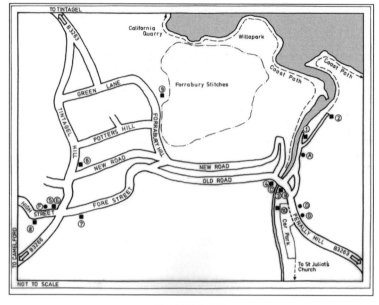

BOSCASTLE

ACCOMMODATION

1   Youth Hostel
2   Pencarmol
3   Rioverside Hotel
4   Wellington Hotel
5   Bottreux House Hotel
6   The Old Coach House
7   Myrtle Cottage
8   St. Christopher Hotel

ESSENTIALS

9   Church
10   Tourist Office & Visitor Centre

RESTAURANTS AND BARS

A   Harbour Restaurant
B   Riverside Hotel
C   Wellington Hotel
D   Old Manor House
E   Bottreux House Hotel
F   Napoleon Inn
G   Cobweb Inn

lookout, from where there are also superb views up and down the coast and inland over the Valency Valley. Just to the south can be seen the stepped cliff face and top workings of *California Quarry* where slate was extracted in the C19. Men and boys were lowered down the cliff face to set the explosive charges. Like many promontories in Cornwall, this was also the site of an Iron Age cliff castle.

Thomas Hardy will forever be connected with Boscastle for it was to the nearby church of St Juliot that he was sent while a young architect to oversee the restoration. He arrived in March 1870 and it was here at the rectory that he met his first wife, Emma. He recalled these events in his book *A Pair of Blue Eyes* in which he has changed the names but the setting is unmistakeably Boscastle and the surrounding area. There is a fine walk from the harbour up the Valency Valley to

THE BOSCASTLE FLOOD

On the afternoon of Monday 16 August 2004, a storm dropped some 2 inches of rain on the hills above Boscastle in just two hours. The ground was already sodden from one of the wettest summers on record, and the Rivers Valency and Jordan broke their banks. In places the water was 10 feet deep and, as it rushed down the valley towards the narrow harbour at Boscastle, it increased in velocity. It poured through the main car park, demolishing the Tourist Information Centre and sweeping dozens of cars and other debris into the lower village and out to sea. In one of the biggest rescue operations of its kind, seven helicopters from the Navy, RAF and Coastguard winched 120 people to safety over a 10 hour period. Miraculously, no-one was killed or even seriously injured, but the lower village around the harbour was devastated by the surge of water, mud and other debris. While some buildings were destroyed outright, most are capable of repair and the long process of drying out, aided by scores of industrial-size de-humidifiers, started within days of the flood. Informed sources are hopeful that most, if not all, of the premises of the lower village will be able to resume trading by the summer of 2005.

St Juliot's Church which also takes in the churches at Lesnewth and Minster. The path starts from the end of the car park and follows the river tumbling over its slate bed. The woods here are some of the most extensive in north Cornwall and are mostly mature oak coppice and noted for their rich variety of lichens and mosses. After a while, you will come to some old granite gateposts in the river which serve as stepping stones. If you cross over these and take the steep path for about 15 minutes you will come to the road by *Minster Church*, which is located in a completely isolated location below the level of the road and surrounded by lush vegetation. In Spring, the chuchyard is awash with daffodils. The church was largely rebuilt in 1869–71, although it is likely that this was the site of a Celtic religious cell which became a monastery or priory in the C12. This building was just downhill of the present church but nothing now remains. The unusual saddleback tower dates from the C19 rebuilding as does the incised stone bearing a pair of scissors built into the tower. Inside, there are some interesting slate memorials and a small brass plate of 1604 to *Hender Robartes*.

Walk to St Juliot

From the bottom of the churchyard, a path leads back down through the woods to cross over a footbridge and rejoin the path along the valley bottom to St Juliot. Alternatively, you can return to Boscastle by following the lane westwards and then following the footpath down the Jordan valley or continue on the lane to the upper village. The path to St Juliot continues up the valley over the narrow road at Newmills and then for another mile or so. *St Juliot's Church* is in another beautiful, isolated position. The church is standard Cornish and must be very much how Hardy left it after his restoration. There are some drawings by Hardy hung in the church and a memorial tablet to his wife, Emma, on the north wall which he designed and had made by a local stonemason when he returned to visit the church in 1912. In the churchyard are two good Cornish crosses, one with cross-arms consisting of four triangles and exceptionally well preserved.

For those with energy left, it is only a short detour to the pretty church of Lesnewth. To get there, return by the same footpath and take the path on the left, where two paths cross, which turns into a lane leading up to the church in its tiny hamlet. The church is set right below the road with only the top of its tower

Lesnewth

visible so it can be easily missed. The church is largely Norman but was restored in 1862 when *J.P. St Aubyn* built a new nave. From here, one can return by the valley footpath or follow the narrow and winding lane to Minster Church and on to Boscastle.

To do the whole route would take the best part of four hours and, as there are many delightful picnic spots along the way, it is tempting to make a day of it. The walk to Minster Church from Boscastle takes about 40 minutes and makes a worthwhile destination in its own right. The churches can also be visited by car but parking is limited and the lanes are very narrow with several steep hills.

Accommodation

There are several good places to stay at reasonable prices and Boscastle makes a good base for exploring the surrounding area. The most atmospheric location is by the harbour where the sunsets throw the harbour into harsh relief and the quiet of the evening allows for a more leisurely appreciation of its charms. Facilities and room rates for those premises affected by the flood may be subject to change.

Youth Hostel   Palace Stables (**0870 770 8868**) *A*, in the old stables and right by the harbour, this small friendly hostel is in one of the best locations in the village.

Pencarmol   The Harbour (**01840 250435**) *B*, if possible, an even better location than the youth hostel. This listed, former harbourmaster's cottage dates from the Georgian period and is at the end of a terrace with superb, uninterrupted views over the harbour. All rooms are en-suite and very good value.

Riverside Hotel   (**01840 250216**) *B*, The Bridge. Right in the centre of the lower village, this converted warehouse has comfortable en-suite rooms. They also have rooms in Bridge House, opposite, a smart new conversion with en-suite rooms at the same price.

Wellington Hotel   The Harbour (**01840 250202**) *C*, large C16 coaching inn, one of the last to be working in Cornwall, and nicely situated near the harbour at the bottom of the road from the upper town.

Bottreaux House Hotel   (**01840 250231**) *B–D*, located in the upper village at the top of Old Road. Pleasant hotel with good value en-suite rooms.

The Old Coach House   Tintagel Road (**01840 250398**) *B*, lovely granite and slate house with all en-suite accommodation. Located on the edge of the village heading towards Tintagel.

Myrtle Cottage   Fore Street (**01840 250245**) *B*, beautiful, old granite cottage on this quiet road linking the two villages.

St. Christopher Hotel   High Street (**01840 250412**) *B*, nice period house in the upper village with a range of en-suite rooms..

Eating and drinking

Boscastle is a quiet place in the evenings and this is one of its attractions. However,

Camel Estuary near Padstow

Regency architecture, Penzance

Church at Towednack, Penwith

Tate Gallery, St Ives

there are several pleasant places to eat and some nice pubs. **The Harbour Restaurant** (**01840 250380**) *M* is right by the harbour but has a rather dim and dark interior that fails to make the most of its setting. There is a varied menu which includes daily fresh fish. They also serve breakfasts and lunch. The **Riverside Hotel** has a separate restaurant which is also open for lunches and teas *M*. The **Wellington Hotel** has a restaurant and they also serve bar food. **The Old Manor House** (**01840 250251**) *M* opposite the car park in the lower village serves a range of fish, seafood and meat dishes in its unpretentious interior. In the upper village the **Bottreaux House Hotel** *E* has a highly-rated restaurant and the nearby **Napoleon Inn** serves food as well.

Of the places to drink the **Wellington Hotel** has a nice bar with real ales and folk music on Monday nights. There is a pleasant and sheltered garden to the rear. The **Cobweb Inn** is a converted wine warehouse – its name derives from the fact that spiders were encouraged to help keep down the flies. It is now a spacious pub with slate floor and exposed granite walls. They serve real ales and bar food, lunchtimes and evenings, and have live music on Saturday nights. In the upper village, the **Napoleon Inn** is an atmospheric old pub which often has impromptu music evenings. There is a beer garden too.

Practicalities

The Tourist Information Centre is located in Cobweb Car Park in the lower village (**01840 250010**). It shares the space with the Boscastle Visitor Centre, open 10.00am–5.00pm daily, which has a good exhibition about the history of the area and its flora and fauna. This building was completely destroyed by the flood and it is not known when it may re-open. If in doubt, contact the TICs in neighbouring Bude or Tintagel for further information. Bus connections are good with regular buses to Tintagel, Bude and Newquay. By car, it is easily located off the main A39 or from Tintagel on the B3263 coast road. There is a large pay and display car park near the harbour. The coast path passes through the village and it is a good place to stop for those walking this route.

Tourist Information Centre

Bocastle Visitor Centre

The Coast, Boscastle to Tintagel

It is an easy walk on the coast path from Boscastle to Tintagel and there are good views of the cliffs and sea along the way. Around here, the underlying strata of slate has resulted in an extraordinary coastline of sheer-sided cliffs, caves, stacks and offshore rocks. Seals can be seen along this part of the coast and Long and Short Islands, just off the coast about a mile from Boscastle, are home to the largest colony of puffins in Cornwall. The walk will take about two hours which allows time to visit the sites in Tintagel and return to Boscastle by bus.

St Nectan's Glen is a local beauty spot on the road halfway between Tintagel and Boscastle. Park by the Rocky Valley Hotel and follow the path away from the sea and down to the wooded valley. After a while you will come to a waterfall, only

St Nectan's Glen

about 60 feet high, but very beautiful with the cascade cutting through the dark slate cliff and then descending in a number of falls. From the coast path, it can be reached by following the footpath up the Rocky Valley to the road and then picking up the path as above. The land around the waterfall is privately owned and access is only between 10.30am–6.30pm (or dusk), closed Tuesdays and Thursdays and there is a small admission charge.

Tintagel

First impressions of Tintagel are of a tacky, over-developed, tourist-ridden town with little or no character and you may well be tempted to pass straight through. However, it is worth visiting for three major sites, the castle on its rocky headland, one of the most dramatic in Cornwall, a fine cliff top church and one of the best preserved early medieval manor houses in the South West. There is also an excellent visitor centre which provides a good background to the history and development of the area and does well to explain the legend of King Arthur and its tenuous links to Tintagel.

Historic Development

Tintagel has been an important place since Roman times. Strangely, there is no evidence of any Iron Age or Bronze Age occupation for the rocky outcrop would have been easily defended. The first evidence of occupation is some pottery and assorted coins from the late Roman period. There are also two Roman milestones found on the mainland on either side of Tintagel. There are no remains of any buildings found from this period and it is likely that this was a small trading centre rather than a more significant community. This Roman connection may have led to its use as a royal seat in the centuries following, for throughout Britain the rulers of the new independent kingdoms re-used the centres of Roman occupation for their own ends. Certainly, the defensive possibilities of the site and the nearby haven for ships would have been reason enough to occupy the site. A substantial wall of earth, timber and stone was built across the neck of land sometime in the C5 or C6 and the remains of large amounts of pottery, tableware, wine jars and so on suggest that the island was a stronghold with royal patronage. Excavations within the castle have revealed a large number of buildings dating from the C5 and C6.

There is little evidence of what happened here during the Dark Ages but a series of myths and fables started to develop about the Cornish kings and their resistance to the Saxon invaders, although very rarely can any of these be linked back to any known events. The myths were given credence by the work of Geoffrey of Monmouth who in 1136 produced a colourful and largely imaginary *History of the Kings of Britain* which linked Tintagel to the birthplace of King Arthur.

Richard, Earl of Cornwall, was an ambitious man. When he came to Tintagel in 1233 it was no more than a wind swept headland but nevertheless firmly linked to the Legend of King Arthur. Keen to establish his reputation with the troublesome Cornish and enhance his position overseas, he saw the possibility of adapting the legend for his own use. There was no strategic value in his building a castle at

Tintagel, the north coast was far from areas of strategic importance and, while easily defended, any castle here could be just as easily besieged by a relatively small number of men. However, he proceeded to build the substantial fortification which is largely what you see today at considerable cost and effort. The Earl may have hoped that this would establish his standing with the Cornish as the natural successor to King Arthur and this connection with the age of chivalry would do him no harm at all in his attempt to be crowned Holy Roman Emperor, for which he would need the support of the European Kings and Princes. The castle that was built was quite old fashioned in its design and construction. This may have been deliberate to enhance its antiquarian qualities and Arthurian connections, but it must also have indicated that the castle was to serve no practical purpose as a fortification.

Richard's successors had little use for the castle he had built and it was left in the charge of the county sheriff. In the 1330s the roof of the Great Hall was removed and put in store – a sure sign that no important visitors were expected. Much of the island was leased out for grazing and it is unlikely that more than a dozen men at most were garrisoned there. By the late C15, the castle was described as being in ruins. By the C19, the interest in the Gothic past and the growth of the legend of King Arthur led to an increase in the number of visitors to the area and famous writers like Dickens, Tennyson, Swinburne and Hardy were drawn to the area to see what had inspired these wonderful, romantic tales. The village itself began to profit from this new interest and re-named itself Tintagel in 1900 – previously it was known as Trevena. Since then, tourist interest in the site has grown apace until today the village is little more than an Arthurian theme park catering for the hordes of visitors.

Tintagel Castle, English Heritage, is located at the bottom of a long steep lane (no vehicles) from Tintagel village. There is a Land Rover shuttle for those who require it. The Castle Beach Cafe is located by the entrance and has lots of outside tables. The small cove of *Tintagel Haven* had been an important trading centre since Roman times and more evidence of pottery and glass from the Mediterranean has been found here than any other coastal site in Western Britain. The Haven continued as an important trading centre until well into the C19 when slate use to be lowered down to waiting boats by a system of pulleys. The large sea cave on the beach which is slowly undermining the island is known as *Merlin's Cave*.

Open daily 10am–6pm (or dusk if earlier). Entry £3.70, conc. £2.80, children £1.90

For most people, the tour of the castle starts from the entrance kiosk by the Haven where there are also toilets and a small exhibition. However, the most logical point to start a tour is from the original castle entrance which is on the hillside above the ticket office and can be reached by taking the path in front of the office that climbs the hill or by taking the higher path along the valley rather than the lane in the bottom. Tickets can be purchased from here so there is no need to go to the ticket office as such.

The castle lies on a finger of land dramatically projecting out into the sea with the larger part of the castle being on an isolated crag virtually surrounded by water and reached via a new footbridge. The cliffs here clearly show the juxtaposition of the dark bands of hard slate above the soft, paler sedimentary layers. At the points of weakness, the sea is carving through the rock and soon the island will be completely separated from the mainland.

The entrance to the castle is dominated by the high crag of rock on your left and this would have served as the earliest defensive point guarding the narrow entrance. Some time in the C5 or C6 a great ditch and wall was constructed across the valley to the right forcing any attackers to approach via the narrow path between the ditch and the high crag. This gave the stronghold its name *Din Tagell*, the Fortress of the Narrow Entrance. When Richard of Cornwall re-fortified the castle in the C13, the Dark Age defences were replaced with a stone wall, the base of which remains today.

On this mainland part of the castle are two medieval courtyards, smaller now than they would have been as substantial parts have fallen into the sea by cliff erosion. The straight wall along the cliff edge was added later in the Middle Ages after the cliff fall. The remains of Dark Age buildings were buried when the land was levelled for the courtyards. From here, you cross the narrow neck of land to the Island. At the top of the steep flight of steps is a battlemented wall built in 1852 when Tintagel was becoming a popular tourist destination. It is on the same alignment as the original C13 wall and was the first line of defence of the Island Courtyard. Again this was once larger. It would have been the heart of the medieval castle – the site of the Great Hall and its attendant service quarters. Through the archway in the battlemented wall, a path leads off down the side of the cliff to the Iron Gate, a defended rock wharf where ships could tie up in calm weather. From here, you have to return by the same path.

The low walls you see along the sheltered east side of the island are the remains of a substantial Dark Age settlement that was only first discovered in the 1930s. The top of the island is covered with a multitude of ruined buildings the date and purpose of many still unknown. Towards the middle of the island is a well-preserved rock cut tunnel which may well have been used as a larder in the Middle Ages. On the mainland side is the remains of a tiny chapel dedicated to St Juliot and dating from around the end of the C11, a time when the Dark Age settlement had long been abandoned and the medieval castle not yet started. The reason for the chapel is a mystery for there was already a small church on the mainland near the present church. However, this must have become the main place of Christian worship for the castle when it was built. There are fine views along the coast and inland from the top of the island and it makes a good place for a picnic in fine weather. In stormy weather you can appreciate just how inhospitable a place this must have been to live.

The cliff top **Church of St Merteriana** is clearly visible from the castle. A path leads from the castle gateway to the church or it is possible to drive there from the village. The site has been a place of burial since at least the C6 and a series of burial mounds have been discovered in the churchyard. It is thought these graves may be linked to the Dark Ages occupation of the nearby castle. The present church is largely Norman and retains its plan form of nave and transepts. There are a number of distinctive Norman features surviving including the south door, while on the north side there is a Saxon-looking doorway and two tiny windows. Inside is one of the two Roman milestones found near Tintagel. It is a pleasant walk back to the village along the narrow lane beside the church.

Open daily April – Oct, 11am – 5.30pm (4pm in Oct). Entry £2.50, children £1.20, family £6.20

The **Old Post Office**, National Trust, is a fantastic example of a small Cornish farmhouse of the C14 and one of the few surviving examples in the South West. Its small size is evidence of the relative poverty of the county compared to other parts of England at this time. A room in the house served as the village post office between 1844 and 1892 and hence the name which has remained. In 1895 the building was put up for auction at a time when much of the old village was being pulled down and replaced by shops and hotels. Luckily a group of artists concerned at the destruction of the village bought the building and it was later purchased by the National Trust in 1900.

The building is of local slate and is long and low but just one room wide. The roof is a fantastic swirl of dips and dives where the heavy roof slates have distorted the rafters supporting them. The plan form is pure medieval with a stone passage leading straight through the house to the rear garden with the parlour or kitchen on one side and a full height hall, surely one of the smallest in the country, on the other. A further room, now furnished as the Victorian post office, comes off the hall. Above, there are two bedrooms and a further tiny space in the "gallery" above the hall – too small to have been a minstrel's gallery, it is most likely to have been a subsidiary bedchamber. The rooms have been furnished with items from farmhouses and cottages in the area, nearly all the furniture being of oak, once common in this part of Cornwall.

The hall is perhaps the most impressive space in the house, rising full height to the smoke blackened rafters. There is a huge slate overmantel to the large fireplace and a clear view of the elaborate "cruck roof" structure which can also be seen close up in the south bedroom, where you can also see that new strengthening beams have been placed alongside the original structure. From the pleasant rear garden, there is a good view of the rear of the house including the semi-circular stair tower with its tiny window carved out of a single piece of local greenstone.

Elsewhere in the village, there is little of interest. One oddity is **King Arthur's Great Halls** (01840 770526), open daily, erected in the 1920s by Frederick Thomas Glasscock. He also founded the Fellowship of the Knights of the Round Table of King Arthur as a personal crusade to keep alive the memory of the "real" King Arthur. The vast hall is constructed of local stone and reputedly can hold over 1000 people. There are 72 stained glass windows depicting the quest for the Holy Grail and other "Arthurian" objects.

Open daily, 10am–5pm (winter 11am–3pm). Admission £3.00, children/OAPs £2.00, family £8.00

There is really no need to stay in the village as the sites can be easily seen in a day and there are much nicer places to stay in the vicinity. If you do want to stay **Ye Olde Malthouse**, Fore Street (**01840 770461**) **B** is a nice C14 building and the **Cornishman Inn**, Fore Street (**01840 770238**) **B** has en-suite rooms. **Camelot Castle Hotel** (**01840 7770202**) **C**, the large, imposing building on the headland was erected at the turn of the century and has an unbeatable, although very exposed, location. All rooms are en-suite and have sea views. The hotel has an amazing, eccentric ambience with the surreal, "fantasy" artworks of artist in residence Ted Stourton and extraordinary mock medieval interiors, such as the wonderfully named Excali Bar, where non-residentgs are welcome to drink. **The Youth Hostel** (**01840 777033**) **A** is located outside the village, in this case a bonus. It is found along the coast path past the church and atop Glebe Cliff with wonderful coastal views. The approach by car is up a narrow lane and then rough track from Tregatta, to the south of Tintagel. It is quite a small hostel and it is recommended to ring to check availability. Apart from these, there are dozens of other places to stay and finding a room should not be a problem.

There are plenty of pubs, cafes and restaurants in the village. **The Cornishmen** is one of the better places to drink and has a terrace to the front and a more secluded garden to the rear. The **Camelot Castle Hotel** has a grand, if rather faded, dining room. On the edge of town towards Boscastle, the **Cedar Tree Restaurant** (01840 770240) *M* has an interesting menu and reasonable prices. It is located in the **Bossiney House Hotel**.

ⓘ **Practicalities**

Tourist Information Centre

Tintagel Visitor Centre

The Tourist Information Centre (**01840 779084**) is located in the admirable Tintagel Visitor Centre on Bossiney Road on the outskirts of the village centre. The centre is open daily from 10.00am–5.00pm, 11.00am–3.00pm between November and February. It provides an excellent introduction to the nature, geology and history of the area including a good explanation of the legend of King Arthur and its connections with Tintagel. There is a large pay and display car park adjacent.

Tintagel is well connected by bus with regular connections to Bude, Boscastle, Wadebridge and Newquay. If arriving by car, there are plenty of pay car parks but very limited on-street parking. The cheapest for those visiting the castle is the one past the castle lane entrance on the road to the Camelot Castle Hotel. The coast path passes through the village.

Trebarwith Strand and South to Wadebridge

Located a mile or so south of Tintagel is Trebarwith Strand, one of the few sandy beaches on this part of the coast. At low tide, the sand and rocks can extend out for almost a mile while for two and a half hours either side of high tide there is no beach exposed at all. It is a popular surfing venue and there is also a summer lifeguard service. The development by the beach is no more than a scattering of buildings with two cafes, a shop, surf hire and toilets. There are two car parks which can get busy at peak times.

The **Port William Inn** (01840 770230) *D* has a superb location overlooking the beach and serves real ales and good bar food. There are tables on the outside terrace that overlook the beach. Accommodation is also available in en-suite rooms which all have sea views. About a mile back from the beach is **The Mill House Inn** (01840 770200) *C*, a bar, restaurant and hotel in a big, old granite building with a big sun terrace and comfortable, smartly-furnished rooms. The bar and restaurant are also worth a visit. Further up the valley and set on the valley floor way below the road level is **The Old Mill Floor** (01840 770234) *B*. This old slate building is surrounded by trees and water and provides a very secluded guest house. It is also open from 3pm for teas and evening meals

The area around here is littered with slate quarries, now mostly closed.

However, just inland is one of the biggest and most celebrated at **Delabole** Tours available May–Aug, Mon–Fri 2pm (**01840 212242**). Slate has been quarried here for 600 years and it is now England's largest working slate quarry. The tour takes around 75 minutes and costs £3.50 and £2.50 for children. Safety boots are provided but you are advised to wear sensible clothing and bring a pair of thick socks. Very young children are not allowed on the tour – check if in doubt.

South of Trebarwith Strand, the coast path hugs the top of the cliffs with no roads or settlements to disturb the tranquillity. There are several steep valleys that cut through the plateau necessitating strenuous descents and climbs for those walking this part of the coast. *Tregardock Beach* reveals a stretch of sand at low tide and is often used by surfers. Swimming can be dangerous and is not recommended. There are no facilities, the beach is remote from any roads and often deserted.

Port Gaverne is a scattering of buildings around a stony cove. It was once a **Port Gaverne** pilchard fishery and major slate shipping port for the Delabole quarries. The road that approaches the village from the east is the "Great Slate Road" constructed in 1807 at the expense of the Delabole Slate Company to allow their carts direct access to the haven. Until the late C19 and the coming of the railway, this was the major port for the Delabole quarries in the summer, while Boscastle which had a more sheltered harbour was used in the winter. The **Port Gaverne Inn and Hotel** (**01208 880244**) *D* is a converted row of C17 cottages and makes a comfortable if pricey place to stay. Off season prices are considerably lower. There is also a well regarded restaurant *M*, a nice bar with good bar food and a garden where cream teas can be taken.

Immediately to the west is Port Isaac, a beautiful fishing village which has **Port Isaac** spread onto the hills above with more modern development. The core of the village is one of tiny cottages tightly packed around narrow lanes. The small sand and shingle harbour is the focus of the town with buildings facing onto it from every feasible direction. There has been a pilchard fishery here since before the C16 and in 1850 there were 49 fishing boats registered and 4 fishing cellars. The port is still used by fishing boats which can often be seen pulled up on the beach. On the hill to the west of the harbour is the *Port Isaac Pottery* (**01208 880625**) in a converted Methodist chapel. There is a large showroom for the pottery, which is all made on the premises, and a range of paintings as well.

The village is a pleasant place to stay with a nice atmosphere, some good hotels and nice pubs and restaurants. **The Old School Hotel** (**01208 880721**) *C–E* is fashioned from the Victorian school house and looks right over the harbour, with many rooms having harbour views. There is a large terrace, also overlooking the harbour, and car parking. Room prices vary markedly depending on the facilities, size and views. **The Slipway Hotel** (**01208 880264**) *D* is located directly opposite the harbour slip. It is a charming building dating from 1527 and full of character with exposed stonework and beams. **The Galley B&B** (**01208 881032**) *B* is opposite The Old School Hotel at 44 Fore Street (above the art gallery). Newly converted, there are two smart rooms overlooking the harbour and garden behind. Following the coast path south for a few hundred yards will bring you to **Hathaway** (**01208 880416**) *B*, an attractive guest house with fine views over the harbour and town, as well as car parking.

There are some good places to eat in Port Isaac with several specializing in fish and seafood dishes. The restaurant at the **Slipway Hotel** has a good reputation for fish and seafood dishes and has a nice old interior *E*. The **Mote** (01208 880237) *M–E* is nearby and specialises in fish dishes, many with an oriental flavour. There are two outside tables and they serve food all day. Lunches are inexpensive. The **Harbour Seafood Restaurant** (01208 880237) *I*, opposite, is a more basic fish restaurant with unpretentious decor. The restaurant at the **Old School Hotel** is also open to non residents *E*. Several of the pubs also serve food, including the **Golden Lion** which has a small terrace overlooking the harbour. This is also a very pleasant place for a drink with several rooms and much character. **Ours**, near the harbour, is a smart cafe which serves coffee, teas and snacks but is not open in the evening. **The Edge**, at the top of the hill going towards Port Gaverne, is a smart bar/restaurant with spectacular sea views.

There are regular buses to Polzeath, Wadebridge and Bude, stopping at Tintagel and Boscastle. By car, Port Isaac is signposted off the B3314 coast road. The roads in the centre of the village are extremely narrow and car parking is very limited. There is a car park on the beach at low tide or there is also a larger car park on the hill to the east of the village. It is a pleasant walk west to Polzeath and onto Padstow along the coast path, 4 or 6 hours easy walking. The return journey could be taken by bus (no.124).

Portquin   Portquin is a one-time fishing village located on a deep natural harbour about 3 miles to the west of Port Isaac. It now consists of no more than a few granite and slate buildings which have been turned into holiday accommodation by the National Trust who own the village. It is notable as a dead or deserted village – there are no local inhabitants. It is unclear what happened to the village but it is known that the fishing fleet ceased to exist near the end of the C19. Stories abound of the whole fleet being lost at sea in a disastrous storm but the truth will probably never be known. It is approached down extremely narrow lanes but the best way to visit is along the coast path from Port Isaac or Polzeath. On the headland to the west is *Doyden Castle*, built in 1827 by one Samuel Symmons as a drinking and gambling den for him and his friends.

Polzeath   Further west and at the entrance to the Camel Estuary is Polzeath, a village of no interest but with one of the best beaches in the area – a big, west-facing expanse of sand growing to enormous proportions at low tide. There are facilities, including a summer lifeguard. The beach is popular with surfers, and you can hire surf equipment and wetsuits. The Tourist Information Centre (01208 862488) is in Coronation Gardens by the beach. Just to the north of the town is *The Rumps*, one of the most impressive cliff castles in Cornwall. It was occupied between 4BC and the C1 and was defended by a series of walls and ditches still clearly visible. The point where the footpath goes through was once a complex defensive entrance. Within the walls have been found traces of hut platforms and pottery, bones and other artefacts suggesting permanent settlement for the site rather than occasional use as a defensive stronghold. *Daymer Beach*, around a mile south of Polzeath, is a beautiful stretch of sand bordered by dunes, with a more secluded character than Polzeath with little development backing the beach. There is a large car park and all facilities. It is signposted off the road from Polzeath to Rock.

Just behind the beach and accessed by public footpath over the golf course is the Church of St Enodoc made famous by association with the poet *John Betjeman* who is buried in the graveyard. The chapel and the associated village which lay between the church and the sea were overcome by the sands and almost completely submerged. Contemporary accounts in the mid C19 record how the only way into the church was via the roof. It was restored in 1863-4 and now constitutes a rare, survival of a largely intact Norman plan form. The nave and transept is added to on the south side by a short south chancel aisle of only three bays. The short tower is capped by an unusual and crooked C13 spire. Inside, there is a very good, crude Norman font and a tablet to John Betjeman's father on the south wall. His mother is buried in the churchyard near the west boundary wall while the poet's own grave is just inside the lych gate, on the right. Many of the recorded burials at St Enodoc are of "unknown" sailors whose ships were wrecked on the Doom Bar just offshore. The shed outside the west hedge was once used as a mortuary for these sailors prior to burial.

St Enodoc

Rock is a largish town of substantial houses and villas. It is reputed to be the home of more millionaires than anywhere else in Cornwall and has an exclusive and retiring nature that is not welcoming to the visitor. However, the beach is fabulous with the finest sand backed by low dunes. When the tide is out, it extends for miles. Padstow is just over the estuary and is a much more interesting place to stay, so the shortage of affordable accommodation need not be a concern. The ferry leaves every 20 minutes (£2.00 return, children and dogs £1.00, cycles £2.00) and runs throughout the year. The time of the last ferry varies with the season (6.50pm in June). Telephone for details (**01208 532239**). On the southern edge of the beach at Rock is the small Norman *Church of St Michael*, beautifully situated on the banks of the estuary. It was heavily restored and rebuilt in the C19 but the beauty of this place is its setting rather than any inherent architectural merit. **The Black Pig** (**01208 862622**) *E* is about a mile back from the beach in an anonymous parade of shops. It is run by an ex Seafood Restasurant (see Padstow) chef and is very highly regarded. A small, inventive menu, mainly fish.

Rock

At the head of the beautiful Camel estuary is Wadebridge, a town with little interest for the visitor. However, it was once a major trading port and crossing point of the Camel River. The magnificent bridge of c1468 is one of the finest in England, 320 feet long and with seventeen arches. The piers are said to have been sunk on a foundation of packs of wool. Unlike most ports on the north coast, the coming of the railway brought increased traffic when in 1837 the Bodmin and Wadebridge Railway linked the harbour to the inland areas of Bodmin Moor. The town now serves as a major service centre for the area and is a hub for local buses with good connections to all the major towns in Cornwall. *The Chase Art Gallery*, Hamilton House, The Platt (**01208 813552**) and the associated *Chase Art Centre* in the centre of town, both have a good range of paintings, prints and contemporary art for sale. *Tristan's Gallery* (**01208 815767**) in Molesworth Street is the only fine art photographers' gallery in Cornwall with both national and international artists on display. To the south east of the town centre is the *Sir John Betjeman Centre*, in effect little more than a room with some interesting curios, news reports, pictures and some books. It does, however, give some insight into

Wadebridge

the extraordinary popular appeal of the one time Poet Laureate. Entry is free.

If you do decide to stay, the nicest place is probably the **Molesworth Arms Hotel,** Molesworth Street (**01208 812055**) *C* where there is a friendly atmosphere, a restaurant and a nice bar with excellent bar food. If this is full, you could try the nearby **Swan Hotel**, Molesworth Street (**01208 812526**) *B* with 6 en-suite rooms. There are few places to eat in the town, the best bet is probably the Molesworth Hotel. The Tourist Information Centre is in the Town Hall (**01208 813725**). Wadebridge sits astride the Camel Trail, a long distance off-road cycle route between Padstow and Bodmin Moor and there are several places to hire cycles. The **Original Bridge Bike Hire**, Eddystone Road (**01208 813050**) have a variety of cycles for hire with mountain bikes from £10 per day. They are located on the northern edge of town by the river. Nearby **Bridge Cycle Hire** (**01208 814545**) has adult bikes from £8 as well as other types of cycles. Bike hire is a competitive business around here and it may well be worth comparing prices and the standard of equipment before hiring.

The area around Wadebridge to the north and east is one of small villages and isolated farms, a gently rolling plateau between the coast and the granite upland of Bodmin Moor. There are not a lot of sites to see, but perhaps the nicest of the villages is St Kew where there is a fine church in a beautiful wooded setting and an excellent inn. The *Church of St James* dates largely from the C15 and is distinguished by the high and lofty proportions of its interior. There are many fine slate memorials both inside the church and fixed to the exterior walls. By the pulpit stairs there is a particularly fine, deeply-carved slate tablet dating from 1601. There is also a C15 lantern cross and a rare Ogham Stone, inscribed with straight lines, a script common in south west Ireland but unusual in Cornwall. It probably dates from the C6 or C7. The massive, oak front door is original. However, the pride of the church is the stained glass. The north east window is dated 1469 and preserved almost completely, while the south east window also retains mainly C15 glass. Both are rare survivals. As if to prolong the tradition, there is a good Victorian stained glass window to the West family on the south wall. The **St Kew Inn** (**01208 841259**), right beside the church, is a lovely C15 granite inn with a separate dining room, a large garden, real ales and good food. Highly recommended.

To the west of Wadebridge and signposted off the main A389 is **Pencarrow House and Gardens** (**01208 841369**). Built between 1765–75, Pencarrow is the family home of the Molesworth family. It has a fine Palladian front of seven bays with a projecting central pediment. It was designed by *Robert Allanson* of York and this is probably his only major work for he died in 1773 at the age of 38. The main interest inside is the Music Room which has a fine Rococo stucco ceiling. The adjoining Entrance Hall, now turned into a library, also has some fine pinewood panelling which came from the old mansion house at Tetcott. On the stair landing, there is a tripartite Venetian window, a classical detail not commonly found in Cornish houses. Throughout the house, there are some unusually fine Molesworth family portraits and, in the Inner Hall, two outstanding paintings by *Samuel Scott* of London Bridge and the Tower of London (1755). The gardens include a formal Italian Garden to the front of the house while the rest is set to a more natural parkland design. There is a tea shop in the courtyard to the rear of the house.

St Kew

Open Apri–Oct, 11am–5pm closed Fri & Sat. Gardens open daily in season. Admission £7, children £3.50. Garden only £3.50, children and dogs free

Redruth and the North Coast, Padstow to Hayle

Introduction

This area is one of the most heavily populated in Cornwall. Newquay is the single biggest resort in the county and a major destination for those seeking its magnificent surf and beaches, while Padstow is a smarter, more chic resort with equally fine beaches nearby. Elsewhere, the coast is one of high cliffs and sand beaches, much of it readily accessible and therefore busy during peak periods. Inland, and around St Agnes, there is considerable evidence of the Cornish mining industry, the remnants of which are now being protected and promoted as a valuable record of England's industrial past. Redruth and Camborne are two of the biggest towns in Cornwall and, while they contain little in the way of conventional tourist attractions, they do represent two of the best Victorian towns in the county. The area is highly accessible with the A30 and the main west coast railway line running through the centre. Camborne, Redruth and Newquay are all major hubs for buses with connections to most of the major towns in Cornwall.

Padstow

A glance at the map will show the River Camel as the only sheltered estuary between Hayle and Devon. As such, it has long been an important port and bad weather shelter and if it was not for the notorious Doom Bar across the mouth of the estuary, it probably would have developed to a much greater extent. Padstow has now become a major tourist destination with its attractive old town and the nearby sandy beaches. It has also become the number one destination in the county for those seeking fine cuisine. Since Rick Stein established his seafood restaurant here some 25 years ago, a multitude of smart restaurants and cafes have followed and they are now a major attraction for the many visitors to the area. The town has a well-manicured appearance with many smart hotels and guest houses and it makes an attractive, if not particularly cheap, place to stay.

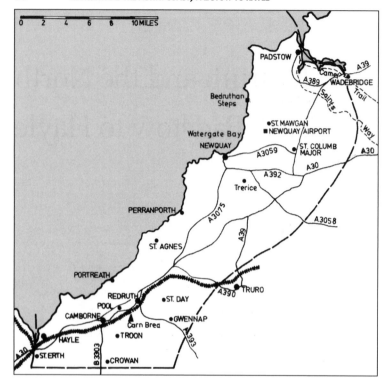

Historic Development

Padstow has a long history. It is thought to have been the northern end of a pre-historic trading route across the peninsula to Fowey and on to the Continent and many prehistoric artefacts have been found along the route to support this theory. However, Padstow itself began to develop as a community with the arrival of *St Petroc*, the patron saint of Cornwall. He landed at Padstow in 518, about 80 years before St Augustus landed in Kent. According to records he spent around 30 years in Padstow and founded a monastery which survived until it was sacked, along with the town and church, by the Vikings in 981. The monastery was subsequently moved to the relative safety of Bodmin and Padstow came under the control of the Priory of Bodmin. Throughout the Middle Ages, Padstow continued to develop as an important fishing and trading port, which gained further impetus when the bridge at Wadebridge was built in 1468 preventing ships from passing further upstream. Some time before 1536, Padstow's first stone pier was constructed.

During the Reformation, the ownership of the land was transferred to the Prideaux family, whose family home, Prideaux Place, was completed in the C16 on the northern outskirts of the town. The development of mining and quarrying during the C17 and C18 led to further development of the port and this was given a further boost in 1899 when the railway arrived. During the C19 the town was an important shipbuilding centre with no less than six yards occupying the foreshore and for a time the town was also a ship owning community. In 1823, there were 27 ship-owning ventures registered in the town. The lifeboat was established here in 1827 and it has been an important station up to the present day. The *Doom Bar*, a notorious shifting sandbank across the mouth of the Camel estuary and the treacherous north Cornwall coastline have kept the lifeboats busy over the years. Since records began, about 200 years ago, over 2000 wrecks have been listed on the north coast with over 600 on the Doom Bar alone.

The arrival of the railway marked the beginning of the tourist industry with the "Atlantic Express" running a regular service from London to Padstow. The line closed in 1967 as part of the "Beeching Cuts", but tourism has continued to flourish and is now the mainstay of the local economy. The port is still used by fishing boats and there has been something of a resurgence in recent years with about 90% of the catch going to the fish auctions in Newlyn or Brixham and the remainder being sold locally to the many fish and seafood restaurants in the town.

The Town

Padstow, today, is a pleasant jumble of old buildings clustered around the harbour and spreading up the valley behind. Many date from the C16 onwards and there are good examples of vernacular buildings of all ages up to the present. Many of them are built of local stone, often rendered or whitewashed and there is also a good deal of slate hanging and, unusually for Cornwall, brick buildings too. The harbour is the focus of the town and there are always boats, some of considerable size, moored against the stone quays. The sparkling new *Padstow Seafood School* on the quay to the south of the harbour is not only a fine contemporary design using traditional and modern materials to good effect but also an affirmation of the continuing strength and vitality of the town as a fishing port. The ground floor of the building is devoted to a number of retailers selling fresh fish and seafood, as well as Stein's fish and chip restaurant and take away. The courses run at the school are geared more at the wealthy enthusiast than the professional. That is not to say that the tuition will not be top class and the residential course does include staying in the Seafood Restaurant or St Petroc's and meals in Stein's various eateries. Telephone **01841 532700** for further details. Nearby, is the newly-opened **National Lobster Hatchery** (**01841 533877**). You can visit the lobster hatchery and learn more about lobsters than you ever thought possible.

The narrow streets behind the harbour are a pleasant place to stroll around with many fine buildings. In Middle Street, there are some good C19 brick almshouses, Victorian Gothic in style and consisting of two rows of terraces at right angles to the street. The nearby Cinedrome has been a cinema since 1924 and is one of the oldest and smallest cinemas still operating in the country (seasonal opening). Down an alley off Lanadwell Street, is *Padstow Contemporary*, 3A Parnell Court (**01841 532242**), a small gallery showing paintings, prints, glass,

Open daily, May–Sept, 10am–6pm (4pm winter). Admission £2.00, children £1.25, family £5.00

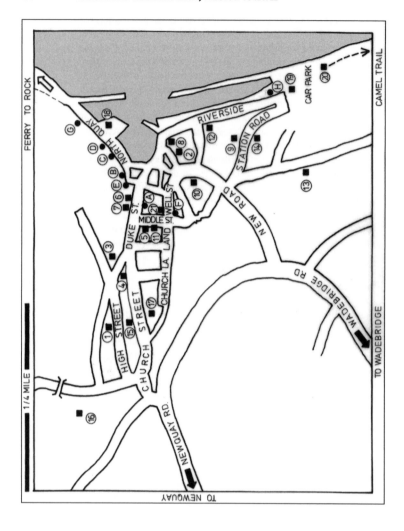

Open Easter–Oct, 10am–5pm (closed 12.30–2pm) Mon–Fri & 10am–12.30pm, Sat ceramics and furniture. The **Padstow Museum** in Market Place is situated on the first floor of the town library and has a good collection of exhibits relating to the history of the town including Padstow's famous "Obby Oss" (see below).

On the South Quay is the C16 court house where *Sir Walter Raleigh* resided when he was Warden of Cornwall. Nearby the *The Old Custom House* dates from the 1800s and was the Custom and Excise building, Padstow being a Customs base for the fight against the smugglers who worked the rugged north coast. Tucked in among the many restaurants, pubs and cafes are shops selling all the essential items

PADSTOW

ACCOMMODATION

ESSENTIALS

RESTAURANTS, BARS AND GALLERIES

a visitor may need. *The Picture House* (**01841 533888**) on North Quay has an interesting display of paintings, glass and ceramics, while the *Middle Street Gallery* on the corner of Landwell Street also has a good range of contemporary paintings. The Quay is also the starting point for numerous boat and fishing trips, including visits to Puffin Island.

The *Church of St Petroc* is located at the top of the old town, well back from the harbour, and in a churchyard surrounded by large trees and with some good, C18 churchyard gates. It is a sizeable church, as befits Padstow's status, and dates largely from the C14 and early C15. The most notable feature is the font, dating from the C15, and a superb carving with angels in the corners of an octagonal bowl and the twelve apostles in the niches between. There is also a very early brass memorial of 1421 on the chancel floor and a large elaborate wall monument to Sir Nicholas Prideaux from 1627.

Just beyond the church, on high ground overlooking the town, is **Prideaux Place** (01841 532411), dating from the Elizabethan period and with some exceptional interiors. The house is open for guided tours only, which are well led and highly informative. If the group is small, there is the possibility that the tour can be fashioned to meet specific interests. Free car parking for visitors is available in the grounds. In the summer, there are occasional open air concerts, theatre and opera.

Open, Easter, then mid-May–Sept, 1.30am–4pm closed Fri & Sat. Admission, £6, children £2 for house and gardens

The house initially presents a rather austere appearance with its dark, stone battlemented walls and steeply pitched grey slate roof. The original house dates from the end of the C16 and the typical E-shaped plan form is still recognizable on the entrance front. The house was remodelled in the early C18, removing the gables to the wings and replacing them with the battlements and hipped roofs seen today. At the same time the grounds were altered to introduce a formal garden including several classical garden buildings. The house was further altered in the early C19 in line with the then popular Regency Gothic, made fashionable by the writer Horace Wimpole at his villa at Strawberry Hill in London. The garden side of the house was transformed with the addition of the big, two storey bow window and the library. They both have elaborate Gothic windows. The stables were built at the same time in the same style.

The major interest in the house is the interiors and furnishings many of which are of exceptional interest. One should note on entering the massive, Elizabethan front door, still with its original lock. The Dining Room, once the Great Hall, is one of the most impressive interiors in the house. The dark panelling is a mixture of Georgian and Elizabethan and displays exceptionally fine carving – the north wall being pure Elizabethan Spanish Oak. To the left of the fireplace is an unusual carving of Queen Elizabeth I standing on a pig, reputedly depicting her stamping out vice. Over the fireplace is a very good portrait of Sir Nicholas Prideaux, who built the house, and believed to be by *Marcus Gheerbaerts the Younger* (1561–1635). The Morning Room contains some of the best pictures in the house with several by *John Opie*, the famous C18 Cornish artist. The most romantic tale is associated with the pastel of Humphrey Prideaux by the Italian artist *Rosalba Carriera* which she painted when he was on the Grand Tour in the mid C18. She was enamoured with her subject and wrote a love letter which she concealed behind the frame. However, the letter was not discovered until 1914 when the picture was being cleaned. Another item of interest is the art deco switch plate dating from 1907 when the house was connected to its own power station.

The Drawing Room is in the part of the house added in the early C19 in the Strawberry Hill Gothic style. Of particular interest is a miniature painting dating from the Civil War, tactfully rendered with a portrait of Charles I on one side and Oliver Cromwell on the other. The Grenville Room was brought complete to the house from the First Earl of Bath's grand manor where it served as his dining room. The room is typical of the lavish, gilded interiors of the late C17 and would have been a very up-to-date addition for Cornwall. The Library is the most lavish expression of the Regency Gothic style in the house with its elaborate stained glass window and ribbed and vaulted ceiling. The fine cantilevered staircase comes from the Grenville house at Stowe and was moved here when that house was demolished. Under the staircase is the earliest English cast iron cannon dating from the reign of Henry VIII. In the hall, there is also a superb C16 chest inlaid with mother of pearl which was salvaged from a Spanish Armada wreck in the nearby estuary in 1585. On the upstairs landing is a dinatron, an early and enormous hi fi from the 1940s, as big as a wardrobe and as unique in its own way as many of the more historic exhibits.

The Great Chamber on the first floor is the architectural highlight of the interior. The marvellous plaster ceiling was hidden behind a false ceiling in the C18 and only uncovered and restored in 1987. It dates from the early Elizabethan house and has many stylistic similarities to the gallery at Lanhydrock, just south of Bodmin. This would have been the family's private quarters away from the communal lifestyle of the rest of the house. The ceiling depicts the biblical story of Suasannah and the Elders, the northern panel showing Moses at the well, but the southern one was destroyed in the C19 and the modern replacement has the family's coat of arms. Above the door is a lozenge shaped picture of the Madonna, dated 1470 and believed to be part of a mobile altar set.

The stables and adjacent service buildings form an attractive courtyard to the north of the main house and give some indication of the self-sufficient nature of the household up to the end of the C19. The gardens are still being restored and there are fine views from the higher parts over the surrounding countryside and coast. The deer park is one of the earliest in the country. At the top of the lawn is a well preserved ancient Celtic cross dating from at least the C9.

The Beaches

There is no beach in Padstow itself and the harbour is not suitable for swimming due to the amount of boat traffic. However, within a short walk there are several superb sand beaches. There is also a public swimming pool on the southern edge of the town by Dennis Cove. Taking the coast path north from Padstow at the top of North Quay, a 10 minute walk will bring you to the small St George's Cove, a lovely picnic spot. It is said that England's patron saint landed here, his horse's's hoof striking the rock, causing a spring to appear which has flowed ever since. Another few minute's walk brings you to Harbour Cove, a lovely stretch of sand and dunes with no development and no facilities. Hawker's Cove just beyond is backed by the old lifeboat station and some old coastguard cottages. In summer, parking is available in a large field near Lellizzick Farm, although it is only 15 minute's easy walk from Padstow. The headland beyond is Stepper Point marking the end of the sheltered waters of the Camel estuary. From here one can see the dreaded Doom Bar and the narrow deep water channel into the estuary. In order to help ships enter the estuary, capstans were erected in the lee of Stepper Point and ships warped around with ropes to ease their passage. The other option for beaches is to take the ferry across the estuary to Rock and use the wonderful sand beaches on that side of the estuary.

St George's Cove

Harbour Cove

Hawker's Cove

Stepper Point

Accommodation

The price coding system that is used throughout this guide is on a scale of A to E and indicates the cost of the lowest priced double room in that establishment during the peak summer period. This is clearly marked by the telephone number of the listing for each establishment. It should be borne in mind that single rooms are likely to be considerably more than half the price of a double. In the off peak months, many establishments reduce their rates considerably and even where they do not you may be able to negotiate a discount.

A –£44
B £45–£64
C £65–£80
D £81–£100
E £100+

There are plenty of accommodation options in Padstow and many of them are in fine old buildings, beautifully furnished and decorated. Many of the hotels and guest houses provide good value for money, albeit more expensive than most other places in Cornwall, and Padstow is one of those places where it is probably worth paying a bit more to stay in a unique and sophisticated setting. There is limited budget accommodation in the town and finding somewhere in the lower price range can be difficult. At peak times it can be difficult to find anywhere to stay at all and it is recommended that you reserve rooms in advance. Prices can be considerably less outside the high season and it might pay to ask around.

MAYDAY AND THE 'OBBY 'OSS

Every year on 1 May (or if this is a Sunday the 2 May) Padstow is witness to one of the most elaborate and ancient May day festivities in the country. Its origins are lost in the mists of time but it is likely that it derives from pagan rites of fertility welcoming the summer and driving out the cold and hardship of winter. The 'Obby 'Oss is a fearsome head mask and body costume with a circular wooden hoop of about 6 feet in diameter. He passes through the streets swirling and dancing with his Teazer, retinue, musicians and dancers. The celebrations start outside the Golden Lion at midnight on the 30 April with the Night Song where the group sing at each house where there is someone sick or elderly. The Blue Ribbon 'Oss sallies forth at 10.00am the next morning, to be followed by the Old Red 'Oss at 11.00am. The whole event is watched by a mass of followers who join in the singing and dancing. It is a major event in the Padstow social calendar and people come from all over the world to witness the celebrations. Accommodation is impossible to find in Padstow over the May Day weekend unless you have booked long in advance.

Treverbyn House   Station Road (**01841 532855**) **B–C**, large Edwardian house with views over the estuary and a few minutes walk to the town centre. All rooms are en-suite and individually furnished to retain their own character. Breakfast is served in the rooms. Car parking to the rear.

50 Church Street   (**01841 532121**) **B**, lovely bed and breakfast in this historic building opposite the church and just a minute's walk from the town centre. The rooms are large, well appointed and comfortable. Breakfast is taken in the family kitchen and prepared to order. Highly recommended.

Tregea Hotel   High Stree t   (**01841 532455**) **E**, extremely comfortable and stylish small hotel located in a C17 building on the edge of the town centre.

4 Riverside   (**01841 532383**) **B**, next to the old Custom House, this comfortable bed and breakfast has a central, harbour-side location.

Armsyde   10 Cross Street (**01841 532271**) **B–C**, a handsome C18 town house on the edge of the town centre. Nicely renovated and decorated, it provides good value accommodation.

Cross House Hotel   Church Street (**01841 532391**) **D**, near the above. Large, Georgian house with 11 en-suite rooms and nicely furnished. There is a garden and terrace to the front.

Number 6   6 Middle Street (**01841 532093**) **E**, three beautifully furnished rooms above this attractive restaurant located in the heart of the old town.

Virginia   20 Duke Street (**01841 532100**) **A**, right in the centre of town, this B&B is one of the cheapest places in town.

Trealaw   22 Duke Street (**01841 533161**) **B**, next door to the above but slightly more expensive.

Treann House   24 Dennis Road (**01841 533855**) **B–C**, smart B&B with stripped wood floors, antique furniture and a comfortable guest lounge. The breakfast is also very good.

The Old Custom House   South Quay (**01841 532359**) *E*, located right on the harbour, this large inn has 25 en-suite bedrooms furnished in a traditional style. Rather overpriced compared to some of the other options in the town.

The Metropole   Station Road (**0870 400 8122**) *E*, an imposing, Victorian Hotel which looms over the town from a hill just south of the town centre. There is a heated outdoor pool and car parking. One of the most expensive place to stay in town.

St Petroc's Hotel   4 New Street (**01841 532700**) *E*, one of the oldest buildings in Padstow and now converted to an extremely comfortable hotel and restaurant as part of Rick Stein's burgeoning empire. There is a lovely garden for residents to use. Prices vary considerably depending on the type of room.

Middle Street Bed and Breakfast   10 Middle Street (**01841 532700**) *D–E*, another Stein establishment with three en-suite bedrooms above the cafe. Nicely furnished and the breakfast is wonderful.

Seafood Restaurant   Riverside (**01841 532700**) *E*, above Stein's flagship restaurant are 13 well furnished rooms including such essentials as fridges stocked with half bottles of wine. Booking a room here guarantees you a table in the restaurant if desired – something which can otherwise be difficult in the season.

Restaurants and cafes

The prices quoted in the guide are inevitably just an indication of costs and represent the price for a meal of two courses with a drink. In the listings, they are indicated by the letter I, M or E, immediately after the telephone number of the establishment.

Inexpensive under £15
Moderate   £16 – £25
Expensive   over £25

Padstow is probably better known for food than any other place in Cornwall. Many people come here just to eat in the town's restaurants. The reason for this is down to one man – Rick Stein, the noted fish and seafood chef who settled in Padstow some 25 years ago and now, through hard work and television exposure, has made a name for himself as one of the best cooks in the country. The success of his restaurant has drawn a wealth of other aspiring cooks and restaurateurs to the town as well as allowing him to expand his own operations, which now include a hotel, delicatessan, cafe and seafood school. He is now the biggest employer in the town. You can check out his empire on www.rickstein.com.

Seafood Restaurant   Riverside (**01841 532700**) *E*, the place to eat in Padstow and one of the finest fish and seafood restaurants in the country. Booking essential.

St Petroc's Bistro   4 New Street (**01841 532700**) *E*, also owned by Rick Stein, this French style bistro serves meat as well as fish dishes from a small menu. There are also tables outside. The cooking is excellent and the prices cheaper than the Seafood Restaurant. Booking recommended.

Rick Stein's Café Middle Street (**01841 532700**) *M*, the third and cheapest part of Stein's empire. The cafe has a pleasant, informal atmosphere with painted wooden walls sporting original paintings and occasional live music. The cafe is open from 10.00am–5.00pm for coffee, cakes and lunches and opens between 7.00pm and 9.30pm for dinner. Prices are reasonable. There are also two outside tables for those warm evenings.

Number 6 Middle Street (**01841 532093**) *M*, inspired by Mediterranean, Pacific Rim and Fusion Food, which means just about everything. The small restaurant has a delightful interior and the food is good with an emphasis on fish and seafood although meat dishes are also featured. Booking recommended.

Margot's Bistro 11 Duke Street (**01841 533441**) *M*, nice bistro style restaurant, highly regarded by locals. Open for coffee from 10am and serves lunches and dinner. Booking recommended. They are also at the Tregea Hotel (Tues–Sat from 7pm).

Rojano's Pizza Restaurant Mill Square (**01841 532796**) *I*, good value pizzas and pasta. There are several tables on the terrace outside for al fresco eating.

Quayside Fish and Chips North Quay, excellent traditional fish and chip shop with tables outside on the quay. *I*

Stein's Fish and Chips South Quay *I*, superb fish and chips in smart modern interior. Restaurant and take-away. Not the cheapest, but worth every penny.

Bars and Nightlife

There are some good pubs in Padstow many of them pleasantly unmodernised and in old, historic buildings. The **Shipwrights** on North Quay is perhaps the nicest with its slate floor and exposed beams and views over the harbour. There are tables on the quayside and a large open terrace to the rear. They serve real ales and bar meals all day. The **Old Ship** in Mill Square is a big pub with a fairly characterless bar. There are however a good number of tables on the terrace to the front. They serve a good range of real ales, serve food lunchtimes and evenings and also have accommodation if required. It also hosts regular live music evenings. The bar at the **Old Custom House** across the harbour is big and soulless but does have screens for watching sport if desired. The nearby **Harbour Inn** has more character. The **Golden Lion** in Lanadwell Street and the nearby **London Inn** are both nice old buildings with unpretentious interiors, real ale and bar food. They also both have accommodation.

Nightlife is restricted to eating in the many restaurants or drinking in the pubs. There will often be live music in one of the pubs and there are concerts and recitals at *Prideaux Place* in the summer. **The cinema** (**01841 532344**), one of the smallest and oldest in the country, shows current releases in the summer months.

Practicalities

Tourist Information Centre   The Tourist Information Centre is on North Quay (**01841 533449**). Bike hire for the Camel Trail (see below) is available from **Padstow Cycle Hire** (01841

533533) or **Trail Bike Hire** (**01841 532594**), both on South Quay by the start of the Trail. River cruises and sea fishing trips are available from the harbour.

Padstow is easily approached by car on the A389. Parking in the town is strictly limited. The most convenient car park is on the south quay, where the bus terminus is also located. There are regular buses to Wadebridge, Newquay and Bodmin. The Bodmin service is timed to meet the trains at Bodmin Parkway, the main west coast line. However, not all trains are met and it is necessary to check first. Several scheduled flights a day land in the summer at Newquay airport and Padstow is only a short taxi ride away. The coast path runs through the town. The ferry to Rock across the estuary runs all year and is a continuous service every 20 minutes. The time of last sailing varies with the season (6.30pm in June). It departs from the harbour by the Tourist Information Centre apart from low tide when it leaves from a landing 5 minutes walk north on the coast path. Fares are £2.00 return, children and dogs £1.00, cycles £2.00.

Around Padstow

The Camel Trail is an off road footpath and cycle track that follows the line of the   **Camel Trail**
old Bodmin to Padstow railway line that was closed in the 1960s. It extends for nearly 17 miles from the estuarine setting of Padstow to the edge of Bodmin Moor at Poley's Bridge, near Blisland. There are plenty of places to hire bikes in Padstow and Wadebridge. The surface is well laid and maintained and anybody who can cycle could complete the route. It is very popular and can get quite busy, the further towards Bodmin Moor the less busy it gets.

The first part of the route from Padstow follows the side of the river with an abundance of bird life and fine views across the water to the north bank. At Wadebridge, there is an unfortunate detour through the town on public roads. The *Sir John Betjeman Centre* is on the route and can be visited. From Wadebridge the route starts to climb slowly and gradually towards the higher ground of Bodmin Moor. However, the railway cuttings, their rock walls now covered with ferns and moss, have taken out any steep gradients and the incline is almost imperceptible. At *Grogley Halt*, around halfway, there is a car park and access to the river and a series of pools. Just beyond here is the *Camel Vineyard*, open Easter to the end of September. There are tours available and wine tasting, as well as a shop. Telephone **01208 77959** for details. At Nanstallon was one of   **Nanstallon**
the few Roman sites in Cornwall. At that time, the river was navigable to this point and this would most likely have been a trading centre for local minerals. *Boscarne Junction* is the terminus of the steam train from Bodmin and makes a good approach from that direction. Cycles can be taken on the train. Beyond here, there are a number of stiles and gates which are rather tedious and interrupt progress. If desired, a detour can be taken into nearby Bodmin.

The trail crosses the busy A389 at Dunmere where the **Borough Arms** makes a   **Dunmere**
welcome break with a good selection of real ales and food. From here, you enter the beautiful *Dunmere Wood* with the stream rushing and tumbling over the rocks in the valley bottom. The trail crosses the next road at *Hellandbridge* which

has one of Cornwall's finest surviving medieval bridges and a cottage serving teas and lunches. A mile or so further on the trail ends at *Pooley's Bridge*, a rather mysterious and inauspicious terminus until one notices the large Wenford Driers belonging to the *English China Clay Company*. The railway line was extended to here to take clay away for export and only closed in the 1980s. From here, it is only **Blisland** a short detour to Blisland with its inn and church and the higher ground of Bodmin Moor. If you are returning, it is possible to leave the trail at Hellanbridge and return via *Pencarrow House*, picking up the trail again near Grogley Halt.

The **Saints Way** is a rather convoluted footpath which supposedly follows the route of the early travellers across the peninsula to Fowey. It follows a mixture of lanes and footpaths but has little in the way of great scenery or remoteness. From Padstow it leaves the town via Dennis Lane where it climbs the hill to the monument to Queen Victoria from where there are good views. It then follows the side **Little** of the creek to Little Petherwick, a lovely village of granite and slate buildings lin-**Petherwick** ing a steep street down the side of a valley. At the bottom of the valley and beside the footpath from Padstow is the *Church of St Petrock*, a tiny church with an astonishingly rich interior. Little remains of the C14 church, the church having been rebuilt in 1858 by *William White* and restored in 1908 by *J.N.Comper*, who provided the lavishly decorated rood screen and loft along with the high altar and reredos. These dominate the interior of the church and while modern in date provide a good example of how medieval churches may have looked before the Reformation. The chapel to the north was added in 1916.

Padstow to Newquay

To the west of Padstow is a low plateau of narrow, winding lanes edged by cliffs and lovely sand beaches. The coast, just north of Trevone, has some remarkably **Tregudda** varied cliff scenery, Tregudda Gorge has been created by erosion along geological **Gorge** faults that has produced a deep chasm with sheer cliffs on each side. Nearby are the *Marble Cliffs*, a limestone outcrop with alternate white and black streaks, a natural arch and the *Round Hole*, a collapsed sea cave. It is only a short walk from Padstow and makes a pleasant diversion.

Either side of Trevose Head, there are a succession of beautiful beaches which have all facilities including ample car parking and summer lifeguards. *Trevone Bay*, the most easterly, is a sandy beach, popular with surfers and families. *Harlyn Bay*, just to the west, is a big sand beach backed by dunes, facing north and therefore more sheltered from the prevailing winds. The Harlyn Inn is the site of an Iron Age cemetery where more than 100 crouched skeletons were discovered. The village is nothing more than a scattering of buildings including several hotels and a surf school (**01841 533076**). As you progress towards Trevose Head you come across the lifeboat station moved here from Padstow in 1967 with the rocky outcrops of the *Merope Rocks* just to the north. *Trevose Head* has a distinct feeling of isolation with its flat, windswept terrain and narrow lanes. The lighthouse was built in 1847. There is a car park and fine coastal views.

To the south is the big, sandy beach of *Constantine Bay* backed by dunes and a golf course. The beach is popular with surfers and is fine for sunbathing and beach games. Swimming can be dangerous and care should be taken. A footpath across the golf course leads to *St Constantine Church*, largely rebuilt in the C15 and then buried in the sands during the C16. It was only re-excavated in 1926. The nearby *St Constantine's Well* was also submerged and uncovered in 1911, the ruins have now been consolidated and covered with a modern shelter. *Treyarnon Bay*, just to the south, is another popular beach and there is the bonus of a natural rock bathing pool which provides safe swimming. It is not safe to swim in the sea here at low water due to a strong off shore current. The **Youth Hostel (0870 7706076)** *A* which is popular with surfers is nearby. Just south of Treyarnon Bay is what appears to be three separate Iron Age cliff castles but in fact are one that erosion has cut into three sections divided by the sea. *Porthcothan* is a nice beach, popular with surfers and with relatively little development. One of the more secluded beaches in this area.

Just inland, St Merryn is an undistinguished village, which just happens to have two excellent places to eat. **Ripley's (01841 520179)** *E* is run by an ex-head chef of Rick Stein's Seafood Restaurant in Padstow. It is one of the few Michelin Star restaurants in Cornwall, and the food is of the highest standard. It is also good value for the quality of food and ambience provided. Open in the evenings only, it is closed on Sunday and Monday, and booking is essential. Opposite is the **Seven Bays Bistro (01841 521560)** *M*, a slightly cheaper option with an interesting menu and also highly recommended.

St Merryn

Bedruthan Steps was developed by the Victorians as a tourist attraction when visitors first started to arrive in the area in the late C19. It is still popular today and many people arrive to look at the spectacularly eroded cliffs with their isolated stacks – the Steps. The slate cliffs here are particularly friable and the exposure to the pounding surf and westerly storms has created this dramatic scenery. There is a National Trust car park, a tea shop, a viewing platform and a staircase down to the beach. Swimming is dangerous here and care also needs to be taken to avoid getting cut off by the tide. There are wonderful walks along the beach at low tide or along the cliff top. A short walk to the north will bring you to the less visited *Park Head* with marvellous views and a good place for a picnic.

Bedruthan Steps

Mawgan Porth is a large and popular beach with plenty of sand exposed, even at high tide. Swimming is generally safe and there are all facilities. Just to the south is the more secluded *Beacon Cove* with no facilities and an awkward approach via the coast path. It is only 10 minute's walk from Mawgan Porth but is often deserted. *Watergate Bay* is a magnificent beach of fine golden sands, two miles long and backed by steep cliffs. This is the first of a succession of fine beaches that lead into Newquay. There are all facilities, most of them gathered around the centre of the beach by the big Watergate Hotel, where there is a large car park. The beach is very popular but its sheer size means that it rarely feels overcrowded. Right on the beach is the excellent **Beach Hut (01637 860877)** *M*, a bistro and bar serving an eclectic menu of international food, cocktails and beers, coffee and snacks. There is an outside terrace and big picture windows to the bar to allow good views even in inclement weather. It has a young clientelle and a relaxed atmosphere. There is also a beach shop, surf hire and tuition in the same complex. Just inland from the

Mawgan Porth

Beach Hut is the **Watergate Bay Hotel** (01637 860543) *E* with lots of sports facilities, including indoor and outdoor pools. They only provide half board accommodation in peak season. The only other option by the beach is the rather grim **Tregurrian Hotel** (01637 860280) *B–C*, which has a pool and car parking. A few hundred yards up the valley is the **White House** (01637 860119) *C–D*, a C19 house in extensive grounds. They have two comfortable guest rooms and two suites, which are very good value. They also have self-catering accommodation. Undoubtedly the best place to stay in this area. There is a regular bus service along this part of the coast between Newquay and Padstow which allows for easy access to all the beaches mentioned above.

Just inland of here is an area of high windswept plateau which is dominated by the presence of Newquay Airport which doubles up as a military helicopter repair base. On the northern edge of the airfield, nestling in the bottom of a steep wooded **St Mawgan** valley, is the delightful village of St Mawgan. The church is big and high and sits in a beautiful wooded setting in the centre of the village. It dates from the C13, the south aisle was added in the C15 and the whole was well-restored and partly rebuilt by the famous Victorian architect *William Butterfield* in 1860–1. It has a light and airy interior and a certain sense of civic pride at odds with its village location. This is perhaps due to the large number of stained glass windows, many dating from the Victorian restoration. The west window to the nave with its 3 small lights dates from around 1300 while the other windows are in the more familiar Perpendicular style. There is a squint from the north transept to allow for views into the chancel during mass. The pulpit dates from around 1530 and there are some good, deeply carved bench ends of the same period. The rood screen and loft is unusual with having no tracery between the openings thus giving a very open effect, which is only marred by the crassly insensitive fluorescent lights fixed to the back of the screen. Elsewhere, there is a badly worn brass of a vicar from the early C15 and a large number of memorials to the Arundell family. Lanherne, the house of the Arundell family till 1794, is nearby with its Elizabethan front. It is privately owned and not open to the public. The rectory and school building were built by Butterfield while he was undertaking the restoration of the church. Opposite the church is the **Falcon Inn** (01637 860225) *C*, a superb, stone inn with a nice terrace and beer garden. They serve a selection of real ales and good quality bar food. They also have good value accommodation and it would make an excellent, quiet base for exploring the surrounding area. There is a footpath from the village which leads up the valley which with the adjacent stream and woods all around makes a very pleasant stroll. After about 20 minutes, it joins a lane. If you turn right, you will come to the road that skirts the airport and you can follow this back to the village or you can return by the same route.

Just inland of here is an area of high windswept plateau which is dominated by
If you turn left, continue along the path and follow the lane at the end you will **St Columb** come to St Columb Major, about an hours walk from St Mawgan. This is one of the **Major** bigger towns in the area and it has a range of shops and facilities. There are some good vernacular buildings from the C18 and C19 lining the narrow streets of the town centre, including a particularly ornate Victorian Gothic brick building, now in use as a bank. The church is of lofty proportions with a high tower, open at the ground floor to north and west. Inside, there is a very interesting octagnal font of around 1300 with crudely carved faces on five of the sides and tracery motifs on

the other three. By the church is *Glebe House*, a nice slate building with projecting bays, now a tea and coffee shop. The **Ring O'Bells** public house in Bank Street has a narrow frontage behind which are three bars of varying character. They serve real ales and have a separate restaurant. Two miles to the east is *Castle an Dinas*, one of the largest and best preserved Iron Age hillforts in Cornwall. There is a car park from where it is a five minute walk to the site.

East of Bedruthan Steps, on the road to St Eval, is the church of *St Uvelus* with an extraordinary location, high on a plateau, totally isolated from any other buildings and almost surrounded by Air Force establishments. Its high tower is so prominent that in 1724–7 Bristol merchants rebuilt it to use it as a landmark for their ships. The church dates from the Norman period and retains a fair amount of Norman structure including the north wall and a window in the nave. The south aisle was added in the C15 with a mysterious lower arch by the chancel. Whereas the tower is high, the aisle and nave are low giving quite distinctive proportions to the building. Inside there is a plain Norman font and many memorials to the RAF squadrons from the nearby airbase, including a modern stained glass window in memorial to the air crews based here during World War II. There are also some good early C18 slate memorials including one particularly decorative one to General Simon Leach, dated 1709.

St Eval

Newquay

Newquay is the biggest holiday resort in Cornwall and has paid the price for its success. The beaches, the reason for its popularity, are extensive and deserving of the reputation they have. Newquay has also become the top surfing venue in the country, although many surfers now prefer the quieter, more secluded beaches. A 1950 guide described it as "a bright and cheerful town possessing all the ingredients for a healthy, happy and interesting holiday." Unfortunately, in the intervening 50 years, the town has become swamped with tourists and new development has tended towards the garish and tacky. The nightlife is raucous and dominated by theme pubs and large clubs with little or no character. If you like this sort of thing, then Newquay will be the place for you. However, if you want to explore the other charms that Cornwall has to offer, there is little need to spend much time in Newquay. The only reason the independent traveller is likely to end up here is that it is a transport hub for this part of North Cornwall and you may well find yourself here to make a connection.

The Town

There is evidence of Iron Age occupation of the area and *Trevelgue Head* to the north of the town is one of the most important cliff castles in Cornwall. The headland was originally defended by a series of seven ramparts – the seaward half is now an island joined by a bridge. On the island are traces of field banks and house platforms. It is thought the castle was occupied from C3BC through to C6AD. To the end of the nineteenth century Newquay was an important pilchard fishing town.

The *Huer's House*, clearly visible on the headland to the west of the town, is a legacy of the industry. The little whitewashed building dates from the C14 and was probably, originally, a hermit's house with a duty to keep a light to direct boats entering the harbour. It was later used by the "huer" who would keep watch for the giant shoals of pilchards and then alert the fishing crews by shouting "hevva" through a long loud hailer. He would then direct the boats to the shoal with a series of semaphore-like signals using long bat-like paddles. It may sound like something from Monty Python but this was the accepted practice throughout Cornwall.

The town takes its name from the new harbour built in 1830 by Joseph Treffry of Fowey for exporting china clay, a trade which flourished for several decades until the purpose-built port at Par on the south coast was opened. The railway arrived in 1875, just in time to alleviate the impact of the decline of the port and the pilchard fishing. The first trickle of tourists began to arrive.

**Apr–Oct
9.30am–6pm
Nov– Mar,
10am–dusk.
Admission,
£6.95, children £4.45,
family £19.95**

There is little of interest in the town itself, but **Newquay Zoo** (01637 873342), to the east of the town centre provides a diversion of sorts. As well as the animals, there is a programme of talks on its conservation work and a play area and maze.

The Beaches

The beaches are what attract most people to Newquay and they are excellent – wide, sandy and with all facilities, including a summer lifeguard service. The town beaches start on the western side of the headland with the magnificent *Fistral Beach*, a wide expanse of sand with a superb west-facing aspect. Directly behind the beach is a golf course, so there is a relative isolation from the town despite its geographic proximity. However, it still gets crowded at peak times, as do all Newquay's beaches. It also produces some of the best surfing conditions in the country and is the venue for regular surfing competitions. Care is required when bathing and the lifeguard instructions should always be followed.

On the eastern side of the headland is Newquay town and a string of fine sand beaches which become one continuous strip of sand at low tide. The harbour is at the western end and is used by a variety of water craft. It is the venue for regattas, gig races and other water sports. There is a small sandy beach at low tide. *Towan Beach* is the most central and extremely popular. It is the most sheltered of all Newquay's beaches and is particularly popular with families. It can get very busy when the other beaches are red-flagged due to the prevailing sea conditions. At the eastern end is *The Island*, a craggy outcrop linked to the mainland by a graceful, suspension bridge. *Great Western Beach* is to the east and is approached by walking across the sands at low tide or via a steep path near the Great Western Hotel. It is surrounded on three sides by steep cliffs that shelter the beach from the worst winds. It is popular with people learning to surf or when the waves are too big on the more exposed beaches. *Tolcarne Beach* is located below the many hotels on Narrowcliff. It is sheltered and sandy and generally considered to be an ideal family beach. Around the next headland is the wonderfully named *Lusty Glaze Beach*, a good, sandy beach with rock outcrops. It can be reached by walking along the sands at low tide or by a steep path from the clifftop. It is usually sheltered from the prevailing winds. Next is *Porth Beach*, an area of flat, golden sand that lies on the eastern edge of the town. Porth Island with its Iron Age castle is to the north and there are many caves at its base that can be explored at low tide. The bathing is generally safe as long as the river on the north side is avoided where there can be strong currents. At low tide, it can pick up a heavy swell in certain conditions and on these occasions extreme care must be taken.

There are also a number of excellent beaches just outside Newquay, *Watergate Bay* to the north and *Crantock Beach* and *Holywell Bay* to the west. These are covered in more detail elsewhere, but are easily accessible to anybody with a car or prepared to walk for a while.

There are several places with surf equipment to hire or buy, along with tuition. Phone around to get the best rates and enquire as to exactly what you will get for your money. **Dolphin Surf School** (01637 873707), **National Surfing Centre** (01637 850737), Fistral Beach, **BSA Surf School** (01637 876474), Tolcarne Beach, **Offshore Extreme** (01637 877083), **West Coast Surfari** (01637 876083) and **Reef Surf School** (01637 879058).

Accommodation

Newquay has literally hundreds of places to stay in all price brackets. At any time outside the peak school holiday period (mid July to the beginning of September) there should be no problem in finding somewhere to stay. Prices vary with season and out of peak season there are often bargains to be had as supply exceeds demand. It is well worth asking around. The Tourist Information Centre has a full list of places to stay. It is pointless to pick out any in particular, but there are a string of hotels in *The Crescent* which have wonderful views out to sea and are very convenient for the bus station. You could try the **Beaconsfield Hotel** (01637 872172) *B*, the **Minerva** (01637 873439) *C* or the **Trenance** (01637 873159) *C*. The **Hotel Victoria**, East Street (01637 872255) *E* is a grand Victorian hotel with elegant public rooms and has recently been extensively refurbished. Newquay's finest hotel is probably the **Headland Hotel** (01637 872211) *E* on the promontory by Fistral Beach. It has a dramatic location but a rather severe presence and a more than slight level of pretentiousness. At the other end of the scale, there are a number of private hostels that provide dormitory accommodation at rock-bottom prices. **Newquay International Backpackers**, 69 Tower Road (01637 879366) *A*, have dormitory rooms and also very good value double rooms. There is free transfer to their sister establishment in St Ives. **Towan Backpackers Hostel** (01637 874668) *A* is at 16 Beachfield Road. **Reef Surf Lodge**, 27 Agar Road (01637 879058) *A* is linked to the surf school of the same name.

Restaurants, cafes and nightlife

Newquay has plenty of places to eat but is dominated by the lower end of the market with innumerable fish and chip shops, burger bars, pizza and kebab bars. The better places include **The Chy**, Beach Road (01637 873415) *I*, a pleasant cafe/bar, right in the centre and directly overlooking Towan Beach. **Finn's Harbour Restaurant** , Newquay Harbour (01637 874062) *M–E*, has a fantastic location right by the harbour and is very smart. Excellent fish and seafood. Highly recommended. **Ye Olde Dolphin** in Fore Street (**01637 874262**) *M*, serves meat dishes and fresh fish, see the daily board. There is an early evening special between 6–8pm. **Skinners Ale House** in East Street (**01637 876391**) *I*, opposite the Hotel Victoria is a comfortable bar with real ales and nice bar food. The **Hotel Victoria** has a grand dining room, as does the Headland Hotel. Expensive.

There is no shortage of bars and places to drink in Newquay but they nearly all verge on the raucous. The **Skinners Ale House** (above) is an exception and has a good selection of ales and a friendly crowd. **Buzios**, next door, is a smart cafe/bar with a large terrace and top floor pool hall. There are also plenty of clubs, including a number of mega-pubs with DJs. Probably, the nicest club in terms of atmosphere is **The Koola**, Beach Road, next to the Chy.

Practicalities

Tourist Information Centre

The Tourist Information Centre (**01637 854020**) is on Marcus Hill, directly opposite the bus station. They can provide full lists of accommodation as well as information on other sights in the area. The bus station is in the centre of town in East Street. There are regular services up and down the coast and to all the major towns. The railway station is on Cliff Road to the east of the town centre. There are trains to Par where there are connections to the main West Coast line. By car, Newquay is on the A392 which connects with the A30 at Indian Queens. The Coast Path passes right through the town. Newquay airport is four miles outside the town and there are regular scheduled flights to London Gatwick and Stansted and to the Isles of Scilly. There is no regular bus connection to the airport but Ryan Air flights are met by a designated bus that goes to Newquay and Truro. Taxis are always available to meet incoming flights.

Trerice

National Trust: Open from April–October, 11.00am–5.30pm (5.00pm in October). Closed Tuesday and Saturday, mid July to mid September, closed Saturday only. Admission £5.50, child £2.75, family £13.75 (01637 875404)

Just inland from Newquay, in an isolated position, is one of the most interesting historic houses in Cornwall. Trerice is located in a secluded valley, protected by trees and high walls and is one of the few, largely unaltered Elizabethan manor houses in Cornwall. It was built for Sir John Arundell in 1571 and has suffered no major changes since, largely due to the fact that it was owned by a succession of absentee landlords who maintained the property but saw little need to invest money in its enlargement or modernisation.

The house is built of local limestone and is a distinguished design with unusual scrolled gables to the front. It is a mystery how these came to be here for there is no other example of this period in the West country. There is a suggestion that Sir John may have had connections with Antwerp through the Mercer's Company with which his wife's first husband was involved. Arundell, himself, served as a soldier in the Lowlands and he would undoubtedly have seen similar gables there. The south front is also something of an architectural puzzle with much of the stonework seemingly coming from an earlier building. The highlight of this elevation is the two-storey, semi-circular bay dating from the C16. The north wing was taken down in the mid C19 after it had become ruinous, but was restored in 1954 which reinstated the building's original symmetry to the east front.

Within the house, the first room entered is the Hall which rises through two storeys and is lit by the great east window containing 576 panes of then enormously expensive glass. Some of the panes date back to the original construction in 1571. The plasterwork is of spectacular quality and innovation, and is unusual for such a remote location. On the wall, above the screens passage, is a secluded Minstrels Gallery with small openings through which the music could be heard. The Drawing Room is at the lower level of the medieval dwelling which preceded the rebuilding of 1571. The semi-circular bay was added in the rebuilding, while the sash windows are early C19. There are two good portraits by *John Opie RA* (1761–1807) that are vastly better than anything else in the room. Opie was born 15 miles away at St Agnes and was launched on London society in 1781 as the "Cornish Wonder." He went on to have a highly successful career. There is also a small picture of Dolly Pentreath, supposedly the last person to speak Cornish as her sole tongue and who is commemorated at the church in Paul, near Penzance.

Above the drawing room is the Great Chamber, one of the most impressive rooms in the house, dominated by the semi-circular window. There is magnificent plaster work on the barrel-vaulted ceiling and an equally good overmantle to the fireplace. The long Gallery connects the two wings and contains the framed Peerage Patent of King Charles II creating Richard Arundell, the first Baron Arundell, as reward for the family's support during the Civil War. There is a good Ecce Homo by *Vincenzo Foppa* on the far wall. The Minstrels Gallery can be seen off to the right. The Court Chamber is in the reconstructed north wing where there are a number of good C16 and C17 portraits. The North Chamber has a picture by Opie, dreadfully over-restored. The Closet in contrast contains another Opie, which is of fine quality despite having suffered serious decay. Outbuildings to the rear contain a tea shop and restaurant and a museum of lawnmowers.

Trerice is accessed down narrow lanes signposted off the A3058. It is around three miles south-east of Newquay and could be walked or cycled via the narrow lanes to Newquay. There is a summer only bus service from Newquay (no.50) that goes on to the **Lappa Valley Steam Railway** (**01872 510317**) a mile to the south. This is a miniature, narrow gauge steam railway that takes passengers the short distance down the beautiful Lappa Valley. Trips are every 40 minutes in the high season, every hour in the low.

The North Coast, Newquay to Hayle

The north coast between Newquay and Hayle is a sequence of spectacular sand beaches separated by rugged cliffs. It has, in St Agnes, one of the most interesting mining areas in Cornwall with plenty of industrial remains and a well-preserved Victorian village. There are also a number of towns that have become over-whelmed by tourism and seem to have no other discernible function. They have grown up alongside the fabulous sand beaches, sometimes swallowing a smaller community in the process but often establishing entirely new settlements.

Gannel Estuary

Immediately south of Newquay and forming the boundary to the town, is the Gannel Estuary, a major salt marsh, rich in winter birdlife. Dunlin, ringed plover, curlew, widgeon and teal may all be seen here. It is also the home of the Gannel Crake, an eerie sound that can sometimes be heard along the estuary. There is a ferry that crosses in the summer months and several footbridges that are usable depending on the various states of the tide. When the ferry is not running and the tide is high, the only route across is via the bridge near Trevemper.

Crantock Beach

At the seaward end of the Gannel, is Crantock Beach, a fine expanse of flat sand between low headlands. There is a car park, shop and cafe and a lifeguard is in attendance in the summer months. Sand dunes provide a refuge in windy weather.

Crantock

The beach can get crowded at peak times. Crantock itself is an attractive village. **The Old Albion Inn** is a lovely, thatched inn serving real ales and bar food.

Porth Joke

Just around the next promontory, is Porth Joke, known locally as Polly Joke, a much more secluded and beautifully sheltered sandy cove, where there is a good chance of seeing the herons that often frequent this area.. There is a car park about 15 minutes walk away, but no facilities.. It is popular with surfers and those keen to escape the crowds of the more accessible beaches around Newquay.

Holywell Bay

Around Kelsey Head lies Holywell Bay, a big sand beach backed by dunes and low cliffs. All facilities are available including a lifeguard in summer. Low tide reveals a natural rock formation, creating a series of basins in a cave on the north side of the beach. The water they contain was reputed to have natural healing properties and was consequently sought out by pilgrims. If visiting the cave, care needs to be

Holywell

taken to ensure that the tide does not cut off your return. The village of Holywell is an undistinguished collection of lacklustre buildings. A particularly grim block of holiday flats mars the aspect from the beach – their architectural inspiration appar-ently deriving from the nearby army barracks. The **Treguth Tavern** is reputedly C13 and right on the beach is the more mundane **St Pirans Inn**. They both serve food and real ales. There are regular buses to Newquay and Truro.

Cubert

Cubert, just a mile inland, has a distinctive church with a low tower and broached spire. The proportions are particularly odd with the spire being almost the equal height of the tower. The entire tower was built around 1300 but was rebuilt in 1852 when George Street remodelled the church. The chancel and aisle have their original wagon roof and there is a particularly fine slate memorial for the "exuviae Arthur Lawrence plebei" and his sons, 1669 and 1699.

From Holywell, the Coast Path continues around the seaward side of the mili-tary ranges. Care must be taken to obey all signs and keep strictly to the path, which is quite high and exposed in parts. There is a cliff castle at *Penhale Point*, just beyond Holywell, consisting of two ramparts across a steep slope. As the path continues south, the huge *Perran Beach* comes into view – a three mile expanse of sand backed by some of the highest and most extensive dunes in Britain. The beach has all facilities, which are concentrated at the town end of the beach. The huge expanse of sand means that it is rarely crowded, with the northernmost end being the most secluded. The beach is good for surfing and generally safe for bathers – a lifeguard is in attendance in the summer. The cliffs at the northern end clearly show the rusty-looking Perran Iron Lode and there are a number of shafts and other mining debris in this area. About halfway down the beach, a footpath leads inland to the site of *St Pirans Oratory*, just to the north of the stone cross clearly visible on its little hill. It is probably the oldest church in Cornwall, but was overwhelmed by the sand in the medieval period. It was excavated in the C19 but was reburied in 1981 to prevent further deterioration of the structure. There is nothing to see other than a memorial stone marking the spot. 400 metres to the east are the remains of the old parish church, itself abandoned to the sand in 1804. Nearby is a fine cross, which may well date from C10.

Perranporth

Perranporth is a more substantial town than many along this part of the coast. Originally a mining settlement, it has now become totally dedicated to serving the tourists who pack the area during the summer months. It has a number of useful facilities, including several places to stay, restaurants, pubs, shops and laundry. The town and surrounding area are the setting for the Poldark novels, the author, *Winston Graham*, having lived in Perranporth. There are regular buses to Newquay and Truro and a summer only service to St Ives..

There is a basic **Youth Hostel (0870 770 5994) A** in the old coastguard station, high on the cliff with extensive views over the town and bay. It is necessary to book ahead in the summer months and you are advised to double check your booking. There are numerous other places to stay including **Cliffside (01872 573297) A**, and **Chy An Kerensa (01872 572470) B**, both in Cliff Road with views over the bay. The more upmarket **Seiner Arms (01872 573118) C** is right on the seafront, with 30 en-suite bedrooms. There are a number of places to eat including Indian and Italian food. The Seiner Arms serves superior pub food and there is a separate restaurant **M**.

Hanover Cove

Beyond Perranporth, there are increasing signs of mining for this was one of the most important mining areas in Cornwall. The many shafts and spoil heaps create an intricate micro landscape while the rocks and stone fragments lying about show clear signs of iron, tin and copper. In several places, the cliffs expose evidence of mineral rich seams and the cliff face itself is dotted with horizontal mine workings or adits. Hanover Cove, beyond Cligga Head, is named after the Falmouth packet that was wrecked here in 1763 with a cargo of gold coins valued at £60,000. Her royal coat of arms is now in Falmouth Maritime Museum. The coast path follows the cliff top until it drops down to Trevaunce Cove and St Agnes.

St Agnes

St Agnes was one of the major centres of mining in Cornwall with production only ceasing in the 1920s. There were over 100 tin and copper mines in the area, employing 1000 miners. Fortunately, for the visitor, the village has retained much of its C19 character and is one of the few places along this stretch of the coast that has not been overwhelmed by tourists. There are still plenty of visitors to the area,

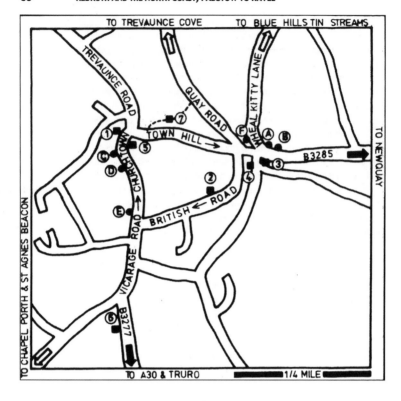

ST AGNES

ACCOMMODATION

1   St Agnes Hotel
2   Cleaders Croft Hotel
3   Grove View Cottage
4   Malt House

ESSENTIALS

5   Church
6   Museum

7   Stippy Stappy

BARS AND GALLERIES

A   Taphouse
B   Aggie Surf Shop
C   Over the Moon Gallery
D   Churchtown Arts
E   St Agnes Pottery
F   Saffron Gallery

but the hilly, dispersed nature of the village means that they seem to be absorbed more easily. With its fine beach, good selection of places to eat and drink and some excellent walks, St Agnes is probably as good a base as any for this part of the north coast.

Mining was the reason for St Agnes' existence and there is evidence of such activity from ancient times. However, serious exploitation only began in the C16

Stippy Stappy, St Agnes

Coast near Bedruthan Steps

North coast near Portreath

Carn Brea, Redruth

and in 1710, after three attempts, a harbour was built to help the export of ore from the area. The cost of constructing the harbour in such an exposed and inhospitable place led to bankruptcy of the Manor of Trevaunance. As a result, the harbour was not maintained and was swept away in 1730. The copper boom at the end of the C18 gave impetus for a new harbour and the St Agnes Harbour Company constructed the last harbour in 1798, allowing for the convenient shipment of ore and also the development of a pilchard fishing industry. The harbour stood throughout the boom years of St Agnes mining, but, again, due to lack of maintenance, it was washed away in the storms of 1915/16. There is no harbour any more, but the scattered granite blocks of the previous one can still be seen at the west end of the beach. The St Agnes Harbour Trust is currently trying to raise money to re-establish the harbour.

The village itself is an attractive jumble of granite cottages interspersed with relics of the mining past and more substantial civic and commercial buildings. The village is spread over several hills and valleys and it is this topography as much as anything that gives St Agnes its distinctive character. This also conspires to make it quite difficult to find your way around the somewhat confusing street pattern. The centre of the village is by the *Chuch of St Agnes*, constructed in 1848 by *Piers St Aubyn* in the traditional Cornish style. It has an unusual position, on a narrow ledge below the road and with views over the rest of the village from the churchyard to the rear. Nearby, are most of the shops and two traditional hotels, the St Agnes and the Porthvean, both big, granite buildings with classical proportions and details. A short walk down Town Hill, brings you to *Stippy Stappy*, a steep terrace of granite cottages that drop down the side of the valley and have become the defining image of St Agnes. Continuing around the "one way system" of St Agnes takes you up British Road, where there is a large Methodist Chapel, not open to the public.

The **St Agnes Museum** is located further out on Penwinnick Road and has a number of artefacts relating to the landscape and history of the area. The area is dotted with mine workings and derelict engine houses. The **Blue Hills Tin Streams** (01872 553341) is a working tin mine that is open for tours and demonstrations of the miners craft. Tours take an hour to an hour and a half and it is best to book in advance. Open all year for group bookings, April–October 10.30am– 5pm (closed Sunday) for individual visits. Admission £4.00, children £2.00. It is located off the B3285 Perranporth Road, follow the signs for Wheal Kitty and turn right at the grass triangle. Follow the road down into the valley and look for signs to the works.

Open Easter-October, 10.30am – 5pm daily. Admission free

Back in the village, the *St Agnes Bakery* produces excellent bread, cakes and pasties. There are a good number of galleries and artist's workshops in the area. In the centre of the village is *St Agnes Pottery*, Vicarage Road (01872 553445), a small gallery attached to the pottery itself, which has ceramics made on the premises at attractive prices. *Churchtown Arts*, Churchtown (01872 553229), opposite the church is a large complex of craft shops with the emphasis very much on craft rather than art. Next door at 6A, the *Over The Moon Gallery* (01872 552251) has a superb range of modern paintings from Cornish artists at reasonable prices. At the bottom of Town Hill is *The Saffron Gallery*, Peterville (01872

553674) with a large display area where the quality of the work can vary considerably. There is also a coffee shop on the premises. At Trevaunance Cove is *Trevaunance Art and Design* (**01872 552404**), a complex of eight workshops and studios with a selection of clothing, glass, paintings and ceramics.

Trevaunance Cove

Trevaunance Cove, itself, is an attractive sand beach hemmed in between towering cliffs. It is approached down a narrow valley and parking at the beach is limited, but there is a larger car park further up the valley. The beach has all facilities, including a summer lifeguard, and is popular with surfers. The sea here is particularly noted for its clarity and colour. Surf hire, equipment and clothing is available from *Aggie Surf Shop*, 4 Peterville Square (**01872 553818**) at the head of the valley.

St Agnes Beacon

Just to the west of the village and easily reached by several footpaths is St Agnes Beacon, 629 feet high and a prominent landmark. There are panoramic views from the top, as far as St Ives to the south and Padstow to the north on a clear day. On a stormy day, the wind feels as though it could blow your head off.

There are several good places to stay in the village including the **St Agnes Hotel**, Churchtown (**01872 552307**) **C**, directly opposite the church in the centre of the village. A large and handsome Victorian granite hotel. **The Porthvean** (**01872 552581**), next door, is only available for holiday lets. The **Cleaders Croft Hotel** at 16 British Road (**01872 552349**) **B–C** is a large and imposing granite house with en-suite rooms. By the crossroads at the bottom of Town Hill is **Grove View Cottage**, Peterville (**01872 553199**) **A**, a small B&B with 4 rooms, no en-suite. The **Malthouse**, Peterville (**01872 553318**) **A**, opposite the above, is also good value.

At Trevaunance Cove itself is the **Driftwood Spars Hotel** (**01872 552428**) **C**, a white-painted, C17 granite building with substantial oak beams evident in the public rooms, many reputedly from the spars of ships wrecked in the cove. A "wreckers tunnel" leads down to the beach from behind the fireplace in the bar. All rooms are en-suite, many with sea views.

There are a number of good places to eat and drink. The **St Agnes Hotel** serves real ales and good food in its pleasant bar, as does the **Driftwood Spars Hotel**. They also both have separate restaurants. **The Taphouse**, Peterville, is a warm and welcoming bar serving good real ales and food with a menu specializing in pizzas and Mexican snacks. Mellow music and chunky wooden furniture add to the atmosphere *I*. Highly recommended by the locals is **Schooners Bistro**, Trevaunance Cove (**01872 553149**) *I–M* which is located right on the beach. During the day it functions as a café with lunches and in the evening as a more upmarket seafood and fish restaurant. The views out to sea are excellent, particularly as the sun goes down.

St Agnes Head

The village is located just off the main A30 on the B3277. There are regular buses to Newquay, St Ives, Camborne and Truro. The Coast Path passes through Trevaunance Cove and then proceeds through increasing evidence of the area's mining heritage to St Agnes Head with extensive views along the coast. The path continues along the cliff top to the *Wheal Coates Mine* and nearby *Towanroath Engine House* dating from 1872–3, both now owned and maintained by The National Trust. There is a car park on the cliff top just above the mine. All the deeper mine workings were plagued by flooding and adits, or tunnels, were dug sloping out to the cliff face or valley side to drain off the water. Many such adits can be seen in the cliffs hereabouts.

Chapel Porth is a dramatic cove situated between high cliffs. It is very exposed to the prevailing storms and therefore was never a major harbour. There is no development other than a National Trust car park, toilets and a seasonal cafe. The beach is sandy and extensive at low tide. However, extreme care must be taken not to get cut off by the incoming tide as the steep cliffs behind prevent any escape from the beach. There are numerous caves that can be explored at low tide. There is a summer lifeguard service. At low tide the sands extend all the way to Porthowan, while the Coast Path climbs and follows the top of the cliffs. **Chapel Porth**

Porthowan has a big car park and a nice, sandy beach, one of the few on this part of the coast which is not in shadow by the evening. However, the village of scattered semis and bungalows has no character and nothing to offer the visitor. **The Unicorn**, just back from the beach, is a charmless pub with grim food. A better option is **Blue** (01209 890329) *I-M*, a bar and cafe right on the beach, and serving food throughout the day. It has a big sun terrace overlooking the beach. In the evenings there is a more upmarket restaurant. Cocktails and tapas are served from 4pm. There are seasonal buses to Newquay and St Ives which make it a convenient place to start or finish a walk along the Coast Path. **Porthowan**

Portreath, three miles south-west, has an interesting history as a major port for the mines of the Basset family who lived at nearby Tehidy. The harbour has a double basin and a long projecting pier and was built in 1760 by Francis Basset. The port was used to ship ore out and Welsh coal in to fuel the pumping engines in the mines. For years the cargo was hauled by horse and mule down a sloping track on the north side of the valley. Then Francis Basset constructed an Incline Railway to allow shipments to be taken to the mines via *The Portreath Tramroad* which operated from 1812 until the 1860s. The Incline is still evident. A footpath now follows the route as far as Scorrier and St Day, a distance of around five miles. The path is waymarked, the first one being by the Portreath Arms. The white "pepper pot" on the cliffs is a daymark for guiding ships into the narrow harbour entrance. **Portreath**

The beach is wide and sandy and has an attractive setting backed by high cliffs and with the outcrop of Gull Rock directly offshore. It is a popular beach, but it is dangerous to swim near the pier or rocks. There is a summer lifeguard service. In January 1895, the beach was the scene of one of the most horrific wrecks on this stretch of coast. The *Escurial* sunk only 50 yards from the shore, but the seas were so big that the Hayle lifeboat, which had been brought 11 miles by road to Portreath, could not launch. An attempt had it thrown back upon the shore. The *Escurial* was overwhelmed by the waves and the lifeboat crew and villagers could only watch as the crew climbed into the rigging before falling from exhaustion or cold to their deaths. Amazingly seven men did make it ashore to be plucked from the surf by those watching, but 11 others died. **Gull Rock**

The village has a couple of pubs, the **Basset Arms**, a rather basic pub that serves bar food and the **Portreath Arms** (01209 842259) *B*, with a friendly atmosphere and lots of pictures of the tramway on the walls. They also have accommodation in en-suite rooms. **Cliff House** (01209 843847) *B*, is next door and provides comfortable B&B accommodation. No children under 12. The best place to eat in the village is **Tabbs Restaurant** (01209 842488) *E* with an interesting menu including fish and vegetarian dishes. It is open in the evenings and for Sunday lunch.

**Tehidy
Country Park**

Tehidy Country Park is located about one mile to the south and can easily be walked from Portreath and the Coast Path. There is a car park at the east lodge on the road to Camborne and a visitors centre and further car parking towards the centre of the park, signposted from the road. There is another car park on the B3301 Portreath to Hayle road. The park extends for 250 acres and has some excellent woodland walks, which are something of a rarity in this part of Cornwall. The land originally belonged to the Basset family who used much of the woodland for hunting. The sheltered woodland provides a welcome contrast to the rugged coastline and moorland found in the rest of this area. It would be an excellent place for a picnic on a bright, windy, day.

The **Aviary Court Hotel** (**01209 842256**) **C** is in a secluded location just half a mile east of Tehidy Park. It is an attractive, small hotel which would be a good base for exploring the area. There is also a restaurant.

The coast between Portreath and Godrevy Point is a continuous stretch of high cliffs with sheer drops to the sea below. The Coast Path follows the cliff top as does the B3301 a little way inland. There are a number of car parks which allow access to the cliff top walk from various points. *Hells Mouth* is a local tourist site with a sheer drop to the sea below. From here to *Navax Point* to the west, the caves below are used as breeding sites by grey seals. At Navax Point, *Godrevy Lighthouse* becomes visible on its rocky island just offshore, the inspiration for Virginia Woolf's *To the Lighthouse*. The lighthouse marks the landward end of a treacherous line of reefs that have claimed many wrecks. Perhaps the most famous involving the loss of some of King Charles I's personal effects in 1646. The goods that were washed ashore were fought over by the Bassets and the Arundells, each claiming wrecking rights as Lords of the Manor.

St Ives Bay

At Godrevy Point the whole of St Ives Bay is open to view, including the sand beach and dunes that stretch to Hayle estuary and beyond. There is a car park and toilet facilities. The beach to the south, *Godrevy Towans*, is sandy with rocky reefs exposed at low water. The Red River flows into the sea here – its name coming from the red iron oxide mine waste that used to be dumped into the river until it ran rust red. There is a further car park and a cafe that is open all year. As with all the beaches here, there is a summer lifeguard service. *Gwithian Towans* is the extension of the beach south and is backed by high dunes and a large caravan park. The beach is popular with surfers.

Gwithian

Gwithian itself is an attractive hamlet with a rather undistinguished church built in 1866. The stone lytch gate incorporates some details from an earlier building. One of the earliest churches in Cornwall was excavated from the nearby sands in the C19, but has since been covered over again. Its existence here is not surprising for Hayle was the favoured landing place for the Irish saints and the start of the overland route to St Michaels Mount. The sands here were so invasive that there is record of Upton Barton Farm being overwhelmed by sand in a single night in 1650, the occupants having to escape by a window. The dunes have now been stabilized with the planting of Marram grass and are closely monitored by Cornwall County Council. The grass and the calcium rich soil that it traps attract a distinctive flora with many rare plants, migrating birds and butterflies. Most of the dunes are a Site of Special Scientific Interest.

The dunes continue south, all the way to Hayle. The middle part was once the site of the National Explosives Works which employed 1800 people during the First World War. Now there are only remnants of buildings, bunkers and tramways scattered across the sand. A number of holiday camps and caravan parks have populated the southern end. Phillack is no more than a small group of buildings nestling under the leeward side of the dunes. The church, the original parish church of Hayle, is C15 but was substantially rebuilt in 1856. It is standard Cornish but there are some fine Celtic crosses in the churchyard and the dunes encroach right into the churchyard providing a dramatic setting. Of particular interest is the small, projecting stone over the gable of the south porch with the inscibed XP, Chi-rho symbol of ancient Christianity. It dates from the C6 or C7. The wonderfully named **Bucket of Blood** next door, is an old white painted granite inn with low beamed ceilings and a warm and welcoming interior. They serve real ale from the cask and bar food.

Phillack

Hayle, at the mouth of the Hayle River was once important as the northern end of the Iron Age route across the peninsula to St Michaels Mount. However, its real growth came in the Victorian period when a number of engineering works were established to serve the booming mining industry. Black's Guide for 1876 described it "a dirtier, squalider, less interesting town than Hayle is not to be found in all of Cornwall." There are still a number of fine buildings of that period and a canal where the, now largely deserted, wharves are a reminder of its busy past. The first steam railway in Cornwall connected Hayle to Redruth and opened in 1837. On the edge of the village, by the estuary, is *The Plantation*, the site of an Iron Age Castle that may have been used for the storage of tin prior to shipping. Henry Harvey, of the famous Harvey Engineering Works of Hayle, remodelled the earthworks in 1844 laying out paths and landscaping. There are good views over the estuary from the top. A C5 inscribed tombstone was found during restoration and has been installed alongside the path. On the road frontage is a mortar dating from The Crimean War and cast at Harvey's foundry. There are a number of pubs and B&Bs in Hayle that provide accomodation, but there is really little to tempt the visitor to stay with the attractions of St Ives so close by. However, if you do want to stay then **The White Hart Hote**l, Foundry Square (**01736 752322**) **B** is an exuberant neo-classical design, beside the Hayle viaduct.

Hayle

The whole of the Hayle Estuary is an important area for birds particularly during the winter months when many species arrive to shelter here. **The Old Quay House Inn** is at the very mouth of the river and has a hide in its garden provided by the Royal Society of Birds which can be used by anyone. The RSPB owns the intertidal mudflats of the whole estuary and over 250 species of bird have been recorded here.

Hayle Estuary

Just a mile upriver is the attractive village of St Erth with a fine stone bridge over the river dating from C14 but much repaired in C17 and widened in 1816. It still provides a pleasant vista with the *Church of St Ercus* in the background, located on the riverbank. The church dates from C14 and was restored in 1874. It is a small church, set among trees and beautifully positioned. The south porch still possesses its old wagon roof and there is a good Norman font of an unusual design. An ancient cross head in the churchyard displays a primitive crucifixion scene. The village itself has a number of attractive cottages and terraces lining the

St Erth

steep slopes to the east of the river. **The Star Inn** (01736 752068) *B* is a nice, C16 building in the centre of the village. There is a pleasant garden and they serve bar food and cream teas. There is a separate restaurant and accommodation in en-suite rooms if required.

Redruth, Camborne and Mining

Redruth and Camborne make up the largest concentration of population in Cornwall. However, until relatively recently both towns had insignificant popula-tions. Their huge growth was triggered by one thing and one thing only – mining. This area had some of the richest mineral deposits in Cornwall and, at one time, was one of the most heavily industrialized in the world. Over 50,000 miners worked in West Cornwall at the height of the boom in the C19 and two thirds of the world's copper came from the County. In the Redruth/Camborne area alone, there were over 300 mines. Now there are none, although the relics of the mining industry continue to dominate the landscape. While its attraction may not seem obvious to the average tourist, there are a number of interesting sites, and the towns of Redruth and Camborne contain many fine Victorian buildings which give them a distinctive character compared to Cornwall's more obvious destinations.

Redruth

Redruth had an ancient beginning. The town is dominated by the massive, heather-covered granite heights of *Carn Brea*. It is the site of the largest Iron Age hillfort in Cornwall, encompassing some 46 acres. From about 3900BC, stone ram-parts enclosed a village occupied by over 200 people. Between the central and eastern summits may be seen several Iron Age hut circles. Traces of wooden build-ings and Neolithic pottery have been found along with a huge number of arrow-heads which suggests that the site may have been under attack at some time. Much of the defences are thought to belong to the Neolithic rather than the Iron Age. At the highest point is a stone memorial erected in 1836 to Lord de Dunstanville, bet-ter known as Francis Basset of Tehidy,. There are panoramic views over the coun-tryside with the remains of mine engine houses peppered across the landscape. The summit has several massive wind eroded boulders and Megalithic tombs. On the eastern summit, is a medieval castle built into the rock outcrop. It was proba-bly built as a hunting lodge but has now been converted into a restaurant and is certainly an atmospheric setting for a meal. **Carn Brea Castle Restaurant** (01209 218358) *M*. It is open from 6.30pm every day and it is necessary to book in advance. There is a small car park by the restaurant. Carn Brea is easily approached by a number of well-defined footpaths. It is also possible to drive to the top from the mining village of Carnkie on the southern slope.

Minerals have probably been worked in this area from the earliest times and by the Middle Ages mining was well established. Tin was obtained from deposits in stream beds or worked on the surface from veins in the granite. By the early C14, streamers were working the brook that ran along the bottom of Fore Street. The iron oxide from the workings would have discoloured the water and thereby given Redruth its name from the Cornish *rhyd* (ford) and *ruth* (red). By 1324 a charter for two weekly markets and two annual fairs had been granted, an indication of the growing importance of the town.

However, the town's population would still have been relatively small and would remain so until the late C17 when mining in Cornwall began to enter its boom years. It was copper rather than tin that was to be the catalyst. Until then, copper had been discarded as a waste by-product of tin mining, but by the late C17 it could be used to make brass. Copper tended to be deep mined and to employ significantly more people than the old tin mining industry. Redruth and the surrounding towns had a boom in population, with many drawn from all over Britain to work in the mines. The mines were now major investments and the gentry who owned them became fabulously wealthy. However, the profits were not shared and conditions in the mines were appalling and dangerous. In 1847, one in five miners in Gwennap, just outside Redruth, died in mining accidents. The life expectancy of men in Cornwall's mining areas plummeted. Wages were low and riots, drunkenness and brawling common. Redruth had more in common with the mining boom towns of the Klondyke than many of the other towns of mainland England. The spread of Methodism helped to quieten things down and the boom years soon passed due to the opening up of international competition in the 1860s. By 1880, an astonishing two thirds of Cornish miners had emigrated to the Americas, Australasia and South Africa. Mining continued for another 30–40 years but there were fewer jobs and the huge, quick profits were gone.

The legacy of this history is seen in the architecture of Redruth, a nineteenth century industrial town, more so than any other in Cornwall. Immediately opposite the railway station, the two single storey buildings (one dated 1891) were offices where stocks and shares in the mines were traded. At the bottom of Station Road in Alma Place is the *Mining Exchange*, dated 1880, where the metal was bought and sold. On the railway station itself, the wooden building on the south side dates from *Brunel*'s linking of the West Cornwall Railway to the Truro Line and is thought to date from the 1850s. The adjacent footbridge dates from 1888. Fore Street is the main street and runs directly east-west through the town centre. On the corner of Alma Place is the distinctive clocktower, almost Venetian in design, and erected in 1828. The arches at ground level were originally open, but they were enclosed, later in the century, and used as police cells. In 1904, the tower was raised in height, supposedly because the construction of a new building opposite obscured the view of the clock from miners living in the top part of the town. The addition is clearly visible. Fore Street, along with the rest of the town centre, contains several fine Victorian and late Georgian buildings, many of which have suffered over the intervening years. English Heritage is investing money in the regeneration of Redruth and its Victorian legacy. In Cross Street is *Murdoch House*, the home of William Murdoch, who came to Redruth in 1779 to work for the firm of Boulton and Watt and proceeded to build the first model of a steam driven, self propelling locomotive in 1784. He also experimented with the use of coal gas for lighting and in 1792 this house became the first in the world to be lit in this manner. In Penryn Street, beside the impressive viaduct, is the *Old Court House*, a fine granite building of 1850. Just beyond the viaduct, turn left up Treruffe Hill and on the corner of Clinton Road is the *Passmore Edwards Free Library*, a typical, granite design of 1894. Opposite, is *St Andrew's Church*, built by the local architect *James Hicks* in 1883. Clinton Road itself and the area around here have a number of substantial Victorian villas. The *Cornish Studies Library* is in Alma Place and is a good place to start a visit. It has a small exhibition about the history of Redruth. Containing over 30,000 volumes, the Library is an invaluable resource for anybody wanting to research more about Cornwall. Many people use the facilities to trace their ancestors, something of a cottage industry with the great Cornish diaspora of the C19.

Churchtown

St Euny, the parish church, lies outside the present town in the little village of Churchtown, just to the west of Redruth and directly under Carn Brea. It dates from 1756 and has a rather curious appearance by virtue of being attached to a C15 tower. Of the original Norman church, there is no trace. There are good views of Carn Brea from the churchyard. The lytch gate has an unusually long coffin rest, supposedly due to the frequency of accidents in the nearby mines. Churchtown has a number of attractive granite houses.

Redruth is well placed as a base for exploring this part of Cornwall with good transport communications. However, there are relatively few places to stay in the town itself and even fewer places to eat or drink in the evening. There is a definite ghost town feel in the evenings. If you do decide to stay **Lansdowne House**, 42 Clinton Road (**01209 216002**) *B* is close to the railway station and town centre. On the edge of town is the **Penventon Park Hotel** (**01209 203000**) *D*, a smart Georgian country house in extensive grounds. There is a also a health centre with a heated indoor pool.

The choice of places to eat is limited. There are a n umber of rather basic pubs in Fore Street that provide bar food. **The Italian Canteen** in Chapel Street (**01209 314430**) *M* is a smart Italian restaurant, and probably the best option in town. You could also try **Gaslights Restaurant and Bar** in Stratton Hill (**01209 218393**) *B*, which has a small dinner menu as well as tapas and baguettes. It also has two en-suite bedrooms. The restaurant at the **Penventon Park Hotel** has a good reputation too. The **Green Room** at 4 West End is a comfortable bar/club with DJs and attractively ramshackle interior decor. It is found at the western edge of the town centre.

Redruth has good bus connections to most of the major towns in West Cornwall and is on the main west coast railway line. By car, it is found just off the main A30.

Mineral Tramways

The Mineral Tramways is the name given to the network of tramways and railways that were established in the early C19 to connect the rapidly developing mining areas around Redruth to the ports of Portreath, Hayle and Devoran. Essential supplies of Welsh coal were brought in via these ports and mineral ore shipped out.

Prior to the tramways, everything had to be transported by pack mules, an incredibly slow and expensive operation. A small display and information centre for the tramways is located at the **King Edward Mine, Mill and Mining Museum** (01209 614681) at Troon, near Camborne. The museum contains much original equipment and shows the processing of the ore from mining through to smelting. It also has an interesting display relating to mining in the area.

The network of footpaths and cycleways is still being established but eventually there will be over 75 miles of pathway which will connect 40 mine sites and 70 engine houses. At the time of writing only three trails are substantially open.

The Great Flat Lode Trail takes in several mine sites in a wide loop around Carn Brea. The Great Flat Lode once being the single, richest source of tin in Cornwall. The Basset and Grenville United mines have the best preserved ruins. The route is about six miles long and quite tortuous. Although signposted, it is advisable to pick up one of the free leaflets available at the Museum or the local Tourist Information Centre.

The *Portreath Tramroad* was opened in 1812 and was the first in Cornwall. It was an immediate success. The wagons were horse drawn and the tramway itself was single track with passing places at regular intervals. The Directors Carriage, in The Royal Cornwall Museum in Truro, is probably the oldest passenger railway carriage in the world. With the coming of the railways, the Incline, a cut up the slope from Portreath, was built to transport goods up to the Hayle Railway, eventually replacing the need for the tramroad. The Hayle Railway opened in 1837 and linked Hayle to Redruth and was West Cornwall's first steam railway. The route goes from Portreath harbour inland for seven miles to Crofthandy near Scorrier, although there are some short on-road sections. The route is generally flat and open to cycles.

The *Redruth and Chacewater Railway* came about because of the great rivalry between the Williams family, owners of the Portreath Tramroad, and John Taylor from Norwich. Taylor had hit upon the richest copper lode then discovered at Gwennap. However, the Williams' charged extortionate rates of carriage to those mines that they did not own. As a result, Taylor built his own line to Point, near Devoran, on the south coast. In its first year, the new line carried 50,000 tons of copper ore and Devoran and Point became the third largest copper exporting port in the world. The tramroad opened in 1815 and converted to steam in 1853–4. The route is open to cycles and hire is available from **Blissoe Tramways Cycle Hire** (01872 870341) including helmets, route maps and directions. They are located near Carnon Downs and are signposted from the A39.

Open April–Sept, Sun–Wed, 11am–5pm. Oct–Dec, Sunday only, 10am–1pm. Admission, £4.00, children uncder 16 free

Cornwall Industrial Discovery Centre and Engines, Pool

National Trust (01209 315027). Admission, £5.00, children £2.50, family £12.50. Open, April–October, 11.00am–5.00pm, shut Saturdays (except in August). The centre is located directly on the A3047 Redruth to Camborne road

Just north of the Mineral Tramways Centre in Pool is the Cornwall Industrial Discovery Centre and two of the best engine houses and beam engines surviving

today. The giant engine house is clearly visible beside the Safeway supermarket. Ample parking is available in the supermarket car park from where there is direct access to the Centre. There is a display relating to the industrial history of Cornwall, including ingots of pure copper and tin stamped with the mines name, and a shop selling books and artefacts. However, the main draw is *Taylors Engine*, commissioned in 1891 and the largest standard size produced. It weighs 125 tons and pumped 27,000 gallons out of the shaft from a depth of 1700 feet every hour. It is the largest beam engine left in Cornwall. It was built by Harvey & Co. of Hayle and was originally set to work at the nearby Carn Brea Mine. When that mine closed it was moved to Pool where a brand new engine house, the last one ever built in Cornwall, was erected in 1924. It continued working into the 1950s.

On the other side of the A3047, just a few hundred yards west, is the beam engine and house of *East Pool Whim*. It was designed for winding, rather than pumping, and lowered and raised miners and ore from a depth of 1,500 feet. It was the last one to be built by Holman Brothers at their Camborne foundry in 1887. The engine has been restored to working order, although now driven by electricity rather than steam.

Camborne

Camborne's growth is similar to Redruth's in that both owe their modern day existence to mining. However, Camborne became synonymous with the development of the engineering skills that grew up to support this local industry. The Holman Brothers Works were one of the largest, employing over 3500 people at their peak. In the early days they produced steam engines to allow the huge expansion of the industry in the first half of the C19 and gradually they expanded into exporting mining tools and machinery around the world.

Penponds

Camborne's most famous son is, without doubt, *Richard Trevithick*, born in 1771 near Pool. His childhood home in the village of Penponds, just outside Camborne, can be visited between Easter and October on Wednesday afternoons between 2.00pm and 5.00pm (**01209 612154**). Trevithick was one of the school of largely self-taught engineering genius who drove the Industrial Revolution forward with their timely response to the increasing technical challenges. His greatest contribution was the development of the principle of high pressure steam and he worked closely with the Holman Brothers to develop his advanced steam engines. In 1801 he test ran the first high pressure steam carriage, "The Puffing Devil" and in 1804, the world's first rail locomotive. He also invented containerisation for ships, the dry dock and the screw propeller. He left Cornwall for South America in 1816, attracted by the lure of the Peruvian silver mines. After many years, he returned to Britain and died penniless in 1833. He is commemorated in Camborne by a statue outside the library and on the last Sunday in April there is the annual Trevithick Day, climaxed by a parade of steam locomotives through the town.

Camborne is an attractive, rather than picturesque, town with many good Victorian buildings and distinctive terraces with prominent first floor bay windows. *The Church of St Martin and St Meriadocus* is the earliest building, dating from the C15, although it was enlarged and restored in 1878. Inside is an unusual altar slab, probably C10 and believed to have come from the chapel of St Ia at Troon. It is a slab of grey stone and has a key pattern border and Anglo-Saxon lettering referring to the donor, Leuiut. In the churchyard there are several noteworthy crosses including one with several holes said to represent the numbers killed in a battle on Reskajeage Downs. Just by the church, is Tyack's Hotel constructed in the late C18. Elsewhere, there is a fine *Literary Institute*, on the edge of Commercial Square, with a grand pillared portico, a number of substantial Victorian civic buildings and several Methodist Chapels, not least the grand *Centenary Wesleyan Chapel*, built in 1839. It is still in use today and terminates the view west from Trelowarren Street. The town has a busy, bustling air and is a pleasant enough place to spend a few hours.

There are a couple of nice places to stay in the centre of town. The **Tyacks Hotel**, Commercial Street (**01209 612424**) *C* is an attractive hotel built around an C18 inn. There are 15 comfortable, en-suite rooms. **The Regal Hotel**, 2 Church Lane (**01209 713131**) *B* is equally centrally placed, just by the church, and is a cheaper option. All rooms are en-suite.

Camborne is decidedly more lively than its neighbour, Redruth, and there are a number of places to eat in the compact town centre. Both the above have restaurants and also serve bar food. In Cross Street, there is a fish and chip restaurant and take-away, while at no.2 is the **Bengal Balti Cuisine** (**01209 710904**) *I* Indian restaurant and take-away. It is unlicensed but you are welcome to bring your own wine. The food is unexceptional but quite tasty. **Tse House**, 39 Commercial Street (**01209 713488**) *I* is a standard Chinese restaurant and take-away. For drinks, you could try the **Tyacks Hotel** which has a comfortable and welcoming front bar. The **White Hart** in Commercial Street is a dimly lit pub with low ceilings. There is often live music at weekends. Further east along Commercial Street is the **Wagoners Arms**, a low, granite building with an attractively dark interior. They serve bar food and real ales. **The Clipper,** at the top of Basset Road, is a small bar with a pleasant interior and real ales. Camborne even has its own nightclub, **Club Euphoria**, opposite Tyacks Hotel.

Due to the number of places to stay, eat and drink, Camborne probably makes a better base than Redruth for exploring the industrial heritage of the surrounding area. It also has a pleasant, bustling feel that is absent in Redruth. Camborne is very well connected by bus to all the neighbouring large towns. Cycling would be a good way of exploring the narrow country lanes around about. The cycle shop in Cross Street hires bikes. Camborne is on the main west coast line and the railway station is a short walk south of the town centre. The main A30 passes directly north of the town.

Around Camborne and Redruth

The area surrounding Camborne–Redruth is an extraordinary landscape of narrow lanes, moorland, hills and valleys dotted with the remains and detritus of the mining industry. The narrow lanes south of Camborne, around Troon and towards   **Troon**

Treslothan

Pool are particularly rich, with many engine houses and isolated terraces of miners' cottages. In Treslothan, the *Church of St John* was once the chapel to Pendarves House, which was demolished in 1955. Inside, is a C15 font believed to have come from Camborne Church. The churchyard contains the Gothic, Pendarves Mausoleum. The nearby Pendarves Park contains the Giant Quoit, a reconstruction of an original megalithic tomb that collapsed in the nineteenth century.

Pendarves Park

Crowan

Further south still, in an exposed position on low moorland is Crowan, a pleasant village of scattered granite buildings. The church of *St Crewenna* is in an isolated, exposed position with its high tower visible for miles over the flat landscape. There are early capitals preserved in the north aisle, the church having been comprehensively restored in 1872. The shield-holding angels on all four sides refer to a St Aubyn marriage in 1398. The church contains many St Aubyn tombs and memorials, their ancestral home at the time being at Clowance to the west. It was destroyed by fire in the early C19 although the replacement house can still be seen. It is now the centre of a holiday home time share complex. Within the church, there are a number of C15 brasses and a good vault tomb of 1714. There is a hideous, but nevertheless impressive, baroque memorial of 1772 to Sir John St Aubyn and an interesting font with carved lions. The churchyard is extraordinarily large with many interesting tombs and headstones.

Clowance

To the east of Redruth, among the narrow, twisting lanes is *Gwennap Pit*, a large semi-circular, grass amphitheatre where *John Wesley* used to regularly preach. There is a visitor's centre but the pit is open at all times. The power of Wesley's message can be gauged by the fact that he regularly used to fill the amphitheatre with up to 10,000 believers. The site is signposted down narrow lanes between Redruth and St Day. St Day is a rather depressed and depressing mining village with no interest other than its church of 1828, extraordinarily large and derelict. It now houses a series of display panels on the history of St Day and the surrounding area. It is open between Easter and October, 10am–5pm. The landscape around here is littered with the remains of the mining industry.

St Day

Chacewater

Chacewater, in direct contrast to St Day is a pleasant, old mining village with several interesting pubs and a fine church on a hill on the edge of the village. The original church dated from 1828 but was entirely rebuilt, with the exception of the tower, by Edmund Sedding in 1892. The tower and the size of the church are impressive, indicative again of how much greater the population of the mining areas used to be and there is a fine view over the surrounding landscape from the churchyard. The interior is notable for the colours of the walls of local stone. The stained glass in the east window is of fine quality and came from St Mary's in Truro when it was demolished to make way for the Cathedral. Just downhill from the church is the granite schoolhouse of 1847.

The Penwith Peninsula, St Ives and Penzance

Introduction

At the far west tip of England, the Penwith peninsula is one of the most distinctive areas within this most diverse country. It was the very last refuge of the Cornish Celts and evidence of their culture still permeates the area. It is an area of low moorland surrounded by high cliffs and interspersed with sandy coves. The cliff scenery and beaches are some of the best in Britain. It is home to two of the most attractive towns in the county, Penzance and St Ives, and has a number of museums and other sites of interest and importance. It is a major centre for the arts and has been since the C19 when artists first came to Newlyn and St Ives. It is also accessible, despite being at the furthest extremity of England. By car the A30 provides a fast approach with most of it now being dual carriageway. Long distance coaches link Penwith to cities throughout the country and Penzance is the terminus for the main west coast railway line. The peninsula, itself, is small, being no more than eight by ten miles at most. This makes it an excellent place to explore by foot or cycle. The South West Coast Path provides some of the best coast walking in Britain and links most of the major sites, while the Tinners Way is an inland route that explores many of the prehistoric sites of the interior and the industrial legacy of the mining industry around St Just. Cycles can be hired at various places and the small size of the peninsula means that cycling is a perfectly viable means of travel, despite the occasional steep hill.

Lelant

Lelant, now a small village on the approach to St Ives, was a seaport till the Middle Ages when St Ives overtook it in importance. It is quite possible that it constituted part of the ancient overland route between the Hayle Estuary and Mounts Bay for trade between Ireland and Brittany. It is now the starting point for the *St Michael's Way*, a somewhat circuitous 13 mile path to St Michael's Mount, taking walkers to areas of historic and religious significance. The route starts from outside the church where there is a direction board.

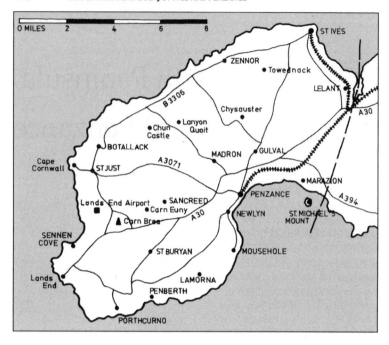

Little remains of the medieval settlement apart from the *Church of St Uny*, prominently located on the shore of the Hayle Estuary. St Uny was one of the many wandering Cornish missionaries, said to have arrived from Ireland in C6. The new church was consecrated in 1424, although remains of the Norman period have been incorporated. The church is typical Cornish, granite, low and solid with a squat tower with diagonal buttresses. The interior has a fine octagonal font of unknown age and two exceptional, deeply carved slate memorials to the Praed (1620) and Pawley (1635) families. The church has fought a continual battle against the shifting sands, in 1679 it was recorded that the vicarage, then positioned between the sea and church had been rendered uninhabitable by sand. Its beautiful location has been compromised somewhat by the adjacent golf course but it is still possible to enjoy the fine panorama across the Estuary.

The adjacent churchyard has several fine granite crosses in the Celtic style and there are good views back to the church. The cemetery chapel was erected in 1879, later a Sunday School and now empty and locked. There is little accommodation in Lelant and it is far better to push on to St Ives just up the coast. The **Badger Inn** (01736 752181) *C* on the main road serves superior bar food and there is a restaurant and accommodation if required.

Lelant Station, has regular trains to St Ives and a small car park. Further out, Lelant Saltings has an official Park and Ride for St Ives which includes the train into St Ives.

St Ives

Located on a narrow spur of land, almost surrounded by white, sand beaches and bathed in a magical, translucent, watery light, St Ives is one of the undisputed highlights of Cornwall. It is home to an artists colony of international fame and importance, it has a plethora of fine art galleries, restaurants and pubs and an atmosphere of bohemia mixed with hard-work that, while, maybe, somewhat tenuous these days, is nevertheless at the core of its essential spirit. The town itself retains the character of its origins as a Cornish fishing village, despite the growth of recent years. The narrow lanes and alleyways are still lined by tightly-packed fishermen's cottages and workshops, clinging together for protection against the elements. Of course, the cottages are now likely to be guest---houses and the workshops, picture galleries, and the narrow streets packed with tourists, but visit any time outside the peak summer months and you will be surprised how much of the original character of St Ives remains. This is essentially a small town and one that is used to welcoming strangers, often of an unconventional manner. It has an open and welcoming nature that puts it above most other destinations in Cornwall.

Historic development

The earliest history of St Ives is uncertain, but it is likely that the area was inhabited in the Bronze Age due to the trade between Ireland and Britanny via the Hayle Estuary and Mount's Bay. Two early, Bronze Age axe heads found at St Erth are likely evidence of this important trade route. St Ives began to flourish as a port due to its natural harbour protected against the westerly storms. It became the most important fishing port in Cornwall with an amazing 285 seines (pilchard businesses), so many that each seine had to be allocated a time when they could net their fish. The often-quoted figure of a record daily catch of sixteen and a half million fish gives some indication of the extent of the industry. Not surprisingly, by the 1920's the pilchards were fished out and the industry was all but dead. The St Ives Museum has a number of exhibits relating to the industry.

Mining, too, had a brief role to play in its development in the C18 and early C19 when exploitation of the local tin gave employment to many in the town. Friction, often leading to violence, was common between the fishermen of the Downalong area and the miners who tended to live in Upalong

Fishing, however, remained the principal commercial interest of the town, long into the C19 when the coming of the London to Penzance railway in 1866, finally opened up this otherwise remote area of England. The first visitors to the town were artists drawn by the quality of light, the beautiful scenery and the richness of the Cornish folk traditions. As communications improved, the onset of tourism began to be felt upon the St Ives community, but it was not until the 1930s and the arrival of paid annual holidays that tourism became a significant force. Interrupted by the war years and post-war shortages, tourism took some time to recover but by the 1960s' it had become St Ives primary source of income. The opening of the Tate

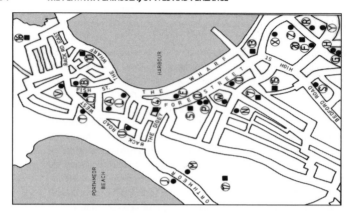

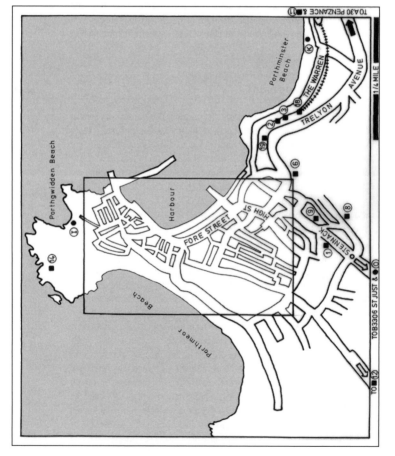

ST IVES

Gallery in 1993 has helped to extend the tourist season beyond the summer months and given a much-needed boost to the arts community in St Ives.

The Town

Despite its growing importance as a port in the Middle Ages, there remained no church in the town till the C15 – the nearest church being Lelant. The town applied for a Papal Bull for a church of its own in 1408. It did not succeed, but a chapel of ease was erected in 1410-34 which is now one of the major church buildings in Cornwall. The **Church of St Ia** is a big church with a high tower, signifying the importance of the town, with a nave of seven bays and identical aisles either side. It is set right on the seafront. The gable ends of the nave and aisles face out to sea while the tower is on the landward side. Inside, the piers of the arcade are of Devon sandstone and display the more intricate carving that the soft stone allows, compared to the more normal granite of Penwith. There is a superb C15 granite font with exquisite carving of this most difficult of stone – the pedestal carving represents demons being cast out by the cleansing powers of baptism. There are some intricately carved bench ends and the pulpit also incorporates some C15 bench ends into its construction. One of the finest memorials is the carving Madonna and Child by *Barbara Hepworth* located in the Lady Chapel to the right of the altar. It was carved by Hepworth in memory of her son, Paul, killed over Thailand in 1953, while serving with the RAF. The piece is infused with the love of a mother for her child and, interestingly, Hepworth modified her later abstract style. Perhaps, she found abstraction too vague and difficult to express the emotions she so clearly felt at this time in her life. The church remained a chapel of ease until 1826 when it finally became the parish church of St Ives.

The *Chapel of St Nicholas* on the Island, the hillock between Porthmeor and Porthgwidden beaches, is the site of an ancient chapel, partially destroyed in 1904, by order of the War Office and rebuilt in 1911. It was further restored in 1971. The floor is made of tiles by Bernard Leach, the famous St Ives artist. There is a magnificent view over St Ives, only partly marred by the public car park in the foreground.

The harbour pier was built by *Smeaton* in 1767–70 and has been subsequently lengthened. The octagonal cupola was designed as a lookout by Smeaton and seems impossibly graceful and flimsy to be in such an exposed position. It has recently been refurbished and the plans and a record of the refurbishment are displayed in the nearby St Ives Museum. A further, even flimsier lookout was added as part of the later lengthening. Between the two lookouts, a plaque to the artist Harry Rountree is set into the wall. There is a small fisherman's chapel at the landward end of the pier, that always seems to be locked, but it is possible to appreciate the simple nature of the space within through the windows.

Tregenna Castle, on the hill to the south of the town, was built in 1774 by the younger Wood of Bath. It is now a hotel, hugely extended and has little of its original character. Further to the south on a hill just outside the town is the Knill Monument, erected in 1782 by *John Knill*, Mayor and, reputedly, smuggler. It is in the form of a pyramid and was probably intended as his mausoleum. There are spectacular views over St Ives and the surrounding area from the hill.

Elsewhere, the town is a jumble of old fishermen's cottages interspersed with net lofts and workshops and the Victorian addition of certain civic buildings in the neo-gothic style, such as the library and a number of Methodist and Nonconformist chapels. The **Western Hotel** was built in the 1850s as a coaching inn and has a fine symmetrical, granite front. Fore Street is the main shopping street, stretching from the church round to the old, fisherman's quarter of Downalong. This area, on the narrow promontory between the harbour and Porthmeor Beach, is one of the most atmospheric in the town and it is a delight to just wander the narrow lanes and alleyways. It is also the home to many art galleries and smart restaurants. The new lifeboat station on the harbour mars the view of the church from Smeatons pier. The building itself is monolithic granite but fit for its purpose with its massive walls standing directly on the sea's edge. The lifeboat can be visited when the main doors are open (donations). There is a plaque on the wall nearest the church, recording the history of the St Ives station, including the tragic loss of the lifeboat in St Ives Bay on 23 January 1939 – only one man of the eight on board survived.

The newest and most spectacular addition to the architecture of St Ives is the **Tate Gallery**, located directly on Porthmeor Beach. Designed by the architects, Evans and Shalev, who also designed the Truro Law Courts, the building is an assiduously worked study in white render and glass. The grand, concave window looking out over Porthmeor Bay allows natural light to flood into the building and emphasises the relationship with nature and the elements that was so important to the St Ives' artists. The building is surprisingly contextual when viewed from the various points around the town and sits happily with its surroundings.

One of the best views of St Ives is from the *Malakoff*, a rather dated piece of urban landscaping opened in 1972. It includes a Hepworth sculpture and is located just above the railway station. There is little public open space in St Ives, the density of buildings being as great as it is. However, the tiny *Trewyn Gardens*, located just off Barnoon Hill is a lush, semi-tropical park in a secluded setting, perfect for a quiet break or picnic lunch. There is a large bronze by the artist *John Milne*.

The **St Ives Museum** (**01736 796005**), located between the harbour and Porthgwidden Beach, contains an interesting range of artefacts and curios relating to St Ives and Penwith. There are photographs and reports of wrecks around the coast near St Ives and a number of press reports relating to the St Ives lifeboat disaster of 1939. Also, just as a reminder that St Ives still has a seafaring tradition and that the sea can never be taken for granted, reports of the loss of the Gorah Lass in March 1997 with all hands. Three local men were lost to the sea.

Open Easter-October, Mon–Sat 10am–5pm (4pm on Sat) Admission, £1.50, children £0.50

The Beaches

The beaches around St Ives are uniformly excellent with fine white sand, good facilities and a different character to each one. Surfing is good from the west facing *Porthmeor Beach* and there is a *Surf School* right on the sands (**01736 793366**). Equipment can be hired here or at the Surf Shop in Fore Street. There is a lifeguard in attendance during the summer and two beachfront cafes to choose from. Probably, the most popular beach in town, it can become crowded at peak times. There is more of a scene on this beach than the others and it is a good place to watch the sun go down while nursing a cold beer. Just around the headland is the smaller Porthgwidden Beach with generally safe bathing. There is an excellent beach cafe and restaurant and the town is only a minute's walk away. The Harbour Beach is very small, although more space is available when the tide is out. It makes a good suntrap and is sheltered from most of the prevailing winds, but tends to be overlooked. Carbis Bay, situated about a mile further around the bay from St Ives, is a long, safe sandy beach which is very popular with families. There are all facilities and it is an easy walk from the centre of town.

Porthmeor Beach

Porthgwidden Beach

Harbour Beach

Carbis Bay

Tate Gallery

Porthmeor Beach (01736 796226). Open every day, March–October 10.00am-5.30pm, November–February 10.00am-4.30pm, closed Mondays. Admission, £5.50, children £2.50. Free guided tour at 2.30pm. A combined ticket with the Barbara Hepworth Museum is £8.50/£3.90 valid for the same day only

St Ives' premier gallery is dedicated to showing modern art created in or associated with Cornwall. There is no permanent collection – it displays selected works from the Tate Gallery's collection – the National Collection of British and

ARTISTS IN ST IVES

The first record of a major artist in St Ives is of **Turner** who painted a view of St Ives from a vantage point above the town in 1811, now in the British Museum. At that time, Cornwall and, particularly, Penwith was a remote and inaccessible place and, perhaps, only an artist of Turner's resilience would be likely to make the journey west, travelling, as he did, on foot, by horseback and occasionally by sea. With the coming of the railway to Penzance in 1866, Cornwall, for the first time in its history, was in direct communication with the rest of England. Attracted by the quality of the light, artists soon followed. From the beginning, St Ives attracted a more international set than the Newlyn Artists. In the winter of 1883–4 the American, **James McNeill Whistler** made an extended visit with his young assistants, **Walter Sickert** and the Australian **Mortimer Menpes**. Whistler was a controversial figure and many of his landscapes and seascapes painted in St Ives came close to total abstraction – an early pointer to the direction that the St Ives School was to take. By the 1890s a number of artists had become residents and an Artists Club was established. Many of the sail lofts, particularly along Porthmeor Beach were converted to artists studios. By 1910 there were about 80 studios. **Julius Olsson RA, John Park** and **Borlase Smart** were among the more successful artists living in St Ives at this time. Olsson also established the town's first school of painting.

In 1920, **Bernard Leach** settled in St Ives with his colleague **Shoji Hamada** to establish a pottery for his Oriental-influenced work. The pottery contained the first Oriental climbing kiln in Europe, where the heat travels up a series of steps giving different temperatures and ceramic effects at each level. A tradition of training apprentices from Britain and abroad was established at the premises located in The Stennack. Leach died in 1979, but the pottery continues.

Despite Leach's arrival, the Great War saw a diminishing in the importance of the Artists Colony in St Ives in the same way that it did in Newlyn and Lamorna.. While many artists still lived in St Ives, their work lacked the impact of their predecessors. The town became something of an artistic backwater during this period. The St Ives Arts Club became less a meeting place for professional painters than a social club for a broader range of talents, including Leslie Stephens , the poet, and his daughters **Vanessa Bell** and **Virginia Woolf** who spent their summers at Talland House, off Talland Road, now converted to holiday flats. Woolf's famous novel *To the Lighthouse*, although set in the Hebrides, was actually based on the Godrevy Lighthouse, clearly visible across the bay.

In 1928 a chance meeting took place that was to reinvigorate the St Ives art scene and provide it with one of its most unique talents. The young painters, Ben Nicholson and Christopher Wood, made a visit to St Ives and walking the back streets of the fishermen's quarter, through the open door of a small cottage, they had their first sighting of the work of **Alfred Wallis** (1855–1942). Wallis was a fisherman, turned rag and bone man. He first went to sea aged 9, working as a cabin boy and cook and by the age of 18 was making trips to Newfoundland aboard the Penzance fleet. He had no real education and could write only with difficulty. At the age of twenty, he married a woman 21 years older, who had already borne 17 children. She had two more by Wallis but both died in infancy. Inarticulate and undersized, he was in many ways inadequate to deal with life. He was given only the most menial jobs on the boats and in 1890 he moved to St Ives to run his scrap business. He retired in 1912 and moved to no.3 Back Road West, where a plaque today marks the house. His wife, Susan died in 1922 and it was about this time that he began to paint, as he said 'for company.' He began to produce a series of paintings on subjects that he knew – the boats, the harbour and sea views, painted in house paint or marine paint on bits of old card, wood or anything else to hand. He was, needless to say, totally untutored and his fresh, naïve approach to painting was a revelation to Nicholson and Wood who were searching for a new way to express their art. The search for simplicity, for a direct form of expression was a key part of the development of the modern art movement. In Wallis the two painters recognized a raw talent that could not be taught, the painting had come from within the direct experience of the artist. Despite his 'discovery' by Nicholson, Wallis was largely ignored by the resident artists in St Ives and became a figure of fun for the small boys in town. He led a solitary, existence beset by personal difficulties and turned increasingly to the Bible for support. He died in Madron Workhouse, a lonely, tormented man and is buried in Barnoon Cemetery, where his grave looks out over St Ives to the sea beyond. His grave is a simple slab decorated with tiles made by Bernard Leach – it shows an old man entering a lighthouse set in a stormy sea with a simple inscription. His funeral was attended by Ben Nicholson, Barbara Hepworth, Naum Gabo, Leach and others. His grave can be visited in Barnoon Cemetery, if you enter through the main gates from West Place it is located along the first path on the left.

Christopher Wood, himself, was a hugely accomplished artist and spent much of 1927 –29 in St Ives and Cornwall producing a series of masterful works of local scenes. However, haunted by personal demons, he committed suicide in 1930 while at the peak of his powers.

In 1939, a few weeks before war was declared, **Ben Nicholson** and his wife, **Barbara Hepworth** came to stay with the writer and painter **Adrian Stokes** in Carbis Bay. They were soon joined by **Naum Gabo**, an artist of the Russian avant-garde who had experienced the upheavals of the Bolshevik Revolution at first hand. His was a unique talent and his mathematical/scientific background led him to create extraordinary, lightweight sculptures that seemed to consist of little more than the flimsiest enclosures of air. Nicholson and Hepworth were already established figures in the progressive art scenes of London and Europe, but after they settled in St Ives their work became more influenced by the landscapes and seascapes around them. Nicholson produced a number of paintings heavily influenced by the work of Alfred Wallis, such as his oil, St Ives, painted 1943–5. Hepworth's sculpture, in particular, began to show the increasing influence of the Penwith landscape with its massive wind-eroded boulders and rocky outcrops being a seminal influence on her later work. She wrote of this time "I discovered the remarkable pagan landscape which lies between St Ives, Penzance and Land's End; a landscape which still has a very deep effect on me, developing all my ideas about the relationship of the human figure in landscape-sculpture and landscape, and the essential quality of light in relation to sculpture, which induced a new way of piercing the forms to contain colour." Hepworth continued to live and work in St Ives until her death in 1975, having spent 35 years in the town, immersed in the landscape of Penwith – the single, most important influence on her work.

After the war, the presence of these influential figures and the reputation of the St Ives artists drew many others to reside in the town and revitalize its art scene. These included **Wilhelmina Barns Graham** (there is a view of St Ives by her on display in the library), **John Wells, Patrick Heron, Terry Frost, Denis Mitchell, Bryan Winter, Sven Berlin** and the only major abstract painter actually born in St Ives, **Peter Lanyon**. The one common element they all had was an affinity for abstraction that was to become the hallmark of the St Ives Artists. At first, the new arrivals were encouraged to join the St Ives Society of Artists, but tensions soon arose over the apparent lack of prominence given to these new artists within the Society. In 1949 there was a split, with the traditionalists staying in the Society and the 'moderns' forming themselves into The Penwith Society of Arts and Crafts in Cornwall. Nicholson, Hepworth and Bernard Leach were among its founder members. Their first meeting was held in the Castle Inn in Fore Street.

Patrick Heron had a long association with Cornwall and as a London critic he did much to publicize the work of the St Ives artists in this post-war period. He established links with painters in New York and many, including **Mark Rothko**, visited St Ives. In 1947, Heron took to visiting St Ives on a regular basis, taking a flat near the church at 3 St Andrew's Street, and painting a series of abstracts inspired by the views over the harbour. In 1958, he gave up professional art criticism and moved to St Ives, taking over Ben Nicholson's old studio overlooking Porthmeor Beach. He continued to develop his abstract work, concentrating on the rich use of colour and strong contrasts.

The Penwith Society became established by the 1960's with an impressive permanent gallery in a converted pilchard cellar. Among the newer members was the St Ives born **Bryan Pierce**, who began painting as therapy for phenylketonuria, the nervous disease he had suffered from since birth. His colourful, primitive paintings of the St Ives scene owe a debt to the work of Wallis, but have a freshness and originality of their own. He has now established a national reputation and his work is much sought after.

By the end of the 1970's the colony had lost many of its most influential members, Nicholson had left for Switzerland in 1958 following the break up of his marriage and Peter Lanyon, Roger Hilton, Bryan Winter, Hepworth and Bernard Leach were all dead. Patrick Heron, Terry Frost and others continued to work, but there was no doubt that the Colony was again to enter one of its troughs. A great boost was given to the arts scene with the opening of the St Ives Tate Gallery in 1993 and many new artists from other parts of the country have been drawn to the area.

Modern Art – which are changed annually in order to display fresh works relevant to St Ives. However, there are always likely to be works by Nicholson, Hepworth, Gabo, Wallis and Leach on display. Many people are disappointed by the annual display and it is true that the size of the exhibition space severely limits the number and range of works that can be shown. However, it is invaluable if you want to understand some of the background and development of the St Ives School and will help you if you are thinking of a tour of the other galleries in the town. The annual display is complemented by a series of exhibitions by contemporary artists throughout the year. One work on permanent display, however, is the huge coloured glass wall by Patrick Heron in the entrance. This is typical of Heron's later style and the transition to the medium of glass is nothing short of spectacular. This can be viewed for free as there is no charge to access the well-provided bookshop on the first floor or the delightful cafe on the top floor.

Barbara Hepworth Museum and Sculpture Garden

Barnoon Hill (01736 796226). Opening hours are the same as those of the Tate Gallery, except that the garden closes at dusk in winter. Admission £4.50, concessions £2.25, under 18/over 60 free

Barbara Hepworth, who died in 1975, asked in her will that her studio and adjacent garden, with a group of her sculptures placed as she wished, be permanently open to the public. The museum is administered by the Tate Gallery and has an excellent collection of her work from all periods of her life. The garden with its lush and dense foliage provides the perfect setting for many of her large abstract pieces and makes a welcome retreat from the busy town just outside the door. There is a small collection of memorabilia on display, including a number of press cuttings confirming the international significance of Hepworth.

In addition to the two main exhibition galleries, there are a large number of commercial galleries of a generally high standard in the town itself. A leaflet, *The Cornwall and Devon Galleries Guide*, available from most galleries (£1.00) lists most of the galleries in St Ives, as well as a good number elsewhere in Cornwall. It is invaluable if you are seriously considering purchasing a work of art. Otherwise, a walk around the centre of the town or the Downalong area will reveal any number of galleries. Some of the better ones are:

Leach Pottery The Stennack (**01736 796398**). Just outside the town centre on the road to Zennor. Founded in 1920 by Bernard Leach and Shoji Hamada, the showroom features many of their Oriental inspired ceramics, as well as work by the late Janet Leach and a number of distinguished apprentices.

Belgrave Gallery 22 Fore Street (**01736 794888**). The gallery is the St Ives branch of the Belgrave Gallery, London. It specializes in the work of St Ives artists of the 50s and 60s including Nicholson, Terry Frost, Patrick Heron, Bryan Winter and Hepworth. Prices for the originals are as you might expect, but there are some good limited edition prints that are more affordable. Worth a visit just to look.

The New Craftsmen 24 Fore Street (**01736 795652**). Opened in the mid 60s by Janet Leach. An excellent range of ceramics is on display as well as work by many of the major artists of the St Ives School. Ask to be allowed to view the upstairs gallery where the best, and most expensive, works are displayed.

The New Millenium Gallery Street-an-Pol (**01736 793121**). Opposite the Tourist Information Centre. Specializing in the work of largely established artists, there are two big exhibition spaces with the top floor gallery particularly good.

The Book Gallery Chapel Street (**01736 793545**). Small, but high class gallery with attached bookshop, dealing in second-hand books associated with the art, literature and history of West Cornwall.

The Penwith Society Back Road West (**01736 795579**). Open Tuesday-Saturday. Founded in 1949 by the 'modern' element of the St Ives Arts Club, it continues today as a spacious gallery, containing a wide range of figurative and abstract painters as well as a range of craft work and ceramics.

The Salthouse Gallery Norway Square (**01736 795003**). Small gallery specializing in largely unrecognized artists with a number of solo shows throughout the year, as well as a continuing display by local artists.

The Picture House Island Square (**01736 794423**). Open Tuesday-Saturday. Small, bright gallery with good glass, ceramics and prints at affordable prices.

The Plumbline Gallery Barnoon Hill (**01736 797771**). Opposite the Hepworth Museum. A small gallery with good, contemporary fine and applied art.

Half Moon Gallery St Andrews St (**01736 798147**). Gallery owned by Michael Quirke showing his own distinctive paintings of London streetscenes, beaches and clowns. One of his paintings hangs in the reception area of The Western Hotel.

Printmakers Gallery Tregenna Hill (**01736 796654**). Open every day, January and February, Friday and Saturday only. Excellent gallery showing a wide range of contemporary work by local artists, specializing in limited edition and monoprints. Prices are very reasonable and work is available either framed or unframed.

Tremayne Applied Arts Street-an-Pol (**01736 797779**). Open Monday-Friday 10.30am-4.30pm and Saturday morning. Good range of C20 artefacts, including Arts and Craft furniture, 1960s pottery and glassware, and contemporary ceramics, all at reasonable prices.

Waterside Gallery Street-an-Pol (**01736 798844**). Smart gallery with a good range of high quality paintings.

If all the above has inspired you to have a go, then consider, **The St Ives School of Painting**, Porthmeor Studios (**01736 797180**) which has been providing tuition for over 60 years. They offer a range of courses for weekend painters, students and professionals.

Accommodation

The price coding system that is used throughout this guide is on a scale of
A to E and indicates the cost of the lowest priced double room in that
establishment during the peak summer period. This is clearly marked by the
telephone number of the listing for each establishment. It should be borne in mind
that single rooms are likely to be considerably more than half the price of
a double. In the off peak months, many establishments reduce their rates
considerably and even where they do not you may be able to negotiate a discount.

A –£44
B £45–£64
C £65–£80
D £81–£100
E £100+

St Ives has literally scores of hotels and guest houses to cater for the hordes of visitors who descend on the town in the peak summer months (mid July to end of
August). In this period, it is recommended, if at all possible, to reserve accommodation in advance. Outside this period, you will have plenty of places to choose
from. The main approach road above Carbis Bay is lined with bed and breakfasts in
the **A–B** category, but unless you particularly want to be in this area, it is far better
to carry on to the town centre where there are dozens of attractive guest houses in
converted fishermen's cottages. Try, for example, the area to the north of the harbour around Back Road East, where every other house seems to be a B&B. Also,
you may want to try:

St Ives International Backpackers Hostel Lower Stennack (**01736 799444**) **A**
Central location opposite the cinema and the Western Hotel. Converted from a
Wesleyan Chapel School, built in 1845, the building has a central courtyard, ideal
for barbecues. Linked to Newquay Backpackers hostel. Dormitory accomodation
for 60 in 6–8 bedrooms with some very good value double rooms available.
Friendly, with good facilities, including bike hire There is free transfer available
to/from the Newquay hostel.

Kynance 24 The Warren (**01736 796636**) **B** No smoking. Delightful, early C19
cottage, run by friendly couple. Conveniently located by the bus and railway stations, a short walk from the town centre. 6 bedrooms. They have some parking
spaces nearby which must be reserved in advance.

Sunrise The Warren (**01736 795407**) **B** next door to the Kynance and similar in
many respects. 7 bedrooms, including 2 singles.

Anchorage Bunkers Hill (**01736 797135**) **B** Early C18 cottage, 6 bedrooms.
Yards from the harbour. The ground floor room boasts a fireplace by Bernard
Leach. There are good views from the top floor attic room, but the stairs are
steep!

Poldhu 60 Fore Street (**01736 794226**) **A** up a narrow alley off the main shopping street. Rooms only. 4 bedrooms, 1 en suite. One of the cheapest in town.

Making Waves 3 Richmond Place (**01736 793895**) **B** Small, centrally-located
vegan guest house near Trewyn Gardens. 3 bedrooms. Evening meals with organic, vegan recipes. The house has been restored with the use of organic materials.

1 Sea View Terrace (**01736 798001**) **D**. Just two delightful en-suite rooms in this
upmarket guest house in a very central location. Breakfast is served in your room.

Trewinnard   4 Park Avenue (**01736 794168**) **B** One of a string of B&Bs with fine views over the town from its elevated position, but still a short, if strenuous, walk to the town centre and beaches. Comfortable and well furnished.

Western Hotel   Royal Square (**01736 795277**) **C** Imposing, granite coaching inn dating from the mid C19, recently refurbished and run by friendly, enthusiastic proprietors. The inn retains some of its historic character, the fireplace in the reception comes from Penlee House in Penzance. Covered car parking is available. 23 bedrooms, 19 en suite. Bedrooms are generally large with high ceilings. Breakfast, carvery at weekends. 3 bars.

Sloop Inn   The Wharf (**01736 796584**) **D** located directly on the harbour front in a medieval building, although the rooms retain little historic character following 'refurbishment' However, there are excellent harbour views from the front rooms.

Tregenna Castle Hotel (**01736 795254**) **E** probably St Ives' best hotel, located on the outskirts of town in extensive private grounds. The house, now much extended, was built in 1774 by the younger Wood of Bath in a castellated, symmetrical form. Little of the interior survives. Golf course, tennis, indoor and outdoor pools, squash, gym – all of the facilities that you would expect for the price. 80 bedrooms.

Garrack Hotel   Burthallan Lane (**01736 796199**) **E** located in a prominent position to the south of the town centre with panoramic sea views, this comfortable hotel has an indoor pool and 18 en-suite bedrooms. Highly recommended.

Restaurants and cafes

The prices quoted in the guide are inevitably just an indication of costs and represent the price for a meal of two courses with a drink. In the listings, they are indicated by the letter I, M or E, immediately after the telephone number of the establishment.

Inexpensive under £15
Moderate   £16 – £25
Expensive   over £25

St Ives has almost as many places to eat as it does places to stay, from upmarket restaurants to fish and chip take aways. The standard is generally good and many of them have wonderful sea views. Many of the hotels also have good restaurants, particularly the Garrack and Tregenna Castle, both expensive.

Blue Fish   Norway Lane (**01736 794204**) **M** beautifully converted from some old fish net lofts, there is a good selection of fish dishes. There is a large outside terrace with views over the harbour.

Mermaid   Fish Street (**01736 796816**) **M** bistro and seafood restaurant in pleasant old premises just back from the harbour in the Downalong area. Many of the dishes are based on Oriental flavours. Another excellent restaurant.

Saltwater Café   Fish Street (**01736 794928**) **M** tiny, welcoming restaurant with a smart "Mediterranean" look and a changing, daily menu of meat and fish dishes. The food is very good.

Russets   18A Fore Street (**01736 794700**) *M-E* open evenings only. Speciality fish restaurant in the centre of town.

Seafood Café   Fore Street (**01736 794004**) *M* smart restaurant with fresh fish and good value.

Isobar   Tregenna Place (**01736 796042**) *I-M* trendy cafe bar, with smart decor and good value wines and food. Snacks, seafood and char grilled meats. Excellent coffee. Five screens usually showing sport, but not too intrusive.

Rajpoot   6 Gabriel Street (01**736 795307**) *I* a good standard Indian restaurant with take-away service.

The Mex   3 Gabriel Street (**01736 797658**) *I* good value Mexican food, including chicken, seafood and vegetarian dishes. Also take-away service.

Porthgwidden Beach Restaurant (**01736 796791**) *M* superb location, right on the beach and with an outside terrace to make the most of good weather. Breakfast, lunch and dinner with a small menu focused on Mediterranean cooking, particularly pasta and seafood.

Porthmeor Beach Café (**01736 793366**) *I* opposite the Tate Gallery and right on Porthmeor Beach. There is a large open terrace for fine days and in inclement weather the glass conservatory-style cafe is as snug as it can get. The view is incomparable. Open for breakfast and lunch, excellent coffee, snacks and cakes. Barbecues on summer evenings.

Porthminster Beach Café (**01736 795352**) *M* another beach front restaurant with a reputation for good and inventive cooking. It is open from 10.00am every day and serves coffees, lunches, teas and dinner till 10.00pm. On Sunday evenings there is a barbecue which makes the most of the wonderful beachfront location. They also serve delicious home made ice cream and there are regular exhibitions of paintings by established artists.

Tate Gallery Café open during museum hours. On the top floor with excellent views over the town and Porthmeor beach. Excellent snacks, teas, coffees and home-made cake. There is also an outside terrace.

Balancing Eel   Harbour Front (**01736 796792**). Fish and chip take away, with restaurant area.

♈ Bars and Nightlife

St Ives has a good selection of pubs and bars, many of which are comfortably old fashioned. Most of them serve pub food and the standard is generally good. Unlike most of Cornwall, there is also something of a nightlife scene in St Ives.

Sloop Inn The Wharf, wonderful, old inn believed to date from C14. Located right on the harbour front with tables outside. A great place for watching the harbour activity. There is a particularly fine bar to the front. Real ales and serves good pub food lunchtimes and evenings.

Golden Lion High Street, big two bar pub in the centre of town. Pool table, TV with a small open yard to the rear. Real Ales and food.

Castle Inn Fore Street, atmospheric pub located on the main street, behind a stained glass front window. It used to be the regular meeting place for artists of the St Ives Colony. Real ales and good pub food, particularly fish.

Queens Taverne High Street, large, friendly locals pub with live music, live sport and pool table. Real ales and standard pub food.

Western Hotel High Street, big two bar hotel, which was originally one of St Ives last coaching inns. The Western is the centre of the St Ives music scene, with different music throughout the week. In winter, a snooker table is brought into one of the bars, which gives some indication of how large they are. Real ales.

Kettle'n Wink next door to the Western Hotel and under the same management. An old smugglers inn, the 'Wink' is reputed to be the nod of recognition that allowed contraband spirits to be served when the bar was empty of excise men. The St Ives Jazz Club meets here every Tuesday, with folk music on Thursdays.

The only clubs in St Ives are upstairs at The Isobar, licensed till 1.00am and the Flamingo, on the outskirts of the town. Every September, the St Ives Fringe Festival is an eclectic mix of music, art, poetry and comedy. The acts are generally a good standard with international, national and local artists performing. Well worth catching if you are visiting around this time of the year. The cinema is located in High Street, near the Western Hotel, and screens current releases.

Practicalities

The well-stocked and helpful Tourist Information Centre (**01736 796297**) is in the centre of town in the Guildhall in Street-an-Pol. The bus and railway stations are both near to each other on the southern edge of the town centre. Getting around St Ives is easy as everything of interest is within walking distance of the town centre. Getting to St Ives is equally easy. There are regular train services to Penzance, with a connection to the main Plymouth–London line at St Erth. There are frequent buses to Lands End, Penzance, Hayle, Camborne, Helston and Truro. By car, St Ives is just off the A30. There are a number of car parks with the largest on the southern outskirts of the town centre, from where it is a steep five minute walk or there are shuttle buses to ferry people into the town centre. Driving in the centre of town is not recommended in the peak summer months. Parking in the

Tourist Information Centre

town can be difficult at this time and you may want to consider using the Park and Ride facility at *Lelant Saltings* station where for £6.00 you can park the car and have return rail fare for up to five people. Alternatively, there is a public car park at St Erth railway station. The coast path passes right through the town, which is also connected to St Just by the Tinners Way and to Penzance by the St Michael's Way. Details of these are available from the Tourist Information Centre. The Penwith peninsula is so small that walking, and most certainly cycling, are perfectly feasible ways of getting around. Cycles can be hired from the *Backpackers Hostel*, opposite the cinema. A variety of boat trips and boat hire is available from the numerous booths around the harbour.

Towednack

Approximately two miles outside St Ives, just off the road to Zennor, in a peaceful, rural setting is the tiny village of Towednack. The *Church of St Tewennochus* is typically low with a squat tower and massive granite walls. The nave and chancel are C13, with a south aisle added in the C15. The low roof and compact interior evoke a vernacular space and give some indication as to the nature of early Cornish Christianity. The early existence of a church in this place is evidenced by the reuse of an incised stone in the porch in one of the side benches. The interior has an interesting carved granite font, with faces at the corners, dated 1720. The base is the inverted bowl of a Norman font. The church is approached up a lane between two stone piers, donated by Sir Edward Hain, Lord of the Manor, in 1914. The church is scenic enough to have featured in the films *Poldark* and *Penmarric*. It lies on the route of the Tinners Way, the overland footpath between St Ives and St Just.

Amalveor Farm, about one mile west of the church, is where a pair of gold bracelets, dated to the Middle Bronze Age (1000 BC) were found in 1931. They are now in the Penlee House Museum in Penzance.

Zennor

Located high above the coast, Zennor, is as picturesque as any of the villages that occupy the windswept Penwith penisula. It can be easily reached by car from St Ives along the scenic B3306 and there are regular buses in summer between St Ives and Lands End that stop here. However, by far the best way to visit is to follow the coast path from St Ives and then either continue on to Cape Cornwall or return to St Ives by the footpath that leaves by the church and crosses over the fields. Alternatively, the bus can be taken back to St Ives. The Coast Path route is 6 miles, but the going is quite hard due to the unevenness of the surface, boggy and stony in equal measures. Proper walking boots are required and at least 3-4 hours should be allowed. The scenery from the coast path is spectacular and well worth the effort.

The area around Zennor is famous for its landscape with hundreds of little fields with the stones cleared and formed into field boundaries – they date from the Bronze or Iron Ages and are still used today. Their survival is largely due to the designation of the Penwith Environmentally Sensitive Area (ESA). This is a voluntary scheme whereby farmers are paid a grant to farm in a traditional manner and, importantly, maintain the ancient field pattern. The Penwith ESA covers approximately 17,000 acres and agreements have been reached for about 95% of the land.

St Senner, the church, was given in 1150 to Tywardreath Priory, one of the chief monastic houses of Cornwall. The south side of the nave is partly Norman, with later additions. The north aisle is C15. The tower is bigger and more impressive than many Cornish churches, perhaps reflecting its early importance. The Mermaid of Zennor, a wood carving of indeterminate date, but possibly 5–600 years old, has been incorporated into a chancel seat within the church. This is the only carving of a mermaid found in a Cornish church and it is thought it may have some connection with St Senner arriving by sea in the C6. Outside the church by the porch, there is a memorial stone to John Davey of Boswednack, died 1891,one of the last practitioners of the Cornish language.

The **Wayside Folk Museum** (**01736 796945**) has a series of exhibitions of different aspects of Cornish life. Outside is one of the more interesting exhibits, the Zennor plague stone. A large granite stone with a bowl in the top, which was filled with vinegar and placed on the boundary of the village. The vinegar was to disinfect money coming into the village from outside. The last main cholera epidemics in Cornwall were in 1832 and 1849. The plague stone gives some indication of how remote Zennor must have been at that time.

Open April and October, daily 11am-5pm , May-Sept, 10.30am-5.30pm. Admission, £2.75, children £1.50

On the hill overlooking Zennor, there are a number of major megalithic chambers, including *Zennor Quoit* and *Sperris Quoit*. There are footpaths leading up to the hill from the village, but they are very overgrown with gorse and bracken. An easier alternative route is to take the track towards Foage Farm and turn up the National Trust path. The views from the top are spectacular.

Zennor's most famous literary association is with *D. H. Lawrence* who came to stay in Higher Tregerthen, just outside the village, with his German-born wife, Frieda, during the Great War. It was here that he wrote *Women in Love*. Harassment from the military authorities and suspicions of being spies signalling to German submarines eventually led them to leave the area. Lawrence wrote of his Cornish experiences in his book Kangaroo.

Zennor makes a good base for exploring the Penwith peninsula, particularly for walkers, and there is reasonably-priced accomodation at the **Old Chapel Backpackers Hostel** (**01736 798307**) **A**, a converted, granite chapel in the centre of the village, it provides dormitory accommodation (max. six per room) and one family room. Meals can be ordered and there is ample car parking. **The Tinners Arms**, an atmospheric one bar pub, next to the church also serves food at lunchtime and evenings. The wood panelled, low beamed bar with its granite fireplaces is as cosy as it gets and Lawrence must have spent many an evening here, under the watchful eyes of his suspicious neighbours. Indeed, it is claimed that he lodged here for some time until the house at Higher Tregerthen was ready for occupation.

Towards St Just and Cape Cornwall

The B3306 continues to *St Just*, with panoramic scenic views over the coastline. Again, the Coast Path is the favoured route with increasingly spectacular coastal views as you approach Cape Cornwall. The walk from Zennor, around Lands End, to Mousehole on the south coast is among the most dramatic and beautiful in Britain and it is well worth trying to do even a short section. There are a string of farmhouse B&B's along the main road, but for something a little different, why not try **Boswednack Manor** (01736 794183) **A**, a mile west of Zennor. Meals are available, vegetarian included, free walk sheets, guided wildlife walks, an organic garden, solar water heating and a meditation room for guests. The **Gurnard's Head Hotel** (01736 796928) **B** on the main B3306, has exceptional pub food, a good wine list and real ales. Accomodation is available. There is folk music in the bar on Wednesday and Friday evenings.

Morvah   The little hamlet of Morvah, has a fine, low church with a typically stumpy tower. The tower is C14 with the nave and chancel dating from 1828, but in the Cornish medieval style. There is a large Wesleyan chapel of 1866 on the main road. Of more interest is **Chun Castle**, one mile immediately south. This impressive double-walled stone built hillfort dates from the Iron Age (3-1 BC) but was reoccupied in the Roman and Post-Roman period. In the C18 the inner rampart was 15 foot high, but much of the stone was taken for building in Penzance in the C19. Nevertheless, the plan form and scale of the structure is still clearly visible with its two concentric walls of stone and single entrance to the south-west. *Chun Quoit*, 300m to the west is a Neolithic chamber tomb, a large, closed chamber of four uprights supporting a massive capstone. The landscape below shows evidence of prehistoric field patterns and there are views over the surrounding countryside. The comparative isolation of the site and the juxtaposition of farms, fort and tomb make this one of the more atmospheric places on the peninsula. The shortest approach is to take the road for Madron, just east of Morvah, and then follow the sign for Chun Castle on the right. Follow the narrow lane to the end, where vehicles can be left. The white stone in the field indicates the path to the fort. This route is heavily overgrown with gorse and bracken and suitable clothes are recommended. An easier, but longer, approach is from the B3318 to the west. A more direct footpath leads from the main road near Morvah for those without vehicles.

Further along the road to Madron, there is a small car park and easy footpath to the Bronze Age monument, the **Men An Tol**, a holed stone with two uprights on either side, much visited and photographed. The site was believed to have magical powers and parents used to pass their children through the stone nine times as a cure against rickets. Locals still know the site as the *Crick Stone*. A few hundred yards further down the road is **Lanyon Quoit**, a large capstone supported by three uprights. The original plan is uncertain, the stones having collapsed in 1815 and been re-erected by public subscription. It is immediately adjacent to the road, but can nevertheless be easily missed. Look out for the layby and National Trust sign on your left. The site is very popular and even seems to do service as a picnic spot.

It has none of the mystery of Chun Quoit.

As the B3306 continues towards St Just, the landscape shows increasing evidence of tin mining, for this area was until recently one of the key areas of production. Ruined engine houses, stacks and mine shafts cover the landscape, none more scenic, nor more photograped, than the two engine houses perched seemingly on the very edge of the ocean west of Botallack. Follow any of the footpaths down to the coast path for a view, walking the coast path you cannot miss them. Alternatively, take the narrow lane from Botallack and follow it to the end where there is a large car park. From here, it is a short walk to the Botallack mines. **The Queens Arms Inn** in Botallack serves food.

Botallack

West of Pendeen is the **Levant Steam Engine**, the oldest working beam engine in Cornwall and sited almost as dramatically as the Botallack mines (National Trust, **01736 786156**). Nearby is the **Geevor Tin Mine** (**01736 788662**) which closed in 1992 and is now the largest preserved mine in the UK. It is clearly signposted from the main road. (Tours are available, 9am–5pm (4pm in winter), closed Saturday. Admission, £6.50, children £4.00, family £17.50.) The tour includes one of the underground mines and sturdy footwear is recommended. There is also a museum, cafe and shop.

Open Jul–Sept daily (except Sat) 11am–5pm, June (closed Sat, Mon & Tues). Restricted opening outside these times. Admission, £5.00, children £2.50, family £12.50

Pendeen Lighthouuse, set on one of Conwalls most dramatic cliffs is also open for visitors, July and August, every day and Easter and Bank Holiday weeks. *Portheras Cove*, just to the east of the Pendeen lighthouse is one of the more sheltered coves along this stretch of the coast and boasts a small sandy beach. However, swimming can be dangerous depending on conditions and the sand can conceal sharp metal fragments from the coaster Alacrity, wrecked in 1963 and later blown up. If you want to stay in this area, one of the nicest places is **Field House** (**01736 788097**) *B* in Trewellard with just three rooms. It is a lovely house with marvellous views out to sea. There is also an excellent cafe with tables in the garden. If this is full, the **Trewellard Arms Hotel** (**01736 788634**) *B*, opposite has en-suite accommodation and serves real ale and meals.

St Just in Penwith

St Just announces its presence from a distance with its church tower visible from afar, unusually tall for a Penwith church and surely built as a beacon for shipping as much as for any other purpose. St Just and the other villages hereabouts were built for the mines and the collapse of tin mining has left the area depressed with some of the highest unemployment rates in England. The villages have little to attract the tourist other than St Just, which has a number of useful facilities, shops, pubs and accommodation as well as some good art galleries. It would make a good base for touring the area were it not for its somewhat grim atmosphere. However, there are some sites of interest for the visitor.

The *Church of St Just* is large and made of regular granite blocks. The porch is particularly flamboyant with buttresses, battlements and pinnacles and a sundial over the doorway. A fine wrought iron gate to the churchyard stands opposite. Inside, the shafts are of limestone from Beer in Devon, rather than the more usual granite, and are decorated with horizontal fruit and leaves. The carving is much finer and delicate than would have been possible with granite. A C5–6 inscribed stone is placed in the north aisle and attests to the early foundation of the site as a place of worship. The shaft of an unfinished cross of the C9–10 has been reused as a lintel over a recess in the north aisle. Restoration in 1866 revealed six C15 wall paintings. However, only two survive – those of Christ of the Trades and George and the Dragon – both have suffered from over-restoration. The large ensign (ship's flag) in the north west corner was flown from *HMS Revenge* at the Battle of Jutland in World War I and is testimony to the area's enduring links with the sea.

Across the square from the church is *St Just Plain an Gwarry* – an arena for performing medieval Cornish miracle plays. A large Methodist chapel is located just to the north-west on a direct alignment to Bank Square.

In recent years, a number of artists and craftsmen have set up workshops in the area, attracted as much by the low rents as the remoteness and the quality of the light. Many of them have their own galleries and there are also a number of independent galleries. Of particular interest are:

The Great Atlantic Mapworks Gallery West Place (**01736 788911**) a large spacious gallery specialising in the contemporary work of West Cornwall artists, featuring paintings, ceramics, sculpture, prints and photography. The standard is excellent and there are normally paintings on display by the hugely accomplished, Kurt Jackson, who lives locally. Open, March to November (closed Mondays and Sundays). In winter, it is only open on Sunday afternoons.

Tregeseal Gallery (**01736 787354**) on the outskirts of St Just on the road to St Ives. The building was formerly an old toll house and offers a selection of paintings of Cornwall and France by local artist Bob Vigg. Closed Sunday.

Navigator Contemporary Arts 41 Fore Street (**01736 787052**) near the Star Inn. Exhibits a wide range of work including painting, sculpture, jewellery and photography. Closed Monday and Sunday.

Nancherrow Studio Gallery 34 Nancherrow Terrace (**01736 788552**) a spacious gallery over two floors showing paintings, sculpture and ceramics by local artists. Open from April to October.

There are several pubs and cafes around the main square, the **Star Inn**, perhaps, being the best. The **Commercial Hotel** (**01736 788455**) *B* and the **Wellington Hotel** (**01736 787319**) *B* provide accommodation if needed. St Just is easily reached from St Ives and Penzance by car and bus. There is also an inland footpath route between St Ives and St Just known as The Tinners Way which links many of the ancient monuments that cover the landscape of Penwith. However, waymarking is poor and the path is badly overgrown in places. The much easier to follow, though longer, coast path is just a short detour as is Cape Cornwall, a mile to the west.

The Tinners Way

Eden Project near St Austell

Jubilee Bathing Pool, Penzance

Botallack mines Penwith

Cape Cornwall

Until relatively recently, Cape Cornwall was thought to have been the most wester-ly point on the English mainland and sitting on the Cape looking south towards Lands End it is easy to see how it may have been so mistaken. The cliffs here are gentler than at Lands End but the view is still stupendous with the full majesty of the Atlantic Ocean before you. Offshore is the looming presence of *The Bisons*, two exposed granite outcrops that have claimed many ships trying to round the Cape. The Cape has a real sense of isolation, of being at the end of something defi-nite and the beginning of something unknown. To come here when a storm is roaring in off the Atlantic is an unforgettable experience. The absence of crowds and commercialisation make this a much more pleasant experience than Lands End. The chimney on the head is a navigation mark and was originally for the tin mine on the south side of the Cape, of which only the count-house remains. There is bed and breakfast accommodation on the Cape itself, though preferable is **Boswedden House** (**01736 788733**) *B*, a large Victorian house on the road to St Just with an indoor heated pool and 8 bedrooms.

The **Lands End Youth Hostel** (**0870 770 5906**) *A* is about one mile down the coast from Cape Cornwall and is located in the beautiful and lush Cot Valley. It makes an excellent base for touring this area or for an overnight stay while walking the coast path. There is dormitory accommodation only and breakfast and evening meals are available on request.

The Cot Valley runs back from the coast in a deep enclave, sheltered from the prevailing winds and warmed by the mild Cornish climate. As a result, the valley is blessed with a micro-climate that allows a rich and luxurious fauna to flourish in direct contrast to the wind-swept, gorse and heather covered cliffs of the coast. The walk from St Just down the Cot Valley to the coast is highly recommended At the end of the valley is *Porth Nanven* beach, a small rocky cove, not suitable for bathing but an excellent spot for a picnic. The beach is a Site of Special Scientific Interest (SSSI) due to the geological evidence at hand in the crumbling cliffs. The granite cliff is exposed at low level, with the boulder-strewn beach of 120,000 years ago, clearly visible in the cliff face. Indeed, erosion of the cliff face is continually dropping boul-ders onto the beach below. They are protected by the SSSI and their removal would constitute a criminal offence. Above the boulder beach, the cliff face displays the smaller ice-fractured stones and rocks of the ice age, approximately 100,000 years ago. There is a small car park at the beach, but the road from St Just is very narrow in places. Walking or cycling is the favoured option if you have the time.

Cot Valley

The B3306 continues southwards towards Lands End, past the **Lands End Aerodrome** (**01736 788771**) where scenic flights and trips to the Isles of Scilly can be booked. Just south of here and just to the east of the road is *Carn Brea*, the most westerly hill in England and with panoramic views across the peninsula taking in the Isles of Scilly, 30 miles to the south-west, both Lands End and The Bisons off Cape Cornwall and the Lizard to the east. Its long been an important landmark, as evidenced by the Bronze Age summit cairn, still clearly recognizable. In the medieval period, the hill was the site of a hermitage and chapel and, during World War II, a military observation post and radar station were positioned here.

The beacon on the summit was built by the fisherman of St Just as a landmark and at midsummer a fire is lit to commemorate the summer solstice. There is a small car park on the minor road to the east (free) which is the first turning on the left after the aerodrome. If you are coming from the Penzance direction along the A30, look for the ancient stone cross and the decorative painted signpost at Crows-an-wra and turn right at the junction. It is an easy five minute walk to the top of the hill from the car park.

Sennen Cove

Sennen Cove sits at the base of high cliffs that back the huge Whitesand Bay, facing due west into the ocean. It is a tiny village, little more than one street facing the sea with the cliffs immediately behind. The main attraction here is the beach with one of the best stretches of sand on the peninsula and the setting is superb. The main beach to the south is sandy with good surfing conditions and safe bathing within the flagged areas. A lifeguard is in attendance during the summer months. The northern beach, Gwenver, provides some of the most spectacular surfing conditions in the country, but is best left to experienced surfers. Bathers need to take care and be aware of local conditions.

The RNLI lifeboat station is at the southern end of the village near the stone quay. The station is open to visitors at certain times and the lifeboat can be viewed. There are occasional launches for practice and testing purposes and these are normally posted on the outside. The station has a particularly steep slipway and the launches are quite dramatic.

Just beyond the lifeboat station is the *Round House and Capstan Gallery* (**01736 871859**). The building dates back to 1876, upstairs is the old net loft with its intricate roof while downstairs is the giant capstan used for hauling boats up from the beach. Since 1983, the building has been in use as a gallery with fine ceramics, glass, jewellery and paintings, all by local artists. The quality and range is generally excellent. Open daily between Easter and November. Just by the gallery are a pair of attractive cottages, one whitewashed with a thatched roof and the other dark, grey granite with a slate roof – the picturesque and the practical side by side.

Sennen Cove makes a good base for exploring the far west of the peninsula. There are some attractive places to stay right in the village and only minutes from the beach. **Myrtle Cottage** (**01736 871698**) *B* is located at the southern end of the village above the cafe of the same name and is a small friendly B&B with sea views. The **Old Success Inn** (**01736 871232**) *D* is a large building, superbly located at the beach end of the village. They have 12 en-suite bedrooms and also two apartments to rent. Just outside the village, on the top of the cliff above Whitesand Bay is **Whitesands Lodge** (**01736 871776**) *A–B*, an attractive and comfortable backpackers lodge with dormitory accommodation as well as individual rooms. Meals are available, along with a lounge, pool table, surf instruction and board hire.

Of the places to eat, the **Old Success Inn** serves good pub food, including excellent fresh fish, as well as a selection of real ales. **The Blue Lagoon** on the sea front is a fish and chip shop, also serving other fast food. **Breakers Cafe and Bistro**, also on the sea front, serves food all day, including seafood and pasta. They also have tables outside on the promenade. All the above are inexpensive. The **Whitesands Lodge** is also developing a reputation for good food that belies its backpacker status.

Sennen Cove is located three miles south of Cape Cornwall and just one mile north of Lands End. There are regular buses to St Ives and Penzance. The coast path passes right through the village which makes it an excellent place for walkers to overnight. There are two car parks, one at each end of the village. The southern car park makes a good starting point for a visit to Lands End. Parking is cheaper and it is a relatively easy half hour walk to Lands End itself. The approach by foot allows for a more gradual appreciation of the majesty of the place and helps to minimize the damage done by the Lands End theme park. Just outside Sennen Cove on the way to Lands End is *Maen Castle*, one of the earliest cliff castles in Cornwall (c500BC). The castle cuts off a small promontory with a ditch protecting an inner stone built rampart.

Driving to Lands End the road passes through the small village of Sennen on top of the cliffs. There is little interest other than the *Church of St Sennen*, the westernmost church of England. It is set in an exposed position with its west tower facing the New World. Again, undoubtedly, built as a landmark for mariners as much as for any other reason. Sennen has some accommodation for those wanting to visit Lands End but it is far better to stay in Sennen Cove. Car parking in the village is cheaper than Lands End.

Sennen

Lands End

Lands End, the most westerly point of England, will always attract visitors who wish to stand on this defining point of the nation's geography. It is also the starting, or finishing, point for all the various Lands End to John'o Groats challenges. It is true that the cliff scenery is spectacular, but no more so than many other parts of the Cornish coast, and there is still that feeling of being at the transition of two great elements, the land and the ocean, but again, no more so than Cape Cornwall, for instance. However, if you have got this far, you are undoubtedly going to want to visit Lands End – it is a 'must do' in travellers terms. To derive any enjoyment from the visit, you need to bear in mind that Lands End is not the wild, remote Cape that you may imagine. The landward side is dominated by the Lands End theme park with a number of 'attractions', children's playgrounds, piped music and so on. On Tuesday and Thursday evenings in August, there is a popular firework display. Car parking is an expensive £3.00, but the site is a public right of way and there is nothing to stop you just walking through the complex and out on to the cliffs beyond. However, your experience of this 'wild and remote spot' will undoubtedly have been tarnished. Far better is to approach the site on foot from either *Sennen Cove* to the north, an easy half hour walk (see above) or from *Porthgwarra* or *Porthcurno* to the south where there are car parks (see below). This is a longer walk but the scenery is more spectacular than that from Sennen Cove.

If you want to stay at Lands End itself, the only place is the expensive **Lands End Hotel** (**01736 871844**) *E*, which is sited right on the cliff top, with many of the rooms having spectacular sea views. There is also a restaurant and bar, open to non-residents.

Porthcurno

Located in a wide valley leading down to a superb white, sand beach, Porthcurno is one of the best places on the south Penwith Peninsula, with several interesting sights, including the world-renowned *Minack Theatre*, a series of magnificent sandy coves and excellent walking.

The beach is undoubtedly the main attraction for most visitors and the sandy cove ringed by steep cliffs is as attractive as any in Cornwall. Bathing is safe, except on some occasions at high tide when the steep shelving beach can cause problems. A lifeguard is in attendance during the summer months and there is a beach cafe and other facilities. The beach car park, which also serves the Porthcurno Museum of Submarine Telegraphy, is located a short walk away. There is free car parking by the Minack Theatre at the top of the hill.

Surprisingly for such an apparently sleepy place, Porthcurno has its own place in history. The site was chosen in 1870 by the Eastern Telegraph Company for the landing point of its first submarine telegraph linking Cornwall to Bombay. Soon, Porthcurno was one of the world's largest telegraph stations with 14 undersea cables fanning out from the beach to all parts of the British Empire and beyond. The Eastern Telegraph Company duly became Cable and Wireless and in the 1950s the Company's Engineering College was based in the valley. When the College moved to Coventry in 1993, Porthcurno was left with many vacant buildings and little prospect of replacement uses. A redevelopment plan was drawn up by the internationally recognized architectural practice of McCormac Jamieson Prichard of which the main proposal was the creation of a museum to record the history of the site and of submarine telegraphy. Five years later in July 1998, the museum opened after £1 million of grants had been made available.

Open Apr–Oct
every day
10am–5pm.
Nov–Mar,
Sun and Mon
10am–5pm.
Entry £4.50,
£4.00 conc,
£3.00 stu-
dents, chil-
dren £2.50.
Family ticket
£11.00

Porthcurno Museum of Submarine Telegraphy (**01736 810966**). The museum entrance is in the Eastern Telegraph Company's offices, while the museum itself is located in the secret, underground tunnels that were built in 1941 to protect the telegraph centre from enemy attack. Telegraphy had certain advantages, even in the Second World War, as it was a more secure method of communication than radio which could easily be intercepted by the enemy. The exhibition is excellent, with a comprehensive display on the history of submarine telegraphy, many artefacts and working exhibits and the preserved telegraph rooms from the last war. There is also an explanation of how in 1902 the Eastern Telegraph Company installed a monitoring wireless station on the clifftop to spy on Marconi's experiments at Poldhu on the Lizard (Marconi having sent the first transatlantic radio message in 1901). The threat from radio must have been alarming to the telegraph companys and within a short time the Eastern Telegraph Company had merged with Marconi to form Cable and Wireless, the hugely successful company that still exists today.

The **Minack Theatre (01736 810181)** located on the cliffs to the west of the beach is world-renowned. It was created in the 1930s, inspired by Greek and Roman cliff theatres. Matinees and evening performances are put on throughout the summer (May–September). The quality of productions vary depending on the theatre company, as the Minack is only a venue and does not have its own resident company. One to keep an eye out for is the Kneehigh Theatre Company, which is Cornish-based and good enough to have appeared at the Royal National Theatre in London. On stormy days the sound of the sea and wind can all but drown out the performance. However, on a warm summer's night, the atmosphere can be magical – don't miss it if you get the chance. Ticket prices are £7.00 and £5.50 (children half price) and seats are unreserved.

Open through the year if you just want to tour the site. Apr–Sept 9.30am–5.30pm, Oct–Mar 10am–4pm). Admission £3.00, OAP £2.20, children 12-18 £1.20, under 12 free

Porthcurno is located just off the B3315 Lands End to Penzance road, approximately 2 miles from Lands End. There are regular bus connections to Penzance and St Ives. The coast path passes right through the village. Surprisingly, accommodation in Porthcurno is somewhat limited with the only options in the valley being the **Porthcurno Hotel (01736 810119)** *B* or **Sea View House (01736 810638)** *B*. The **Cable Station Inn**, opposite the museum, serves food and is a pleasant place for a drink. There are regular buses to Penzance and Lands End.

Porthchapel, Porthgwarra and the Walk to Lands End

Much better than staying in Porthcurno, is to continue along the cliff top for half a mile to St Levan, where the old vicarage has been converted into a magnificently-located guest house, **Grey Gables (01736 810421)** *B*. Open mid-March to mid-October, there are six bedrooms, some with sea views. Evening meals are available on request. The house is located in its own extensive grounds and there is a footpath leading down to Porthchapel beach, a beautiful, small cove of white sand. The path is quite steep in places but well worth the effort. There are no facilities on the beach and care needs to be taken when bathing due to the steeply shelving beach. Due to its relative isolation, the beach is often less crowded than Porthcurno. A small car park is located next to the *Church of St Levan* on top of the cliff. In contrast to Sennen, the church here is located in a sheltered position, nestling against the hillside and with the eastern side half buried in it. The church is all but invisible until you are almost upon it. The setting is everything here with the church and its churchyard sitting high above the sea and yet sheltered in its own tiny valley. It contains the graves of a number of victims of the Khyber, wrecked off Porth Loe in 1904.

St Levan

Porthchapel

A short walk west is Porthgwarra, a tiny village with two equally tiny coves connected by a tunnel through the rocks. One, boulder strewn and rocky, the other sandy. There is a car park, a shop selling teas and ice creams and toilet facilities.

Porthgwarra

There is no overnight accommodation in the village. Porthgwarra is accessed down a narrow lane off the B3315 Penzance to Lands End road. There is no bus service to the village, but you could ask to be dropped off on the main road, from where it is about an hour's walk. The coast path passes through the village.

Porthgwarra and Porthcurno both make excellent places from which to walk to Lands End along the Coast Path. There is car parking in both villages and the walk takes approximately 2–3 hours from Porthcurno from where there is the option of returning by bus. From Porthgwarra, the walk is two hours, but there is no bus service. The coast path is easy going and the cliff scenery spectacular. Just outside Porthgwarra, is *Gwennap Head* with panoramic views – the two daymarks are to help seamen locate the position of the Runnel Stone just offshore and the site of many shipwrecks. This is a good area for bird watching, particularly in spring and autumn when a south-westerly gale can bring the twitchers out in numbers. The walk continues along the clifftop till the broad sweep of *Nanzijal* or *Mill Bay* appears. Lands End, itself, is still hidden by the lie of the land, but the Longships lighthouse is now visible. The cliffs from here to Lands End are high, sheer and dramatic. There is a particularly fine view from *Pordennack Point* looking back towards Nanzijal.

As you approach Lands End itself, the hotel and theme park on the headland detract from the otherwise magnificent setting. However, continue around in front of the hotel and down to the cliff top where you can still look out to sea, over the outcrops of rock scattered across the ocean, towards the Longships lighthouse, with the Wolf Rock lighthouse further out to the south west. This is one of the most exposed lighthouses on the coast and waves frequently break over the top of the 35m tower in stormy weather. This, apparently, drove one of the early keepers mad with fear and the rule was set that there should always be at least two keepers on the lighthouse at any one time. The lighthouse is now automated. On a stormy day, the power of the sea is palpable with huge waves crashing into the foot of the cliffs and spray flying hundreds of feet into the air. Salt spray can be taken miles inland on the gale force winds. Even on a calm day in summer the underlying swell may be a metre high and can bring in powerful freak waves. The sunsets here can be particularly beautiful. Charles Dickens described a Lands End sunset in *A Christmas Carol*: "down in the west the setting sun had left a streak of fiery red, which glared on the desolation for an instant, like a sullen eye, and frowning lower, lower, lower yet, was lost in the thick gloom of darkest night."

St Buryan

Located some three miles inland from Porthcurno, St Buryan, is something of a local centre for the south Penwith peninsula. It has a store and general post office and a friendly, if basic, inn that serves food lunchtimes and evenings. It sits astride the B3283 Penzance to Lands End road, along which there is a regular bus service.

The only site of interest is the *Church of St Buryan*, a large church with an unusually big tower, some 92 feet high. The church is English Gothic, later than many of the chuches on the peninsula, the C13 church having been pulled down, apart from the tower, and rebuilt in the late C15/early C16. The circular church-yard has been found by excavation to be within an Iron Age/Romano-British earth-work. Tradition has it that the church was founded by King Athelstan in the C10 as a collegiate church which explains the scale and lavishness of the plan. However, there is evidence also of a C6 oratory on the site and the stone cross just outside the church dates from this period and would have marked the spot as consecrated ground. The glory of the church is its rood screen which runs right across the nave and aisles, with each of the three sections having a central opening. The workmanship is particularly fine and probably came from a Devonshire workshop. Originally constructed during the C16, it was torn down during the C19 renova-tions but restored at the beginning of the C20. Traces of the original overpainting can be seen in places.

The South Coast, Porthcurno to Mousehole

As you move eastwards from Porthcurno, there is a gradual transition away from the storm battered cliffs of the west coast to the more sheltered, south facing bays of this part of the peninsula. Just beyond Porthcurno, on the prominent headland is the famous *Logan Rock*, a large block of granite that could be rocked by push-ing it gently. In 1824 a Lieutenant Goldsmith dislodged it. Such was the outcry from locals that the Admiralty ordered Goldsmith to replace the rock in its original position at his own expense. The rock was duly replaced at great expense which led to the bankruptcy of Goldsmith. However, the rock now only moves with great difficulty.

Penberth

The coast path continues east to Penberth, an impossibly scenic fishing cove with boats often drawn up on the stone slipway. There is a scattering of cottages and some very discretely located toilets, but no other facilities or accommodation. Parking is strictly limited and is located on the roadside outside the village itself.

St Loy's Cove

As the valleys become more sheltered from the prevailing westerly winds, they become more lush and sub-tropical, none more so than St Loy's Cove. The beach here is boulder-strewn and covered at high tide, but the setting is fabulous. There are only a few properties in St Loy and no facilities. The coast path passes right along the back of the beach – it is a half hours walk from either Penberth or Lamorna and both walks have exceptional coastal views. Halfway to Lamorna, is the *Tater-du lighthouse*, erected in 1965 after a spate of shipwrecks on this part of the coast.

Lamorna, its cove and the valley leading back from it, has an inescapably romantic quality. The harbour, itself, with its granite pier was built for the export of stone from the local quarries which was used to build many of the lighthouses hereabouts. The valley that leads back from the harbour is deep and lush, heavily-wooded and with a profusion of wild flowers in the Spring. The artist Laura Knight described her first visit, "we had suddenly entered Paradise; a densely wooded valley filled with lichen-covered trees of a greenish grey; whose branches threw a bluish tracery of shadow over the rich tufts of grass already speckled with the yellow of early primrose and white anemone. Violet-tinted grey granite boulders bordered a stream that found its way to Lamorna Cove."

Lamorna   Lamorna is, perhaps, best known for the group of artists who came to stay here in the early years of the C20. They revelled in the lush landscape and painted the natural beauty of the area, often in the open air and often in the most appalling weather. They were influenced by Impressionism, but not to the extent that it submerged their own individual expression of the Cornish life and scenery around them. *Lamorna Birch* (1869–1955), born *Samuel John Birch*, came to live in the valley in 1902. He was a romantic naturalist who worked all times of the year in the open air. His best known subjects were the Lamorna valley and its cove, hence the name 'Lamorna'. Until 1902, he lived at St Buryan, where he met and married a local girl, whereupon they moved to Flagstaff Cottage, formerly the Harbour Master's house at the seaward end of Lamorna Valley. *Laura* and *Harold Knight* came to Newlyn in 1908 and lived there until 1912 when they moved to Oakhill, a house in Lamorna. One of her more famous pictures is Lamorna Birch and his Daughters, now in the collection of Nottingham University. Her work was inspired by the Cornish landscape and coastline and in the years leading up to the First World War she portrayed Cornwall's beaches as an idyllic pleasure ground. In 1910, they were joined by the larger than life figure of *Alfred Munnings* (1878– 1959), who formed a close relationship with Laura Knight and resided for some time at the Lamorna Inn, now the Lamorna Wink. Munnings made a studio in the stables of the inn, where he also kept his horses which served as models for his paintings. Munnings left the valley in 1917 to go to war, never to return to this idyllic place. However, he prospered as a painter, culminating in his election to the Presidency of the Royal Academy in 1944, beating Augustus John into second place by 24 votes to 17. Munnings died in 1959 and, showing no bitterness, John described him as "greater than Stubbs. He made it move, had greater narrative quality and his groupings are better."

Other artists who came to live in the valley were *Dod* and *Ernest Proctor*, *Charles* and *Ella Naper, Robert* and *Eleanor Hughes* and others who gave the Lamorna colony its own particular character. The life of these young artists in the years leading up to the First World War had an idyllic quality that is expressed in the works they produced. They lived the simple life, valuing each others company and revelling in the Cornish landscape. The First World War, however, saw the disintegration of the community as they were either taken away to war or restricted from painting due to war time shortages. Any painting out of doors near the coast was banned in the paranoia about German spies – the same paranoia that drove Lawrence away from Zennor. The community never survived the War.

Accommodation in Lamorna is limited with the **Lamorna Cove Hotel (01736 731411)** *C*, once the home of Alfred Munnings, being the only place available, other than a number of holiday lets. The **Lamorna Wink** public house serves food and has a pleasant atmosphere, while there is a cafe down by the harbour. There is a small car park at the seaward end of the valley. Lamorna is located just off the B3315 Penzance to Newlyn road. The coast path passes alongside the harbour,

Mousehole is an easy hour's walk. In public transport terms, Lamorna is almost as isolated as it was at the turn of the century – there are four buses per day to Penzance, Mondays to Saturdays.

Just to the west of Lamorna and accessible by footpath from the valley are the *Merry Maidens*, a perfect circle of regularly placed stones. The legend is that they are the fossilized remains of young girls who were caught dancing on the Sabbath. The *Pipers* nearby are the tallest standing stones in Cornwall and are reputedly the two pipers who lured the maidens to dance. Both are located just off the B3315, look out for the small layby car park.

As you progress east along the coast path, the great expanse of Mount's Bay opens up with views across to the Lizard and St Michael's Mount. The tiny fields around here were used for early crops, particularly daffodils. Point Spaniard, just before Mousehole is reputed to be where the Spaniards landed in 1595 before destroying Mousehole, Paul, Newlyn and Penzance.

Mousehole

Mousehole, pronounced Mowzul, if you do not want to upset the locals, is the archetypal Cornish fishing village with its tiny harbour surrounded by the encircling arms of its granite piers. There is a small, sandy beach within the harbour walls at low tide. The village is a cluster of small cottages stepping up the hills behind the harbour and set around an intricate network of tiny lanes and alleyways. There are some excellent pubs and restaurants, some good art galleries and a variety of tea shops to entertain the visitor. *Dylan Thomas* stayed here with his wife-to-be, Caitlan, in 1937. They were married on 11 July in Penzance and spent their honeymoon at the Lobster Pot on the harbour, now, unfortunately, closed. Wyn Henderson, the landlady, was a friend of Thomas' and lent the penniless poet the money for his marriage licence. The poet, aged 22, wrote of being "with no money, no prospect of money, no attendant friends or relatives and in complete happiness." If *Under Milk Wood* had not been based on Laugharne in South Wales, it could just as easily have been Mousehole. Every Christmas, people crowd the harbour to see the famous display of lights.

Mousehole was sacked by the Spanish in 1595, the only building that is said to have survived the attack is Little Keigwin, just to the west of the harbour. There is a plaque on the wall commemorating the fact. There are a number of shops and craft studios. Of particular note are *The Millpool Gallery* (**01736 731115**), open March–November, with a good collection of paintings, ceramics and glass and the *Essex Tyler Gallery* (**01736 731109**), run by an ex-Cornish surfing champion and displaying work by Cornish-based artists as well as his own raku ceramics. However, the most significant local artist was *Jack Pender*, born in Mousehole and resident from the late 1950s. The activity of the fishing village and its tiny enclosed harbour was the main subject of his paintings which are noted for their bold use of colour within black outlines.

There are several attractive places to stay including a number of small B&Bs in the narrow streets behind the harbour. The **Old Coastguard Hotel** (**01736**

731222) **D** is on the edge of the village on the road to Newlyn and has excellent sea views and nice gardens. The **Ship Inn** (**01736 731234**) **B** is a hugely atmospheric inn with impressive timber framing and is located right on the harbour. There is a plaque on the wall in memory of Charles Greenhaugh, landlord, lost on the Solomon Browne in 1981 (see below). **Tremayne** (**01736 731214**) **B** is a cafe/restaurant with en-suite rooms and car parking, something of a rarity in Mousehole. It is located just back from the harbour on the road to Penzance. **Sunrise** (**01736 731457**) **A** in Commercial Road is a cosy, little B&B in an old fisherman's cottage and good value. It is set just back from the harbour, past the clock tower.

Good places to eat include the **Old Coastguard Hotel** (**01736 731222**) **E** with an AA red rosette seafood restaurant. The **Cornish Range** (**01736 731488**) **E** in Chapel Street also specializes in fish and is highly rated. There are also three very smart en-suite rooms, which are good value. There is a fish and chip takeaway, **Lewis**', near the clock tower, open at lunchtimes and evenings. Also, the **Ship Inn** serves inexpensive pub food, lunchtimes and evenings.

On the road to Newlyn, there is a plaque on the front wall of a house commemorating the fact that the first Cornishman to be awarded the Victoria Cross was born there on December 1835. He was awarded England's most important medal for valour while serving in the Crimea War in 1855. Continuing on the

Penlee Point   coast road to Newlyn for a few hundred metres brings you to Penlee Point where there are expansive views over Mounts Bay and towards Penzance and St Michael's Mount. The lifeboat station, here, and the small memorial garden next door pay tribute to one of the saddest losses in the history of the Royal National Lifeboat Institute (RNLI). On 19 December 1981, the Penlee lifeboat, the *Solomon Browne* was launched in atrocious conditions to help the stricken coaster *Union Star* off Lamorna. Conditions were so bad that the rescue helicopter was unable to assist, the winds of such force that the helicopter was driven inland. However, the pilot was able to witness the extraordinary bravery of the volunteer crew of the Solomon Browne as they tried again and again to pull alongside the coaster in the mountainous seas. Almost unbelievably, four people were seen to jump from the deck of the *Union Star* onto the lifeboat, before the helicopter was finally driven inland. Nobody knows what happened next, but neither ship was seen again and the crew and passengers of the *Union Star* and *Solomon Browne* were all lost to the sea. The memorial garden is a peaceful place to contemplate the force of nature and the capacity of man for bravery and self-sacrifice. There is an extraordinary painting by Geoffrey Hubbard, a local artist, of the Lifeboat Evening Service on 16 August 1981 to celebrate 21 years on station of the *Solomon Browne*. The painting shows the St Ives Junior Silver Band, the Mousehole Male Choir and a number of onlookers, undoubtedly including the lifeboat crewmen. The *Solomom Browne* is moored directly behind. Within four months, the boat and crew were lost. The painting is in private ownership, but postcards of the picture are available in the village. The new, larger lifeboat is now stationed in Newlyn harbour.

Paul   Up a steep hill, about half a mile from the harbour in Mousehole is Paul where the *Church of St Paulinus*, the parish church of Mousehole, is the main attraction.

It is a big church, wide and long, but low, like most of the Cornish churches. Unusually, the interior is whitewashed. The church has undergone much restoration, not least after it was sacked by the Spaniards in 1595. The piers to the rear of the stone pulpit still bear scorch marks from when the Spaniards set fire to the church. The new windows on the north side are the result of bomb damage in the Second World War. In the north-east corner is a memorial to the crew of the *Solomon Browne*. In the churchyard wall, near the south-east gate is a monument to Dolly Pentreath, died 1777, and supposedly the last Cornish speaker. The memorial was erected in 1860 by Prince Louis Lucien Bonaparte, a nephew of Napoleon, who was born and brought up in England and studied old languages. However, a rival claim is lodged outside Zennor church and the truth may never be known. Just by the church are the *Hutchens Almshouses*, dating from 1709, heavily restored and extended. **The Kings Arms (01736 731224)** *B* opposite the church is a pretty, ivy clad, granite inn which serves food lunchtimes and evenings. Accommodation is also available.

Sancreed

Three miles to the west of Newlyn lies Sancreed, a small hamlet of granite buildings and one exceptional church, *St Sancredus*. The circular shape of the churchyard indicates a much earlier foundation for worship than the existing church, which is largely C13-15. The church is typical Cornish – granite, low, squat tower and set in a beautiful churchyard, contained by huge granite block walls to the roadside. Inside the church (often locked) is a memorial to Alec Forbes killed in the First World War, only son of Stanhope and Elizabeth Forbes, key figures in the Newlyn colony of artists, who are also buried in the churchyard. The churchyard also contains two of the most important Celtic crosses in Cornwall. The first is C10 and has the name RUHOL carved on the front with superb interlace work. The second was originally an inscribed stone, turned upside down in the C13 and recarved with a unique design of a lily in a vase. Both have the same unusual shape of heads, with a figure of the crucifixion on one side. *Sancreed Beacon* lies just to the west and offers panoramic views over Mounts Bay and the Penwith peninsula.

A mile to the west of Sancreed lies Carn Euny, a village of the Iron Age and Romano-British period established before 400BC and occupied into the C4. The site was unknown until the C19 when it was discovered by miners prospecting for tin. The layout of the houses is more haphazard than at Chysauster, a similar site north of Penzance, and has suffered from much rebuilding and stone robbing. However, it is still possible to ascertain the layout of the village and the plan form of the individual houses. The compartmented house-form that is so clearly evident, the same as at Chysauster, is peculiar to West Cornwall, but not unlike others in Wales and the highland zones of Britain. These 'courtyard house' villages are confined, in Cornwall, to the Penwith peninsula and are generally found between 350 and 600 feet above sea level. Perhaps the most significant structure at Carn Euny is the magnificently preserved fogou. A fogou is an underground or

Carn Euny

partly underground structure of unknown purpose, possibly a hiding place in times of trouble, a storage area for goods and livestock or perhaps for religious purposes. The one at Carn Euny is particularly impressive, with a long underground passage leading to a round chamber, that may well have been linked to an earlier cult before the passage was ever built. The massive stone construction is particularly well-preserved here. Carn Euny is owned and managed by English Heritage, entrance free. There are footpaths to the site from Sancreed or, alternatively, take the lane to Brane, just east of Sancreed, from where there is a much shorter walk.

Newlyn

Newlyn's pride is its harbour – the reason for its existence and continuing success. It dates from 1885 when the current piers were built. Since then, Newlyn has become one of the most important fishing ports in the country and an early morning visit is still an interestingly fishy experience. Its early existence as a port is recorded by the fact that the *Mayflower*, en-route to the New World, put into Newlyn for water on 16 August 1620. Plymouth at that time was plagued by a cholera epidemic, thus making Newlyn the ship's last port of call in the Old World. The town, subsequently, became a major centre for pilchard fishing, being ideally placed for the approaching shoals from the Atlantic but also sheltered from the worst of the storms on the west side of Mounts Bay.

Open Easter to end October, weekdays 10am–6pm. Admission, £3.25, children £1.95, family £10.00

The Pilchard Works, The Coombe (**01736 332112**) is an award winning factory and museum – the last, working salt pilchard factory in Britain. It is now open to visitors who can follow the whole process of salting, curing, pressing and boxing. Much of the product still goes to the Italian market where they have been considered a delicacy for generations. These works themselves have been exporting pilchards for over 90 years.

Towards the end of the C19, increasing competition in the fishing industry was leading to heightened tensions among the Newlyn fishermen when in 1896 things came to a head. The East Counties fleet driven by commercial pressures had commenced fishing on Sundays – a day that the devout Cornish considered their day of rest. When they tried to land their catch at Newlyn, the fishermen took over the piers and prevented the catch from being landed. The Newlyn fishermen marched on Penzance in protest but were beaten back by the police. Troops were eventually summoned from Penzance and they cleared the North Pier and removed the chains that the fishermen had strung across the harbour entrance.

The people of Newlyn have always been known for their independent spirit and endeavour and two episodes in their history epitomize these attributes. In 1854, during one of the many depressions to hit Cornwall in this period, a 16 ton craft, *The Mystery*, with 7 men set out on a remarkable voyage to Australia, arriving 116 days later. They had left their families behind to seek their fortune in this new land. However, their hopes were unfulfilled, no fortunes were made and 5 of the 7 eventually returned to Newlyn. More recently, in 1937, the town was threatened with a plan to clear much of the old village and redevelop it with modern housing. The plan caused an outcry in the village and as part of the opposition to the proposal *The Rosebud*, a Newlyn long-line trawler, sailed to Westminster with a petition to save their town in true Ealing Comedy fashion. The national publicity of the voyage, and more pragmatically, the onset of the Second World War led to the dropping of the plans. There are plaques on the wall of the Seamen's Mission commemorating these exploits.

In 1915, Newlyn acquired another sort of attribution when it was chosen by the Ordnance Survey as their datum point. Ever since, all heights in Britain have been calculated from the mean sea level at Newlyn. The Newlyn Tidal Observatory is located in the insignificant little building next to the lighthouse on the south pier.

Newlyn's other lasting claim to fame is associated with the artists who started to settle and work in the area towards the end of the C19 and became known as the Newlyn School, one of the most influential art movements that England has produced. However, there is little evidence of this rich artistic legacy today with the great majority of artists and galleries now being located in nearby Penzance. The only commercial galleries in Newlyn are the *Helen Feiler Gallery*, 36 The Strand (**01736 330796**), open Thursday–Saturday 11am–6pm, and *Badcocks Gallery* (**01736 366159**), shut on Sunday. The former exhibits paintings, jewellery and pottery from the next door studio and there is also a small cafe. It is located directly behind the Star Inn. Badcocks is more recent and has quickly established a reputation for showing the best of Cornwall's artists.

The **Newlyn Art Gallery**, New Road (**01736 363715**) open Monday–Saturday 10am–5pm. Admission free. It was established in 1895 for the exhibition of works by the Newlyn School of Artists. The facade incorporates four art nouveau copper relief panels in the style known as repousse, examples of the Arts and Crafts copper work once produced in the town. The Newlyn Society of Artists continues to exhibit three times a year. Now, however, the gallery is primarily an exhibition space devoted to modern art and many touring exhibitions originate here. There is a small shop selling prints and other original artworks, some by well-established artists.

The port, and Newlyn itself, is still very much a working harbour and town and those looking for the picturesque may be disappointed. Having said that, there are attractive rows of cottages on the hills leading back from the harbour. There is little point in staying in Newlyn as Penzance is so close and a nicer place to stay for any time. There are several pubs near the port that cater largely for the fishing trade – certainly atmospheric. If you are interested, try **The Swordfish** or **The Star Inn** right on the dockside. Further up the hill, towards Mousehole is **The Red Lion** which serves food and has views over the harbour. Perhaps the nicest is the **Tolcarne Inn** on the seafront, although the high sea wall blocks any views to sea. They serve real ales and good pub food, lunchtimes and evenings. The inn used to be a regular haunt of the Newlyn School artists and there are still displays of artists work around the bars. There is also often jazz on Sundays.

Newlyn is easily reached from Penzance, regular buses ply the short journey from Penzance bus station along the Promenade. The same route can be easily walked in half an hour and it makes a pleasant or bracing walk depending on the weather conditions.

THE NEWLYN SCHOOL OF ARTISTS

With the coming of the railway to Penzance, Cornwall was opened up to easy communication with the rest of the country and among the first to arrive were artists that had studied in the "plain air" studios of Brittany and Belgium. On returning to England, they were keen to repeat their experience and the small, fishing port of Newlyn with its good light, cheap lodgings, attractive scenery and wealth of working class subjects proved an adequate replacement.

The first "Newlyn School" painter to settle in the town was **Walter Langley** who arrived in 1882. Like many of the early arrivals, he came from the Midlands, which, at this time, was the centre of manufacturing and jewellery. However, Langley, unlike many of the others, did not hail from a prosperous, professional background but from a poor working class family. He had established a reputation in Birmingham as a fine artist, while still working in a lithographic studio. His dream of becoming a full-time painter was realised by a proposal from a Birmingham photographer who paid him £500 for one year's work. This provided Langley with all he needed and by January 1882 he had found a house in Newlyn. With his working class background, he readily identified with the hardships of the working people of Newlyn. He went on to produce a series of masterful watercolours depicting the hardships and tragedies of the seafaring community – they were infused with sympathy and understanding for his subjects and rate among some of the finest in English art.

Edwin Harris was a childhood friend of Langley's and moved to Newlyn around the same time. His pictures dwelled more on the happiness in the villager's lives, rather than the tragedy and had a tendency towards the sentimental. His work, while accomplished, does not put him in the first league of Newlyn painters. **Frank Bramley** also hailed from the Midlands and arrived in Newlyn in the winter of 1884. Arguably the most talented and dedicated of the Newlyn artists, he painted a series of superb oils of Newlyn villagers – none more accomplished than *A Hopeless Dawn* (1888), one of the most famous paintings of Victorian art. The picture shows two women alone in a room, grieving for the loss of their loved one at sea. Dawn rises over the bleak sea and casts a cold light over the room, with its uneaten last meal on the table. The painting was an instant success and now hangs in the Tate Gallery in London.

Around the same time that Bramley arrived, **Stanhope Forbes** took up residence in the town. He was to become the most influential artist in Newlyn and was to live in the area until his death in 1947. He settled in the Union Hotel in Penzance in January 1884, while he searched the Cornish coast for a suitable painting venue. He decided to stay in Newlyn, attracted by the number of other artists already resident in the town as much as by the opportunities for painting. Forbes was a dedicated open air painter and despite the many hardships of working outdoors he persisted with the technique. Throughout 1884, he worked on what was to become one of his finest paintings, *Fish Sale on a Newlyn Beach*, a masterful study of a figure-filled beach scene. It was widely acclaimed and displayed at the Royal Academy in 1885. Public acclaim for the picture led to a public recognition of the Newlyn artists and encouraged other young artists to move to the town.

The town was now developing as an artistic community and the Cornishman reported 27 artists residing in Newlyn in 1884. **Ralph Todd, Henry Tuke, Fred Hall, Chevallier Taylor, Fred Millard** and **Thomas Gotch** were among the more notable. However, one of the great characters of the Newlyn artists, as well as one of the most original, was **Norman Garstin**. He was born in Ireland and was already 31 when he decided to take up painting. He led an adventurous early life and studied art in Paris for a time, where he became familiar with the work of the Impressionists. He married and moved to Newlyn in 1886 where he and his wife soon became popular members of the artists group. In 1890, they moved to 4 Wellington Terrace, Penzance where he lived until his death in 1926. His finest painting of this period is the masterful *The Rain it Raineth Every Day* which is in the collection at the Penlee House Gallery in Penzance. The painting displays a feeling for space and subdued colour that singled him out from his contemporaries. **Elizabeth Armstrong** visited Newlyn many times but did not reside in the area until she married Stanhope Forbes in 1889. She was an accomplished artist and made the lives of the local children her particular theme.

During this period, Newlyn grew in importance and major works were undertaken to expand the fishing port. By 1894 the harbour walls were completed enclosing an extent of water of 40 acres. The new harbour road backed by sheds for the sale of fish swept away the slips and little beaches that had served as landing places. The town grew with the increasing prosperity and for many artists it became less interesting, less picturesque.

One important event in the artistic year was the March "show day" when a private view would take place in the artist's studios before the pictures were submitted to the Royal Academy. However, in October 1895 the Newlyn Art Gallery opened and was intended to give the artist's a more satisfactory place to display their pictures before sending them to London.

Around this time, many artists started to drift away from Newlyn. Some had personal ambitions that took them away, but there was also a feeling that the Newlyn artists had had their day. St Ives was becoming more popular with aspiring artists and it had a more thriving social scene too. Partly in response to this dispersal of talent, Stanhope and Elizabeth Forbes opened their school of painting in 1899 which continued until the Second World War. In 1902 it was recorded that only three of the Newlyn painters still resided in the town – Forbes, Langley and Ralph Todd.

Around this time, the *Newlyn Copper Works* were established, a philanthropic attempt to provide alternative employment to the young men of the town. **John Pearson**, a founder member of C.R.Ashbee's Guild of Handicraft in Whitechapel became the driving force and his Arts and Crafts-influenced training was evident in much of the output from the works which were characterised by the designs and motifs of ships, fish, flowers and birds.

Although their numbers were less, artists continued to be attracted to the town. In the years before the First World War **Harold** and **Laura Knight** settled in Newlyn before moving on to the burgeoning artistic community in the Lamorna Valley. They were highly accomplished artists, particularly Laura who went on to become a prominent Academician.

Harold Harvey is one of the few Cornish-born painters to make a reputation for himself. He lived his whole life in or near Newlyn and received his early training from Norman Garstin. His work was characterised by a simplification of form and bold use of colour. In the 1920s he converted to Roman Catholicism and increasingly incorporated symbolism and religious subjects into his work.

Dod Proctor studied at the Newlyn School where she met her future husband, **Ernest Proctor**. They were both accomplished artists, Dod Proctor, in particular. She established her reputation as one of the finest woman painters of her time with a series of portrait and figure studies she carried out after the First World War. Ernest was a devout Christian and he carried out works in a number of Cornish churches including St Mary's in Penzance and at St Hilary. The couple lived in Newlyn, Dod dying at the age of 80 in 1972. One other artist of note is **Aletha Garstin**, daughter of Norman Garstin. She was a successful painter in her own right and produced a series of sparkling scenes of Cornish life and landscape. In 1978, the year of her death, Patrick Heron described her as "England's leading Impressionist painter."

Penzance

Penzance and Newlyn have now virtually merged into one town, but they still retain their separate characters. While Newlyn is the working, fishing port, Penzance is a little more refined. It may have started out as a tiny fishing port, but today it is one of the largest towns in Cornwall (pop. 18,000) and the unchallenged capital of Penwith. It is the administrative and social centre and while its shops cannot compete with Truro, they are still the best in the Penwith peninsula and include a large number of excellent art galleries. It has an exceptionally mild climate, the mildest in England, and this has long been one of its main attractions. The 1939 Penguin Guide unfairly described the town as "so uninspiring. Not only has it no buildings worth even one glance, but much of it is distinctly ugly." The town, now, is a bustling, pleasant place with many fine C18 and C19 buildings, a number of exotic gardens and a lively social scene. It has a magnificent outlook over Mounts Bay with fine views of St. Michaels Mount to the east. While there are no real beaches in the town itself, it still makes a good base for exploring the surrounding area with a range of accommodation of all prices and standards and many excellent places to eat and drink.

Historic development

For many centuries, Penzance was nothing more than a tiny fishing port, overshadowed by its more important and established neighbours of Marazion and Mousehole. The earliest evidence of Christianity in Penzance is the C10 cross, now displayed in front of the Museum in Penlee Park. It is known that a chapel of ease was erected some time in the C12 or C13, for the parish church was located some 2 miles inland at Madron. Its location is unknown, but is thought to have been at the west end of Barbican Street, later converted into a fish cellar. It was rebuilt about 1850 when a badly damaged cross was discovered and later placed in St Mary's churchyard where it remains today.

By the C15, the population and trade of Penzance was beginning to increase when the plague struck in 1578. No sooner had the town recovered, than it was sacked by the Spaniards in 1595 in the same raid that destroyed Mousehole. However, the citizens of Penzance were resolute in their rebuilding and they were rewarded in 1614 when James I incorporated the Borough by charter which increased the power and privileges of the town and allowed it to forge ahead of its neighbours. In the Civil War, Penzance declared for the King and in 1646 it was plundered for two days and two nights by Fairfax's Parliamentarian forces. To cap it all, the plague struck again in 1647.

Things looked up after the restoration of the Monarchy when Charles II rewarded the town with a coinage charter in 1663, allowing it to assay tin and collect dues. The town began to prosper. In *A Description of England and Wales* published in 1769, Penzance was described as "a place of considerable note; many of the Cornish gentry have houses here and a great trade is carried on by the inhabitants, who are owners of several ships. The town consists of about 600 houses and the streets are paved." By 1789, the Penzance Grammar School had been re-established in a new building.

The Napoleonic Wars saw many skirmishes in Mounts Bay and a big increase in naval traffic using the port. It also saw the start of the development of Penzance as a health resort as the war prevented the rich and influential from going to the Continent for the winter. Penzance's mild climate must have been a huge draw for the town as Cornwall was still relatively remote and inaccessible. A number of Regency terraces and squares date from this period, including North Parade (1815–1826), Regent Terrace (1815–1820) and Marine Terrace (1826). Penzance was rapidly becoming a fashionable cultural and social centre despite, or perhaps because of, its isolation from the rest of England. To a large extent, its society had to be self-sustaining due to the distance from other sources of education and entertainment. The Royal Geological Society of Cornwall was founded in 1814 with Davies Gilbert as its first president. Four years later the public library was established.

The population was now increasing rapidly from 3382 in 1801 to 9500 by 1859. The railway line arrived in 1852 linking Penzance to Truro and in 1859 the direct link to London was established. Work started on the current railway station in 1879, to a design by Lancaster Owen. From then on, Penzance's importance as a holiday town grew steadily. In 1935 the bathing pool by Battery Rocks was completed in the then fashionable art deco style.

The Town

Penzance has a wonderful position on a bluff of high land overlooking Mounts Bay. The skyline is dominated by the twin landmarks of the dome of the Market House, indicating the town centre, and the tower of St Marys Church, marking the seaward end of the town. Surprisingly, no other high buildings have intruded on the dominance of these two historic landmarks.

The Penzance of today owes much of its character to the development of the C18 and C19. The Regency terraces and squares provide an elegant backdrop to the town, notably those to the south and west of the town centre. Regent Square is a perfect example of an informal grouping of classical architecture with the road winding through the square on the diagonal and the houses set back behind long front gardens. Elsewhere, more formal compositions line the narrow streets and Clarence Place, Clarence Terrace, North Parade, South Parade and Regent Terrace are all full of good examples of late C18/early C19 architecture. This part of Penzance makes an interesting walk with the sub tropical **Morrab Gardens** making a fine place to rest for a while. The Palladian style, Victorian house in the middle of the gardens is the **Morrab Library**, one of only a few private libraries in the country. It has a collection of over 45,000 volumes, including some 2000 printed before 1800 and a rare collection of 3000 Napoleonic memorabilia. The collection is particularly strong on Cornish and Celtic books and also has a photographic archive of 10,000 negatives and prints. Subscriptions are very reasonable and daily membership is available too. Morrab Terrace and Morab Place, just to the north, are an attractive group of regency buildings around a network of narrow lanes.

**Open
Tues– Fri
10am–4pm,
Sat 10am–
1pm**

Chapel Street is one of the nicest in town and leads from the Market House down towards the docks. The street is lined with good Georgian and Regency houses including the **Regent Hotel** and **Union Hotel**. The Trafalgar Room of the latter used to be the Assembly Room and is where the news of the Battle of Trafalgar and the death of Nelson was brought to the mayor who was attending a ball. One can just imagine him in all his pomposity climbing up to the balcony to announce the bitter-sweet news – England's greatest naval victory and the death of her greatest naval hero. It also contains the second oldest theatre in Britain. Nearby, the **Egyptian House** is a remarkable construction of 1835 in the style made fashionable by Napoleon's Egyptian campaign of 1798 and one of the finest examples in the country.

A plaque on no.25 Chapel Street identifies it as the home of the mother and aunt of the Bronte sisters. The big, Italianate building nearby, set back from the street, is the rather pretentious **Weslyan Chapel** of 1864. *The Chocolate House* at no.44 has an elaborate, carved shopfront. The large building, opposite the church, with its classical facade facing out to sea is now the home of the **Penzance Arts Club** and was once the Portuguese Embassy, a legacy of Penzance's importance as a trading port and point of embarkation. *St Mary's Church* and its tower command the seaward end of Chapel Street. The church dates from 1832-5 and was built by *Charles Hutchins*. It is big, grey and grim with an enhanced sense of grandeur due to its heightened position. Inside, is a spectacular altar dating from 1934 and executed by Ernest Proctor, one of the important Newlyn artists.

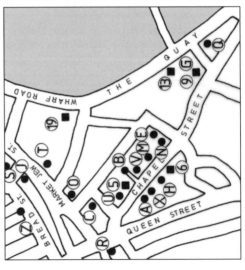

PENZANCE

The *Market House* dominates the centre of town and the long view up Market Jew Street from the east. The road narrows and is forced to detour around it such is its prominence within the street. It was built by *H.J. Whiting* in 1837 and is a dignified granite structure with a giant portico to the upper floors and the landmark dome above supported on rows of Tuscan columns. The ground floor is now a bank – you can go in and admire the finely proportioned interior and ceiling, which can still be appreciated despite the modern bank fittings.

Outside the Market House is a statue of *Sir Humphry Davy*. Born in Penzance in 1778, he was one of the great chemists of his day, isolating sodium and potassium and forming the first coherent theory of electro-chemical reaction as well as inventing the miner's safety lamp, the deed for which he is most well known. He used to meet regularly in the *Star Inn*, directly opposite the statue. Market Jew Street is now the principal shopping street of Penzance, its principal feature being the raised terrace on the north side. Halfway down on the north side is the Arcade, an attractive flight of steps lined by small shops. *Victoria Square* just to the north of Market Jew Street is a handsome composition of white, rendered workers houses. The nearby, 1 Leskinnick Place on the corner of Adelaide Street, is an extraordinary battlemented and pinnacled little house – a fine example of Victorian Gothic extravaganza played out on a miniature scale. Causeway Road is the pedestrianized street leading north from the Market House. It is lined with an interesting range of small shops including the excellent *Penzance Rare Books* which boasts a glass fascia sign preserved from the previous occupants, *J.C.Rogers*. Waves coffee shop has a 1930s Art Deco influenced shopfront. The *Savoy Cinema* claims to be the oldest in Britain, having been showing movies without interruption since 1912.

To the west of the town centre is the **Penlee Memorial Park**, purchased by public subscription in 1946 as a war memorial for the town. The park is now a pleasant haven in the town. There is an open air theatre which stages productions in the summer months. The large, Italianate house in the park was built in 1865 and now houses the town's museum and art collection. The cross outside is one of the most important in the Celtic world – the complex set of inscriptions has allowed it to be dated precisely to 1007.

Open Mon– **Penlee House Gallery and Museum**, Morrab Road (**01736 363625**). The
Sat 10.30am building was completely refurbished and extended in 1997 and now provides excel-
–5pm lent display space for the town's museum and art collection. There is also a nice cafe
(4.30pm in with plenty of outdoor seating and a small shop, selling cards, prints and books.
winter).
Admission, The museum has an interesting collection of artefacts and memorabilia relating
£2, concs £1, to Cornwall's history and in particular West Penwith and Penzance. Exhibits
under 18s include the safety lamp invented by Humphry Davy. There is also a photographic
free, Sat free archive and image database with over 10,000 images. The gallery also stages spe-
cial exhibitions of art works, often associated with Cornwall and the Penwith area. However, the main strength is the Gallery's own art collection – the largest in West Cornwall and one of the most significant in the country with its fine collection of paintings from the Newlyn School.

The collection consists almost entirely of English paintings from the early C19 onwards. The earliest painting is *Mounts Bay from Ludgvan* from 1794 by William Brooks. There are some early C19 paintings of the locality including Richard Pentreath's *View from Madron Carn* which clearly shows the Madron workhouse where Arthur Wallis was to spend his last days. There are also a number of paint-ings of St Michael's Mount, more important for their historical record than their artistic significance. Collectively, these paintings provide an important record of the area at that time and highlight its remoteness and undeveloped character.

The remaining pictures in the collection are from the Newlyn School. Seeing the pictures together in such proximity to their setting greatly enhances the under-standing and appreciation of their quality. The subject matter of these pictures was the lives of the ordinary working people of Penwith – the fishermen, farmers and tradesmen, their wives and children, all painted in naturalistic settings, generally in the open air. The use of light, colour and reflection in the finer paintings is little short of superb.

It should be Stanhope Forbes is widely accepted as the leader of the Newlyn School of
borne in mind Artists. His work is not well represented in the collection with his major works
that there is being elsewhere. *The Young Apprentice, Newlyn Copperworks* was painted early
no guarantee in the C20 and, while not one of his better works, it is an intriguing historical
that all these record as it shows John Mackenzie, artist, designer and founder of the Newlyn
paintings will Industrial Classes for the young people of Newlyn. It shows him overseeing the
be on display work of 15 year old apprentice, Johnny Payne Cotton who later became a master
at any one craftsman and partner in the Newlyn Copper Works. They produced repousse
time, as metalwork, much influenced by the Arts and Crafts movement with patterns based
special on the village and its industry – the fish, flora and fauna of the area. There are a
exhibitions or number of examples of their work on display in the collection.
the normal
rotation of
displays may
require their
removal.

Possibly the collection's finest painting is *The Rain it Raineth EveryDay* by Norman Garstin and selected for the Royal Academy in 1889. It depicts a rainy, stormy day on Penzance promenade and is executed in a sombre palette of black, browns, silver and grey. The handling of light and reflection from the rain soaked promenade is masterly and the sparse composition with almost two dimensional figures against the flat background of the promenade seems to owe something to Oriental art. The picture is the most requested in the exhibition and is, occasionally, on loan to other galleries. Elizabeth Forbes is represented by, probably, her finest and certainly her most popular work. *School is Out* is a beautifully observed scene of the end of the day in the village school. The slightly idealized representation is compensated for by her use of colour and warm light.

Walter Langley was a major figure of Victorian art and the collection has one of his best watercolours, *Fishwives*, a medium in which he excelled and is not to be bettered. Alexander Chevallier Taylor is represented by an exquisite portrait *Girl Shelling Peas* painted in 1886 and a rare example of his work. Percy Craft has a couple of works in the gallery, most notably the large *Tucking a School of Pilchards* painted in 1897. This colourful, figure filled picture depicts a scene that must have taken place regularly and a good number of the fishermen would have been known personally by Craft. Written in pencil on the back of the canvas are the names of many of the fishermen portrayed, many of whom still have descendents living in the area today. Harold Harvey is the only member of the Newlyn School to have been born locally. *Girl on the Cliff* is a particularly fine example of his later work, painted in 1926 and there is also *Marazion Marshes* showing his unrestricted use of bright colours.

Lamorna Birch has never really been considered one of the Newlyn School as he concentrated on landscapes and seascapes producing some of the most beautiful Cornish views ever painted. There are four paintings by Birch in the collection, including the wonderful *January, Clapper Mill, Lamorna*, a large canvas beautifully evoking the icy cold atmosphere of a sharp winter's day.

On the Promenade is the **Jubilee Bathing Pool**, designed in the art deco style and opened in 1935. There are good views of the bay from the war memorial to the east. The large stone building opposite is the Barbican which houses the idiosyncratic museum of mechanical objects **Around The Bend (01736 331933)**. (Open seven days in summer, 11am–5pm. Admission £2.50, children £1.50.). The Docks, just around the headland are normally full of boats of various types and make an interesting walk. Cruises and fishing trips are available from **The Quay (01736 368565)**. The ferry service to the Scilly Isles leaves from here.

Open daily, 10.30am–6pm, mid May–mid Sept. Admission £2.30, children £1.70

Opposite is **The National Lighthouse Centre (01736 360077)**. Located in an old warehouse, it contains an interesting collection of artefacts, including a recreation of a typical lighthouse room and numerous types of optical equipment. The centre provides an interesting history of the lighthouse. It explains how the earliest lights were often kept by monks. With the dissolution of the monasteries by Henry VIII, there was suddenly nobody to maintain these primitive lights. In response, Henry, in 1514, granted a Royal Charter to Trinity House to maintain safety around the shores of England. It was not until 1836 that Trinity House

Open Easter–Oct, daily 10.30am–4.30pm. Admission, £3, children £1, family £6

assumed total responsibility.

There is a video presentation on the history of the Eddystone Lighthouse, the first offshore lighthouse erected in 1698 on the notorious Eddystone Reef, off Plymouth. In 1703 a huge storm washed it away, but it had already proved its worth as no ship had been wrecked on the reef in those five years. Two days after its destruction, a ship was wrecked on the reef. A new lighthouse, made of oak, was opened in 1709 and stood for 49 years before it was destroyed by fire. The replacement by *John Smeaton* was the archetype of the new breed of lighthouses built of massive granite blocks. It stood for 123 years until replaced by the new lighthouse in 1882. Smeaton's original was reconstructed on The Hoe at Plymouth where it still stands.

Perhaps the most powerful exhibit in the whole exhibition is the shattered door from the Bishop Rock lighthouse which was ripped off its hinges by a huge storm on 3 February 1994. The massive steel door must have seemed almost indestructible and the resultant damage is evidence of the awesome power of the sea.

Penzance has a large number of interesting shops dealing in antiques, collectibles and second hand books. There is a particular concentration in Chapel Street, although a stroll around the town centre will reveal many more. There are also a large number of art galleries, as Penzance has now become a major centre for the arts in West Cornwall. Many of them are of excellent quality. Among the best are:

Belerion Gallery, Bread Street (**01736 351249**). Open in summer, Tuesday–Saturday and in winter, Wednesday–Saturday. Located at the top of the Arcade from Market Jew Street, it has a good range of paintings, ceramics and jewellery as well as reclaimed and restructured period furniture.

The Rainyday Gallery, 116 Market Jew Street (**01736 366077**) Located above the Pioneer Supermarket, this long-established gallery has a good selection of paintings many by well-known local artists. There is an ongoing programme of exhibitions throughout the year.

Shears Fine Art, 58 Chapel Street (**01736 350501**) Upmarket gallery specializing in the works of the early Newlyn and St Ives Schools. There is a permanent exhibition of works by many of the leading Newlyn painters.

Goldfish, 56 Chapel Street (**01736 360573**) Excellent gallery displaying paintings, jewellery, ceramics, pottery and prints by local artists. Also stages a number of solo shows throughout the year.

Tony Sanders Gallery, 14 Chapel Street (**01736 366620**) Extensive gallery over three floors with antiques predominating on the ground floor and paintings and sculpture on those above. Vast selection of work, many of high quality.

Penzance Arts Club, Chapel Street (**01736 363761**). Open 9.30am–11.00pm, Tuesday–Saturday, 7.00pm–11.00pm on Sundays and Mondays. Members only after 5.30pm. Opposite St Mary's Church at the seaward end of Chapel Street. The walls of this private club are lined with paintings by its members, of which most are normally for sale. There is also a small gallery space in the foyer which has regular exhibitions. Prices are very reasonable and the quality consistently good. Ring for entry. The club also offers painting holidays with tuition which are designed to suit beginners as well as the more experienced. Telephone for further details.

Lighthouse Gallery, 25 Causeway Road (**01736 350555**). Excellent selection of paintings and ceramics, many by Cornwall's top contemporary artists.

Bread Street Gallery, Bread Street (**01736 363334**) Tiny gallery but with a good selection of very high quality work. The owner runs his violin workshop from the same building.

Accommodation

Penzance is full of hotels, hostels and bed and breakfast places of all standards and prices. It is a major tourist destination and finding somewhere to stay should not be a problem outside the peak season, school summer holidays. Due to the number of rooms available, rates are often keenly priced, especially out of high season. The Tourist Information Centre (**01736 362207**) by the bus station can provide a full list of accommodation. There is a concentration of places to stay in Morrab Road,, Regent Terrace and Alexandra Road to the south and west of the town centre. In Morrab Road, just 5 minutes west of the town centre, try the **Lynwood Guest House** at no.41 (**01736 365871**) *A*, **Con-Amore** at no.38 (**01736 363423**) *A* or **Woodstock House** at no.29 (**01736 369049**) *B*, all similar and very good value. The **Estoril Hotel** at no.46 (**01736 362468**) *C* is a bit more upmarket. All rooms are en-suite. Open from February to November. Regent Terrace is a whole street of upmarket B&Bs and hotels in lovely Georgian buildings with good views over the bay. Try **Chy-an-Mor** (**01736 363441**) *C*, **Lombard House** (**01736 364897**) *C* or the **Stanley Hotel** (**01736 362146**) *B*. Alexandra Road is a quiet tree-lined street around 10 minutes walk west of the town centre. Try the **Penmorvah Hotel** (**01736 363711**) *B* or **Pendennis Hotel** (**01736 363823**) *B*. Also worth trying are:

Penzance Backpackers, The Blue Dolphin, Alexandra Road (**01736 363836**) *A*, dormitory accommodation in this lovely, Victorian house. Also double room available. The best, budget accommodation in town.

YMCA, The Orchard, Alverton (**01736 365016**) *A*, well-appointed hostel with pool and snooker/table tennis facilities. About 20 minutes walk from the town centre.

Penzance Youth Hostel, Castle Horneck, Alverton (**01736 362666**) *A,* rather inconveniently located on the edge of town just off the bypass. This lovely Georgian mansion in landscaped grounds has been converted into a comfortable hostel. Lounge, dining room and TV room, ample car parking.

Tourist Information Centre

It is also possible to camp here.

Holbein House, Alexandra Road (**01736 332625**) **A**, big Victorian house opposite Penzance backpackers. Very good value.

Wymering Guest House, 15 Regent Square (**01736 362126**) **B**, lovely house, the only place to stay in this beautiful Regency square, Good value and very central.

Tarbert Hotel, Clarence Street (**01736 363758**) **C**, comfortable hotel in the town centre.

Union Hotel, Chapel Street (**0800 136885**) **C**, located right in the heart of town on one of the nicest streets. Penzance's oldest hotel, the present building dates largely from the Georgian period. The Trafalgar Dining Room, where breakfast is served, is one of the finest examples of a Georgian Assembly Room in Cornwall. There are two bars and a separate restaurant. The hotel is filled with comfortable old chairs, antique furniture and memorabilia of Nelson and the Battle of Trafalgar.

The Georgian House Hotel, 20 Chapel Street (**01736 365664**) **B**, just down the road from the above. Smart Georgian building with own car park.

The Summerhouse, Cornwall Terrace (**01736 363744**) **C**, superb, elegant hotel with only 5 bedrooms. Highly recommended, if it is within your price range or if you want to treat yourself. The restaurant is very good too.

The Queens Hotel, The Promenade (**01736 362371**) **E**, large, Victorian hotel right on the seafront. Comfortable, if a bit faded in grandeur. There is complimentary membership of the adjacent health club.

Penzance Arts Club, Chapel Street (**01736 363761**) **C**, this private club located in the former Portuguese Embassy has four rooms available to non-members on a bed and breakfast basis. The rooms, and club, are beautifully furnished and the walls covered with artworks. There is a comfortable lounge, bar and terrace. All rooms have sea views. Highly recommended.

Restaurants and cafes

Penzance has a good number of places to eat although the standard is variable. There are, however, a number of very good restaurants and several pubs that serve good food also.

Cocos, Chapel Street (**01736 350222**) **I**, large, friendly cafe bar with smart modern interior. Open all day for coffee and lunches. Excellent tapas and main meals in the evening. One of the most "fun" places to eat in town.

The Bakehouse, Chapel Street (**01736 331331**) *M-E*, down an alley opposite Cocos. Smart décor, over two floors with a few tables in the courtyard for al fresco dining. There is a cheaper lunchtime menu.

Harris's, 46 New Street (**01736 364408**) *E*, behind the Star Inn on Market Jew Street. Upmarket cuisine in pretty interior. The food is good, but the atmosphere slightly pretentious. Considered to be one of Penzance's best restaurants.

The Summer House Restaurant, Cornwall Terrace (**01736 363744**) *M-E*, in the hotel of the same name. Beautiful, stylish surroundings and great food make this an excellent choice for a treat. In the summer, one can eat by candlelight in the walled garden. Highly recommended. Open, Tuesday to Sunday evenings and Sunday lunch. Restricted opening in the winter.

Abbey Restaurant, Abbey Street (**01736 330680**) *M*, just off Chapel Street, this smart restaurant and bar is open for morning coffee (from 11.00am), light lunches and dinner. The downstairs bar has comfortable sofas and tub chairs while the restaurant is upstairs.

Gino's Spaghetti House, The Promenade (**01736 350447**) *I*, next to the Queens Hotel. Italian restaurant, very popular with locals.

Oliver's, Chapel Street (**01736 332555**) *M-E*, located underneath the Penzance Arts Club, this intimate restaurant features modern English cuisine with a Mediterranean influence..

Ganges Restaurant, Chapel Street (**01736 333002**) *I*, standard Indian cuisine in friendly atmosphere with bizarre interior. Take-away service also.

Poolside, Jubilee Pool (**01736 366955**) *I*, open air, poolside cafe with evening barbecue including fresh fish.

Terrace Café, Market Jew Street, on the corner with The Arcade. Smart, modern coffee and sandwich shop with friendly service.

Waves, Causeway Road, opposite the above. Traditional cafe/teashop behind original art deco facade.

First Servic e, Penlee Park (**01736 367627**) *I*, part of the new tennis pavilion in Penlee Park, this smart cafe provides inexpensive lunches and refreshments throughout the day. There is a large terrace for sunny daye.

Bars and nightlife

Penzance has a large number of pubs and nightlife venues as befits its size and status. However, many of the pubs have been ruined by alterations and have little character. The better ones include:

The Turks Head, Chapel Street (**01763 363093**), reputed to date from 1233 and to be the first so called in England following The Crusades. Cosy and lively front bar with an excellent selection of real ales. The pub has a large restaurant area and serves superior pub food. It is extremely popular and reservations are recommended.

Admiral Benbow, Chapel Street. The upstairs bar has a bizarre interior with a massive, exposed timber frame and numerous ships' figure heads. Caters predominantly for a young crowd. There is a restaurant downstairs.

The Star Inn, Market Jew Street, reputedly where Humphry Davy used to meet his associates, although the opened-up interior with its games machines and banks of television screens would make it unrecognizable to him. The old ale house bar at the rear has a good selection of real ales. Pub food served.

Farmer's Arms, Causeway Road, small, low granite building with wooden floors and beamed ceilings and a tiny snug bar at the front. Very popular with locals.

The Dolphin Tavern, Quay Street, right by the Docks. Large pub with real ales and decent pub food. Open all day. Convenient for those waiting for the ferry to the Scillies.

Globe and Ale House, Queen Street, good selection of real ales. Dylan Thomas held his wedding reception here after marrying at the nearby Penzance Registry Office.

There are two nightclubs in Penzance, **Club 2000** at Branwells Mill, near the bus and rail stations and the **Barn** on the eastern edge of town near Tesco's supermarket. **The Bosun's Locker** on the harbour front opposite the Docks has occasional live bands and DJ's. **The Acorn Theatre**, Parade Street (**01736 365520**) runs a year round programme of theatre, dance, comedy, music, exhibitions and workshops in a small, but welcoming venue. The **Savoy Cinema** in Causeway Road has regular screenings in its three screens. The Penwith Film Society also present films here. The **Penzance Arts Club** (**01736 363761**) in Chapel Street has a regular programme of entertainment's, many of them open to non-members. Temporary membership is available at £10.00 per month – a good investment if you are staying here for any length of time. The **Golowan Festival** of arts and community is held each year to celebrate the traditional Feast of St John in June. Further information is available from the festival booking office (**01736 365520**) or the Tourist Information Centre.

(i)   ## Practicalities

Tourist Information Centre   The Tourist Information Centre (**01736 362207**) is prominently located next to the bus and rail stations at the eastern edge of the town centre. Penzance is the terminus for the main West Coast line and there are regular trains to Plymouth, Exeter, Bristol, London and beyond. It is a major terminus for buses in the Penwith area and there are regular buses to Lands End, St Just, St Ives, Helston, Camborne and Truro for onward connections. There are also direct express coach services to London and other major towns in England. Getting around Penzance is easy as all the sites of interest are within walking distance. For trips further afield, the **Cycle Centre** in Bread Street (**01736 351671**) rents bikes for £10.00 per day. Penwith and the Lizard are both small enough for cycling to be a feasible way of getting around. There are also a number of interesting sites within easy cycling distance of Penzance.

Around Penzance

Just two miles north-west of Penzance, Madron was until 1871 within the parish of Penzance. This explains the extraordinary scale and richness of the *Church of St Madern*, the mother church of Penzance. It is also unusual, for Penwith, by having been added to over many different periods. The present building was completed by C16. The oldest part is the Lady Chapel, where the Saxon church stood, the south aisle was added by the Normans and the Sanctuary is Early English. Further enlargement and alterations were consecrated in 1336 and the north aisle was added in 1507. Legend has it that the vicar of the time supported Perkin Warbeck in his misguided bid for the throne. When Perkin was defeated, he chose to placate Henry VII by building the north aisle with plenty of Tudor Rose roof bosses and the timely addition of the Royal Coat of Arms to the Lady Chapel. The church steps down across its width with the natural slope of the land. The interior is interesting with a rood screen across all three aisles, similar to St Buryan. Only the bottom 3 feet are original and date from the mid C15. There is an unusual Jacobean tower screen and a brass memorial to John Clies, Mayor of Penzance,1623. Also, in the Lady Chapel are two finely carved tombs and C15 bench ends. Above the door to the south porch is the famous Nelson Banner. It was made and carried up from Penzance by the mayor and people on hearing of the Battle of Trafalgar and the death of Nelson. Penzance was the first place in Britain to hear the news when local fishermen intercepted HMS Pickle as she sailed towards Falmouth with the official communique for the King. There is still an annual remembrance on the Sunday closest to 21 October.

There is an attractive churchyard with some spectacularly large memorials. The view across Mounts Bay is only partially marred by the hideous extension to the otherwise picturesque, Church School of 1878. The stone and timber lychgate nearby is a memorial to the dead of the Boer War 1899–1902. The village has some fine granite buildings, including Landithy Hall, a semi-circle of almshouses built in 1909. The **King William IV** pub serves food lunchtimes and evenings. There is no need to stay in Madron as Penzance is so close and generally a better option. However, for those who wish to there is **Tregoddick House** (**01736 362643**) **A**, a picturesque period house B&B in the centre of the village.

On the outskirts of the village heading north-west is the old Madron Workhouse where *Alfred Wallis* spent his last days. Rather unromantically, the building is now part of the Madron Meat Company Abbatoir. Further along the same road, is the extraordinary *Madron Holy Well and Chapel*. It is signposted and there is a small car park from where it is a short walk through woodland to the Holy Well, a place of ancient pilgrimage that is still in use today as evidenced by the scraps of cloth, handkerchiefs and scarves tied as votive offerings around the well head. The water is reputed to cure rickets and assist in divination. A few hundred yards further on are the remains of the Baptistry Chapel, in ruins for 200 years but now largely restored. In the right hand corner opposite the entrance is the font or place of baptism. The altar and lower courses of the walls may date from the C12 but the chapel and well are part of a complex that has a much earlier origin.

Open mid-Feb–Oct, Sun-Thurs 10am-5.30pm (5pm in March and October). Admission, £4.40, children £2.20, family £11.00

Trengwainton Garden (01736 363148) National Trust. Located one mile south-west of Madron, are these beautiful and exotic gardens, first established in the C16 when the walled gardens were built. The property changed hands in 1867 but the present garden owes most of its existence to the period after 1925 when Lt. Colonel Sir Edward Bolitho took over. Notably, he bought a share of the 1927–8 expedition of the famous plant hunter Kingdon-Ward to North East Assam and Burma. Many of the exotic plants at Trengwainton originate from this expedition, including the extensive rhododendron collection. The garden is ostensibly a linear walk alongside the stream with a large area of walled gardens to the north as one first enters the garden. The climate and sheltered aspect help the large number of exotic plants to flourish and the walled gardens are particularly splendid in this respect. Towards the end of the walk is the restored terrace and new summerhouse with superb views over Mounts Bay. Light lunches and teas are available from the new and rather smart tea room in the grounds.

Gulval

Just behind the Penzance heliport and just a few hundred yards from the sea is the tiny, picturesque village of Gulval. The square is ringed by Victorian granite buildings, including the **Coldstream Inn**, originally the Gulval Institute, erected 1895. There is a 1910 granite, drinking fountain in the centre of the square. The *Church of St Gulval* is on the main square, open for visitors, June–September, 2.00–4.30. The tower dates from 1440. The beauty of this church is its setting within a circular churchyard and unusually, heavily landscaped with many exotic trees and plants. There is a large stone lych gate constructed from arcading taken from the C13 transept. It was erected in 1897 to commemorate the Jubilee of Queen Victoria. On the main B3311 is a large, granite Methodist Chapel.

Open daily Apr–Oct, 10am-6pm (or dusk if earlier). Admission £2.00, children £1.00

Further along the B3311, heading north, is **Chysauster**, signposted from the main road. The site is owned and managed by English Heritage. There is a car park and toilet facilities beside the road. The site, itself, is a short walk away. The site can be approached by footpath from Gulval along the beautiful Trevavior Valley. The site is the best preserved and displayed example of a courtyard house hamlet in Cornwall. It appears to have been constructed relatively late in the Roman period and abandoned shortly after, which may explain its excellent state of preservation. The layout of the houses shows an unusual degree of planning with eight houses being arranged in pairs on either side of a 'street,' and a single house set apart from the others. The houses are easily identified with stone walls 4–5 feet high, clearly defined entrances, hearths and other details. However, what is most impressive is the planned nature of the settlement and the clear expression it gives of the communal life of that time. There is a fogou on the site, but it is not as impressive as that at Carn Euny. Towards the end of June each year, a local school build a replica hut within the village and live on-site for a week.

Just under a mile due east is *Castle-an-Dinas*, one of the largest and best preserved Iron Age hillforts in Cornwall. Nearby is *Castle-an-Dinas West*, otherwise known as Rogers' Tower. Erected by a local landowner in c1800, it is a sham castle with towers, built for the magnificent views over Mounts Bay. Both sites can be reached by footpath from the B3311 or from Chysauster, itself.

Ludgvan is an appealingly pretty village, located just off the A30 east of Penzance. The *Church of St Ludgvan and St Paul* is set within its own churchyard with massive encircling granite walls. There are some interesting memorials inside and, below the battlements of the tower, a series of head-like gargoyles. The **White Hart**, directly opposite the Church is a scenic, granite inn with plants trailing over the front. Real ales and food served, lunchtimes and evenings.

Ludgvan

Marazion and St Michael's Mount

Approximately two miles east of Penzance is *Marazion* and one of the most visited places in Cornwall, *St Michael's Mount*. Marazion is now just a small town, but was once of much greater importance, owing much to the nearby St Michael's Mount. A market has existed here from the C11 and in 1595, the town was granted its charter from Elizabeth I, some 19 years before Penzance and 44 years before St Ives. The town is spread along the shoreline, with any centre that there is being around the small, but flamboyant town hall of 1871.

The town is quite picturesque with a number of attractive cottages and houses, but little else of interest. A plaque on a house directly opposite the Mount states that Prince Charles (later Charles II) stayed there on the night of 2 March 1646 before escaping to the Scillies after the battle of Nazeby – St Michael's Mount being one of the last Royalist strongholds in England. The town, now, has some attractive places to stay and several good art galleries.

There is really no need to stay in Marazion as Penzance is so close and convenient. However, if you do wish to, there are a number of rather upmarket hotels along the shore road, many with fine views of the Mount. One of the nicest and certainly the one with the best view is the **Godolphin Arms**, West End (**01736 710202**) *D*, directly opposite The Mount. The hotel has recently been completely refurbished and there is a restaurant and bars serving superior pub food and real ales. There is an outside terrace, perfect for summer days. On the other side of the road is the **Marazion Hotel** (**01736 710334**) *C* with comfortable rooms and a restaurant and bar serving good food. The nearby **Rosario B&B** (**01736 711998**) *C* has nice en-suite rooms.

Many of the hotels have restaurants open to non-residents including the two above. The restaurant at the **Mount Haven Hotel**, Turnpike Road (**01736 710249**) *E* is reputed to be particularly good. The **Ferryboat Café**, opposite the Godolphin Arms is open all day and serves breakfasts, lunches and dinners. The **Corner House**, Fore Street (**01736 711348**) *M* is open in the evenings only and serves fresh fish. The **Kings Arms**, next to the Town Hall, is a pleasant pub frequented by locals. On the Mount itself, is the **Sail Loft Restaurant and Café**, open for lunches and teas. Inexpensive.

There are several good art galleries in Marazion including:

Avalon Art, West End (**01736 710161**). Open every day in summer, winter Tuesday to Saturday. It has an excellent range of paintings and prints by local artists, also ceramics and jewellery.

Out of the Blue Gallery, The Square (**01736 719019**). Open, every day in summer, closed Sundays in winter. Bright blue painted building opposite the Marazion Hotel. There is a fine selection of paintings and ceramics. The upstairs gallery hosts an ongoing series of solo exhibitions by major local artists.

Market House Gallery, Market Place (**01736 710252**). Open every day in summer, telephone for winter opening times. This recently-opened gallery specializes in the post-war St Ives period including artists such as Alfred Wallis, Terry Frost and Jack Pender. Also, a good selection of pottery and glass.

Praed Gallery, Market Place (**01736 711400**) In winter, it is closed Saturday to Tuesday. Exhibits the paintings of the well-known Cornish contemporary artist, Michael Praed as well as guest artists, ceramics and jewellery.

Seagrove Gallery and Tearoom, The Square (**01736 710732**) Has a range of ceramics, clothes, fabrics, jewellery and paintings.

Marazion is easily reached from Penzance, there is a regular and frequent bus service from the Penzance bus station which goes on to Helston. Alternatively, it is a pleasant hour's walk along the beach path or an even easier cycle ride. There are car parking facilities in Marazion, although at peak times finding a space can be difficult.

St Michael's Mount

National Trust. (01736 710507) Open, April–October, daily (closed Saturday, except July and August) 10.30am–5.30pm. Outside these times, you must phone to determine when it may be visited. Admission £5.50, children £2.75, family £13.75. At low tide the Mount can be approached on foot over the Causeway, at high tide the approach has to be by boat which leaves from various points in Marazion depending on the state of the tide. Signs are clearly posted in the town. The ferry costs £1.00p for an adult, 50p per child and is the more atmospheric way of arriving on the island. Information on tides and ferries is available on 01736 710265 or 710507

St Michael's Mount has an ancient history – it is widely considered to be the ancient port of Ictis from which Cornish tin was exported to the Greek trading communities in the Mediterranean. It certainly would have formed part of the ancient trading route between Ireland and the Continent, terminating the southern half of the short overland route to Hayle. The Mount is dedicated to the Archangel St Michael who, according to legend, appeared in the year 495 to some fishermen who saw him standing high on the Mount. From then on the site became one of Christian pilgrimage and a Celtic monastery is said to have existed on the site from the C8 to the C11.

The origins of the present priory are not clear, but it seems that the Mount may have been granted to the *Abbey of Mont St Michel* in Normandy for a cell of Benedictine monks to be established, some time just before the Norman Conquest in 1066. Certainly, no buildings materialized as a result of this before the Conquest. The first definitive evidence of construction of the present priory is from 1135 and it was included in the possession of Mont St Michel in a papal bull of 1155. However, the priory never reached the magnificence of the Abbey of St Michel, catering as it did for a prior and only twelve Benedictine monks. After the plague in 1362, only the prior and two monks survived.

The community on the Mount was suppressed in 1425 and the land given to Syon Abbey. After the Reformation, it was held on lease from the Crown by various Governors. The Mount had a strategic significance and featured in many of the Cornish uprisings of the early medieval period, but its importance was to grow with the threat from foreign sea powers. In 1587, the beacon on top of the church tower was lit to signal the approach of the Spanish Armada.

In the Civil War, it was to play a strategic role. Sir Francis Basset, a leading Royalist, had purchased the Mount in 1640. When war broke out in 1642, he immediately set about improving its defences. The harbour was invaluable to Royalists as arms and munitions could be imported from France and paid for by the sale of Cornish tin. However, the Parliamentarians were to prove too strong and by 1645 the Royalists were all but defeated. St Michael's Mount was one of the last strongholds to surrender on 23 April 1646. In 1647, Parliament appointed Colonel John St Aubyn to be Captain of the Mount, thus beginning an unbroken line of ownership that extends to today.

The Mount must have seemed an inhospitable place once the need for defence had receded and the St Aubyn family continued to spend much of their time at their family home of Clowance, near Camborne. This was badly damaged by fire in the C19 and the family moved to take up more permanent occupation of the Mount. Much of the present appearance of the building dates from this time and was designed by *Piers St Aubyn*, an architect by profession, who carried out much work to Cornwall's churches as well as his family home.

By whichever means you approach the Mount, you will arrive at the harbour, the present jetty and pier dating from 1824, but replacing much earlier structures. There are fewer buildings around the harbour now than in the past when it was a busy working port. It was only in the middle of the C19 that Penzance harbour overtook the Mount in importance. The buildings lining the harbour date from the C17 onwards. The path up towards the main buildings is steep and extremely uneven in places. Outside the entrance, is an unusual Celtic cross with a circular head with an equal-armed cross, a crucifixion figure in a circular recess below and below that a Latin cross – evidence of early Celtic occupation of the Mount.

The buildings are approached through the west door, a C15 archway with the St Aubyn arms added later. The Hall contains a C17 chest of John St Aubyn, installed as Captain of the Mount after the Civil War. Off the hall is St John's Room, which has a fine carved fireplace with a Delft tile surround. This and the Armoury are comparatively recent C19 additions. The breakfast room is one of the older parts and was originally higher and longer. The next room, the large banqueting hall is known as the Chevy Chase Room after the plaster frieze of hunting scenes that runs around the room. This is also one of the earliest parts of the castle with medieval walls and a C15 roof. The date of the frieze is unclear but there is a date of 1641 on the Royal Coat of Arms which is unexplained and could possibly relate to the date of the frieze. The Coat of Arms, itself, dates from 1660, tactfully placed there by Colonel John St Aubyn to celebrate the restoration of King Charles II.

You now pass through a small room to the South Terrace, part of the large Victorian wing of the castle. There are extensive views over Mounts Bay. The tour leads to the North Terrace and into the *Priory Church*. One of the earliest remaining parts of the complex, the Church is largely C14 with C15 windows, although it has been much restored and the furnishings and ornamentation are largely modern. The fine gilt brass chandelier was installed in 1811, but is thought to be Flemish dating from the late C15. There are some good alabaster carvings behind the altar, but otherwise the interior is sadly lacking in interest.

The tour route leads back out onto the North Terrace and into the former Lady Chapel, now the Blue Drawing Rooms, a startlingly pretty and accomplished interior within this otherwise rather bleak and cold building. The ruined chapel was converted in the 1740s into an extraordinary, Rococo-Gothic creation with Oriental influences and elaborate plasterwork. This must have been an early example of the style which was to reach its peak at Strawberry Hill in London, but there is no evidence as to whose hand it was or indeed how such a remote area as Cornwall became home to such fashionable design. Access is sadly limited and the smaller drawing room is all but invisible.

The tour continues on to the Map Room with maps of Cornwall from 1612 onwards, along with a rather bizarre model of the Mount carved from champagne corks by one of the butlers. A series of passageways leads to the Museum. In the passageway outside is Thomas Martyn's inch-to-the-mile map of Cornwall, published in 1748 and considered to be among the best of the County. From here, one leaves the castle and the route is retraced back down to the harbour.

Trelissick Garden near Truro

Beach and cliffs at Porthcurno

Falmouth

Fowey

The Isles of Scilly

Introduction

Located some 28 miles from Lands End, the Isles of Scilly are a group of more than 100 islands, only five of which are inhabited. Around 25,000 years ago they were one land mass connected to the mainland, part of the same granite outcrop as Penwith and Bodmin Moor. As the sea levels rose, the higher parts were left as the islands. However, a fall in sea level of 5 fathoms would still see most of the larger islands rejoined and it is estimated that as late as the C11 most would have been connected at low tide. Each of the five inhabited islands has its own character, but they all share the same wonderful scenery, climate and beaches and a distinctly, relaxed pace of life. They are relatively untouched by the trappings of modern commercialism and there is a pleasing air of small, self-reliant communities. Flower growing and tourism are now the main sources of income for the islanders. There are many reasons for visiting – the area's prehistoric remains are significant, the birds, sea life and flowers astonishing in their range and variety and the beaches some of the best anywhere. The clear water and many shipwrecks make the area a major destination for divers.

For those seeking relaxation in beautiful surroundings, the Isles make a wonderful holiday destination. The only drawback is the high cost of getting to the islands and the shortage and cost of accommodation. It is always essential to book travel and accommodation in advance. Due to the accommodation problems, the guide in this instance includes details of campsites as they may be the only cheap, and often the only available, accommodation. Many of the tours and services provided for tourists are carried out by enthusiastic individuals, rather than established companies, which is part of their charm and attraction. However, times, rates and availability can change at short notice and it is advisable to telephone to confirm arrangements in advance.

Getting There

The islands are accessible by both sea and air. Boats leave Penzance, South Pier for

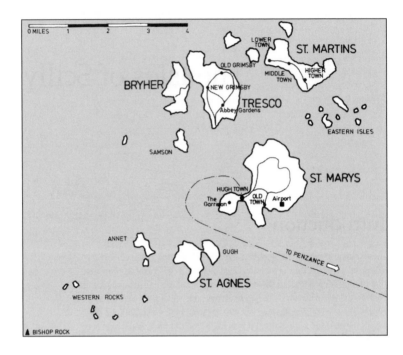

St Mary's every day, except Sunday, between mid April and October. There are no sailings in the winter months when the only access to the islands is by air or by the regular freighter. Departure from Penzance is generally in the early morning (9.15am) and returns from St Mary's in the afternoon (4.30pm). The journey time is 2 hours 40 minutes and fares are £78.00 return, children £39.00. There are also day trip fares which are good value at £32.00 and £16.00 for a child, but would only give you about 4 hours on the islands – hardly enough time to even begin to explore what they have to offer. An alternative day trip is to fly one-way (from Land's End) and use the boat for the return (or arrival). This would give you the best part of the day on the islands and costs £53.50 return, children £29.75. Short breaks allowing 1-3 nights on the island are £60.00, children £30.00. The boat is comfortable and well furnished but can be nauseatingly rocky in anything like rough conditions. Be warned, the nature of the sea in these parts means that it can take several days for a big swell to develop, so there may be no wind and yet the crossing rough and similarly a stiff wind but no swell. Ask the locals what the weather has been like for the previous few days. A recent windy spell virtually guarantees a rough crossing. Bookings and further information are available from *Isles of Scilly Travel* (**0845 710 5555**).

Luggage is carried in containers on deck and needs to be clearly labelled with your final destination. If you want your luggage delivered to your door in St

Mary's, just leave the bags on the dock to be collected by *Island Carriers* who will deliver them to where you are staying. Charges are very reasonable. They also provide a collection service for your return which can be arranged on the island. If you are travelling to the off islands (ie other than St Mary's) you will need to clearly mark your bags and collect them from the quay.

Air services to the islands are operated by the same company with the majority **Air services** of flights from Lands End and Newquay. The journey takes 15 minutes from Land's End and there are frequent flights, Monday to Saturday. During the winter months, flights are restricted to 4 a day. Return fares are £108.00 and there are also day returns for £75.00 and short breaks for £85.00. Children travel at half price. From Newquay, it is approximately 30 minutes flying time. Fares are only slightly more than from Lands End at £125.00, £85.00 day return and £100.00 for short breaks. There are also flights from Exeter (50 minutes, 1–2 a day, £199.00 and Bristol (70 minutes, 1–2 a day, £245.00). There are no flights on Sunday. Winter flights are only from Lands End and Newquay. Standby fares are also available and are considerably cheaper.

The third way to reach the islands is by helicopter and services are run by **Helicopter** British International (**01736 363871**) from Penzance to St Mary's and Tresco. There are frequent flights throughout the day to St Mary's and 3–4 a day to Tresco. In winter, services are less frequent, 2–3 a day to St Mary's and 1–2 to Tresco. Fares are £130.00 return, £89.00 day return, £100.00 short breaks (max. 4 night stay), children under 12 are half price. The heliport in Penzance is located on the eastern edge of the town just behind the seafront road. There is a secure car park where cars can be left for £3.50 per day.

Some History

The Isles of Scilly have a quite distinct history, which is largely due to their remoteness from the main centres of power coupled with their strategic location guarding the western approaches to England. Their role in the history of England has fluctuated from one of major importance during times of crisis and conflict to almost complete insignificance during times of peace and stability.

Once a single land mass, by 3000BC rising sea levels led to the formation of a number of separate islands. The biggest contained all the current main islands apart from St Agnes, which with Annet and the Western Rocks formed separate islands to the west. There is much evidence of pre-historic occupation and a remarkable number of Bronze Age monuments. For example, of the 250 known **Bronze Age** chambered tombs of this period in England and Wales, 50 are in the Scillies. Roman occupation of England left the islands comparatively untouched although **Romans** significant finds at Nornour, in the Eastern Isles, have puzzled historians. It is thought, perhaps, the site was a shrine to a marine goddess and attracted votive offerings from travellers between Gaul and North and West Britain and Ireland. There is no evidence of any Roman occupation of the islands.

Settlement of the islands remained largely undisturbed until the Norman **Normans** Conquest when they became the property of the Crown of England and thereafter the Duchy of Cornwall. From the C12, the administration of Scilly was split, with Tavistock Abbey controlling the north part and the de Wika family of North Cornwall the southern. St Nicholas' Priory on Tresco was the centre of the ecclesiastical administration of the islands although by the C15 it appears to have become a ruin. The Old Town on St Mary's was the centre of secular administration. It had a natural harbour and in 1244 a small castle was erected on a rocky outcrop. In the early C14, Ranulph de Blanchminster was tenant-in-chief and he had to pay a yearly tribute to the King of 300 puffins or 6s 8d. Throughout this time, the strategically-placed, but poorly-defended, islands were attacked by raiders and pirates.

In 1547, the whole of Scilly was acquired by Thomas Seymour, the Lord Admiral. However, within two years he was accused of plotting against the King and using the islands as a base for piracy. His execution led to the long association of the Godolphin family with the Isles. From the mid C16, and the wars with Spain and France, the strategic significance of the Isles became of major importance. Not only did they guard the main sea approaches to England, but their safe anchorage could be used to prepare an invasion force for the mainland, only 28 miles distant. Major fortifications were subsequently built to guard the main approaches, harbours and anchorages.

Civil War   During the Civil War, the islands became a Royalist stronghold. In March 1646, Prince Charles (later Charles II) and most of his council sailed to Scilly where they stayed until mid April before slipping away past a Parliamentary fleet to the safety of Jersey. Scilly, itself, surrendered to the Parliamentarians on 12 September. In September 1648, there was a revolt and the Islands declared once more for the King. Sir John Grenville became Governor and presided over a period of piracy when passing ships were plundered regardless of nationality. In 1651 a Dutch fleet sailed to capture Scilly arriving at the same time as a Parliamentary fleet under Admiral Blake. The Dutch withdrew and Blake subsequently retook the Islands for Parliament. The fortifications were further strengthened to ensure Parliament's hold did not slip again.

Further wars with Spain and France saw the Islands' defences being strengthened, but by 1863 the Garrison defences had been disbanded. However, both World Wars saw many servicemen billeted on the Islands. In the First World War, a naval and seaplane base was established. In the Second World War, Scilly became a centre of activity against German submarines and fighter planes and air sea rescue operations were launched from the Islands. Tresco was also used as a secret base for covert operations into France.

Life on Scilly was often harsh and, in particular, there was much distress during the period after the Napoleonic Wars. Farming and fishing were the mainstay of the economy. In 1834, *Augustus Smith* took over the lease of the Islands and gradually his autocratic but philanthropic rule increased the fortunes of the islanders. He reallocated farmland which had become minute and scattered by sub-division and introduced a system of inheritance by which land only passed to the eldest son, all other offspring being forced to find alternative employment. He financed new industries and built schools on all the main islands, making schooling compulsory some 30 years before the mainland. He was the first to become a resident landlord and built his house on Tresco next to the ruined Abbey. The same family still lease Tresco from the Duchy today.

St Mary's

St Mary's contains the great majority of the island's population, commerce and shops and also most of its tourist accommodation and facilities. The only town of any size is Hugh Town, the de facto capital of the Scillies, and it barely numbers more than a few thousand residents. The rest of the island is very sparsely populated and there are many fine walks to deserted coves and beaches. The island itself is barely one and a half miles by three.

Practicalities

Airport

The airport where both planes and helicopters land is a mile outside Hugh Town and buses meet incoming flights to shuttle passengers and their luggage the short distance into Hugh Town and the quay for onward travel to the off islands. Ferries dock at the quay on the north side of the town and from here leave all the inter-island boats and cruises. The ferries between the islands are extremely well organized and run by the St Mary's Boatmen's Associations. Departures are clearly marked on blackboards on the quay and outside the Isles of Scilly Steamship Company offices in Hugh Town. The first departures from St Mary's to the off islands are generally at 10.00am–10.15am and returns vary depending on the state of the tide. The only uninhabited island where the ferries land regularly is Samson, deserted since 1855. There are some fine beaches, no crowds and no facilities – don't miss the ferry back! There are also a large number of round trips to look at sites of interest including the puffin and seal colonies, the Bishop Rock lighthouse and Western Rocks. On Sundays, there is a Seabird Special cruise which spends two hours visiting many of the rocks and islands where the many seabirds nest and roost. There is a commentary by local wildlife expert, Will Wagstaff. Fares are £5.80 return to the off islands and £7.50–£9.50 for the circular trips. As many of these will drop you off at one of the off islands and the fare will still cover your return to St Mary's, they can be exceptional value. Tickets can be bought from the kiosk on the quay and there is no need to book as there is always enough capacity. If one boat is full, another is simply brought into service.

Ferries

Samson

Getting around St Mary's is no problem. The island is small and flat and lends itself to walking or cycling. A footpath follows the coast and allows for a complete circuit of the island – allow a full day for this with stops for refreshments. A number of footpaths and quiet lanes criss cross the centre of the island providing easy access to all sites of interest. *Buccabu Bike Hire* (**01720 422289**) are located near Porthcressa Beach in Hugh Town and rent bikes for a very reasonable £6 per day, £35 per week.

If you do want to use the island's bus service there are nine buses a day from the park in the centre of Hugh Town which do a circuit of the island. Taxis are also readily available if required. *Heritage Tours* (**01720 422387**) run scenic tours of the island in a 1948 Austin K2 Coach and *Classical Tours* (**01720 422479**) have similar car tours in a 1929 Riley and a 1952 Riley Saloon.

Tourist Information Centre

The Tourist Information Centre (**01720 422536**) is located in the Old Weslyan Chapel in Garrison Lane, Hugh Town. It can provide much useful information, including full accommodation lists which can be invaluable given the shortage of accommodation on the Islands.

Hugh Town

By far the single biggest town on the Islands, Hugh Town is beautifully located on a narrow spur of land with wide sandy beaches to either side. Indeed the neck of land linking the granite islands of the Garrison and St Mary's proper is itself formed by blown sand – a common feature of the Islands. However, it was not the original settlement on the island and its importance only began to grow with the development of the Garrison on the easily defended spur of land to the west.

The Garrison

The Garrison, itself, is of national importance for the range and complexity of its surviving fortifications, providing evidence of military architecture and development since the late C16 to the C20. The site is largely open to the public and there

Star Castle

is no admission charge. The first fortification was Star Castle which still dominates the town and surroundings from its elevated position. It was built by the Godolphins, with the help of the engineer *Robert Adams* in 1593–4. Its name derives from the distinctive eight-sided star plan of the central keep, curtain wall and moat. It is a rare, complete example of an Elizabethan fort built to a common Renaissance plan. The building has served as a fort, governor's residence and prison and is currently in use as a hotel. While access to the hotel is restricted to the public rooms, there is public access to the wall walk from where there are good views over Hugh Town and beyond. The garrison walls along the neck of land linking the promontory to Hugh Town were built soon after the castle as an essential addition to the fortifications. They are constructed of large rubble granite and incorporate the garrison gate which was rebuilt in 1742. The flanking build-

Rocket House

ings, now cottages, were the guardhouse and barracks. The nearby rocket house is an early C17 powder magazine and blast walls with adjoining prison. There is an interesting English Heritage display on the history and development of the Island's fortifications.

The extension of the breastwork and fortifications around the seaward side of the garrison dates largely from the Civil War period in the mid C17, when the site was heavily fortified as a Royalist stronghold, and the C18 when the walls were further extended by the master gunner, *Abraham Tovey*. There are batteries dotted the length of the sea defences and it makes a fine walk around the walls with marvellous views out to sea. Heading south from the rocket house, there are a number of modern houses which do nothing but detract from the historic setting of

Veronica Lodge

the castle. Veronica Lodge, a white painted house of c1790 was built for the Commanding Officer of the garrison, while just to the south is the handsome,

Hugh House

grand classical facade of Hugh House, built in 1792, the original Offiicer's Mess and later in 1835, Augustus Smith's first residence. Slightly further on are *Trinity Cottages* dating from 1858. They were built by Trinity House for lighthouse keepers, and display the clean lines and symmetrical proportions of other Trinity House properties. As you progress around the walls, you will notice many concrete pill boxes and fortifications dating from the two World Wars of this century. Set within the centre of the site are a number of batteries including the well-preserved *Woolpack Battery* which dates from the 1900s. On the northern tip of the site, below the star castle, is *Newman House* (1716–18) an impressive granite house of two storeys with an attic storey and dormers, now a private residence.

Elsewhere, the town is a pleasant collection of houses and commercial properties, many dating from the C17 and with many good C18 and C19 villas. Church Street, in particular, has many fine buildings including a fine Regency town house, *Lemon Hall*, on the north side and a good row of three storey white render Regency houses with attractive fanlights over the front doors, opposite the museum. The **museum** (**01720 422337**) is a bold modern design that sits uneasily with the more vernacular buildings around. It contains many interesting artefacts, including old photographs, salvage and finds from the many wrecks around the Islands, brief records of the history and geology of the Islands as well as their flora and fauna.

Open Easter to October, Mon–Sat, 10am–4.30pm (winter 10am–12 noon). In July and August it is also open in the evenings, 7.30–9.00pm. Admission, £2.00, children £0.50

The nearby *Methodist Church* was designed in 1899 and has remained unaltered with its first floor gallery supported on cast iron columns. At the end of Church Street, the *Church of St Mary the Virgin* was built between 1836–8 but has little architectural interest. The adjacent *Chaplaincy* is an elegant two storey house of around 1830. The Parade contains a number of fine C18 and C19 houses around the small park making a pleasant ensemble. The *Roman Catholic Church* on Lower Strand was designed in 1860 as a girl's school which explains its unusual ecclesiastical design. The *Bishop and Wolf Public House* in Silver Street is one of the earliest surviving houses on Scilly dating from around 1700 and originally built for *Thomas Ekins*, first land agent for the Godolphin Estate who was resident on the islands from 1683. The front has been badly altered by the addition of a full length bay window and other internal alterations have detracted from its character. The post office in Hugh Street (1897) is an unusual design with massive granite boulder surrounds and dressings to the front elevation. The roof has two big projecting gables with cantilevered granite brackets and scissor trusses. The *Waterloo Book Shop* behind the post office sells second hand books and prints, many with a Scilly connection. Nearby, the *Atlantic Inn* dates from the late C18 and C19 and is a typical vernacular design with coursed granite walls, slate roof and small, sash windows. The Town Hall in The Parade was built in 1889 and is a solid granite edifice in the classical style – it serves a multi-functional purpose as public hall, theatre, local authority offices, council chamber and magistrate's court.

The two beaches on either side of the town have quite different characters. The Town Beach on the north side overlooks the harbour and is more of a working beach with many boats pulled up on the sand and buildings backing onto the sands. Porthcressa Beach on the south side is a wide sweep of sand with good, safe bathing. The buildings here are set a bit further back from the beach and this

Town Beach

Porthcressa Beach

is by far the best of the two for bathing.

Apart from the beaches and wandering around the town itself, there is little else to see in Hugh Town which is, of course, its attraction. The shops provide all the basic necessities. The Co-op supermarket opens seven days a week and stays open to 10.00pm. Throughout the summer, there are many events put on by the active community including regular slide shows, concerts and amateur theatre. Details are available from the Tourist Information Centre. On Wednesdays and Fridays in the summer, there are gig races, the traditional sport of the Scillies. The gigs are long oared rowing boats, sleek and fast, which were used to take the pilots out to the waiting ships. The first one there got the job, hence the legacy of gig racing. Boats leave from the quay to follow the races and normally end up in a pub on one of the off islands before returning to St Mary's – well worth doing.

Gig races

Diving

The clear waters and large number of wrecks around the Islands combine to make this one of the best places for diving in Britain. There are a number of operations that provide equipment hire, tuition and underwater safaris including *Mark Groves* (**01720 422732**) and *Jim Heslin* (**01720 422595**) on St Mary's. *The Isles of Scilly Wildlife Trust* (**01720 422153**) provide guided snorkelling trips to look at the rich marine life of the area. Trips are undertaken between May and September, weather permitting. *Scilly Walks* (**01720 423326**) lead walks on Tuesdays and Thursdays to look at the archaeological and historic heritage of St Mary's. They start from opposite the Catholic Church on The Strand at 10.00am and there is no need to pre-book. Adults £3.50, children £2.00, under 10 free. Duration around 2–3 hours. *Will Wagstaff* (**01720 422212**) leads wildlife tours around the Islands visiting all the inhabited islands as well as some of the uninhabited ones. The itinerary varies week by week and is posted on the board by the quay. Tours start at 9.45am and start either from the quay or the Town Hall. Pre-booking is not required. Charges are £4 for a morning and £3 for an afternoon tour. For tours to the off islands, the ferry fare must be added to the cost. Sailing and windurfing is available at Porthmellon Beach (**01720 422060**).

Walking

Sailing & Windsurfing

Outside Hugh Town

The rest of the island is devoid of towns with just two small settlements at Old Town and Porthloo and a scattering of isolated buildings. One of the best ways to see the island is to walk the well-maintained path that goes all the way around the coast. From Porthcressa Beach, it is an easy 45 minute walk around Penninis Head to Old Town (by following the road it is a 15 minute walk from the church in Hugh Town). There are a series of spectacular rock formations near the lighthouse and this makes a wonderful spot for a picnic. The unusual steel lighthouse was built in 1911 and replaced the light on St Agnes.

Old Town

Old Town was the site of the original settlement on St Mary's – remains of the harbour can still be seen at low tide. The castle here was first mentioned in 1244 but it has been largely demolished and its stone used for building Star Castle in 1593. *Old Town Church* dates from the C12, a north and south aisle were added in the C17. However, the church was rebuilt in the 1830s and restored in 1890. All that remains of the medieval church is a nave and vestry. The round-headed arch to the vestry is part of the original Norman church. There is some good C19 glass over the altar. The large graveyard is surrounded by a wall of massive, lichen encrusted boulders. The big obelisk at the top is in memory of *Louise Holzmaister*, one of 328 passengers lost on the wreck of the *SS Schiller* in 1875. There are a number of other victims of the same disaster buried in the churchyard along with a memorial to Augustus Smith. In the extension to the churchyard, is the unpretentious grave of *Sir Harold Wilson*, the Labour Prime Minister between 1960–70 and 1974–76 who lived on the Isles of Scilly.

The beach is a nice, sweep of clean white sand although the foreshore can be rocky. There are plenty of good rock pools at low tide. There is a small community of houses with one guest house, two cafes and a public house (see listings). The *Old Town Gallery* (**01720 423358**) is off the main road, near the pub and clearly signposted. It has a good selection of pastels, etchings and pictures in its studio gallery. It is open Monady to Friday, 10am–5pm.

Continuing along the coast path, you skirt the end of the airport runway before reaching Porth Hellick, a lovely crescent of sand. There are few people and no facilities. Either side of the bay are giant rock stone outcrops like Easter Island statues staring out to sea. At the top of the beach is a simple stone memorial to *Sir Cloudesley Shovel* marking the spot where his body was temporarily buried after being washed ashore, before being reinterred in Westminster Abbey. In October 1707, an English squadron of 21 ships, sailing home from Toulon in thick fog and gathering darkness struck the rocks west of the Isles of Scilly. Two thousand men died including Admiral Shovel in one of the worst disasters of the Royal Navy. The disaster motivated the Admiralty to offer the famous prize for a device that could accurately determine a ship's longitudinal position, leading to the creation of the Harrison clocks, the first accurate sea-going chronometers that are now housed in the Greenwich Observatory in London. On Porth Hellick Down, just to the north, is a group of seven entrance graves and two cairns. The most impressive entrance grave is slightly apart from the main group. It has been heavily restored but nevertheless gives a good impression of how such tombs would have looked.

Porth Hellick

Porth Hellick Down

Pelistry Bay is one of the finest beaches on the island, a large, white sand beach with safe bathing at low tide. There are no buildings by the beach and no facilities. At high tide, bathing can be dangerous and great care should be taken. If you have a vehicle or cycle, it is accessible from Pelistry Lane to the west. Bar Point on the northern tip of the island has two nice sand beaches on either side which face across the water to St Martins and the Eastern Isles. Just inland are the prehistoric *Innisidgen Entrance Graves*, one of which is in particularly good condition.

Pelistry Bay

Bar Point

As the path continues south, a large clearing opens up on the slopes above, the site of the *Hallangy Down Settlement* – the remains of an Iron Age and Romano-British community. There is a complex of stone built houses with clear evidence of drains, hearths, stores and partitions. The settlement was probably occupied for up to 500 years from 200BC onwards. A few hundred yards up the hill is *Bant's Carn Entrance Grave*, the most famous of all the Scillonian entrance graves and a very fine example. It dates from around 1300BC, some 1100 years before the nearby settlement was established. There are fabulous views across to Tresco and the other islands from here and the site makes a good spot for a picnic. There is a nice, secluded sandy cove below the site as well. The site can be easily approached from the main road around the island, from where it is signposted down a footpath from near the telegraph tower. The tower was erected in 1805 on the highest point of the Islands as a gun and semaphore tower and later adapted as a signal station. It was here, in 1898, that *Marconi* first heard wireless signals transmitted from Porthcurno on the mainland.

Porthloo   Porthloo has a pleasant, sandy beach but the road and a rather scruffy car park and yard immediately behind detract somewhat from its setting. Porthmellon Beach is nicer with fine sand, sailboats and *The Isles of Scilly Windsurf and Sailing Centre* (**01720 422060/423399**) which hires sailboards, kayaks and dinghies. Tuition is also available. Just above the beach are *Harry's Walls*, one of the earliest fortifications on the island. They were begun in 1551 but only the south-west side was ever completed. The focus of the defences was soon moved to the Garrison and this area abandoned. The site is in the care of English Heritage and admission is free. Beyond Porthmellon, one returns to Hugh Town via the school and church.

While most of the interest for the visitor is concentrated around the coast, the interior of the island still warrants a visit, if only to gain a different perspec-

Lower Moors   tive on the island. Just to the east of Hugh Town is an area known as the Lower Moors, rich in wildlife with heron, moorhen, mallard and greenshanks particularly prevalent on the low lying marsh. There is a well laid out nature trail which includes bird hides. A footpath between Porthloo and Old Town travers-

Carreg Dhu   es the Lower Moor as well. Continuing along Telegraph Road brings you to the
Garden   Carreg Dhu Garden virtually in the centre of the island. It is a community garden created and run by local volunteers and planted with many sub-tropical species that thrive in the sheltered location. There are plenty of benches and

Open   grassy areas for picnics and entrance is free. Nearby is the *Longstone Heritage*
May–Oct,   *Centre* (**01720 423770**) which has old photographs of the Scillies and ship-
Mon–Sat,   wreck and other local artefacts. There is also a licensed cafe, one of the few
9.30am–   places to eat or drink in the centre of the island. The rest of the interior is a
5.30pm.   mixture of moorland and farmland with relatively few buildings and no settle-
Admission   ments.
free

Accommodation

The price coding system that is used throughout this guide is on a scale of A to E and indicates the cost of the lowest priced double room in that establishment during the peak summer period. This is clearly marked by the telephone number of the listing for each establishment. It should be borne in mind that single rooms are likely to be considerably more than half the price of a double. In the off peak months, many establishments reduce their rates considerably and even where they do not you may be able to negotiate a discount.

A –£44
B £45–£64
C £65–£80
D £81–£100
E £100+

Accommodation on all the islands is strictly limited and advance booking is essential. The more popular accommodation can be fully booked up to six months in advance in the high season. Much of the accommodation is in rented properties and the Tourist Information Centre can provide a list. *Island Properties* (**01720 422082**) also have a large number of properties to rent. Prices vary widely with the property and location but rates are considerably more than for comparable properties on the mainland. The island's only campsite is on the *Garrison* (**01720 422670**) and may well be the only budget accommodation available. Hugh Town has by far the great majority of hotels and guest houses on the island. There is a particular concentration in the roads to the east of the town centre. Many people use St Mary's as a base for exploring the other islands and in that case Hugh Town is the logical place to stay, as it is the hub of all inter-island communication. It should be noted that many hotels and guest houses shut for the winter period and many will also only let rooms on a half board basis. All those listed below provide bed and breakfast terms unless stated otherwise.

Veronica Lodge, Garrison (**01720 422585**) *B*, a historic building with marvellous views over Hugh Town and a large garden in a quiet location. One of the best value places in town. Closed January and December.

Scillonia, The Bank (**01720 422101**) *B*, excellent location near the quay and town centre. Open May to October and good value. In peak season the minimum let is four days.

Evergreen Cottage, The Parade (**01720 422711**) *B*, central location, 300 year old traditional cottage with five rooms all en-suite. Open all year.

Lynwood, Church Street (**01720 423313**) *B*, located in a handsome Regency house. Three en-suite rooms. Open all year.

Westford House, Church Street (**01720 422510**) *B*, next door to the above. Five rooms, all en-suite. Closed November to March.

Crebinick House, Church Street (**01720 422968**) *C*, located in a nice, granite cottage. Six rooms, all en-suite. Closed November to March.

Tolman House, Old Town (**01720 422967**) *B*, a big granite house overlooking the bay, a short distance outside Hugh Town.

Old Town Inn, Old Town (**01720 422301**) *B*, three newly converted en-suite bedrooms in this nice pub, a short distance outside Hugh Town.

Atlantic Hotel, Hugh Street (**01720 422417**) *E*, a hotel since the 1860s, one of the oldest on the island. It is a nice granite building with good views over the harbour from some rooms. The restaurant and terrace have particularly fine views. Closed December and January.

Bell Rock Hotel, Church Street (**01720 422575**) *E*, a rather overpriced establishment but with the benefit of an indoor swimming pool. Closed December and January. B&B rates are available at an unattractive discount of £6 per night.

Tregarthens Hotel, Garrison Hill (**01720 422540**) *E*, located right next to the quay with views over the harbour. One of the most expensive hotels on the island but it is difficult to see why – the public rooms are poorly furnished and lacking in character. Closed November to February.

Star Castle Hotel, The Garrison (**01720 422317**) *E*, if you are going to pay the sort of prices demanded by the above hotels you might as well pay a bit more and stay in the most, atmospheric hotel in town. There are eight bedrooms in the castle itself with the majority of the rooms in a discretely located annexe nearby. There are four acres of grounds, tennis court and an indoor swimming pool. Closed November to February. The rooms in the castle are slightly more expensive than the annexe but probably worth the extra.

Restaurants and cafes

Inexpensive *under £15*	The prices quoted in the guide are inevitably just an indication of costs
Moderate *£16 – £25*	and represent the price for a meal of two courses with a drink. In the
Expensive *over £25*	listings, they are indicated by the letter I, M or E, immediately after
	the telephone number of the establishment.

While there are not a huge number of restaurants on St Mary's, with many visitors self-catering or staying on a half board basis, the quality is high with most offering a menu featuring fresh fish and seafood. In contrast, the pub food is well below normal Cornwall standards, with the notable exception of the Lock, Stock and Barrel in Old Town.

The Galley (**01720 422602**) *M*, near the Town Hall in the centre of town. Probably the best place for fish on St Mary's, this small, unpretentious restaurant serves wonderful fresh fish and seafood dishes at very reasonable prices. Advance booking essential. The fish and chip take-away downstairs is also meant to be good.

Chez Michel (**01720 422871**) *M*, opposite the above. A small, comfortable restaurant with adventurous cooking by the Swiss chef. Booking recommended. Also open for morning coffee and inexpensive lunches.

Pilots Gig Restaurant (**01720 422654**) *M*, near the quay. Fresh fish and grilled meat dishes. At 6.00pm they serve very good value "early evening specials."

Atlantic Hotel (**01720 422417**) *M*, waterfront location with views over the harbour. There is a large open terrace for warm evenings. Also open for breakfast, coffee and lunches. Not to be confused with the adjacent pub which serves basic bar food.

Juliet's Garden, Porthloo (**01720 422228**) *M*, on a warm summer's evening this is the only place to be. Located just north of Porthloo Beach, about 15 minutes walk from Hugh Town, this early C19 farm has been skilfully converted to a rustic restaurant with exposed timber roof trusses. There is also a large terrace with tables overlooking the bay from which to watch the setting sun. The menu is adventurous and has a good number of vegetarian dishes. Closed Monday.

Old Town Inn, Old Town (**01720 422301**) *I*, about 15 minutes walk from Hugh Town. Excellent pub with good food in the bar or the restaurant.

Star Castle Hotel (**01720 422317**) **E**, for an upmarket meal in authentic historic surroundings you cannot beat the Star Castle, where you can dine in the officer's messroom with its beamed ceiling and magnificent granite fireplace. The food has a high reputation and is good value for the four course menu.

Bars and nightlife   ☿

While St Mary's can hardly be described as having a vibrant nightlife, there is nevertheless a good choice of evening entertainment. There are a number of attractive pubs and a social scene which includes regular slide shows, concerts, theatre and the weekly gig races. What these may lack in sophistication, they gain by being informal, welcoming and unpretentious. It is a rare chance to feel part of this essentially remote community.

Atlantic Inn, beautiful, old granite inn in the centre of town with a small terrace overlooking the harbour. Real ale, but the food is poor.

The Mermaid, right by the quay. Busy pub with one large bar, rather lacking in character.

Bishop and Wolf, located in one of the oldest buildings on the island but the interior has been altered to lose most of its historic character. Nevertheless a friendly atmosphere with occasional live music makes for a pleasant evening.

Porthcressa Inn, right on Porthcressa Beach, this modern inn has a long, narrow terrace overlooking the sands but no character.

Old Town Inn, Old Town. A recently renovated farm building, this is one of the best pubs on the island. They serve real ale, the food is good and inexpensive and there is a regular programme of live music. It is around a 15 minute walk from Hugh Town but worth the effort.

Tresco

The largest of the off islands and the most visited after St Mary's. Many day trippers use the helicopter service from Penzance to come and visit the Abbey Gardens – one of the few set piece attractions on the Islands. Tresco is leased from the Duchy by the Dorien-Smith family and, while it would be wrong to suggest it is run as a private fiefdom, it does have a manicured and exclusive air which gives it a decidedly different character to the other islands. The south of the island, in particular, is plagued by a network of overly-maintained footpaths and large numbers of visitors who come to visit the gardens. The regular helicopter service can also be intrusive at times. The north, in contrast, is wilder, less visited and the nicer for it. The beaches, however, are uniformly excellent and some of the best on the Islands.

Boats

Boats arrive at one of three quays depending on the state of the tide, New Grimsby or Old Grimsby in the centre of the island or Carn Near in the south. The

Heliport

heliport is just north of Carn Near beside the Abbey Gardens. If you are staying on the island arrangements can be made to have luggage transported to your accom-

Bike Hire

modation. The island is easily small enough to walk everywhere, but bike hire is available from the Estate Office if required.

By the quay at Carn Near is a rock outcrop, once used as a Parliamentary gun position during the Civil War, and known as Oliver's Battery. There is nothing to see now but it provides a good viewpoint over the southern part of the island.

Appletree Bay

Appletree Bay, to the east, is a wide sweep of fine sand backed by grassy dunes and one of the best beaches on the island. At low tide, it may be possible to see the remains of a prehistoric field system indicated by lengths of boulder wall. They were covered as the sea levels rose to isolate the granite heights that now form the islands.

Open daily 10am– 4pm. Admission £8.50, chil– dren free

The **Abbey Gardens** are the major attraction on Tresco and many visitors come just to see them. There is a cafe and small shop. The gardens were established in the early C19 by Augustus Smith who chose the island as his home. Today, they constitute one of the best sub-tropical gardens in the south-west with formal plant-ing around a series of paths on different levels. The remains of *Tresco Priory*, dat-ing from around 1300 are incorporated into part of the gardens. The priory was disused by the C15 due to the continual threat from pirates. In one corner of the gardens is *Valhalla*, an open air museum of figureheads from shipwrecks around the Islands. It is now owned and run by the National Maritime Museum. Most date from the second half of the C19 and form an interesting collection. Unfortunately, a lot of the figureheads were over-restored in the 1960s and have lost some of their antique character. The island's heliport is immediately next to the gardens and the peace and quiet one would normally associate with an island garden of this sort can be rudely shattered by the arrival and departure of the helicopters. Next to the

Tresco Abbey

gardens is Tresco Abbey, designed by Augustus Smith for his own home. It was habitable by 1838 and was twice further extended before the end of the C19. The gatehouse is in a particularly distinctive Gothic Revival style building. The house is not open to the public.

To the east of the gardens is the huge, white sand beach of *Pentle Bay* with fine views across to St Martins and the Eastern Isles. To the north is *Rushy Bay*, another beautiful boulder-strewn beach. The blockhouse on the northern end of the beach is one of the many fortifications that have been built upon Tresco over the years. Constructed in 1554, it is still substantially intact and provides magnificent views.

Old Grimsby

Old Grimsby, just to the north, is a not particularly attractive settlement of holiday cottages and the island's only hotel. There is a small sandy beach. A short walk across the island to the west brings you to New Grimsby and most of the facilities. The church dates from the late C19 and was designed by one of the Dorien-Smiths. It is an undistinguished design but the stained glass windows are by the noted Victorian artist C.E.Kempe. There is also a post ofice and stores and the quay shop. *Gallery Tresco* (**01720 424925**) has a good range of ceramics and paintings and regularly holds exhibitions and one man shows. The **New Inn** is a nice pub with a large sun terrace to the front. They serve real ales, coffee, cream teas and bar meals at lunchtime. There is also a seperate restaurant which serves highly regarded food. Expensive. There is a sheltered, sandy beach which makes a good place to wait for the ferry at the nearby quay.

The northern part of the island has a very different character with more rugged, windswept moorland and a less manicured appearance. The area shows signs of continuous occupation since prehistoric times with a large number of cairns and fragments of prehistoric field systems. On the higher ground is King Charles' Castle, built in 1550–54 as an artillery fort overlooking the narrow channel to Bryher. However, it turned out to be badly sited as its guns could not depress enough to fire down into the Channel. It was soon abandoned and much of its stone re-used to build Cromwell's Castle, lower down and nearer the shore. This dates from 1651–2 and forms part of the Parliamentary fortification of the islands. It is still substantially complete. There is a gun platform and small guardroom at ground level but the rest of the structure is a large stone tower some 60 feet high with another gun platform for six cannon. Within the tower itself were the garrison's living quarters. Immediately below the tower, *Castle Porth* is a beautiful, small sandy cove but with difficult access. On the coast path back to New Grimsby, you will come across a small plaque on a rocky outcrop. It commemorates the fact that this area was a secret naval base between April 1942 and October 1943 when British vessels, disguised as French fishing boats, sailed to Brittany to make contact with the French Resistance.

**King Charles'
Castle**

**Cromwell's
Castle**

Options for staying on Tresco are strictly limited and expensive. The exclusive **Island Hotel** (**01720 422883**) *E* is located by the sea in Old Grimsby. It is pleasant enough but spectacularly overpriced. The only other place to stay is the **New Inn** (**01720 422844**) *E*, which is cheaper, but still expensive. There is no campsite, of course, and the only other option is to hire a cottage from the **Estate Office** (**01720 422849**) but expect to pay premium prices. Far better to stay on one of the other islands and visit Tresco on a day trip.

Bryher

Bryher, the smallest of the inhabited islands with less than a hundred residents is located directly opposite Tresco and separated by a narrow channel which can be walked across at low tide. Regular ferries connect Bryher to Tresco, St Mary's and the other inhabited island. For further details telephone **01720 422886**. The island is small enough to walk everywhere and there is only a short length of road anyway. It is one of the most peaceful and relaxing of the islands with a pleasing mixture of moorland and beaches.

Visitors are dropped off on one of the two quays on the sheltered east side of the island. There is a scattering of buildings and what passes for the centre of the tiny community. The *Church of All Saints* was built in 1742 and extended in the C19. It is of little architectural interest but has a pleasant setting by the shore. The strip north of here contains most of the few places to stay and eat, as well as the shop and post office. The island is pleasantly rugged with the west coast being exposed to the full force of the Atlantic gales while the east coast is more sheltered and overlooks the narrow channel to Tresco. In Spring, there is a profusion of wild flowers, while in the Autumn, gales can lash the west coast and the island becomes a resting place for many migratory birds

Shipman Head Down

Shipman Head Down occupies the north of the island and is an area of low moorland with no buildings or roads. Several footpaths cross the Down and it is no more than a 10 minute walk from the post office to the point overlooking Shipman Head where the remains of an Iron Age cliff castle can be clearly seen. The promontory here is called *Badplace Hill* while the rugged bay to the west revels in the

Hell Bay

name of Hell Bay. Come here during a storm and you will understand why, as huge waves roll in from the Atlantic to break upon the rocky shore. In calm weather, it is utterly peaceful with the sound of birds probably the loudest sound to be heard.

Gweal Hill

Further south, towards the centre of the island, is the low Gweal Hill with the island of Gweal, just offshore. There is a sheltered bay with a sandy beach on the north side of the hill. There is a scattering of buildings here with the islands only hotel and the *Golden Eagle Studio* (**01720 422671**). It was originally a gig shed built for the pilots of Bryher from money donated from the USA in thanks for saving the crew of the *Award* wrecked on Gweal Island. The money was paid in US gold dollar pieces with the American eagle on the back of the coin – hence the name. It is now the studio and gallery of the talented painter Richard Pearce who was born on the islands and paints local scenes in his own distinctive style. Prices are very reasonable and he is always happy to discuss his work with visitors.

Droppy Nose Point

A path continues south from here towards the wonderfully-named Droppy Nose Point. Just to the east of here on the southern tip of the island is *Rushy Bay*, a lovely sandy bay and the best beach on the island. The water is shallow and at low tide there are good rock pools full of sealife. The area of low moor just inland of here is known as *Samson Hill* and is littered with rock cairns and strangely shaped granite outcrops.

If you want to stay on Bryher, and it is a supremely relaxing place to spend a few days, there are a number of good value options. On the east side of the island near the quay is **Soleil d'Or** (**01720 422003**) **B**, with views across the water to Tresco. A short walk away, on the other side of the island, is **Bank Cottage** (**01720 422612**) **E** with views out over the offshore rocks. Rooms are only available with evening meal and are expensive. The island's only hotel is the pleasant **Hell Bay Hotel** (**01720 422947**) **E**, situated by Gweal Hill on the west side of the island. It consists of a series of low buildings around a central garden courtyard and is discretely and sensitively located. There is a nice lounge and bar and the restaurant has a good reputation. All rooms have a private sitting room and en-suite facilities. There are good value Autumn short-breaks for 3 or 4 nights. There are also a number of self-catering cottages and chalets for hire and details are available from *Bryher Holiday Information* (**01720 422003**). There is a campsite at *Jenford Farm* (**01720 422886**).

Given the size of the island, it is surprising that there are several places to eat. The **Vine Farm Cafe** (**01720 423168**) is little more than a converted greenhouse – they serve breakfasts, lunch and teas. They also serve evening meals but it is necessary to book before 4.00pm. The **Fraggle Rock Cafe** (**01720 422222**) is licensed, has an upstairs restaurant and a large outdoor terrace overlooking

Tresco. They are open from breakfast through to evening meals. The **Hell Bay Hotel** has a very pleasant dining room and a good reputation for food. Expensive. Sail boats can be hired and tuition arranged with *Blue Boats Sailing and Boat Hire* (**01720 423095**).

St Martin's

Located some two miles east of Tresco, St Martin's has a distinct community with three small settlements at Higher Town, Middle Town and Lower Town. The island is a mix of tiny cultivated fields enclosed by high windbreaks and windswept downland covered with thick bracken. It has some of the biggest and best beaches on the islands and this is one of its major attractions. Ferries land at New Quay on the south of the island, although some also stop at the Hotel Quay at the western end. *St Martin's Boat Services* (**01720 422814**) also provide trips to the other islands and tours. **New Quay**

Directly on leaving the ferry, you come across the magnificent Par Beach, one of the best on the island. There is no development nearby and it is backed by sand dunes. There are public toilets by the quay. Just behind the beach is the all weather cricket pitch and a tennis court that is available for hire. A path leads along the back of the beach towards Chapel Down, an exposed area of high ground thick with bracken and heather. A prehistoric field system covers much of the Down along with stone cairns and the remains of entrance graves. The dominating presence though is the red and white striped Daymark at the northern end of the Down. It was erected in 1683 by *Thomas Ekins*, first steward of the Godolphin family and is the earliest surviving dated example of a beacon in the British Isles. Adjacent are the barely visible remains of the small C8-C10 chapel that give the Down its name. The nearby remains of the signal station date from the Napoleonic Wars and was used to send orders to naval warships offshore. There are good views and the nearby cliffs are home to many seabirds. It is an easy 20 minute walk from the quay. **Par Beach** **Chapel Down**

To the west of the Daymark is a sandy and very secluded cove. Further to the west, the magnificent sweep of Great Bay is one of the best beaches on the islands. There is crystal clear water and good bathing with absolutely no buildings or development to intrude on the unspoilt setting. White Island can be reached on foot for two hours either side of low tide, but it is otherwise cut off by strong currents and swimming should not be attempted. At the western end of the island, there are good views to the lighthouse on Round Island and the nearby uninhabited islands of Tean and St Helen's. The lighthouse was built in 1887 and although only 46 feet high, it is built in an elevated position 180 feet above sea level. The light is still operational but was not enough to stop the huge oil tanker *Torrey Canyon* hitting the Seven Stones Reef in 1967, one of the world's worst oil spills. This end of the island is dominated to some extent by the new hotel, built in 1989 and one of the newest buildings on the Isles of Scilly. Its construction was highly controversial and one has to question whether this is the direction that tourism in the Scillies should take. It is notable that the islands only street lamp is directly outside this hotel. **Great Bay** **White Island** **Round Island**

Lower Town   Lower Town consists of no more than a few farms, a shop and the only pub on
the island. From the hotel to Yellow Rock, below Middle Town, is a nice sandy
Middle Town   beach. Low tide reveals a huge area of sand, perfect for ball games. Middle Town
is no more than a string of granite buildings along the island's only road. The
Middle Town Gallery (**01720 422521**) has a small range of pictures and prints,
as well as paper hand-made from the plants and flowers of the islands. Higher
Town, further along near the quay is the centre of the island's tiny community
with the church, Methodist chapel, shops and post office and the bulk of the
island's accommodation. The *North Farm Gallery* (**01720 423028**) is artist Sue
Lewington's own gallery and workshop. She produces watercolours in her own
distinctive style and has published a number of books with illustrations of
Cornwall and the Scilly Islands. Sketching and painting classes are also run using
the gallery as a base.

Accommodation on the island is limited to two guest houses, the hotel, a campsite and a number of self-catering cottages. Details on cottages to hire is available
from the Tourist Information Centre on St Mary's. The campsite is well-sheltered
by high windbreaks and is located just back from the big sand beach below
Middletown (**01720 422888**). **Polreath** (**01720 422046**) *D*, near the Methodist
chapel and **Ashvale** (**01720 422544**) *C*. near the pub in Lower Town, are the
guest house options. The **Island Hotel** (**01720 422090**) *E* is very expensive and
not particularly attractive. There is an indoor swimming pool and games room.

Underneath the Polreath guest house is a cafe that serves lunches and snacks
and opens as a restaurant in the evenings. There are several tables on the sunny
terrace. Moderate. The bakery at Higher Town also serves filled rolls and pizzas.
There is also a wholefood cafe at *Little Arthur Farm* in the valley to the east of
Higher Town. The **Seven Stones** public house at Lower Town is a modern stone
building with superb views over the other islands from its terrace. They serve real
ales and good bar food. Inexpensive. The restaurant at the hotel has a high reputation and there are wonderful views over the offshore islands. Expensive. They also
serve inexpensive bar food and lunches which can be taken on the large sun terrace outside.

At Higher Town, there is a diving school (**01720 422848**). There are regular
guided walks to look at the birds on the island and these are posted on notice
boards around the island.

St Agnes

The most south westerly of the islands, St Agnes is a small flower-growing community that has retained its tranquility, largely untouched by the commercialization of
the C20. It is no more than a scattering of granite buildings and tiny cultivated
fields. There is no village as such, though there is a concentration of facilities
towards the quay. There is only a very limited stretch of single track road and very
few vehicles to disturb the peace. In the Spring, the island is awash with flowers
while in Autumn many migrant birds visit the island. At all times of the year the

lack of light pollution makes it one of the best places to see the night sky. Ferries land at the quay on the north east side of the island. The island has its own boat service (**01720 422704**) as well as the regular ferries to St Mary's.

The northern part of the island is where all the island's properties and scattered farmsteads are located, the southern half being windswept moorland. The lighthouse dominates the island with its stumpy but solid 60 foot high whitewashed granite walls. It is one of the earliest in the country and was erected for Trinity House in 1680. The cupola on top was added in 1806. The first floor is distinguished by four gun ports and is testament to the dual role that many early lighthouses played. It is now in private ownership and not open to the public. Periglis Beach is found down the road beside the lighthouse and is a sandy cove with a rocky foreshore. The nearby church was built in 1821 but is of little interest architecturally. From here, there are good views over the Western Rocks and the *Bishop Rock lighthouse* beyond. It was built between 1852 and 1858 and is the tallest lighthouse in the British Isles. Annet Island, just offshore, is a bird sanctuary and one of the best places to see puffins. There are regular boat trips to both Annet and the Bishop Rock.

Periglis Beach

From beside the church, a footpath leads around the coastline to the Troy Town Maze, a circular maze of rounded beach stones forming a complex pattern known as the Game of Troy. It is reputed to have been laid out in 1729 by the bored son of a local lighthouse keeper but may well have earlier origins. It is unique in Britain but similar to the stone mazes of Scandinavia. It was rather unsympathetically rebuilt in 1988. Further along the path, past St Warna's Cove is the tiny St Warna's Well, a holy well allegedly capable of attracting shipwrecks. It may well be medieval but has probably been substantially restored since 1890.

Troy Town Maze

South of here is Wingletang Down, an area of low moorland covered with gorse and heather and surrounded by the sea on three sides. There are many pre-historic cairns and large, naturally moulded granite outcrops. At the southern end are the two small, sandy coves of *Porth Askin* and *Beady Pool*, the latter named after a C17 shipwreck which still occasionally reveals beads buried in the sand.

Wingletang Down

The best beach on the island is the narrow neck of fine white sand between St Agnes and Gugh. There are beautiful sheltered bays on either side and crystal clear water. Gugh is accessible on foot at low tide and has a number of pre-historic remains, including the *Old Man of Gugh*, an upright stone some 2.4 metres high and a prominent feature on the skyline. The two houses with their distinctive wave-shaped roofs date from 1920. The roofs are made of concrete and their distinctive shape was meant to resist "lifting" during severe gales.

Gugh

There is a good range of reasonably-priced accommodation on St Agnes, with perhaps the best option being **Coastguards** (**01720 422373**) *C* which has beautifully furnished, en-suite accommodation in two of the three coastguard houses. It is located in the centre of the island near the lighthouse. Accommodation is on a half board basis only. **Downs Cottage** (**01720 422777**) *B* nearby is another attractively furnished traditional granite house. **The Parsonage** (**01720 422370**) *B* is located on the road down the side of the lighthouse and is a big, early C19 house in large gardens. **Covean Cottage**

(**01720 422620**) *B* is located close to the sand bar to Gugh and provides comfortable accommodation. There is also a separate cottage which affords greater privacy. The **Turks Head** (**01720 422434**) *C* near the quay has one twin room on a bed and breakfast basis. There are a number of cottages available to hire on a self-catering basis and a list is available from the Tourist Information Centre on St Mary's. The campsite (**01720 422360**) is on the western side of the island and has superb views over the western rocks with frequently spectacular sunsets. The site is exposed to westerly gales though and tents need to be of sturdy construction.

The **Covean Tea Garden** (**01720 422620**) *I* provides snacks, lunches, cream teas and dinner. It is necessary to book before 5.00pm for dinner. The **Turks Head** is one of the finest pubs on the islands and is a beautiful old granite inn with slate floors, exposed beams and small, interconnecting rooms. There is a wealth of naval memorabilia on the walls and ceiling and an outside terrace with an incomparable view over the sheltered cove to Gugh. They serve real ales and good bar food, lunchtimes and evenings as well as coffee and cream teas.

The Lizard
and the Helford River

Introduction

Almost surrounded by water, the sparsely-populated Lizard has its own distinct character. Its geology is also unusual, for it is believed to be an ophiolite, a piece of the ocean floor that has been thrust up by enormous forces to its present level. The serpentine rock which constitutes most of the southern part of the peninsula is considered to be a slightly altered slab of the earth's mantle. It weathers very slowly and is covered with a layer of clay which is barren and almost impermeable to water. The result is an extraordinarily flat and stable surface but one which is rarely suitable for cultivation. As such, the landscape of the Goonhilly Downs is unique in Cornwall. Where it meets the sea, it forms the sheer cliffs of Mount's Bay and provides some of the finest coastal cliff walking in the country. The Lizard also boasts some excellent beaches with Kynance Cove being considered by many the most beautiful in Cornwall.

Goonhilly Downs

Kynance Cove

Lizard Point, itself, is the southernmost point of mainland England and is a wonderful place, unspoilt and with marvellous views. It is something of a turning point for the Cornish landscape, to the west, wild and rugged while to the east it is lower, more rounded and sheltered from the worst of the south-westerly storms. The Helford River defines the northern edge of the Lizard and could not be more different from the wild, gale-lashed west coast. It is a wonderfully evocative landscape of tidal creeks and estuary views with some of Cornwall's rare woodland lining its banks. The south bank is relatively isolated with few settlements of any size, very narrow lanes and little public transport. The north bank on the other hand is more cosmopolitan, with its proximity to Truro and Falmouth, and has a number of important country houses and the famous sub-tropical gardens at Glendurgan, Trebah and Penjerrick.

Lizard Point

Helford River

Helston is the only town of any size and is a fine country town with many good historic buildings and a welcoming atmosphere. Nearby Porthleven has an impressive harbour and a number of highly-rated restaurants. Mullion, Cagdwith, Coverack and St Keverne are interesting villages with good accommodation and nice places to eat and drink. The Lizard is not particularly well-served by public

Helston

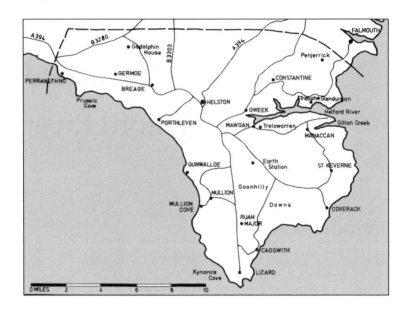

transport, although it is possible to get to most of the main places of interest by bus and distances are relatively short. With a car, it is easy to find your way around, although the lanes around the Helford River are particularly narrow. Due to the flat nature of much of the terrain, this is one part of the County that definitely lends itself to cycle touring and places to hire bikes are listed in the text. For coast walking, the area is one of the best in the country with a nice contrast between the steep cliffs of the west coast and the sheltered landscapes of the Helford River.

Helston

Helston is the transport hub for the area and easily the biggest town – very much the gateway to the Lizard. It was one of the five Stannary towns of Cornwall and during the early Middle Ages tin was brought here for assaying and taxing, before being dispatched from its then thriving port In the C13, a bar of sand and shingle formed across the mouth of the River Loe and access to the sea was cut off. The seaborne trade was diverted to Gweek at the head of the Helford River, some 3 miles to the east. Helston, however, continued to prosper as the main town of the area , even though its size was small by today's standards – even in the late C14 being less than 300 people. The town was described in the 1530's as a good market town, making the most of its coinage rights and the privileges that came with them.. The town continued to prosper, though its fortunes tended to fluctuate with the success of the surrounding mines. The C18 saw a growth in lawlessness and the tinners of Helston, along with those from the Lizard, were notorious for wrecking – the practice of luring ships onto the shore and then plundering the wrecks. The C19 was one of general decline, the town lost its status as a coinage town in 1838 when the system was abandoned. Mining declined with the last mine at Wendron closing in the 1920s. Today, Helston remains a busy market town helped by tourists and the nearby RNAF base at Culdrose.

The town is a pleasant collection of Georgian, Regency and Victorian buildings lining the wide main street and the narrow streets that lead off it. At the bottom of Coinagehall Street is the mock gothic Grylls Monument, a memorial gateway **Grylls** erected in 1834 to Humphrey Millett Grylls whose actions kept open the local tin **Monument** mine, saving 1200 jobs. The archway leads through to a small park, once the site of the castle, but now long gone. The bowling green here is one of the oldest in the country dating from 1764. Coinagehall Street, whose name relates to Helston's days as a Stannary Town, is lined by a number of fine buildings including the **Blue Anchor Inn**, originally a monk's rest house which became a tavern in C15. The building is an extremely picturesque and largely unaltered inn with a distinctive thatched roof. Miners used to collect their wages in the pub which has a colourful history with two landlords dying violently and another being seriously injured by a bayonet in a brawl. Things have quietened down a bit now and it is an excellent place for a drink and a bite to eat. Further up the hill is the *Methodist Chapel* of 1888, big, grey and granite with a central gable over a projecting porch and further still is the Angel Hotel, the C16 town house of the Godolphins. It has been an inn since the mid C18 and was the meeting place for local society. Beside the road are small water channels, or kennels, which divert stream water from the top of the town down either side of the street. Note too, how the granite paving slabs have been tooled to divert water naturally into the kennels. At the top of the street is the Market House, 1837–8, a classical composition in granite and not unlike the **Market House** one in Penzance of the same date.

Continuing up Wendron Street, will take you to the *Godolphin Hall*, built in 1888, a rather grim exercise in granite gothic. Just beyond is a small C17 thatched cottage, that is the reputed birthplace of Bob Fitzimmons, born in 1863, who was the first boxer, and only Briton, to be world heavyweight, light heavyweight and middleweight champion. He retired in 1914 and died in Chicago three years later.

To the north of the Market House, along the narrow, winding Church Street is St Michael's Church, one of the few C18 churches in Cornwall and an indication of the importance of Helston during those times. It was erected between 1756 and 1763 at the expense of the Earl of Godolphin, by now spectacularly rich from his tin mines. The designer was *Thomas Edwards* of Greenwich and the church has a decidedly metropolitan feel. The interior originally boasted a gallery around three sides supported on cast iron columns, but C20 restoration has cruelly removed most of this C18 feature, leaving a gallery at just one end. A stained glass window behind the altar depicts angels at the top indulging in the Furry Dance, the ceremony for which Helston is perhaps most famous (see below). The brass chandelier was a gift from the Earl on the church's opening in 1763. Behind the altar is a fine mosaic reredos depicting the last supper. Outside the porch is a monument to *Henry Trengrouse*, the Helston cabinet-maker who, after witnessing the

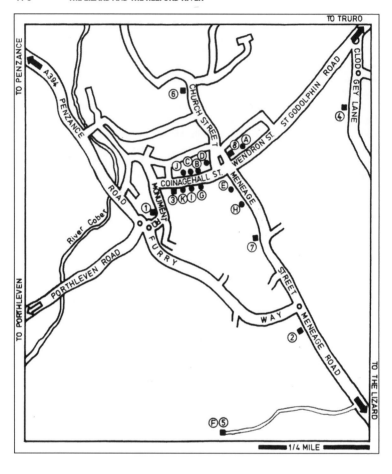

HELSTON

ACCOMMODATION

1 Strathallan
2 Lyndale
3 No. 52 Coinagehall Street
4 Mandeley
5 Nanslowe Manor

ESSENTIALS

6 Church
7 Tourist Office
8 Museum

RESTAURANTS AND BARS

A Morley's
B Pinocchio's
C Figs Bistro
D Red Lion
E Thurley's
F Nansloe Manor
G Angel Hotel
H The Rodney Inn
I Fitzimmons Arms
J Trelawneys
K Blue Anchor

appalling wreck of the *Anson* on Loe Bar in 1807, devoted his life to the invention of life-saving equipment for use in shipwrecks.

Adjacent to the churchyard is the 1828 National School, a fine Georgian composition in granite, now a public hall. There are a number of good Georgian buildings in this part of the town, none more so than *The Willows* on the corner of Cross Street and Church Street. Note the fine decorative fanlight and porch, only marred by the crassly insensitive sign erected by the current occupiers, Kerrier District Council. In Meneage Street, there is a rare example of good C20 design with a marvellous art deco shopfront to Eddy and Sons premises, reputedly brought from Birmingham in the 1930s.

Besides the above buildings, the town is full of delightful streets and good groups of C18 and C19 vernacular frontages. A free leaflet is available from the Tourist Information Centre and Museum on the Helston Town Trail which includes many of the above buildings.

Helston Folk Museum, Church Street (**01326 564027**) is located just behind the Guildhall and occupies the old meat market and drill hall. It displays a fairly mundane collection of artefacts and photographs of old Helston, including a collection of "hot marks" for branding the blocks of tin ore with the owners name. There is also an exhibition about *Henry Trengrouse* 1772–1854, who invented the life savers rocket apparatus, the breaches bouy and the life jacket. There are exhibits of the early inventions and of his life in Helston.

> Open 10am– 5pm (closed Sunday & Bank Holiday). Admission £2, under 16 free

Many of the old photographs on display relate to the Furry, or Flora Dance. It is held every year on 8 May, unless that day falls on a Sunday or Monday when it is held on the preceding Saturday. This is the Christian feast day of St Michael, Helston's patron saint, although the origins of the Furry Dance almost certainly pre-date Christianity, the early church having adopted and transformed many pagan rituals for its own purposes. It celebrates the triumph of Spring over Winter, life over death. The town is decorated with flowers, gorse and laurel leaves for the festivities. Dancing starts at 7.00am and at 8.30am the mummer's play, known as the Hal-an-Tow, is performed at several venues in the town. There are further dances throughout the day, with the principal dance at midday, when invited participants in top hats, tails and dress gowns dance in and out of the shops, houses and gardens behind the Helston band playing the Flora Dance tune. The town is packed for the festival and people come from far and wide to witness the spectacle.

> Flora Dance

The range of shops will provide most of the essentials that any visitor will require. *The Creftow Gallery*, 6 Church Street (**01326 572848**) is opposite the museum and is a surprisingly spacious gallery run as a co-operative by local artists. There is a good range of high quality contemporary work, including paintings, ceramics and jewellery. The *Helston Bookworm*, 9 Church Street (**01326 565079**) is an excellent second hand bookshop which also displays some artworks of varying quality. Bike hire is available from *Family Cycles*, 7 Church Street (**01326 573719**).

> Cycle hire

The RNAF base at Culdrose, just to the south of the town, may be visited for those interested in this sort of thing. It is open to visitors from April to October for tours at 10.45am and 1.40pm (morning only on Fridays). The cost of the tour is £5.00, children £2.50. Opening times are liable to change at short notice, so it is

> RNAF Culdrose

Flambards
Theme Park
advisable to telephone **01326 565085** to check. Nearby is Flambards Theme Park (**0845 6018684**), with a reproduction Victorian village, a funfair and other amusements. It is open from Easter to the end of October. Admission £9.95, children £8.95, OAP £5.75.

Accommodation

Helston has surprisingly little accommodation, most tourists seeming to prefer to stay in the coastal resorts. The local Tourist Information Centre has a full list of accommodation but you could try:

Strathallan, Monument Road (**01326 573683**) *B* an attractive granite, Georgian house with comfortable en-suite rooms. Located just a few minutes walk from the town centre, it has some limited parking. Good value and the breakfast is excellent.

Lyndale Guest House, Greenbank, Meaneage Road (**01326 561082**) *A*. Standard B&B on the road to Lizard on the edge of town, but good value.

No. 52 Coinagehall Street (**01326 569334**) *B*. Next to the Blue Anchor public house in the main street. A comfortable B&B, though the front rooms can be noisy.

Mandeley Guest House, Clodgey Lane (**01326 572550**) *A*. Large guest house on the bypass to the east of the town centre. No en-suite rooms.

Nansloe Manor, Meneage Road (**01326 574691**) *E*. Located just outside Helston, on the road to the Lizard. A comfortable hotel set in a grade II listed building with extensive grounds.

Restaurants and cafes

There are a number of pubs that serve food but a rather limited number of restaurants. It may well be worth making the short journey down to Porthleven where there are some excellent restaurants.

Morley's, The Mews, 4 Wendron Street (**01326 564433**) *E*. Located down a tiny alley, there is an adventurous menu of meat and fish. Probably the best in the town itself.

Pinocchio's, 3 Cornagehall Street (**01326 565633**) *I*. Italian cafe/restaurant with a rather soulless interior

Figs Bistro, Cobbled Ope (**01326 565649**) *I–M*, found down an alleyway behind no.15 Coinagehall Street. There is also a nice courtyard for al fresco dining. They serve sandwiches and snacks as well as full meals.

Red Lion, Church Street (**01326 572293**) *I*, behind the Guildhall. Bar food with pizzas a speciality.

Thurleys Fish Restaurant, Meneage Street (**01326 572991**) *I*, fish and chips to eat in or take-away.

Nansloe Manor, Meneage Road (**01326 574691**) *E*, elegant dining in a country house hotel. Located just outside the town.

Bars and Nightlife

There are a surprising number of pubs and bars in Helston and the weekend scene can verge on the raucous, partly due, no doubt, to the nearby air base at RNAF Culdrose. Many of the pubs are in interesting historic buildings, although more often than not the interiors have been unsympathetically modernised. Some of the better ones are:

Red Lion, Church Street, comfortable and central pub with real ale and food.

Angel Hotel, Coinagehall Street, the historic town house of the Godolphin family, but now with a sadly mutilated interior. Basic pub serving standard bar food.

The Rodney Inn, Meneage Street, another historic building with no remaining internal features.

Fitzimmons Arms, Coinagehall Street, on the main street with DJs and music at weekends.

Trelawneys, Coinagehall Street, opposite the above. Young clientelle, music bar with late licence on Fridays and Saturdays. At weekends, queues start to form as the evening progresses.

Blue Anchor, Coinagehall Street, superb, atmospheric old pub consisting of several small rooms divided by a central passageway. The pub has its own micro-brewery and serves its own ale. Food and occasional live music. Highly recommended.

Practicalities

The Tourist Information Centre (**01326 565431**), 79 Meneage Street, is well-stocked with leaflets and local interest books. Helston is connected by bus to Camborne, Truro, Falmouth and Penzance and to all the major towns and villages on the Lizard. The nearest main line railway station is Camborne from where there are regular buses to Helston. For those using the coast path , there is an easy walk from Loe Bar which takes about 45 minutes. By car, Helston is on the main A394 Truro to Penzance road, while virtually all the roads to the Lizard pass through Helston. On-street car parking is limited in the town, but there are a number of signed car parks just outside the town centre. Cycling is an attractive option as the distances around the Lizard are relatively small and the going generally flat. Cycle hire is available in the town.

Tourist Information Centre

Around Helston

Helston's primary interest for the visitor is as the gateway town for the Lizard peninsula and nearby Mounts Bay. However, there are several interesting sights in the vicinity which are worth seeing if the time allows. To the west of Helston, just **Breage** off the main Penzance road is Breage, an undistinguished village but with a fine, lichen-covered church, containing some particularly good medieval wall paintings dating from the C15. There is a Roman milestone inside with an inscription referring to *Marcus Cassianus Posthumus* (258–68). He was a usurper who ruled only part of the Empire (Britain, Gaul and Spain) and it is the only surviving stone dedicated to him in Britain.

Open Apr–Sept, Tues, Thurs & Fri, 11am– 5pm, Sun, 2–5pm. Open Bank Holiday Mon, 11– 5pm. Admission £6.00, children £1.50. Gardens only £2.00, children free

Two miles to the west is **Godolphin House** (01736 763194), the ancestral home of the powerful Godolphin family. They rose to prominence under Henry VIII and made fortunes from the mineral wealth of the area. The house is largely C17, although there are some earlier C16 remnants. Though relatively small, the house is one of the most important in Cornwall, and is currently undergoing a four year programme of restoration. However, this does not preclude visits, and in many ways enhances the experience as you can see the work in progress and appreciate more of the exposed structure than you may otherwise be able to. The restored interiors, including the King's Room (circa 1630) and the Dining Room (circa 1530) are very impressive, with the latter having wonderful Elizabethan carving and panelling. They are sparsely furnished with period pieces and all the better for it. Lunches and teas are served in a large marquee in the grounds. The gardens, still undergoing restoration, are also attractive, and a North American tipi and pony rides help keep the children amused. Everything here has a pleasant understated atmosphere and makes for a very relaxing visit. The estate around the house is owned and managed by the National Trust and is open to visitors every day between 10am–5pm. Godolphin Hill is the focal point of the estate and there are several paths to the top from where there are fine views. *Godolphin Cross*, just to the south is a pleasant granite village with the *Church of St John the Baptist* dating from 1849-50 by J.P.St Aubyn. The **Godolphin Arms** opposite the church serves good pub food.

Tregonning Hill   Just south of Godolphin Cross is Tregonning Hill, showing signs of Iron Age and Romano-British occupation. There is a hillfort at the western end with two stone ramparts, now largely reduced. However, there are panoramic views from the top and it would be a pleasant place for a picnic in fine weather. The easiest **Balwest** approach is from Balwest from where it is a 10 minute walk along an established path. Balwest, itself, is a tiny hamlet with a huge Methodist Chapel, an indication of the much greater population of these areas during the mining boom of the C18 and C19. From Balwest, it is only a short distance through narrow lanes to Germoe, a delightfully picturesque hamlet tumbling over the hills **Germoe** around a narrow valley. The *Church of St Germoe* is a beautifully simple design of granite with stained glass windows of the palest green, pink and blue. The earliest parts of the Church are Norman, including the font which is very primitive, with three carved faces, one hardly recognizable. In the churchyard is *St*

Germoe's Chair, an extraordinary, little structure built into the churchyard wall. It is assumed to date from the medieval period and despite its name, its purpose is unknown.

Around two miles to the north west of Germoe, just off the B3280, is St Hilary, a lovely hamlet of stone cottages and houses with a beautiful church in an unspoilt setting. The church dates from 1854, but the tower is C13 and is unusual for Cornwall in having a broached spire. The top cornice displays some primitive carved faces. The decoration of the pulpit is by *Ernest Proctor*, one of the leading Newlyn artists.

St Hilary

Mounts Bay and Lizard Point

The Lizard coast to Mount's Bay is a succession of glorious high cliffs and sandy coves. With its south-westerly aspect, it is one of the biggest and most lethal lee shores in the country. Given the Lizard's exposure to fierce Atlantic storms and the large number of offshore reefs and outcrops, it is not difficult to see how the coast has proved fatal for so many. Added to these natural hazards, the area had a grim and deserved reputation for wrecking in the C18. Today, the coast has a less sanguine character and is popular with tourists who come for its fine beaches and magnificent scenery. However, on a stormy day the seas bring enormous waves onto the shore and it is only too easy to imagine the dangers of this coast for sailing ships with primitive navigation and poor charts. The coast path provides some of the best coast walking in England and there are several, excellent places to stay and many interesting sites on or just by the path.

Perranuthno, just east of Marazion is a pretty village with an attractive church and pub, but not much else to detain the visitor. From the shore near here, there are excellent views of St Michael's Mount. There is a fine coastal walk past Perran Sands towards *Cudden Point* from where there are more good views. Just beyond is Prussia Cove, a small stony beach surrounded by cliffs. The name comes from John Carter "King of Prussia," a notorious smuggler in the C18, who used the cove as his base. The ruts across the beach are claimed to be formed by cart wheels carrying contraband. On the cliff top was a small battery to discourage the revenue boats and close by a "kiddleywink" selling smuggled liquor. In 1947, *HMS Warspite*, en route to the breakers yard broke free from her towing lines in heavy seas and was wrecked here. She remains the largest wreck to occur on the Cornish coast – the salvage operation lasted six years. Nearby is Porth-en-Alls, an Arts and Crafts influenced house built by *Philip Tilden* between 1910–14. The house is now used as a centre for music masterclasses. Towards the end of the summer there is normally a programme of concerts in local churches. Telephone **01872 262466** for further information and booking. Prussia Cove can be approached by car down a narrow lane off the A394. There is a small free car park, from where it is an easy five minute walk to the cove.

Perranuthno

Prussia Cove

Continuing east for a few hundred yards brings you to Kenneggy Sand, a long bay of sand and scattered rocks. There are no facilities. The path continues on to Hoe Point, from where a view opens up of the extensive beach at *Praa Sands*. The

Kenneggy Sand

beach is fine, but the village has been built to cater predominantly for the tourists who stay in the nearby caravan and holiday camp sites. There is little character, but there is an inn and a fish and chip shop beside the beach. A lifeguard is on duty in the summer months. The coast path continues past *Rinsey Head* with its cliff top mines towards Porthleven.

Porthleven and Loe Bar

Porthleven is a pleasant mix of seaside town and working port. The focus of the town is the huge harbour, started in 1811 and completed in 1825. A deeper inner basin was created in the 1850s and is protected by the massive timber gates still in use today. The Council Office with its clock tower perched on the seaward end of the harbour is the most distinctive building in the town. There are many postcards and pictures in the village of the spectacular winter storms of 1989 with the waves breaking right over the exposed building. The harbour was built primarily to meet the demand for coal and other supplies for the nearby mines, but, once constructed, fishing and boat building became important local industries. Away from the harbour, the town is largely undistinguished although the long, sweeping row of C19 houses in Peverell Terrace form a notable backdrop to the south side of the harbour. The beach is sandy and extends over two miles south to Loe Bar and Gunwalloe. It is excellent for sunbathing and the further south you go the more secluded it is. However, bathing can be dangerous, especially around Loe Bar where it is not recommended under any conditions. Just to the north of the village by *Tregear Point* is a monument dedicated to all the men, women and children who were drowned and buried in common, unmarked graves on the cliffs around here. This was common practice, at the time, so as to prevent the non-baptised from being buried in consecrated ground. It took the dreadful and very public wreck of *HMS Anson* in 1807 before the law was changed with the Grylls Act of 1808. On the beach below, is the Giant Rock, made of garnet-gneiss and unique in Cornwall. No-one knows how it got here, but it is believed to have been deposited by a glacier during the last Ice Age. The rock and the area around it is now a Site of Special Scientific Interest.

Giant Rock

Porthleven has a number of interesting shops and galleries. The *Old Customs House* (**01326 564010**) has a selection of photographs and pictures, including the work of *David Hosking*, a local artist who produces brightly coloured semi-abstracts of Cornish scenes. The *Net Loft Gallery* (**01326 564010**) has two large rooms with a range of paintings and ceramics. Both the above can be found on the harbour front. The *Cober Valley Stained Glass Studios* in The Shipyard at the head of the harbour has a small collection of stained glass for purchase and commissions are undertaken. In Fore Street, a few hundred yards from the harbour is the *Julia Mills Gallery* (**01326 569340**) with a good collection of stained glass, as well as ceramics and paintings. Nearby is *Tombodama* (**01326 560200**), a small jewellery studio. *Quayside Fish* (**01326 562008**) on the north side of the harbour sells excellent fresh fish and have their own smokehouse producing salmon "roast" and smoked prawns, excellent for picnics. The nearby *Porthleven Angling*

Centre, Harbourside (**01326 561885**) can arrange fishing trips and coastal cruises and hires fishing gear.

There are a number of excellent restaurants around the harbour. **Critchards** (**01326 562407**) *E* is one of the most established and specializes in seafood and fresh fish. It has featured in numerous good food guides as well as on several TV programmes. The food is excellent. Booking is recommended. The **Lugger Bistro** (**01326 562761**) *M*, next door, has daily fish specials and a few tables outside by the harbour. The **Smokehouse**, Harbourside (**01326 563223**) *M* is a distinctive green building by the harbour with a smart, modern interior and a large outdoor terrace. The menu features fish and other local produce. There is a summer barbecue and smart bar area.

In addition to the above, there are several tea shops and cafes around the harbour and Fore Street, including **Nauti But Nice** on the south side of the harbour, which has ice cream and also home-made cakes, teas and coffees and **The Galley** in Fore Street which also serves evening meals. There are several good pubs, including The **Ship Inn**, a snug and friendly C17 whitewashed, granite inn overlooking the entrance to the harbour, serving real ales and good pub food. The **Harbour Inn** is a large C18 building on the south side of the harbour, which retains some of its original character. It has a pool table, occasional live music and good views over the harbour and serves real ale and food. The **Atlantic Inn** in Peverell Terrace is on a prominent position on the hill to the south of the harbour. An undistinguished building, but a friendly, locals pub with excellent views over the harbour and Mount's Bay. Good pub food and a selection of real ales.

Accommodation in Porthleven can be somewhat restricted and many of the guest houses close down out of season. There are a number of B&Bs in Peverell Terrace, on the south side of the harbour, including **Seefar** (**01326 573778**) *A* and **An Mordros** (**01326 562236**) *A*. There is a tiny guest house on the harbour at **1 Harbour View** (**01326 573713**) *B* with just three rooms. **Critchards Restaurant** (**01326 562407**) *B* also has two superior rooms, both en-suite, which are good value. The **Harbour Inn** (**01326 573876**) *C* has   rooms, many with sea views.

Walking south along the beach or the cliff top, one soon comes across Loe Bar with The Loe, the largest natural fresh water lake in Cornwall, behind its natural, shingle barrier. Before the Bar was formed the Loe was not a pool but the estuary of the River Cober which connected Helston to the sea. However, by the C13 the bar was fully formed and Helston cut off from the sea. It is likely that the Bar was created by a combination of onshore and longshore drift causing a spit to develop on each side of the estuary mouth. The process was aided by deposits from mines that were dumped in the slow-moving Cober. Eventually, the spits were joined and the Loe Pool created. One unsolved mystery is the origin of the shingle which is 86% flint – the nearest onshore source of this material being in East Devon, 120 miles away.

As the Bar became consolidated, less fresh water percolated through to the sea and after heavy rainfall it was common for the Loe to flood the lower parts of Helston. In such circumstances, the Mayor of Helston would apply to the Lord of Penrose Manor for permission to cut the Bar, thus releasing some of the dammed up water. This was carried out by teams of men with shovels, the last such time

Loe Bar
The Loe

being in the winter of 1867-68. However, the last time the Bar was breached was in 1979 and 1984 when channels were excavated with bulldozers by South West Water.

The Loe is a haven for birds, in particular, over-wintering wildfowl. Widgeon, teal, mallard, shoveller, tufted duck and coot are among those regularly seen, and even rare migrants like osprey are occasionally sighted. There is a bird hide near Helston Lodge, which is also suitable for wheelchair occupants. At the head of the **Loe Marsh** Pool is Loe Marsh, now crossed by a causeway constructed in 1987. The tangle of water-tolerant trees, including willow and alder, along with a profusion of wild flowers provides a lush and secluded habitat for many species.

Penrose Estate The Pool and the surrounding Penrose Estate is owned by the National Trust. Access is allowed around the shore of the Pool and through the Estate on the signed paths. It is an excellent walk through fine woodland and with good views over the Pool. There is a footpath that links the Pool to Helston, a short distance to the north and a number of car parks around the edge of the estate. The easiest to access from Porthleven is just off the B3304 near the main entrance to Penrose **Penrose House** House. Penrose House itself, originally C17 but much added to in the C19, is not open to the public, but it can be clearly seen from the walks, along with a solid-looking bridge of 1847 and the adjacent bath house, where it was the custom to take cold baths in accordance with the fashion of the times. The stables pre-date 1788 and are the fine group of service buildings to the south of the main house. *Helston Lodge* on the path to Helston is standard Victorian with exaggerated, over-hanging eaves. Much more flamboyant is *Bar Lodge*, beside the Bar which was built between 1895–98 to the plans of the London architect *G.H.Fellowes Prynne*. **Parc Mean (01326 574290)** *C* is a big Edwardian house on the estate, which is now a very comfortable guest house.

Anson Memorial At the southern end of the Bar is the Anson Memorial, erected in memory of those drowned and buried in the fields hereabouts when *HMS Anson* was beached in a storm in December 1807. The 44 gun frigate had been on its way to take up station on the Brest blockade when it was caught in a fierce south-westerly storm. The captain attempted to beach her on the comparatively safe Loe Bar, but over 100 people were lost to the sea while hundreds of bystanders watched from the beach unable to do anything to help the stranded ship. One of those watching the spectacle was *Henry Trengrouse*, a Helston cabinet maker, who was so appalled that he devoted the rest of his life to inventing life saving apparatus to help in shipwrecks. Most famously, he invented the rocket apparatus and breeches bouy, which was used for generations to rescue people from stranded ships. Like many inventors, he died penniless in 1854 – the grateful government having awarded him just £20.

Gunwalloe The sands continue for another mile or so to Gunwalloe, a small hamlet with a highly rated pub, the **Hazelphron Inn (01326 240406)** *C*. There is bar food, a separate restaurant and a terrace with views across Mount's Bay. There are also two en-suite rooms.

The Coast, Gunwalloe to Lizard Point

Beyond Gunwalloe, the long sand beach ends and a series of rugged cliffs and small coves lead all the way to Lizard Point. The first, and perhaps the nicest, is

Maze at
Glendurgan Garden

Serpentine workshop,
Church Cove, Lizard

Portloe

Harbour at Coverack, Lizar

National Maritime Museum, Falmouth

Gunwalloe Chuch Cove, a small sandy beach between low cliffs. There is no development other than a refreshment kiosk and the spectacularly-sited *Church of St
Gunwalloe*, which is right on the seashore with the earlier, free-standing tower
half-submerged by the sands. In stormy weather it can seem that the very fabric of
the church is under attack. It was founded by St Winwaloe, a Breton missionary, as
the Church of the Storms. Rebuilt in the C14–C15, it is low and extremely atmospheric. Within the church are two remnants of a C15 rood screen with painted figures of the apostles below, reputed to have come from a Portuguese wreck in the
C16. The churchyard has a number of interesting gravestones, many to those lost
to the sea hereabouts. A number of ships have been wrecked on this part of the
coast including several reputed to have been carrying treasure. There have been
occasional finds of gold coins in the sands around but as far as anyone knows the
bulk of the treasure still lies under the shifting sands. The cove has toilet facilities
and a lifeguard during the summer months and there is a small car park. All in all,
it is a delightful and secluded spot and one of the nicest beaches on this stretch of
the coast. Located at the end of a narrow lane signposted off the A3083 Helston to
Lizard road, it can also be reached by a 30 minute walk from Mullion via Poldhu
Cove and the coast path.

**Gunwalloe
Church Cove**

Heading south around the low headland lies Poldhu Cove, a sandy beach
backed by some scrubby dunes and an intrusive car park. When the wind is
from the south-west the surf can be sizeable. A lifeguard is on duty during the
summer months and care needs to be taken when bathing. There is a cafe and
toilet facilities, but nothing else. Just inland is Cury, a rather undistinguished
village but with a fine church, small, low and with an interesting interior.
However, the Norman doorway inside the porch is of most note with a key
band on one side and zigzag on the other column. The tower doorway, dating
from the 1400s is also of interest with the carved faces still clearly visible in the
door surround.

Poldhu Cove

Cury

On the cliffs above Poldhu is a memorial to *Marconi* and the remains of the
wireless station from where the first Transatlantic radio message was sent in 1901.
Marconi's company was in vigorous competition with the Eastern Telegraph
Company based at Porthcurno, but the government at the time was keen to see
both methods of communication developed and the two companies soon amalga-
mated as Cable and Wireless.

Mullion is the largest village on the Lizard and makes a good base for exploring
the area. It is located half a mile inland, sheltered from the worst of the south-
westerly storms. The village consists of a number of attractive, granite buildings
gathered around the *Church of St Mellina*, open Monday-Saturday 9.00am-
4.00pm. It is set within a circular churchyard and made from massive granite and
serpentine blocks with a low tower and slate roof. The most important feature is
the carved bench ends which probably date from the early C16. There is a good
C13 font and a finely carved Royal Arms of Charles II.

Mullion

In the C18, Mullion was notorious for wrecking and smuggling which went
largely unchecked by the authorities. John Wesley brought his new code of
Methodism to Mullion in 1762 and gradually a more civilized demeanour settled
on the place. The large and imposing Methodist Chapel, by the church, is

testament to these times. There is little else to see in the village itself, but there are shops, a post office, a good B&B and a very nice pub. The sandy *Polurrian Cove* is only 15 minutes easy walk from the village centre.

Of the few places to stay, the best are:

The Old Vicarage (01326 240898) *B*, beautiful C19 building in extensive gardens located on the edge of the village. The building is reputed to be featured in the Sherlock Holmes' story *The Devil's Foot* by Sir Arthur Conan Doyle.

Stocks Restauran t (01326 240727) *C*, has a double room with lounge which is let on a bed and breakfast basis.

Polurrian Hotel (01326 240421) *E*, high on the cliffs just outside the village and above the sandy Polurrian Cove. Set in 12 acres of grounds, with its own leisure centre including indoor and outdoor pools, this is probably the most luxurious place to stay on the Lizard and the prices are correspondingly high. Clark Gable stayed here in 1952 while filming *Never Let Me Go* on location.

Stocks Restaurant and Tea Room (01326 240727) *I*, is one of the few places to eat in the village and has rather a basic menu. The **Old Inn** is a hugely atmospheric, old thatched inn with a delightful cosy interior and good pub food. The dining room at the **Polurrian Hotel** is lavish and has a fabulous view over the bay. Food is good but prices are expensive, children under seven are not welcome either.

Mullion is located just off the main Helston to Lizard A3083 road. There are regular buses to Helston and Lizard. It is a short walk from the coast path.

Mullion Cove   Mullion Cove, the harbour for Mullion, is extremely picturesque with massive greenstone piers, completed in 1895, and spectacular cliffs to either side of the narrow harbour. Offshore is the bird sanctuary of Mullion Island along with several sea stacks of serpentine. A small beach is revealed at low tide. A lifeboat was stationed in the harbour from 1867–1909 and with good reason – in the six years up to 1873 there were nine wrecks under Mullion cliffs alone. There is a car park, toilet facilities and a cafe.

On the cliff to the north is the large and imposing **Mullion Cove Hotel** (01326 240328) *E*, a comfortable hotel with excellent views across the bay. The restaurant is recommended and good value for the quality of food and ambience. Well worth it for a special treat. Just beside the hotel is the cheaper **Henscath House** (01326 240537) *B*, with equally superb views.

Kynance Cove   The coast from Mullion Cove to the Lizard is a series of high cliffs with tiny coves, many inaccessible from land. The finest, perhaps, is Kynance Cove, considered by many to be the most beautiful beach in Cornwall and correspondingly popular. It is now owned by the National Trust, along with the surrounding cliffs. There is a car park about 10 minutes walk away and a steep descent to the beach. The car park is accessed down a narrow lane off the A3083 Helston to Lizard road. The cove is completely immersed at high tide. The sand is fine and firm and the many islands and sea stacks of serpentine create a dramatic setting. There is a cafe and facilities, but no lifeguard. Care needs to be taken when swimming and, in particular, one needs to be alert so as to not get cut off by the incoming tide. The National Trust have gone to considerable efforts to control visitors and their impact on the area. A concerted programme of protection has resulted in the preservation of much of the rare Lizard flora and an Europa Nostra Award for their work.

The coast path continues along the flat top of the cliffs towards Lizard Point **Lizard Point** where the lighthouse forms a landmark for miles around. The Lizard is the most southerly point in mainland Britain and was the last point at which ships could receive messages from land. It was therefore of some importance before the days of radio communication and Lloyds Signal Station can still be seen at Bass Point on the east side of Lizard Point. The Armada is supposed to have been first sighted on mainland England from The Rill to the west. Polpeor Cove is the most southerly in **Polpeor Cove** England. It is reached by a wide, steep path and there is a small, stony beach, uncovered at low tide. The redundant lifeboat station which operated from 1859–1961 dominates the cove. It is almost inconceivable how men could have launched a boat in storm conditions into this narrow and treacherous bay surrounded by offshore reefs. However, hundreds of lives were saved from this most dangerous part of the coast. On the night of the 17 March 1907, the White Star Liner *Suevic* became stranded on the Maenheere Reef. Along with others, the Lizard lifeboat rescued all 524 people on board – the biggest rescue operation ever undertaken by the RNLI.

In contrast, Pistol Meadow to the west was witness to one of the most horrific **Pistol Meadow** wrecks on the Cornish coast. In November 1720, the *Royal Anne*, a transport heading for Barbados, went down on the off-lying reefs – 704 men were drowned and only 3 survived. Bodies were washed ashore for days afterwards and, as was the practice of the day, they were buried in unmarked graves in Pistol Meadow. The low mounds can still be seen today. Contemporary reports increase the horror with packs of dogs attacking the bodies on the sea shore before they could be buried. For generations afterwards, it was said that the people of the Lizard were so ashamed that dogs were banished, even from farms. When the Victorian writer, Wilkie Collins, visited the Lizard in the mid 1800s he noted the absence of dogs as confirmation that the story was true.

Above the lifeboat station, there are a couple of cafes and serpentine workshops and the whole is pleasantly understated compared to the excesses of Lands End. The lighthouse is one of the most famous in the world. A warning light was first established here in 1612, but it had mixed success to the extent that there is a report of the captain of a Falmouth packet firing a cannon in anger at the recalcitrant keeper who had let the light go out. A regular light was established in 1752 when the present twin-towered structure was built. Originally coal fires provided illumination, then in 1812 oil lamps and reflectors greatly improved the range. Electricity was installed in 1878, along with the powerful foghorn still in evidence today. The light is so powerful that in clear weather it can be seen 29 miles away. It is due to re-open to visitors in 2005 after complete renovation. There is a car park at Lizard Point but the lane from Lizard Town, half a mile inland, is narrow and can get very congested at busy times. It is better to park in the town (no charge) and walk the half mile to the lighthouse along a well-established footpath.The Youth Hostel (**0870 7706120**) *A*, immediately adjacent to the lighthouse has been newly converted from an old Victorian hotel. The views are magnificent and it is a wonderful spot to stay.

Lizard Town, Goonhilly Downs and the Coast to Nare Point

Lizard Town Lizard Town, itself, is a rather undistinguished collection of buildings grouped around a central crossroads. *Wilkie Collins* visited in 1850 and wrote that whoever named the group of cottages, "Lizard Town must have possessed magnificent ideas indeed on the subject of nomenclature." There are a number of serpentine shops displaying various ornaments made from this most spectacular of rocks. It is well worth looking around as price and quality vary significantly from shop to shop – the cheapest by far being the serpentine workshop in Church Cove. *Anne's Pasty Shop* is reputed to be one of the best of its kind. **The Top House** is a pleasant pub in the village centre with good food. There is not really a lot to detain the visitor, but if necessary **The Caerthillian** **(01326 290019)** *B* is a pleasant B&B in the centre of the village. The **Housel Bay Hotel** **(01326 290417)** *D–E* has fine views and is located on the edge of the town. The restaurant has a particularly good reputation. There are regular buses to Helston for onward connections.

Back on Lizard Point, to the east of the lighthouse, is *The Lions Den*, a massive conical hole in the cliff-top that was created when a sea cave collapsed in 1847. It should be approached with extreme caution. The coast path continues along the **Housel Bay** cliff top to Housel Bay, a small and popular beach in a beautiful setting. There are **Bass Point** no facilities and it can only be approached by footpath. Bass Point is the location for the *Lloyds Signal Station*, erected in 1872. By 1878, more than 1000 ships a month were using the service, coming in close to the point to register their names and collect messages and instructions. It has now been restored to recreate the original radio room and is open throughout the year. It is advised to telephone **01326 290384** to confirm opening times. There is also a coastguard **Pen Olver** lookout and on the adjoining headland of Pen Olver a simple bungalow with a plaque commemorating the fact that *Guglielmo Marconi* set up an experimental wireless station here in 1900 to work with the larger station at Poldhu. On 23 January 1901, a new record for wireless communication was set between Lizard and the Isle of Wight of 186 miles. The next year, the famous trans-Atlantic signal was sent from Poldhu. The station was finally closed in 1920. It is now open to visitors in the summer, Tuesday, Thursday and Friday between 1pm and 4pm. In winter, it may open on Sunday afternoons. Telephone 01326 561407 to confirm opening times.

A fine coast walk leads around Bass Point to *Kilcobben Cove* where there is a **Church Cove** dramatically-sited lifeboat station. A little further on is Church Cove, an almost perfect Cornish fishing cove with only three buildings of massive granite and serpentine blocks – the boathouse, the winch house and the round house, now all converted to residences. From here, a lane leads up a narrow, lush valley dotted with attractive cottages and a bright blue, serpentine workshop which has a limited range of work but very reasonable prices. The *Church of St Wynwalloe* is perfectly situated – a low, typical Cornish design with a tower of local serpentine and granite, providing a distinctive chequerboard effect. It is thought that a church existed here from the C6, but the earliest part of the existing building is the C12 doorway with its typical Norman zig zag decoration. The porch, itself, is battlemented and has a rib vault inside resting on angel corbels with a larger angel as the central boss. Inside there is a simple barrel vault roof and a squint, between the south chapel and chancel, enabling those in the chapel to still see the main altar. There is a good C15 font with serpentine pillars added in the C19. Serpentine, the Lizard's 'local' stone, has also been used for the pulpit and lectern.

Goonhilly Downs

Inland from the Lizard are the Goonhilly Downs, a poorly-drained plateau with thin soils rich in magnesium. This, with the mild climate, has resulted in a unique flora with many of the plants being of a south European origin. Most prevalent is the Cornish Heath, *Erica Vagens*, a type of heather which is only found in any quantity on the Lizard. Trees are few and far between and the flat top of the Downs present an eerie and sometimes bleak aspect. There have been attempts to enclose and farm the Downs over the years but on the whole they have remained remarkably untouched by the hand of man. However, in the last 25 years over a quarter of the unique heathland has been lost to agriculture. Fortunately, this process has now slowed due to the general decline in agriculture in the country as a whole.

North of Lizard Town and just off the A3083 Lizard road, is the extraordinary ruined church of Ruan Major. Located down a narrow lane and in a remote location, there is limited parking. As recently as 1970, *Pesvener* wrote of a deserted church, "so little visited that…. a white owl was nesting in the timbers of the south porch roof." Deterioration has been so rapid that now there is no south porch, let alone roof, and all the internal features of note have disappeared along with the roof and substantial parts of the structure.

Ruan Major

Located in the centre of the Downs is the looming presence of the **Goonhilly Downs Earth Station** (0800 679 593), the biggest satellite communication centre in the world. The site was chosen because of the extremely stable subsoil and has a pleasing continuity with the area's history of advanced communications from the days of telegraphy and wireless. There is a visitors centre and guided tour.

Open daily from 10am(11am in winter, closed Monday). Admission, £5.00, children £3.50

Just north of Cadgwith is the small village of *Ruan Minor*, largely undistinguished, but with a tiny church, one of the smallest in Cornwall. The low tower is C15 and built of enormous blocks of serpentine, while the earliest part dates from the C13.

The Coast, Church Cove to Nare Point

As one progresses east past the Lizard, the coastline begins to change perceptibly. High, rugged cliffs and storm-lashed coast give way to a gentler, more rounded coastline, sheltered from the prevailing storms by the land mass of the Lizard itself.

Cadgwith, about one mile north-east of Lizard Town is the quintessential Cornish fishing village with its tightly clustered cottages sheltering in a narrow

Cagdwith

valley. The two tiny coves are still dominated by fishing and the boats are pulled up onto the slipway as the village has no harbour as such. Many of the cottages are still thatched as here is about as far as one can get from the slate mining areas of Cornwall and, until relatively recently, thatch would have been the cheaper materi-al. Immediately to the south of the village is the *Devil's Frying Pan*, a huge crater created when the roof of a sea cave collapsed. The small hut on the cliffs to the north of the cove was once a coastguard lookout. The village has a post office, shop and art workshop/gallery and the **Cadgwith Cove Inn** (**01326 290513**) **B**, a won-derfully, picturesque building situated directly opposite the slipway. They serve good pub food and have good value accommodation. The village is approached down extremely narrow lanes and there is limited parking at the cove. Drivers are strongly advised to park in the car park on the Lizard road and walk. The nearest bus service is in Ruan Minor to the north. The coast path passes through the village and it is a pleasant 45 minute walk from Church Cove to the south.

The slopes above *Kildown Cove* to the east are the site of an experiment by the National Trust to reinstate the natural flora – grassland rich in wild flowers is reap-pearing and the area is beautiful in the early summer. Poltesco is a tiny valley with a stream bubbling down to the cove. It used to be the site of a serpentine quarry and the abandoned workings are still evident. Continuing east brings you to **Kennack Sands** Kennack Sands, a popular beach, especially with divers. The beach itself is quite nice, sand with large boulders set between low cliffs, but it is spoiled somewhat by the large, holiday park nearby. The south end of the beach has a certain geological interest as gneiss, serpentine and gabbro are juxtaposed along with veins of asbestos and talc. There is a large car park, toilets and cafes that are open in sea-son. The **Kennack Sands Inn** (**01326 290547**) **B** is a grim looking edifice over-looking the bay and has real ale, food and accommodation. However, if you are looking to stay, far better to push on to Coverack, two miles east and one of the nicest places on this part of the coast. Following the coast path, the route follows the cliff top to *Lankidden Cove*, a tiny and secluded sandy cove with footpath access only. At *Black Head*, there are extensive views towards Falmouth and the headlands beyond.

Coverack Coverack sits on the sheltered side of a wide sweeping bay. It was once an important fishing village and also a notorious centre for smuggling. The first coast-guard noted in his annual report that 7000 casks of brandy had been successfully landed in the bay, although some exaggeration would no doubt have been helpful in his plea for more men. The lower village is a picturesque jumble of fishermen's cottages set around the harbour and its massive serpentine pier. The harbour is still a working port and fishing boats are moored among the pleasure boats. The beach is rocky and narrow at high tide, but low tide reveals a wide expanse of sand. Bathing is generally safe in the centre of the bay, but care should always be taken as there is no lifeguard. The bay is also very popular with windsurfers and tuition and hire is available from the *Coverack Windsurfing Centre* (**01326 280939**) Open, March – November. There are a number of shops that provide essential services and several places to stay and eat, making it an attractive base for explor-ing this part of the coast.

YHA Youth Hostel, School Hill (**0870 770 5780**) **A**. Coverack's youth hostel is one of the best in the county and as good a place to stay as any if you do not mind the dormitory accommodation. The hostel occupies a large Victorian house set on the cliffs above the harbour. The views are spectacular. There is a large lounge, dining room and conservatory with pool table and table football, garden and ample car parking. The stair balustrade and balcony come from the *SS Mobegan* wrecked on The Manacles, a notorious offshore reef, in 1898. A copy of *The Cornishman* of 20 October 1898 is framed nearby with the original report of the disaster. The hostel is linked to the Coverack Windsufing Centre and many wind-surfers stay here giving the place a more lively feel than many other youth hostels.

Boak House (**01326 280608**) *A*, overlooking the harbour. Attractive brick, dou-ble fronted house with sea views.

Fernleigh, Chywbloth Way (**01326 280626**) *B*, set back just off the beach towards the centre of the bay.

The Paris Hotel (**01326 280258**) *B*, on the promontory by the harbour with sea views on all sides. Named after the SS Paris stranded on The Manacles in 1899. Four en-suite rooms, but the bar can be noisy.

The Bay Hotel (**01326 280464**) *E*, right on the beach road with extensive views over the bay. This large, family-run hotel provides somewhat overpriced accom-modation.

Of the places to eat, the best is **The Old Lifeboat House** (**01326 280899**) *M*. Located in the eponymous building, this is one of the most atmospheric restau-rants in Cornwall. It has no pretensions, with simple seating and decor and the simply cooked fish is excellent.. There is a fine view through the glass wall that replaces the slipway doors. Fresh fish and steaks are the speciality and the fish is fresh. Stormy weather will severely reduce the size of the menu. Ron, the chef, not only cooks fish, he catches them and the pictures all around the wall testify to this. There is a take-away service from the landward end of the building. Booking for the restaurant is strongly recommended. Open in the evening only.

The **Paris Hotel**, opposite the above serves real ales, although the bar lacks any real character. They also serve bar food. The **Café** towards the beach serves teas and lunches and meals until 8.30pm in summer. The **Bay Hotel** restaurant is open to non-residents. *The Mill Gallery* (**01326 280844**) is a tiny space with exhibi-tions of local artists' work.

Coverack is easily reached by car along the B3293, the road that runs past Goonhilly Earth Station and over the Downs. There are regular, but not frequent, bus connections to Helston. The coast path passes right through the village.

North of Coverack, the Goonhilly Downs start to break up into gently rolling countryside with a network of tiny lanes and villages as the land dips down towards the Helford River. St Keverne is the largest village and has an attractive **St Keverne** central square with a number of shops, two pubs and the *Church of St Akeveranus*, a large but low church with a tower of two stages and an octagonal spire. An unusual feature in Cornwall, but perhaps intended as a landmark for mariners to help avoid the dreaded Manacles reef, a mile and a half offshore, almost a mile square and virtually covered at high tide. The church was built in the C15, but appears to have re-used much material from earlier structures. It is believed to have been a place of Christian worship since the C6. Beside the altar are some carved stone remnants from Tregonning Priory, a one time Celtic monastic community. There are no less than three rood stairs in the north wall, indicating that the church was extended at least twice. There are some good, carved bench ends and a nice C15 font with angels at the corners. The pulpit is Jacobean with ornamental panels.

Manacles Reef

Over 400 souls who perished on the Manacles Reef are buried in the churchyard. There is a memorial to those lost when the liner *SS Mohegan* was wrecked in 1898. The liner struck as the passengers were settling down to dinner. She sank within ten minutes and 106 lives, including all her deck officers, were lost. Only 51 people survived. The reef was the scene of countless wrecks, but none more infamous than that of the emigrant ship *John*, wrecked on the 3 May 1855, with 263 people on board bound for a new life in Canada. The master and crew seemed curiously unconcerned about hitting the reef and, breaking open the ship's liqour supplies, proceeded to get drunk while sitting in the rigging. They fought to prevent the passengers joining them and, although there were only 70 survivors, not a single crew member died. In a famous trial, Captain Rawle was convicted of manslaughter and sent to prison. The entire crew, but one, were publicly censured for cowardice, selfish and inhuman behaviour.

Two of the many Cornish rebellions had their origin in St Keverne, one in 1497 and the other in 1547. On the church wall, facing the square, there is a plaque to the village blacksmith, Michael Joseph, leader of the first uprising. He led a Cornish army to march on London to protest at punitive taxes levied by Henry VIII. The Cornish were routed at Blackheath and Joseph was subsequently, hung, drawn and quartered.

There are two good pubs on the main square. The **White Hart Inn** (**01326 280325**) *B* is an attractive slate roofed building with en-suite rooms. The pub serves real ales, good bar food and there is a restaurant serving more expensive meals. The **Three Tuns** (**01326 280949**) *B*, next to the church also has accommodation and serves real ales and superior pub food.

There are the same regular, but infrequent, buses to Helston as Coverack. For those walking the coast path, St Keverne is located 1 mile inland – the easiest route from the west being from Polcries, which avoids the large, active Dean Quarry. From the east, it is easiest to take the narrow road from Porthoustock, where there is a beach of grey sand and stones surrounded by abandoned quarries. Its attractions are hard to discern, but the beach is much used by divers as a base for exploring the wrecks on the Manacles, just offshore at this point. *Dive Action* have learn-to-dive courses, telephone for details (**01326 280719**). Porthallow, just to the north, is approached by very narrow lanes. To the south, is Porthallow Vineyard, one of the few in this part of the country. Wine and cider can be tasted. The village itself is attractive but with limited facilities. The beach is of dark stones and grey quarry shale thrown up by the sea. The **Five Pilchards Inn** is an attractive place and has real ales and food. **Oscars** café and restaurant is right on the beach. Inexpensive. The coast path continues due north towards Nare Point. The cliffs are

Porthoustock

Porthallow

now lower and from the small headland to the south, there is a good view back to Porthallow of the narrow raised beach on the foreshore. This area forms the transition from the exotic rocks of the Lizard, the serpentine, schists and gneiss to the slate and granite that makes up most of Cornwall. Nare Head is the last point **Nare Head** before the coast turns inland to the more lush and tranquil landscapes of the Helford River. In 1891, one of the last big clipper ships then afloat, the *Bay of Panama*, was wrecked in a blizzard. The alarm was raised by a shepherd looking for his sheep in the snowdrifts – he summoned the Coverack Rocket Brigade, who rescued 18 of the crew by breeches bouy. The Head itself is the location of a now defunct naval tracking station built in the 1950's. Another raised beach is visible just around the point at Men-aver.

The Helford River

The Helford River is not a conventional estuary, but a ria or drowned valley which was flooded when the sea level rose after the last Ice Age. It is tidal up to Gweek and no large rivers dilute its tidal waters. The river and its many tributaries are remarkably unspoilt by C20 development and the area has the feel of an idyllic England long since gone. As such, it has become a haven for the rich and fashionable with some of the most expensive house prices in Cornwall. New development is strictly controlled. There are few places to stay, or eat for that matter, and certainly no campsites. However, there are some wonderful walks and good sailing on the many narrow creeks. The south bank is more remote than the north for its geography isolates it from much of the rest of Cornwall. The north bank with its geographic proximity to Falmouth and Truro is more refined, with a number of distinguished early C20 houses and fine gardens. The south bank, in particular, is not very accessible by public transport with a regular, but infrequent, bus service to Helston. By car, the road layout can be confusing and the roads themselves, narrow. However, the effort to get here is rewarded by one of the most individual and attractive areas in Cornwall.

On the south bank, Gillan Creek leads back from Nare Point and is almost a **Gillan Creek** Helford River in miniature. Gillan and Flushing are approached down extremely **Flushing** narrow lanes and there is no car parking provision in either. It is much better to park outside the villages and walk. The **Tregildry Hotel** (**01326 231378**) *E* is one of the few places to stay in this area. It is an elegant, small hotel with 10 en-suite rooms, many with river views. The restaurant is also reputed to be good. Gillan Creek can be crossed on foot for about one hour before and after low tide by the stepping stones which are located just upstream of the grassy banks that narrow the river, directly to the east of Gillan. Otherwise, walkers will have to walk around the creek. This involves cutting back inland to the road that leads towards Manaccan. Halfway there, the road crosses the head of the creek and proceeds directly along the north bank of Gillan Creek with superb views across the water to the wooded slopes of the south bank. The lane is very narrow and can be busy in the summer months. It makes a perfect walk or cycle ride. St Anthony in Meneage **St Anthony in** is an idyllic waterside hamlet with a fine church and boatyard and no other facili- **Meneage** ties. The *Church of St Dunstan* has a picturesque location on the water's edge and is built of a fine grade of granite found only in Normandy. Legend has it that the church was built as a thanksgiving by Norman sailors who had been shipwrecked and were washed ashore at this spot. The church is tiny, with a large tower reaching some 65 feet. Boat hire, as well as tuition, is available from *Sailaway St Anthony Ltd*. (**01326 231357**). Beyond St Anthony, a footpath leads to *Dennis Head*, the site of an ancient cliff castle that was refortified in the Elizabethan times during the threat from Spain. It was held by the Royalists during the Civil War, falling to General Fairfax in March 1646. There are fine views from the promontory. The coast path continues along the south side of the Helford River to Treath and Helford, although no dogs are allowed on this part of the path.

Helford

Helford itself is a delightful village of picturesque cottages of granite, slate and thatch clustered around its own tiny inlet. It can be extremely popular and in the summer months no cars are allowed into the village other than those belonging to local residents. A large car park is located on the outskirts of the village. Out of high season, it is quiet and peaceful and this is by far the best time to visit. **Rose Cottage** provides light lunches and teas, while the **Shipwrights Arms Inn** is an old thatched inn located right on the riverside. They serve real ale and bar food and they have tables on the waters edge. Highly recommended. There is no overnight accommodation in the village. The *Helford River Ferry* (**01326 250770**) leaves from beyond the pub and connects Helford to the north bank at Helford Passage. It is a daily summer service between Good Friday and the end of October. Boats leave Helford Passage on the hour and return from Helford 10 minutes later. Boat hire is available too. Helford Passage is an easy two hour walk from Falmouth and it would be quite feasible to walk to Helford for lunch and then return to Falmouth.

Frenchman's Creek

Helford is a good base for a walk to Frenchman's Creek and Pengwedhen. Frenchman's Creek is a typical Helford inlet, but has gained fame as a result of *Daphne du Maurier*'s novel of that name. She described it "still and soundless, shrouded by the trees, hidden from the eyes of men." Certainly, when the tide is in and the water laps at the fallen trees, there is a sense of mystery and intrigue. In contrast, when the tide is out the inlet becomes a muddy strand where wading birds and herons feed waiting for the next tide to bring in further riches. It was here in de Maurier's book that the French pirate, *Jean-Benoit Aubery*, hid his vessel *La Mouette*. The origin of the name of the creek is unknown but it is possible that there could be some connection with an incident with a French ship in the C18 or early C19. A fact of which de Maurier would presumably have been aware.

From Helford, the walk commences from the Shipwrights Arms Inn. Walk past the pub towards the ferry landing and take the footpath on the left, by the signpost for the ferry. Continue up the hill till the next footpath sign on the right and follow this through to *Penarvon Cove*, itself a beautiful and peaceful spot with just one house by the tiny beach. From here, the path splits – straight on for *Pengwedhen* or take the track beside the house to the top and follow the sign to the left. Pengwedhen is a wooded slope above the Helford River with views across to the north bank. The circular path drops down to the water where there is the tiny *St Francis'Chapel* built in 1930 by workmen on the nearby oyster farms. Just outside the entrance to the wood, there is a clearly defined track which can be followed to join up with the path to Frenchman's Creek described above.

Once rejoined, follow the path around till it forks and then keep left. Ahead is a panoramic view of the upper Helford River with *Merthen Wood* in the centre foreground. The path then drops down to Frenchman's Creek and winds along its eastern bank. The landscape is lush, quiet and sheltered and in direct contrast to the exposed, high fields above. At the end of the Creek, the path continues over a small footbridge and then proceeds up onto the high land above. This can be followed on to Tremayne Woods, another delightful spot on the river. The stone cottage at the head of the creek, almost completely surrounded by dense trees and totally isolated, is Frenchmann's Pill. The way back to Helford continues up the steep path just before you reach the cottage. The path continues straight over the road and through the farmyard. Follow the signs, keep to the right of the field boundary and proceed down to the valley bottom over a stile by the tree line. In the valley bottom, you join the footpath to Manaccan. Turn left and follow the path down the picturesque valley to the head of the inlet at Helford.

Merthen Wood

Manaccan, located just inland from Helford and at the head of Gillan Creek is an attractive village with cottages dotted around its hilly centre. The only building of note is the *Church of St Manacca* with a particularly fine barrel vaulted roof with embossed heraldic shields. There is a nice, though not particularly old, granite font and a characteristic squint between the chancel and south transept. In 1690, the *Reverend William Gregor* discovered Manachanite, a variety of titanium, in the stream leading to the old mill – further evidence still of the mineral wealth of the Lizard. The **New Inn** is a lovely thatched pub on the outskirts of the village.

Manaccan

Tremayne Woods, west of Frenchman's Creek is owned by the National Trust and has a woodland walk through to Tremayne Quay, one of the many granite landing stages throughout the Helford River. This one, however, was graced with a Royal Visit by Edward, Duke of Windsor (later Edward VIII) in 1921 when he visited the great house at Trelowarren. The woods are accessible from the narrow lane between Manaccan and Mawgan, although there is only very limited roadside parking. The lane itself is an attractive drive alternating between the high, exposed fields and the narrow, sunken lanes with overhanging, aged oaks in the valleys.

Tremayne Woods

Trelowarren, located just off the B3293, dates from the mid C14, with a fine Rococo Gothic chapel being added in the mid C18. The house was further extended in the C19. The house is not open to the public, but the gardens and chapel are open every day. Within the gardens is the Halligye Fogou, the largest in Cornwall and well preserved. The service buildings to the house contain a bistro, pottery, information centre and gallery.

Trelowarren

Halligye Fogou

Mawgan is a pleasant jumble of buildings around the *Church of St Mawgan* which is big and distinguished with a high tower. The earliest parts are C13 with further significant additions in the C15. There is a particularly fine, heavily carved barrel vault roof and an elaborate squint, the cut-off corner being replaced by a shaft with a carved shield-holding angel. There are some particularly, fine memorials mainly dedicated to the Vyvyans, whose ancestral home is at nearby Trelowarren. The **Old Courthouse** is a traditional inn that serves real ales and good pub food. There is also a pleasant beer garden.

Mawgan

Gweek

Gweek, is the limit of navigation on the Helford River and once an important port. It is now used mainly by boat owners to over-winter their craft, though some surprisingly big ships do still dock at the small port. Just outside the village is the

Open 10am–5pm daily. Admission, £8.50, children £5.50

National Seal Sanctuary (01326 221874). There are a number of pools where seals recovering from injury are kept before release and also a number of resident seals and sea lions who cannot be released into the wild.

Just outside Constantine, to the north east of Gweek, is the **Trengilly Wartha Inn** (01326 340332) *C–D*, voted Pub of the Year by *The Good Pub Guide* in 1999. It is signposted down narrow lanes off the road to Gweek. The pub itself has an attractive interior with real ale served from the barrels behind the bar. However, their reputation is based on their wine and cooking – the pub and restaurant stock a list of over 250 wines with more than a dozen being sold by the glass in the bar. The food in both the bar and restaurant (moderate/expensive) has a fine reputation and there is also accommodation if required.

Helford Passage

Narrow lanes lead around the north side of the river, via *Porth Navas*, a tiny hamlet in a luxuriant setting, to Helford Passage, little more than a line of buildings facing the river. There is very restricted car parking in the village but there is a free car park just outside from where it is a short walk to the river front. There is a small, sandy beach exposed at low tide. The **Ferry Boat Inn** has tables overlooking the river and serves food and real ale. The ferry to Helford leaves from here on the hour between 9.00am and 5.00pm (later in July and August).

Open daily, 10.30am–5pm. Admission £5.00, children £3.00. In winter, £2.50, children £1.50

Trebah Gardens (01326 250448), just to the east, is one of the most important sub-tropical gardens in the country. The 25 acre garden is set in a steep valley that leads down to a private beach on the river. The changes in level are fully exploited to create vistas and views across the gardens and over the river. The gardens were first planted in the 1830s by Charles Fox, an extraordinarily energetic man who would direct teams of gardeners to build massive scaffold towers to check the effect of the fully grown plant before placing the seedling. It became recognized as one of the most important gardens in England with many rare and exotic plants. However, in 1939 the estate was sold and split up and the gardens neglected. Restoration work began on the gardens in the 1980s and they are now fully restored. A series of paths lead down to the beach with the rhododendrons , hydrangeas, bamboo and giant Brazilian rhubarb particularly noteworthy. The small beach is available for visitors to use. It is not particularly attractive although there are nice views over the river. American forces embarked from here for the D-Day landings, hence the name Yankee Beach.

Open mid-Feb–Oct, daily except Sun & Mon (open Bank Holiday Mon) 10.30am – 5.30pm. Admission £4.50, children £2.20, family £11.20

Glendurgan Gardens (01326 250906) owned by the National Trust, is almost immediately adjacent to Trebah. Another valley garden running down to the river and another creation of the energetic Fox family, this time Alfred Fox. It was first planted in the 1820s and 1830s. The garden contains many fine and exotic plants and has many similarities to nearby Trebah. Of particular interest, is the large, laurel maze, which dates from 1833. At the bottom of the garden is the impossibly scenic hamlet of Durgan, no more than a few granite houses scattered around a tiny shingle beach. It is entirely owned by the National Trust and many of the properties are available to rent as holiday homes. There is no overnight accommodation nor any facilities. The only parking is in the car park further up the hill. The coast path passes through the village and it is an easy and very attractive walk from Helford Passage or Mawnan. Much of the land around here is owned by the National Trust and there are several good walks and footpaths as well as the coast path that leads around to Falmouth. There are a number of tiny coves along the north shore and from *Porth Saxon* there is the pleasantly wooded Carwinion Valley with a series of walks to the car park by Mawnan Church.

Mawnan Church lies outside the village in a peaceful setting with good views towards the sea. The churchyard extends right to the cliff top and there are benches to allow the views to be fully appreciated. The church is typical Cornish with a low tower and a rather unusual roof structure inside. The font is an unusual C15 design and there is an excellent piscina, a basin for washing Mass vessels, in the chancel wall, thought to be C13 and with intricately carved heads as labelstops. There is a small parking area and a footpath to Durgan and the coast path.

The coast between Mawnan and Falmouth is one of low cliffs and small coves with Pendennis Castle claiming the skyline in the distance. *Bream Cove* is one of the nicer ones, a small beach of sand and rocks at the end of a wooded valley. It can only be approached by footpath from the Mawnan to Maenporth road or via the coast path. Maenporth is a rather undistinguished place but the beach is sandy and sheltered and can get busy at peak times. All facilities are available along with windusfing and diving tuition and equipment hire.

Maenporth

Just inland is **Penjerrick Garden** (**01872 870105**) almost unbelievably another creation of the Fox family, whose shipping interests allowed the easy importation of species from overseas. The gardens were developed around the 1840s and contain some large specimens of these early plantings, including a round Brain Coral thought to have come from Charles Darwin's expedition aboard the Beagle. The gardens have a more natural, less-manicured appearance which is at variance with many of the others in the area. The gardens are privately owned, and are found on the road between Mawnan Smith and Budock Water.

Open Wed, Fri & Sun through summer, 1.30pm –4.30pm. Admission £2.50, children £1.00

Falmouth, Truro and the Coast to St Austell

Introduction

This area is not one that may immediately appeal to the visitor but there are a number of key sites and some wonderful river and coastal scenery. Falmouth and Truro are two of the biggest and most interesting towns in Cornwall. Falmouth is the major seaport and Truro, the commercial and administrative centre. Truro has some of the best Georgian architecture west of Bath and one of the twentieth century's more impressive cathedrals, while the recent opening of the National Maritime Museum Cornwall in Falmouth is destined to increase both the number and profile of visitors to the town. The Fal Estuary is one of the largest and deepest in the country and the many rivers and creeks that feed off it provide a delightful setting for the tiny villages and isolated churches that dot the landscape hereabouts. The Roseland is relatively remote and little visited with the major sailing centre of St Mawes at its southern tip and a number of attractive but understated villages along the coast including Portscatho and Portloe. While the area is not particularly noted for its beaches, there are a number of good ones in remote locations that rarely, if ever, get busy. Mevagissey is a busy fishing port and major tourist destination. The gardens of Heligan and the Eden Project, near St Austell, are two of Cornwall's most visited attractions to the extent that finding accommodation in their vicinity can be difficult without pre-booking. Apart from the main towns, the public transport connections are not good and it requires a bit of forward planning to get around without your own transport. Around the Fal Estuary, ferries become the key link in an otherwise fractured transport system.

Falmouth

Falmouth sits on one of the finest natural harbours in the country. This and its proximity to the shipping lanes of the Atlantic has been the defining factor in its

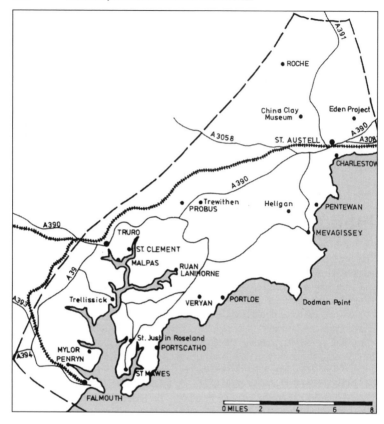

history. It still maintains a maritime connection, with its ship repair yards and docks, but is now also one of the major urban centres and tourist destinations in Cornwall.

Historic development

Falmouth's history as a town is surprisingly recent. There was no mention in the Doomsday Book and the earliest depiction of the area is a map of c1540 which shows only one building on the site – the medieval manor house of *Arwenack*. This was the home of the Killigrews, Falmouth's foremost family. The house was largely rebuilt in 1567–71 but then destroyed by Parliamentarians during the Civil War, the Killigrews being prominent Royalists. The building now is largely late C18 and more modern reconstruction. There is little to see of the original Elizabethan mansion. It is now divided up into residences but can still be seen in Grove Place, opposite the *Killigrew Monument* on the harbour front – a simple stone pyramid without date or inscription and originally erected on a different spot in 1737–8, some 12 years after the last of the Killigrews had left Falmouth.

In 1542–6, Henry VIII built Pendennis Castle to strengthen his coastal defences. It presented the Killigrews with the chance to develop Falmouth as a rival to the much longer-established Penryn, located just upriver. John Killigrew was appointed the Castle's first Governor and was succeeded by his son, also John. This position was very convenient for the Killigrews as their other activities of piracy and smuggling must have dovetailed in nicely with being the King's man on the spot. The Castle saw little action during these early years, but was subjected to a siege that lasted five months during the Civil War.

Pendennis Castle

The Killigrews created Falmouth. At the end of the C16, a licence was obtained to build 4 houses – by 1613 a plan had been formulated for building a whole town. There were objections from the established towns of Truro, Penryn and Helston which were also key trading ports. A map of 1630 shows no settlement and town status was only granted in 1661 by Royal Charter from Charles II. By 1664, however, the town was recorded as having some 200 houses and a new church with the timely dedication of King Charles the Martyr, Charles I having been executed in 1649.

The church was a substantial undertaking and must have seemed impossibly grand for a community of only 200 houses – the Killigrews were making a statement of their future intentions for Falmouth. The church was built in 1662-4 and sits on a small hillock above Church Street, commanding the slight deflection in the road at this point. From outside, it looks typically Cornish; low, granite but with a curious tower, narrower in one dimension than the other, and having an unusually slim and graceful line. The square plan of the church is not evident from the outside due to the restricted nature of its setting. It is only once inside that the superb proportions of the church reveal themselves – the nave, originally 66 by 66 feet and divided by tall granite columns. This classical splendour is oddly contrasted with the two tiers of typically Cornish medieval windows and the three separate roofs. It is this mixture of classical and medieval that gives the church its distinctive interior – you can see the new concept of classicism wrestling with the still strong forms of medievalism, lingering in this remote corner of England. Galleries were added in the late C17 but have now been removed with the exception of the west end. The new east end was constructed in 1813 and contains a fine, Venetian window over the altar. There is a heavily carved pulpit and some, bright modern glass.

Church of King Charles the Martyr

The church is notable for the number of memorials to soldiers, sailors, civil servants and entrepreneurs of the burgeoning Empire. Falmouth's importance as a point of embarkation during the C17–C19 is evident from these sombre accounts of young lives lost at sea, many of them packet captains. A marble and alabaster memorial to *Thomas Corker*, dated 1700, is a testament to Falmouth's importance as a trade centre – the inscription states how he died trading with Africa for gold, ivory and precious timber. Another memorial of 1810 commemorates the New Yorker *L. N. Malcomb* mortally wounded on H.M.Packet *Princess Charlotte* in an action with a French privateer off the Isles of Scilly. A slate memorial on the floor in front of the entrance is dated 1694, the earliest in the church.

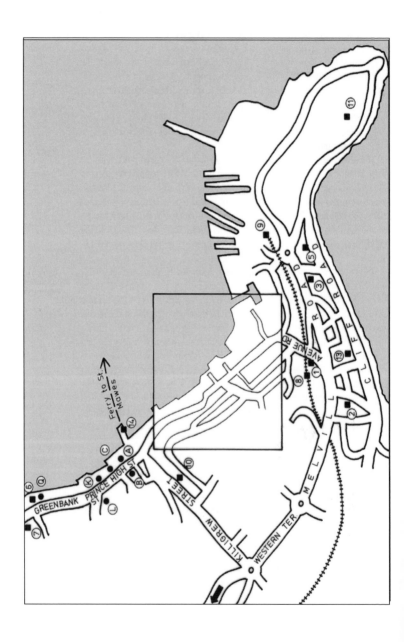

FALMOUTH

ACCOMMODATION

1 Camelot & Headlands Hotel
2 Gyllyngvase House Hotel
3 Ivanhoe
4 Grove Hotel
5 Falmouth Hotel
6 Greenbank Hotel
7 Goodwinds

ESSENTIALS

8 Dell Railway Station
9 Falmouth Docks Railway Station
10 Tourist Office
11 Pendennis Castle
12 Maritime Museum
13 Princes Pavillion
14 Prince of Walles Pier
15 Church

RESTAURANTS AND BARS

A Pepe's
B Thai Orchid
C Café no. 33
D Mings Garden
E Bistro de la Mer
F Hunkydory
G The Hut
H The Seafood Bar
I De Wynns Coffee House
J 5 Degrees West
K Star and Garter
L The Boathouse
M Cork and Bottle
N King's Head
O Quayside Inn
P Chain Locker
Q Working Boat Pub

GALLERIES

R Beside the Wave
S Ocean Contemporary
T Demelza's

Another member of the Killigrew family, Thomas, was a well known playwright, writing three plays before the Civil War, all of which were performed at the Cockpit in Drury Lane. After the Civil War, he gained a charter for a *Theatre Royal* in Drury Lane, London. It opened in 1663 but was destroyed by fire in 1672. Killigrew engaged Sir Christopher Wren to design the new Theatre Royal. He died in 1683 and is buried in Westminster Abbey. The last of the Killigrew's left Falmouth in 1725, by which time the town was well established.

The Post Office Packet Service arrived in 1689 and initially carried mail and bullion to Corunna in Spain. The packets were sleek, fast brigantines crewed by no more than 30 men and designed to flee with their precious cargos rather than fight and risk capture. They were an instant success and soon the service was extended to include the West Indies, the Americas and the Mediterranean. By 1782, 22 packets were in service and by 1808 this number had risen to 39. Most were privately owned vessels, hired by the Post Office, and controlled by the Falmouth-based Packet Agent. For a time, this was located in Bell's Court, still in existence up an alley off Church Street, opposite Marks and Spencers. The building is distinguished by its bold projecting front porch. The packet service led to huge growth in the importance of Falmouth, as the town catered for the trade, passengers and crews. Falmouth became an important harbour with many ships calling in to collect directions for their final port of call. Between 1811 and 1861,

Packet Service

the number of houses almost doubled to1252.

However, when the railway connected Southampton to London, it became quicker to transfer mail and goods from the south coast and Falmouth ceased to be a packet port in 1850. The establishment of the Lloyds signal station on the Lizard in 1872 meant that ships no longer needed to put into port to collect orders, a further blow to Falmouth's fortunes. However, Falmouth's geographic advantages could not be diminished and it remains England's most south-westerly safe anchorage. To capitalize on this, the foundation stone of the docks was laid in 1860 and two dry docks were completed by 1863. Further dry docks were built during and after the First World War and the last was added as recently as 1958. Falmouth became an important centre for shipbuilding and more recently repair and maintenance.

The railway arrived in 1863 and directly connected Falmouth to London for the first time. However, it was too late to tempt back the Packet Service which was now well established in the ports of Southampton and Liverpool. The railway hastened the development of the tourist industry which capitalized on the extraordinarily mild climate and proximity of beaches and estuary.

During the Second World War, Falmouth had a significant role to play in the Battle of the Atlantic and as a port of embarkation. Survivors from Dunkirk were landed here and the famous raid on St Nazaire was launched from Falmouth. It was also a major port for the D Day landings and there were many military bases in the area in the build up to the biggest sea-borne invasion in history. Not surprisingly, Falmouth was a target for enemy bombers and some 2000 houses were damaged during the raids with 31 civilians being killed and 91 injured.

Pendennis Castle

English Heritage (01326 316594). Open April–October, 10am–6pm (5pm in April, June and Sept.), November–March, 10am–4pm. Admission £4.50, children £2.30, family £11.30

The castle is on the southern edge of the town and is well signposted. There is a scenic drive around the perimeter of the site which affords good river and sea views and also allows access to some of the fortifications outside the ramparts. The castle, itself, is one of the most important defensive installations in the country. It has been well maintained and restored by English Heritage and they have installed a number of tasteful and informative tableau to represent the various periods of the castle's history.

Pendennis Castle is the westernmost of the string of fortifications that Henry VIII built along the south coast against the threat of invasion. It is one of the biggest and most elaborate and it continued in more or less continual use until 1956. As such, the fortifications provide a good example of how the defences have been adapted to respond to the changing technology of warfare. The earliest structure was probably *The Blockhouse* (Little Dennis) on the very tip of the headland near the water line. This was built in 1538 and was probably a short-term measure to mount cannon over the harbour entrance while the main fort was built. This lies outside the ramparts and can be visited (no charge) from the car park on the perimeter road. The main *Henrician Castle* was built between 1540–45 and consists of a central round gun tower, an encircling lower gun platform and a projecting entrance block. The design of these forts was a response to the new principles of warfare and they were specially designed to mount cannon and resist bombardment. Enemy cannon balls would be deflected off the curved and immensely thick walls, while the squat profile provided a small target for enemy ships.

The central round tower is the oldest part, the forebuilding with its projecting bay window was added in the late C16. Above the entrance to the castle is a fine carving of the Tudor royal coat-of-arms. The empty niche below would have been for the governor's own coat-of-arms. There are also some finely carved grotesque waterspouts – a good example of the craftsmanship at work on these castles. The castle is divided up into basement kitchen, gun rooms on the ground and upper floor and the rooftop gun platform that would have been the most important. Fully armed the castle would have provided considerable and concentrated firepower. There are panoramic views from the roof across to the neighbouring castle of St Mawes. From the roof the wider spiral stairs go down to the first floor of the forebuilding which would most probably have been the governor's quarters. The interiors have been fitted with furniture and artefacts typical of the period.

It quickly became apparent that the castle was poorly defended from attack by land and with the increased threat of invasion from Spain, Elizabeth I ordered the strengthening of the defences. The earthen *ramparts* date from this period (1598–1600) and, again, were at the cutting edge of military technology The slope of the rampart was designed to absorb the impact of cannon balls while the projecting bastions allowed smaller guns to give covering fire on anyone attempting to scale the wall. The *gatehouse and guardroom* were added in the late C17 – the guardroom is possibly the earliest purpose-built barracks in Britain. They have now been fitted out to represent how they would have looked during the First World War. Within the ramparts, the storehouse, now the shop, was built during the Napoleonic Wars and the barracks in 1902. The battery observation post was constructed in the C19 to control the guns at Half Moon Battery located outside the ramparts. This was used during the Second World War and the interior has been reconstructed to how it would have looked during those times.

To the south of here, a tunnel leads under the ramparts to *Half Moon Battery*, built in 1793 and thereafter the principal offensive firepower of the fort. It remained in use up to the Second World War when it formed the principal line of defence for Falmouth, in association with the battery on St Anthony's Head opposite. The battery is armed with 6-inch naval guns, similar to those mounted during the war. They had a formidable range of 12 miles.

National Maritime Museum Cornwall
Discovery Quay (01326 313388). Open every day, 10am–5pm. Closed January.
Admission £5.90, children and concessions £3.90, family £15.50

Located by the sea at the southern end of the town centre, the newly-opened Maritime Museum has become one of the major attractions in Cornwall. The purpose-built museum is a distinctive building clad in green oak boarding by master shipwrights. It has a sweeping glazed wall to the sea providing views over the harbour from the main boat gallery. A "lighthouse" tower provides more panoramic views across Falmouth and the harbour, while the basement has windows to allow views below the tidal waters.

The museum's primary purpose is to display the National Maritime Museum's collection of more than 120 small boats. Two large boat galleries have been created, where the exhibits are hung from wires and viewed from ramped walkways. Each year, the exhibition will be changed to present a different theme from the collection with up to 40 boats being displayed at any one time. They range from an Inuit kayak of skin and driftwood to the latest laser-cut racing craft, but, perhaps, the biggest draw is *Bluebottle*, the last remaining Royal Yacht that has been donated to the museum and meticulously restored.

In addition to the boat galleries, there are displays on weather forecasting, tides, navigation, Cornish maritime history and everything that pertains to the world of small boats. There are inter-active opportunities to plot charts, navigate boats and even sail miniature, radio-controlled yachts against a fan-generated wind. There is one of the best maritime libraries in the country, a waterside cafe, lecture theatre and a large square to the front of the building which hosts regular outdoor events.

The Town

The old town is long and narrow and follows the line of the harbour along *Grove Place, Arwenack Street, Market Street* and *High Street*, in effect one continuous road. Narrow lanes and alleys lead down to the quays and harbour immediately to the east. The street is lined with an interesting collection of buildings, many dating from the C18 and C19. At the southern end is Arwenack House and the Killigrew Monument. Further north, is a terrace of C18 brick houses, set back from the street, and with a chequerboard pattern of red and dark brick. The *Custom House* dates from the early C19 and is a distinctive, low classical design with a series of columns supporting an entablature along the front facade. The whole is painted stark white and, rather pleasingly, is still used by H.M. Customs and Excise. A nearby chimney was used to burn contraband tobacco.

Arwenack House

Royal Cornwall Polytechnic

Falmouth Arts Centre

Further to the north, is the Royal Cornwall Polytechnic, which was established in 1833 and is the third oldest cultural institution in Cornwall. Its classical facade with large central pediment sits comfortably in this streetscene of different styles and periods. It is now occupied by the Falmouth Arts Centre (**01326 212300**) with a regular programme of talks, exhibitions, film, music and theatre.

The C17 church, described earlier, commands the sharp turn in the street as it enters Church Street. At no.54 and 55 are two remarkable C19 shopfronts with huge bowed windows. One is the de Wyms coffee house and the other John Maggs Prints. Opposite is *St George's Arcade*, built in 1912.

Where the street widens, the large *Prince of Wales Pier* is the base for ferries and boat excursions throughout the Fal Estuary. Cruises are available to Flushing, Helford River and Frenchman's Creek, Truro, the River Fal and Smugglers Cottage. Fishing trips can also be arranged. A number of companies provide cruises including *Enterprise Boats* (**01326 313234**), *K & S Cruises* (**01326 211056**) and *Newman's Cruises* (**01872 580309**). These and other operators have come together to form Fal River Links in an attempt to better co-ordinate and promote ferry services throughout the area. There is a free leaflet that has details of all the available ferries.

The Prince of Wales Pier is also the landing place for the year round St Mawes Ferry (**01326 313201**). It takes 25 minutes and is a good way to see the bay. Services are every 30 minutes in summer (hourly on Sunday) and less frequently in winter. Return fares are £4.80, children £2.40. There is also a ferry service to Flushing, Monday to Saturday, every half hour in the summer, less frequently in the winter (**01326 317637**). There are good views of the estuary from the pier and also of the Falmouth shoreline, now much built over.

Beyond the pier, the road climbs steeply uphill until it reaches *Greenbank*, *Stratton Terrace* and *Tehidy Terrace*, with a number of fine C18 and C19 houses looking out over the Penryn River towards Flushing. Many have good doors and porches, distinctive bay windows and fine brickwork and stucco. This was the more exclusive area of town where the well-to-do built substantial villas enjoying the river views and fresh air. The Greenbank Hotel has a prominent position on the river's edge. The earliest part dates from the late C18 and the hotel originally catered for the packet ship captains. The granite quay below is reputed to be C17. Kenneth Graham stayed here while writing *The Wind in the Willows*.

The Town Hall and Public Library on The Moor in Killigrew Street was opened in 1896. The library contains Cornwall's Maritime Collection, including sets of Lloyds List, charts and almanacs as well as books on all aspects of sailing and maritime history. The upper floor now contains the *Falmouth Art Gallery* (**01326 313863**), which has visiting exhibitions and a small permanent collection. Opposite, on the other side of The Moor is *Jacob's Ladder*, a flight of 111 steep, stone steps.

Open Mon–Sat 10am–5pm. Admission free

The town contains many interesting shops including several antique shops, secondhand bookshops and galleries. *Beside the Wave*, 10 Arwenack Street (**01326 211132**) has a good selection of contemporary paintings in its rather cramped gallery and prices are reasonable. *Ocean Contemporary*, 29 Church Street (**01326 210300**) has a good collection of paintings by local artists and *Demelza's Gallery* (**01326 316472**), next door, is a compact space with some interesting work. The *Fox Rosehill Gardens*, a legacy to the town from the Fox family contains many exotic and sub-tropical plants brought back from various parts of the globe by captains in the Falmouth shipping trade. It is located a short walk from the town centre near The Dell railway station. *Falmouth Arts Centre* also often has exhibitions of art work. *John Maggs*, 54 Church Street is in a magnificent Victorian shop and sells traditional prints, framed or unframed.

The Beaches

Falmouth's beaches are something of a disappointment, certainly compared to those of North Cornwall and Penwith. They are found on the south facing shore along Cliff Road with Pendennis Castle to the east. There are no beaches on the

Fal Estuary side of the town. Swanpool Beach is at the extreme west end of the
Swanpool town and can be accessed from Cliff Road by footpath or by car via Swanpool
Beach Road where there is a large car park. The beach is sandy and fairly extensive, but
nothing special. Most facilities are provided, although there is no lifeguard service. However, the beach is generally safe for bathing. Behind the beach, there is a
Gyllynhvase large lake where rowing boats can be hired. Gyllyngvase Beach is Falmouth's
Beach biggest and most popular. It is located directly below the hotels and boarding
houses of Cliff Road and has a pleasing southerly aspect. However, the sand is
rather coarse and the whole beach is overlooked by the road and a continuous
strip of development. There are all facilities, including a summer lifeguard service. Bathing is generally safe and the sands slope quite gently. Further along Cliff
Road are thin strips of sand, largely covered at high tide and not particularly
pleasant.

Accommodation

Falmouth is a major tourist destination and there are a large number of places to
stay in all price ranges. The main concentration is to the south of the town centre
along and behind Cliff Road and the beaches. The Dell railway station is nearby.
There are almost too many to attempt to make a selection. However, you could try
Camelot, 5 Avenue Road (**01326 312480**) **B** or the **Headlands Hotel**, 4 Avenue
Road (**01326 311141**) **B**, right by the railway station or **Gyllyngvase House
Hotel**, Gyllyngvase Road (**01326 312956**) **C**, near the beach. **Ivanhoe**, 7 Melvill
Road (**01326 319083**) **B** is one of a string of guest houses in this road near
Pendennis Point. Directly opposite the Maritime Museum is the **Grove Hotel**,
Grove Place (**01326 319577**) **B** in a period, Georgian building. **The Falmouth
Hotel**, Castle Beach (**01326 312671**) **D–E** overlooks the beach and is an impres-
sive, white, Victorian building with very comfortable facilities including a pool and
gym. To the north of the town centre, the **Greenbank Hotel**, Harbourside
(**01326 312440**) **E** is one of the most luxurious in town. It is located on the shore
road and has extensive views across the Estuary. Rooms are attractively furnished
and the restaurant is reputed to be very good. Just to the north is the **Goodwinds
Guest House**, 13 Stratton Terrace (**01326 313200**) **B**, a lovely Georgian house
with beautiful gardens and estuary views. 10 en-suite rooms, most with harbour
views and very good value.

Restaurants and cafes

Falmouth has scores of places to eat, many of them with a reputation for good
food. Most are concentrated on the main route that runs north-south through the
town. Most of the pubs in the following section also serve food and are generally
cheaper than the restaurants.

Pepe's 29 High Street (**01326 311212**) **M**, snug restaurant with a small, but
enterprising menu with a choice of fish and meat dishes.

Thai Orchid High Street (**01326 211028**) *I–M*, opposite the above. Good value Thai cuisine.

Café no 33 33 High Street (**01326 211944**) *M–E*, lovely, wood floored interior with many pictures and a bistro atmosphere. Good food with an eclectic menu, including Japanese food on Wednesdays. Open evenings only.

Mings Garden 40-41 Church Street (**01326 314413**) *M*, standard Chinese in large Victorian building with high ceilings. Evenings only.

Bistro de la Mer Arwenack Street (**01326 316509**) *M–E*, French influenced cuisine in attractive bistro.

Hunkydory Arwenack Street (**01326 212997**) *M–E*, opposite the Custom House. Smart restaurant with exposed timber beams and a small menu of imaginative fish and meat dishes.

The Hut 12 Quay Street (**01326 318229**) *M*, tiny restaurant with a bright interior and a small menu of fish, meat and tapas.

The Seafood Bar Quay Street (**01326 315129**) *M–E*, opposite the above. Highly regarded, fish and shellfish restaurant

De Wynn's Coffee House 55 Church Street (**01326 319259**) *I*, traditional coffee and tea shop, cakes and light lunches. Coffee freshly ground on the premises.

5 Degrees West Grove Place (**01326 311288**) Near the maritime museum. this smart bar and grill also has regular live music. There is also a large outside terrace.

Bars and Nightlife

There are some good pubs in Falmouth, many in old, character buildings and with views over the harbour and estuary. There are also a number of clubs.

Star and Garter High Street. A friendly locals pub with marvellous views over the estuary from its raised position just to the north of the town centre. Real ale from the cask and bar food. The walls are covered with paintings of the pub regulars by local artist Steve Taylor. Commissions undertaken. Occasional live music.

The Boathouse Trevethen Hill. Near the above. Equally fine views from this popular pub with real ales and good pub food. There is live music on certain nights.

Cork and Bottle Church Street. Comfortable pub with spacious, modernised interior serving pub food..

Kings Head Church Street, big pub on the corner next to the church. Somewhat lacking in atmosphere.

Quayside Inn Arwenack Street, one of the nicest pubs in town. Two bars and nice views over the harbour from the upper bar. The lower gives access to the harbour where there are tables available for customers' use. The pub has a warm and welcoming interior and serves a good selection of real ales and pub food.

Chain Locker   Lower Quay Hill, near the above and sharing the outside tables. A charming old pub on several levels.

The Working Boat Pub   Harbourside, below the Greenbank Hotel, an old inn directly on the river front, just north of the town centre.

A number of places around town have live music on an occasional basis. The *Falmouth Arts Centre* in Chapel Street (**01326 212300**) has a full programme of film, theatre, talks and exhibitions. The *Princess Pavilion* (**01326 2112220**) near the beaches caters for the more mainstream shows. *Shades* in Lower Quay Hill and *Remedies* on The Moor, near the bus terminus, are the local clubs.

ⓘ   Practicalities

Tourist Information Centre

The Tourist Information Centre (**01326 312300**) is at 28 Killigrew Street, near the bus terminus. They can provide a comprehensive list of accommodation. Trains connect with the main West Coast line at Truro, although the service is not frequent. However, the line is particularly scenic. Somewhat confusingly, there are three stations in Falmouth. *Falmouth Docks* is the largest and the terminus and is located to the south of the town. *The Dell*, an unmanned halt is the closest to the town centre and is a few hundred yards from the southern end of Grove Place. It is also the closest station for the beaches on the south shore. *Penmere Halt* is again unmanned, but beautifully maintained by volunteers. It is at the western end of Killigrew Street, about 15 minutes walk from the town centre. Buses stop in the centre of town on The Moor. There are regular buses to Truro, Camborne and Helston for onward connections. Falmouth is on the A39 from Truro. There are a number of car parks in the town centre but they can be full at peak times. Ferries operate from the Prince of Wales Pier and carry passengers only to St Mawes and Flushing throughout the year. There is a summer, passenger ferry service to Truro which makes a pleasant trip and can be linked with a return journey by train. Details of ferry operators are provided above.

Trains

Buses

Ferries

The Fal Estuary to Truro

The Fal is an area of sheltered, deep water tidal inlets surrounded by rolling hills and some of Cornwall's rare woods. It has few towns and little development and is a complete contrast to the wind lashed north and west of the county. It is a mecca for sailors and of national importance for the waders and wildfowl who winter in its sheltered creeks. The estuary, itself, is also rich in wildlife with its oyster fisheries, and the rarer maerl beds, a calcareous seaweed which provides a home for many unusual plants and animals. In places, just below low water, are eel grass beds, Britain's only flowering marine plant. The Fal is now recognized as an internationally important wildlife site and is destined to become a marine Special Area of Conservation.

Just a few miles upriver from Falmouth is Penryn. It predates Falmouth and was an important town and port in the early Middle Ages. A market charter was granted in 1236 and in 1265 the great *Collegiate Church of Glasney* was erected. It was dissolved in the C16 and is now completely gone. Much of the stone was used to construct the buildings of Penryn. The town is pleasant enough and there are some attractive buildings along the main, Market Street and in the narrow lanes and alleys leading off it, but otherwise little to detain the visitor. The *Town Hall* of 1839 is the most notable landmark sitting astride the main street and dividing the traffic either side. The **Kings Arms** in the main street is a 200 year old coaching inn and has a distinctive, projecting bay over its entrance. It serves real ales and food. There are several cafes in the main street and a couple of art galleries, *Penryn Fine Art* (**01326 376839**) in Lower Market Street and the Malcolm *Sutcliffe Glass Gallery* (**01326 377020**) at 2 West Street. *Tremough*, on the western edge of the town, has been selected as the site for the first University of Cornwall and phase 1 of the innovative design was expected to be finished by autumn 2004.

Penryn

Flushing lies on the opposite bank to Falmouth and can be reached by passenger ferry (see under Falmouth). It was once the home to many of the sea captains working out of Falmouth and it has several fine buildings dating from the C17 onwards. It provides an exceptionally pretty backdrop to the river and there are good views across to Falmouth. There is a small, sandy beach at the southern end of the village. **The Seven Stars** (**01326 374373**) *M* is a beautifully situated pub and restaurant right on the riverside.They have tables outside which make a wonderful place to watch the sun set over the river. Right on the quayside is **The Sticky Prawn** (**01326 373734**) *M*, a small fresh fish restaurant with marvellous views from the outside terrace.

Flushing

Just to the north, is Mylor Churchtown, a small hamlet with nice river views and a big yacht harbour which used to be a naval dockyard. However, the main interest is the *Church of St Melorus*, one of a number of exquisitely located churches around the Fal estuary. This one is located in a large churchyard on slightly higher ground, just back from the river. The design is unusual, with a turret on its west gable with thick supporting buttresses the same width as the nave, giving the odd impression of a large chimney. Nearby is a free-standing belfry with a weatherboarded top dating from the early C17. The church possesses two Norman doorways, the one on the north side, in its original position, with a Maltese Cross and zigzag moulding and the other moved to the west side, also with a cross above. The south doorway is of soft Caen stone, unusual for Cornwall, and exceptionally well carved, as is the south porch itself. The same French stone has been used for the piers inside. The entire floor of the church is paved with old, slate memorial slabs. There is a very good, carved Elizabethan pulpit and an equally good rood screen. A riverside path to Flushing alongside the Carrick Roads makes a pleasant walk from where the ferry can be taken to Falmouth.

Mylor Churchtown

Just north of Mylor Bridge and approached down a steep narrow lane is one of the most attractively sited pubs in the area. **The Pandora Inn** (**01326 372678**) is a C13 thatched inn in a waterside setting. It serves real ales and food and can get very busy in the summer.

Come-to-Good

On the way to Feock, the road passes the intriguingly-named Come-to-Good where there is a rare *Friend's Meeting House* dating from 1710. The walls of cob (dried mud) and the big thatched roof are more in the tradition of Devon than Cornwall. An open stable at one end would have been for the congregation's horses. The simple, plain interior and utilitarian timber furnishings are typical of the Quaker philosophy. The building is open daily and you are welcome to look around.

Feock

Feock is a large village for the Fal with houses set within large gardens and a lush landscape. There is a small sand and shingle beach that offers sheltered bathing and is popular with locals. The *Church of St Feoca* is below the road level and highlighted by the detached C13 tower on the road side, the only remains of the early church. The present church is largely C19. However, inside there is a well carved Norman font and a pulpit with four C16 Flemish panels depicting religious scenes. The lytch gate with its slate hung upper storey is similar to examples elsewhere in the County. *Creekvean* in Pill Lane is an early work (1967) by the now celebrated architects *Richard Rogers* and *Norman Foster*. There is not much to see from the lane as the main elevation faces out over the creek.

Trellissick

Gardens open all year daily, mid Feb–Christmas, Jan–mid Feb, Thurs–Sun, 10.30am–5.30pm. In winter 11am–4pm. Woodland, open daily all year. Admission (gardens) £5.00, children £2.50, family £12.50

Trellisick is a grand country house with superb gardens and woodland. The house is privately owned and not open to the public. The gardens and woodland are owned by the National Trust (**01872 862090**). There are two restaurants and a shop and plant sales when the gardens are open. The *Trellissick Gallery* (**01872 864084**) is located in another of the house's service buildings and has a large and well-presented range of paintings, prints, ceramics and pottery. A regular programme of events is held throughout the year including open air concerts and theatre. Telephone for further details. It is also possible to visit Trellissick by boat from Truro, Falmouth and St Mawes in the summer months. For further information on sailings, telephone 01872 862090 or the local Tourist Information Centre.

The house was designed in 1750 by *Edmund Davey* as a simple and rather severe two storey neo-classical villa with a recessed veranda on the south front overlooking Carrick Roads, the main river channel. In 1825, the architect *Peter Robinson* added a giant pedimented portico across the veranda and another portico to the west front, which gave the building a more impressive appearance, particularly from the main river views. In the late C19 the single storey wings had another floor added to give the simple, but impressive building seen today. Although the house is not open to the public, there are good views of it from the surrounding gardens and woodland.

The gardens extend to 25 acres and are to the east of the house running down to the River Fal, while the woodland extends to some 500 acres, much of which is open to the public. The garden is young when compared to many National Trust properties and dates largely from 1937 onwards. It is planted within the sheltered framework of the earlier woodland planting which help to give it a more mature aspect than one might otherwise expect. It has a wide range of hydrangeas, rhodo-dendrons, camellias, maples, magnolias and other exotic shrubs and plants. It is par-ticularly colourful in Spring, but retains interest throughout the year. It is unusual compared to many other Cornish gardens with its areas of mown lawn and flower borders. Much of its drama comes from its riverside location and the views over the large expanses of water to the wooded hills on the other side. There is a particularly good viewpoint from the Victorian-style timber summerhouse at the south end of the garden. The parkland which forms the foreground to the house from Carrick Roads was planted from 1820 and is a fine example of the English landscape style.

The woodland has many good walks to take advantage of the river views. North of the house, a walk skirts the side of Lamouth Creek, a typical Cornish estuary with trees hanging over the sides and wide mudflats at low tide. At the mouth of the creek, on the north bank, is *Roundwood Quay,* an C18 granite quay for shipping tin and copper. It was meant to be able to take 300 ton boats, even at the lowest tide. Just inland from here are the remains of an Iron Age promontory fort, the earthworks and ditches still visible. Paths continue along the south side of the creek and extend southwards along the edge of the River Fal. The character now changes for this is no longer a shallow creek - the Fal being Britain's largest deep water harbour with a depth of 80 feet in mid-channel. It is quite common to see large ocean-going ships laid up in the channel here. The wood drops down to a small, attractive hamlet and the ferry.

The *King Harry Ferry* (**01872 862312**) is a key link in the transport system of the estuary, saving a long road detour to the north. There has probably been a ferry here since before the Norman Conquest and it used to be on the old coach road between Penzance and London. The name probably refers to an inscription to Henry VI in a woodland chapel near Tolverne. In 1888, a steam ferry replaced the rowboats used previously. The ferry is fixed to chains on each bank and pulls itself back and forth. Steam has now been replaced by diesel power.

The ferry runs every 20 minutes in summer with the last sail-ing at 9.30pm (10.30pm on Sat). Cars £3.50, motorcycles £1.00, foot passengers £0.20

The woodland walk continues into South Wood which is rich in bluebells in the Spring and has a large variety of ferns in the damp, shady areas. At the south-ern end of the wood, a magnificent view opens up of the Carrick Roads, the main estuary channel and the third largest natural harbour in the world. While the main channel is very deep, other areas are covered by only a few feet of water at low tide. It is here where the famous oyster farms are. Oyster men are still permitted to dredge under sail or oar from October to March. They are the last working fish-ing vessels in the country to use sail. The path continues along the shoreline for a while and then returns to the car park through an area of grazed parkland.

Immediately south of Truro and approached down a pleasant riverside lane is Malpas. The **Heron Inn** serves real ale and food and has tables outside to take full advantage of the river views. Just north of Malpas, but not accessible without going via Truro is St Clement, one of the most picturesque villages on the whole estuary. The church has an extraordinary approach via a two storey lytch gate with its slate hung first floor extending out from the end of a terrace of cottages. Adjacent, is another cottage terrace with thatch roof and little, thatched rustic porches. As you

Malpas

St Clement

enter through the lytch gate, the church tower is directly in front of you blocking the approach and forcing the visitor to detour around to the south porch. The tower dates largely from the C14, although the church was heavily restored in the C19. There is little of special interest although there are some C18 and C19 monuments inside and good Victorian tiles on the floor behind the altar. The east window, a bright design of anchors and ropes, is a rare example of enamel painted glass. Within the churchyard, there is a tall, inscribed stone of the C6 which was remodelled as a cross some 200 years later. There are no facilities in the village and only a handful of houses. The bus service is limited to only four per week! For those without a car, it is a pleasant cycle ride or walk from Truro and a riverside **Pencalenick** path continues on to Pencalenick to the north, from where a bus could be taken back to Truro from the main A390. Alternatively, a path from just west of the church cuts inland and then down to the river at Malpas where there are facilities and buses back to Truro. Either route would make a pleasant diversion from Truro and provide some good river views.

Truro

Truro is the administrative, ecclesiastical and commercial heart of Cornwall, though Bodmin remains the county town. Sitting in a wide valley, surrounded by low hills and at the head of a meandering river, Truro has an appealing setting that is matched by the many attractive streets and buildings within this busy market town. It is Cornwall's premier shopping centre with a range of shops that cannot be matched anywhere west of Plymouth. It is the transport centre of Cornwall with direct connection to the West Coast line and the major terminus for buses in the county. As such, it makes a good base for the visitor, with plenty of interesting and reasonably-priced places to stay, a lively nightlife, by Cornish standards, and plenty of good places to eat and drink. Even if you are not staying here, the city has enough attractions to warrant at least a day visit.

Historic development

The city's location gave it a strategic significance from early times – a navigable port, but far enough upriver to be easily defended against seaborne attack. The town grew up under the Norman Castle which commanded the crossing point of the river. **Castle Hill** Nothing remains of this structure, but Castle Hill and Castle Street are evidence of its location. A merchants guild was established in the town around 1250 and the official stamping of tin dates from c1300, when it was made one of the Duchy's Stannary Towns. The town was an important port for the shipping of tin and other trade and, in the reign of Queen Elizabeth I, a new charter was granted confirming the privileges and standing of the town, including control over the port of Falmouth.

With the outbreak of the Civil War in 1642, Truro raised a large contingent of troops for the King and for a short while the Royalist mint was located in the town before being transferred to Exeter. Prince Charles passed through the town in

1646 as he fled via nearby Falmouth. Rivalry between Truro and Falmouth surfaced soon afterwards and in 1663 control of the whole river was invested in the new Corporation of Falmouth. In 1709, Truro re-asserted its rights over Falmouth Harbour, much to the dismay of the now established town of Falmouth. The matter was settled by the courts who divided control between the two rivals.

Throughout the C18, tin was transported through Truro for control and taxation purposes and the town became prosperous as a result. The wealth transformed Truro into a stylish and fashionable town, perhaps the most important west of Exeter, and most of Cornish society would have a town house in Truro. Much of the development of Truro took place during this period and there are many fine examples of Georgian architecture and town planning still in evidence. In 1830, Truro had 3,000 inhabitants and was becoming the centre of a major mining and manufacturing area. The railway arrived in 1859 and for the first time connected Truro directly to London and fashionable society. There was an inevitable weakening in the social role of the town as London society became more accessible. In 1876, Truro was made the centre of a new diocese and soon afterwards construction began on the cathedral. Around this time, the mining that had sustained Truro's wealth for so long collapsed, but the city has transformed itself into the administrative and commercial centre of Cornwall and remains one of the economic hotspots of the County with comparatively low unemployment.

The Town

Despite its medieval origins, Truro is very much a Georgian or Late Georgian town, with little remaining from before this period. Indeed, it is considered to have the best Georgian architecture west of Bath. The Tourist Information Centre stocks a leaflet (20p) which gives a short guided tour of the best buildings in Truro. The earliest surviving medieval structure is probably the retained south aisle of *St Mary's*, the rest of the church being demolished to make way for the cathedral in 1880. Other than that, the enduring legacy of those times is the medieval street pattern of the town centre.

There are a number of fine C18 houses in the centre of the town including *The Mansion House*, in Princes Street opposite the Coinage Hall, and *Princes House,* next door but one. They were both built by the London architect *Thomas Edwards* in c1751 and c1737, respectively. The former is built in imported Bath Stone, a more sophisticated and fashionable alternative to the native granite, and has an elegant entrance hall with an impressive staircase. The building is currently in office use and you should ask whether you can look inside the hall. The Princes House was built for Mr William Lemon, whose fortune was made from copper, and who went on to give his name to Lemon Street. Opposite is an unusual hexagonal, post box of 1888. Between the two houses, there is an exuberant Victorian building of stone and brick. The *Old Mansion House*, further down Princes Street, is a fine C18 town house of yellow stucco with a big central pediment and heavy moulding of the eaves. The *Old Ale House* nearby is a good example of Victorian pub architecture in red brick and terracota, designed by *Sylvanus Trevail.*

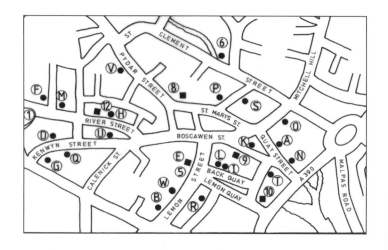

Truro

TRURO

Opposite, is the building that once housed *Bishop Phillpott*'s collection of ecclesiastical books. At the rear, is a fine projecting, oriel window. The *Assembly Rooms* of 1772 was probably the best individual building of this period. Only the south facade of Bath Stone with its medallions of Handel and Shakespeare remain. It is located by the main entrance to the cathedral,

In 1794, the building of *Boscawen Street* and *Lemon Street* commenced. The former was once two narrow streets, cleared to make way for this early bit of town planning, and explains the unusual width of the street today. Lemon Street was a planned expansion of the town and a speculative development designed to provide better housing for the wealthier families that were being attracted to the town. It is one of the finest Georgian streets in the country. It marches straight uphill from the town centre, a wide, handsome street, dominated on the horizon by the twin landmarks of the Lander Memorial and the dome of *St Johns Church*. It is flanked by a series of good, Georgian buildings in a rich, honey coloured stone. Many have superb details of porches, doors and fanlights as well as many well-preserved examples of Georgian wrought iron railings. The cinema on the west side of the street has been skilfully inserted into the streetscene. Through an arch, just by the cinema is *Lemon Street Market*, originally a stable block and carriage house for the residents of Lemon Street.

St John's Church is a small classical design of 1828 with a distinctive open sided dome on the skyline. Nearby is the *Lander Memorial*, a tall Doric column erected in 1835 to commemorate the explorers, Richard and John Lander, who discovered the source of the Nile in the 1830s. *Strangways Terrace* nearby is an early C19 terrace of four storey houses with original wrought iron railings to the front. The high kerb to the pavement was to assist horsemen when dismounting and the steps for ease of entering carriages.

To the rear of Lemon Street Market is *Walsingham Place*, a curved street of early Regency houses, those on the east side rendered and classical with lion heads as corbels to the door canopies, while those on the west are more rustic with stonework, simpler detailing and arched brick heads to the windows.

The *City Hall* on Back Quay, built in 1846, is a classical, granite composition with five arches to the ground floor. The building was extensively renovated in 1997 and is now one of the best performance halls in Cornwall. The *Market Inn* next door has a facade of terracota, faience and tile with an elaborate gable. The *Municipal Building* to the rear, fronts onto Boscawen Street and houses the *Tourist Information Centre.* Opposite is the *Coinage Hall* built in 1848 when the original of 1351 was demolished. This building was where locally mined tin was brought to be tested and assayed for its purity before being shipped out via the port. The present building is a high, Gothic stone edifice which successfully terminates the view to the western end of Boscawen Street. A plaque on the wall commemorates the fact that John Wesley frequently preached on this spot.

Off the north side of Boscawen Street, *Cathedral Lane*, picturesque and narrow with interesting shopfronts, leads towards the Cathedral. The large windows and white glazed bricks above some of the shops were to allow the maximum light for tailors who used to work here.

**Truro
Cathedral**

Truro Cathedral is one of the more modern in the country having been commenced in 1880 and largely completed by 1910. At the time, it was the first new cathedral to have been built in England for 800 years. The Diocese of Truro had been created in 1876 and in 1877 Edward White Benson was consecrated first Bishop of Truro in the medieval parish church of St Mary which was to serve as the cathedral. However, this was not to be grand enough for the new bishop and it was swept away to make room for the new cathedral. The beauty and richness of what was lost can be seen from the retained south aisle which has been incorporated into the new structure. The architect was *John Loughborough Pearson* and it was completed after his death by *F.L. Pearson*, his son. It is designed in the Early English style with the exception of the towers which are French Gothic and unlike anything else in Cornwall. Indeed, the whole composition pays little respect to the traditions of Cornish church architecture and has the hallmark of a building designed on a drawing board and transplanted to the site. The design is certainly accomplished and the proportions of the fine interior and the spectacular vaulting are impressive. However, the whole, and particularly the interior, has a rather stilted and wooden feel.

Once one has admired the lofty proportions of the interior, the rest is mildly disappointing. The furnishings are generally undistinguished although there is an elaborately carved, stone reredos behind the High Altar. In the North Transept are some memorials that have been relocated from the old church including a large alabaster memorial of 1620 to John Robartes and his wife. Figures of Time and Death flank the central figures and the pickaxe, shovel and miner's lamp show how the family wealth was acquired. The stained glass is a fine example of Victorian work by *Clayton* and *Bell* of London and constitute a complete cycle depicting God revealing himself to the world. Elsewhere, the interior is badly served by poor lighting, seating and fixtures and a panoply of insensitively located signs. There is a hideous painting by John Miller in the North Transept showing an aerial view of Cornwall with a heavenly light cast upon the churches of the Diocese.

The ornate, south aisle is a remnant of *St Mary's Church* which was demolished to make way for the cathedral. Dating from 1504–18, it is one of the finest pieces of medieval architecture in Cornwall. The exterior stonework is particularly decorative with the plinth in two tiers and niches for statuary. The contrast with the plain stonework of the new Cathedral is marked. There is also a beautiful painted and gilded barrel roof. Fragments of old glass have been re-used in some of the windows. One can only imagine at the beauty of the building that was destroyed.

From outside and around the city, the cathedral dominates all views. The tall spires soar over the low buildings that make up the rest of Truro and the comparison serves to make the cathedral seem even more dominant than it actually is. Like all good cathedrals, it is tightly packed into the surrounding streets and gains much of its drama from this juxtaposition, particularly on the south side where it abuts the narrow St Mary Street. On the north side, within the cathedral grounds, is the most hideous *Chapter House*, erected in 1967, of concrete on stilts over a grim car parking area. The cathedral shop is almost equally hideous. The *Cathedral School* of 1908 is a more satisfactory design of stone with long ranges of leaded light windows.

Just around the corner from the Cathedral, behind Marks and Spencers, is the big, Methodist Chapel of 1830 with a pretty street of early C19 houses in *Union Place*. Near the railway station, is the *Old County Hall*, a handsome granite building. The new County Hall completed in 1966 is on the outskirts of town on Treyew Road – it is an undistinguished, block like structure only saved by the fact that it is low and relatively unseen. There is a *Barbara Hepworth* statue in the courtyard.

The Royal Cornwall Museum

Open Mon–Sat, 10am–5pm. Admission free. Telephone 01872 272205

Located in River Street in a handsome granite building formerly used as a bank, the Royal Cornwall Museum has recently been extended into the Methodist chapel, adjacent. It is the foremost museum in Cornwall and is dedicated to the history and culture of the county. As well as the exhibitions, there is the Courtney Library, the oldest Cornish Historical Research Centre in the county, and a cafe serving lunches and teas. The Museum has a programme of visiting exhibitions as well as a permanent collection on display. The building has recently been completely refurbished. There are exhibits relating to the archaeology and natural history of Cornwall, an excellent minerals collection and some good paintings. Within these collections there are some outstanding, individual artefacts.

In the main gallery, directly as you enter, is the wooden *Director's Carriage* from the Portreath Tramroad. The line opened in 1812 and the wagons were drawn by horses. The line was used for the transport of ore, coal and other essential supplies between the port at Portreath and the mining areas inland. The Director's Carriage was to allow the mine owners to inspect their investment and is probably the oldest passenger railway carriage in the world. In the same room is the *Trewinnard Coach*, one of the earliest in existence in Britain and certainly the oldest in Cornwall. It is thought to be of Eurpoean origin, perhaps French or Spanish, from around 1700. Nobody is quite sure how it came to be in Cornwall, but by 1757 it was housed at Trewinnard, and such were the state of the roads, that it was only used on Sundays to travel the half mile to St Erth Church and back. Before the mid C18, it was extremely rare to see a coach in Cornwall – the roads were dreadful and horse and pack animals were the main means of overland transport. The introduction of the turnpike trusts (in effect, toll roads)   revolutionized Cornwall's roads and mail coaches were introduced by 1785 and stage coaches by 1790. The museum has a number of plaques from Truro Inns which were installed at this time in lieu of the hanging signs which were lethal for the coachmen in Truro's narrow streets.

The *Rashleigh Gallery* contains an extensive and important collection of minerals, the core of which was formed by Philip Rashleigh of Menabilly, near Fowey, who died in 1811. Also on display are early, tin ingots from the Third or Fourth Century and a massive ingot, probably C17, which was recovered from Fowey harbour.

Upstairs, there is a small collection of paintings, many of them from the Newlyn School, and several of extraordinary quality. There are three pictures of St Ia church by the modern, naïve painter *Bryan Pearce* and works by *Elizabeth Forbes, Julius Olsson* and *Borlase Smart*. There are two good paintings of miners by *Harold Harvey* and a Newlyn harbour scene by *Frank Heath. Henry Scott Tuke* who lived in Falmouth for much of his life is represented by several works including *The Run Home*, an idealized picture of boys sailing, typical of his style. There is a big *Stanhope Forbes, Against Regatta Day*, which is very accomplished and utterly typical of the Newlyn tradition of painting local scenes from life. *Norman Garstin's A Steady Drizzle* is a superb evocation of a rainy winter's night in Penzance owing as much to the influence of Whistler, with its dark, almost monochromatic, use of colour, as to the Newlyn School. Perhaps, finest of all is a picture by *Lamorna Birch, Morning Fills The Bowl*, painted in 1926. The view of Lamorna Cove in the early morning displays an exquisite handling of light and a superb composition with tall cliffs surrounding the astonishing turquoise blue of the sea. A small painting by *Christopher Wood* of the china clay workings near St Austell is equally impressive. Of an earlier period, there is a good portrait by *John Opie* who was born near St Agnes. These pictures may be removed at certain times to make way for other exhibits.

The C20 contribution to Truro's development has been largely negative, with a grim collection of car parks, shopping developments and warehouses. The worst of these, perhaps, is by the docks where a large Tesco superstore turns its back on the riverside and leaves a mean strip of walkway for the public to use. The derelict warehouses opposite stand testimony to the decline of Truro's port. Beyond them, can just be seen *The Parade* in Malpas Road, a terrace of early C19 houses. The river, itself, has been cut off from the centre of Truro by the invasive ring road and one has to negotiate a series of underpasses to find the river walk. The original harbour was covered over in the 1930s with, of all things, a car park. This, in turn, has now been pedestrianized to form a much-needed public square and civic space for the city. The art deco facade to Woolworths on Back Quay is a rare survival and must have been completed about the time that the dock to the front was removed. More recently, things have improved with the completion of the *Law Courts* by Evans and Shalev, the architects of the Tate Gallery in St Ives. The building has a prominent location just to the north of the town centre and there are excellent views over the town and the Cathedral from the public terrace within the courtyard. The design has similar references to the Tate Gallery with its rough rendered walls and circular plan forms.

Truro is Cornwall's main shopping centre with many shops, including many national chain stores, in the compact town centre. There are also a number of interesting, independent shops including several good art galleries.

Lemon Street Gallery Lemon Street (**01872 275757**) located in a beautiful Georgian building at the bottom of Lemon Street, it has a good selection of high quality paintings and prints.

Glass House Gallery Kenwyn Street (**01872 262376**) excellent range of paintings and ceramics at very reasonable prices and one of the largest displays of craft jewellery in the county.

The Guild of Ten 19 Old Bridge Street (**01872 274681**) run by a co-operative of local artists who display and sell their own work. Works include pottery, jewellery, textiles and wood carvings.

Bishop Phillpots Gallery Green Street (**01872 263977**), good displays of paintings, ceramics and sculpture in this historic building.

Pydar Gallery Pydar Street (**01872 223516**), located down an alley off Pydar Street, in one of Truro's oldest buildings. It displays the work of local artist, Melanie Mcdonald as well as a good selection of work by other Cornish-based artists.

Lander Gallery Lemon Street (**01872 275578**), located in the Lemon Street Market, this large gallery occupies the whole top floor of this converted garage with a good range of paintings, prints and ceramics.

Accommodation

The price coding system that is used throughout this guide is on a scale of A to E and indicates the cost of the lowest priced double room in that establishment during the peak summer period. This is clearly marked by the telephone number of the listing for each establishment. It should be borne in mind that single rooms are likely to be considerably more than half the price of a double. In the off peak months, many establishments reduce their rates considerably and even where they do not you may be able to negotiate a discount.

A	–£44
B	£45–£64
C	£65–£80
D	£81–£100
E	£100+

Truro has a good number of reasonably-priced places to stay, many of them located in Georgian properties, as well as some up-market options. Most are located in three specific areas of the town.

In Ferris Town, just to the west of the town centre and near the railway station are **The Bay Tree** (**01872 240274**) **A** at no 28, and **Crescent Rise** (**01872 274005**) **A** at no 6, both located in historic, Georgian houses and very similar. These are probably the closest budget accommodation to the town centre.

On Treyew Road, some distance to the south of the town centre, are a number of substantial B&Bs that front onto this rather busy road. **Gwel-Tek Lodge** (**01872 276843**) **B** at no 41 and **The Fieldings** (**01872 262783**) **B** at no 35 both have off street car parking and may suit those touring by car. However, the town centre is a good 10–15 minute walk down a steep hill.

The third area is Tregolls Road, just five minutes walk to the east of the town centre. A number of large Edwardian and Victorian villas have been converted into comfortable guest houses. **Cliftons** (**01872 274116**) **B** at no 46 is a detached Victorian residence with car parking. The **Brookdale Hotel** (**01872 273513**) **C**, conspicuously signposted, is a more expensive option on the same road. Directly opposite is the **Alverton Manor Hotel** (**01872 276633**) **E**, a large, Victorian country house in landscaped gardens. The hotel has much character with its mellow stone walls and leaded light windows and is, probably, the nicest place to stay in Truro. Rooms are comfortably furnished and the public rooms have all the large squashy sofas and armchairs you would expect of a country house hotel.

Elsewhere in Truro, you could try:

Royal Hotel   Lemon Street (**01872 270345**) **D**, located in the middle of town in a beautiful C18 stone building. This completely renovated hotel is the most central option available. There is a small fitness room and snooker room.

The Town House   20 Falmouth Road (**01872 277374**) **C**, large Victorian hotel, a few minutes walk from the Lander Memorial.

Palm Tree House   8 Parkins Terrace, St Clement Street (**01872 222733**) **B**, centrally located Victorian house with car parking.

 ## Restaurants and cafes

		The prices quoted in the guide are inevitably just an indication of costs
Inexpensive	*under £15*	and represent the price for a meal of two courses with a drink. In the
Moderate	*£16 – £25*	listings, they are indicated by the letter I, M or E, immediately after
Expensive	*over £25*	the telephone number of the establishment.

There are some good places to eat in Truro, many of them of high quality and with very reasonable prices. There are also plenty of cafes and teashops.

Saffron   Quay Street (**01872 263771**) **M**, excellent food based around an interesting menu of meat, fish and vegetarian dishes served in a cosy interior. They do an excellent value menu of two courses and a glass of wine between 5–7pm. Booking strongly recommended. One of the best places in town.

Bustopher Jones   62 Lemon Street (**01872 279029**) **I**, warm, welcoming and unpretentious wine bar with a large menu, including a good range of vegetarian dishes. Extremely popular, particularly at weekends. Booking recommended.

Baba   32 Lemon Street (**01872 262694**) **I**, good Indian restaurant. Open evenings only.

Pieros Ristorante and Pizzeria   Kenwyn Street (**01872 222279**) **I–M**, Italian food in modern setting. Popular with locals.

Mannings Brasserie   82 Lemon Street (**01872 222666**) **M**, linked to the Royal Hotel. Comfortable cafe/restaurant.

Shanaz 1 Edward Street (**01872 225895**) **I–M**, smart Indian restaurant in period, Georgian building.

The Feast 15 Kenwyn Street (**01872 272546**) **I**, highly-rated vegetarian restaurant with a small garden to the rear. Also, serves a large range of Belgian beers. Voted by a national newspaper as one of the 50 best vegetarian restaurants in Britain.

Stingi Lulu's River Street (**01872 262300**) **I–M**, next to the museum in a converted Methodist chapel, this large and very smart cafe/restaurant offers an Asian-based cuisine. There is also a large, open terrace to the front.

Stars Restaurant Back Quay (**01872 262389**) **M**, situated within the Hall for Cornwall. Serves inexpensive lunches and more upmarket food in the evenings.

Alverton Manor Hotel Tregolls Road (**01872 276633**) **M–E**, the restaurant at this country house hotel is a lovely setting for the modern English cuisine that they serve. They do a very good value Sunday lunch.

Pizza Express 1 Boscawen Street (**01872 263617**), located on the ground floor of the historic Coinage Hall. Excellent pizzas and pasta from this national chain.

Bars and nightlife

As the social and cultural centre of Cornwall, Truro has a bigger than normal range of evening activities for sleepy Cornwall. The **Hall for Cornwall**, Back Quay (**01872 262466**) is the county's premier performance venue and has a comprehensive range of theatre, dance, music and comedy. It has recently been completely renovated and is an extremely comfortable venue. In Lemon Street, there is the **Plaza Cinema** (**01872 272894**) with four screens. The cathedral also has a programme of music throughout the year and it provides a suitably atmospheric setting. A leaflet is available in the cathedral or you can telephone **01872 262466**. There are also two nightclubs, the **Eclipse**, a relaxed, gay club down an alley off St Marys Street and the **Loft** in Calenick Street. A number of attractive pubs are dotted around the town centre, many serving food.

m.j. bar Back Quay, conveniently located next to the Hall for Cornwall. Behind the wonderful brick, terracota and tile facade is a trendy bar with cutting edge decor. There are also tables and chairs outside on the new Lemon Quay "piazza." Food served all day.

The Globe Frances Street, big pub set in a large Georgian building. The inside is a succession of rooms and intimate spaces with comfortable sofas and chairs. Occasional live music. Food is served lunchtime and evenings.

Old Ale House Quay Street, big pub with impressive terracota and brick frontage. Nice interiors, although the furnishings are a bit contrived. Real ales and food served, lunchtime and early evening (not Saturday).

The Crab and Ale House New Bridge Street, lovely, old pub with low ceilings and a warm and cosy interior. No television, pool table or jukebox. Real ales and food are served lunchtimes and early evenings. Highly recommended.

Barley Sheaf Old Bridge Street, big, Victorian pub by the cathedral. Conveniently, it serves food all day from 12.00–7.30pm.

William IV Kenwyn Street, large, modernized pub with a predominantly young clientele. It has a large conservatory and open yard with tables which make it a pleasant spot in summer. A wide range of food is served at lunchtimes.

ⓘ **Practicalities**

Tourist Information Centre
The helpful Tourist Information Centre (**01872 274555**) is in the Municipal Building in Boscawen Street. They have comprehensive lists of accommodation, restaurants and public houses as well as general information about the area. Truro is on the main West Coast railway line and there is a branch line to Falmouth. The station is located 10 minutes walk to the west of the town centre. Truro is the main terminus for buses in Cornwall and has regular connections to all the major towns in the county as well as to other towns throughout the country via the National Express network. The bus station is in the centre of town in Green Street at the east end of Lemon Quay. By car, Truro is easily approached off the main A30. There are a large number of car parks in the town centre and parking is not normally a problem. Getting around Truro is easy as all the sites of interest are within walking distance.

Boats
Enterprise Boats (**01326 374241**) run a summer only passenger service to Falmouth from Town Quay, located just the other side of the ring road from Back Quay. The trip takes around an hour and is an extremely pleasant journey. It can easily be linked with a return trip on the scenic, branch railway line. When tides do not permit sailing from Truro, a connecting bus takes passengers downriver to board at Malpas.

The Roseland Peninsula and the Coast to St Austell

The Roseland is the name given to the east bank of the Fal Estuary and the land running back to Tregony and beyond to St Austell, one of the biggest towns and industrial centres in the county. It has few towns and villages and is relatively unspoiled and unvisited. A good proportion of the land alongside the southern part of the estuary is owned by the National Trust and there is good public access to the riverside which is not always the case elsewhere. From Truro, access to the Roseland is either by the King Harry Ferry at Trelissick (see above) or by road around the north of the estuary at Tresillian and Tregony. There is also the passenger ferry from Malpas which operates on demand from dawn to dusk in the summer. Public transport in the area is limited and it can be quite difficult to get around by bus with only the larger villages having anything like a regular service.

South of Tresillian, is an area of narrow lanes with very limited access to the riverside. The manor of Tregothnan occupies most of the southern part of this area and is not open to the public. The estate belongs to the Earls of Falmouth, the Boscawen family, one of the country's most famous seafaring families. The original C17 house was enlarged and encased by the noted architect *William Wilkins* in 1816–18 and again in 1845–8 by *Louis Vulliamy*. The resulting building is a large and elaborate Victorian Tudor. The village of St Michael Penkevil is no more than a scatter of buildings around the entrance to the manor. The church has an undisturbed cruciform plan, although the C13 church was largely restored by *George Street* in the C19. The remaining C13 elements, the niches for seats in the transepts and the piscina in the north transept show noble C13 proportions indicating a high status for the church at that time. There are also two fine reredos' of the transept altars dating from the C13 (south transept) and C15 (north). There are a large number of memorials to the Boscawen family, none of any particular interest although that to Admiral Boscawen (1763) is by the famous artist *Rysbrack* who produced many funerary memorials.

Tregothnan

St Michael Penkevil

The road from here to Ruan Lanihorne is heavily wooded and the steep and hilly terrain open up many fine views and vistas. There is a beautiful, quiet and verdant feel to the area. *Lamorran* is a tiny hamlet with a small, cruciform church. Ruan Lanihorne is a small village in a beautiful setting overlooking a tiny inlet of the Fal River. The church contains an early, but badly decayed, C13 monument with a priest lying with his hands in prayer. The **Kings Head** provides a welcome facility in this otherwise barren area. It serves real ales, food at lunchtimes and evenings and has a beer garden for the summer and log fires in the winter.

Ruan Lanihorne

Continuing south brings you to Philleigh, once on the main coach route between Penzance and London and now a quiet backwater. The *Church of St Filius* is a small church with a low tower of two and a half storeys. Opposite are some attractive cottages, one with two round bays showing similarities to the round houses of Veryan. Glebe House, nearby, has graceful Georgian proportions and an entirely slate-hung front elevation. The **Roseland Inn** is a C16 building with slate floor and exposed beams. They serve real ales and food and there is a nice patio to the front for use in fine weather.

Philleigh

The road continues on towards the King Harry Ferry and Tolverne. The **Smugglers Cottage**, either reached by a vehicle track or footpath from Tolverne, is located beside the River Fal. The thatched building is meant to be 500 years old and serves lunches, coffees and cream teas. The area around here was used extensively in the build-up to the D Day landings and there is a collection of memorabilia of these times on display. There is a passenger ferry between Falmouth and the cottage in the summer months. Telephone **01872 580309** for further information.

Tolverne

St Just in Roseland is one of the most visited churches in Cornwall, hence the large car park at the top of the churchyard. The church is located at the bottom of a steep, wooded valley at the water's edge. The church is of no special interest

St Just in Roseland

and it is its setting that is the main attraction. However, the over-manicured churchyard with its profusion of palms and exotic shrubs gives the curious impression of graves set within a rather lavish garden. The large number of visitors can also detract from the tranquillity of the site. In truth, the church and its riverside setting are no finer than many others around the estuary.

From here, there is a footpath south to St Mawes which provides fine views over the river towards Falmouth and Pendennis Castle.

St Mawes

St Mawes has an attractive setting, located on the southern tip of the promontory with water on three sides and views across to Falmouth and out to sea. The village is a picturesque collection of houses and cottages spread out along the sea shore and up on to the hill behind. There is an affluent feel to the place and many wealthy people retire here or have summer homes. It is a major sailing centre and there are small, sandy beaches exposed at low tide. The only historic site of interest is Henry VIII's castle on the western edge of the town.

St Mawes Castle

English Heritage (01326 270526) Open daily July and August 10am–6pm (April–June and September, 10am–5pm). Winter, closed Tues–Thurs Nov–March. Admission, £3.20, children £1.60

St Mawes Castle is the partner to Pendennis on the opposite shore and together they provided protective fire to the safe anchorage of the estuary. It was built in 1540–43 and is one of the finest examples of its type, having been little altered and undamaged in battle. It is a unique combination of Tudor technology and decoration, for while its purpose was purely functional as a military installation, great care was lavished on its masonry decoration and carving. The castle comprises a circular central tower with three lower bastions arranged like the leaves of a clover. The design has a pleasing symmetry and harmony of composition which is more Renaissance than Tudor and yet we must assume that it was dictated by the military thinking of the day rather than any aesthetic considerations. Certainly, the design was intended to present a low, squat profile to enemy guns and yet to allow the maximum firepower to be trained on any enemy ship.

You approach the castle from the ticket office, once the original guardhouse. The main entrance is surmounted by a fine carving of the Tudor Royal Coat of Arms, just as at Pendennis. Above this, is the first of a series of carved inscriptions composed for the castle by the King's antiquary, *John Leland*. The entrance leads onto the second floor of the castle where the original Tudor partitions remain. This floor with its fine decoration and private rooms was probably used as the private quarters of the captain. At the far end of these quarters is the forward gun platform which would have contained four cannon. Above the door is more carved ornamentation. The wall walks around the side bastions were designed to be used by hand-guns and were intended for defence from land attack. Similarly, the top internal floor was a combined gun and barrack room, designed for hand guns only. The stairs from here lead up to the roof which would originally have been the main gun platform. The turret would have been used by the look-out. The basement room was the kitchen evidenced by the large fireplace and separate bread oven and the floor above, the main mess room and living quarters for the garrison. On the lower floor of the forward bastion is the forward gun room. Most of the gun's on display are ship's cannon from around 1800, but in the centre is a bronze saker of c1560 cast by the Venetian gunmaster, *Alberghetti*. It was recovered from the sea off Teignmouth in Devon and contemporary accounts reveal that the castle had three such bronze sakers among its armaments. The ground floors of the side bastions were also designed to take heavy cannon.

As at Pendennis, the favoured position for mounting the guns became the foreshore and not the castle itself. During the Napoleonic Wars, this area was remodelled to form the Grand Sea Battery which held up to 12 cannon. Below the battery, on the shore line are the remains of the original Tudor blockhouse that preceded the building of the main castle. The ramparts now provide a pleasant walk with excellent view across the river and out to sea. There is a small sandy beach beside the castle.

There are a number of shops in the town that provide the essentials that a visitor may need. The *Waterside Gallery* (**01326 270136**) has a permanent exhibition of paintings and some excellent glass. *The Square Gallery* (**01326 270720**) opposite The Rising Sun has a very good range of paintings and stained glass. There are a good number of places to stay, but prices tend to be on the steep side with little budget accommodation in the village.

St Mawes Hotel (**01326 270266**) *E*, on the sea front. This smart hotel has eight en-suite bedrooms, with a pleasant ground floor bar and first floor brasserie.

Hotel Tresanton (**01326 270055**) *E*, one of the most stylish and expensive hotels in Cornwall. Originally a yachtsmen's club from the 1940s, the hotel was totally renovated and redesigned in the late 1990s. There are 26 rooms, some with their own terraces and all have sea views. There is also a cinema, bar, restaurant, sitting rooms and conference facilities. There are also a number of boats for guests to use, including a 48 foot classic yacht.

Idle Rocks Hotel Harbourside (**01326 270771**) *E*, traditionally, furnished hotel with a large terrace overlooking the river.

The Ship and Castle Hotel (**01326 270401**) *D*, large hotel on the river front with rather basic decor and somewhat overpriced.

The Rising Sun Hotel (**01326 270233**) *E*, located on the river side, very comfortable and welcoming hotel.

The Victory Inn (**01326 270324**) *D*, attractive, old granite pub in a street just back from the harbour. Good value for St Mawes.

Newton Farm (**01326 270427**) *B*, located up a steep hill at the back of the village. It is more easily located from outside the village from where it is the first turning on the left after taking the turning for St Mawes castle. Comfortable B&B with fine views over the town and estuary. Good value.

Little Newton Farm (01326 270664) *B*, next door to the above and similar.

There are some good places to eat in St Mawes. The **Idle Rocks Hotel** (expensive) and the **St Mawes Hotel** (moderate) both have good restaurants. The former has a large sun terrace on the river where cream teas and lunches can be taken. The **Rising Sun Public House and Brasserie** (moderate) is located on the seafront with a big sun terrace and serves good value food. The **Victory Inn** serves bar food as does the **Fountain Bar** in the St Mawes Hotel (both inexpensive). The last three establishments also serve as bars and make good venues for an evenings drinking. The **Fountain Bar** is particularly pleasant with its brightly painted decor and comfortable sofas and chairs. For a special treat you could consider the restaurant at the **Tresanton Hotel** which has an excellent reputation and prices to match. If you cannot afford to eat here, you could at least have a drink in the stylish bar.

There is a regular passenger ferry to Falmouth, every hour (times vary with season). Return fares are £5.50, children £3.00 (**01326 313201**). There is also a summer, passenger ferry to Place where the coast path continues east to St Austell and beyond. It leaves every half hour on the half hour. There is a small pay and display car park on the quay but larger car parks in the village and by the castle. Street parking in the village is strictly limited, but there is a large, free car park by the castle. Bus services are also limited with just one service to Truro. It is often easier to take the public transport connections to Falmouth and the ferry across to St Mawes.

The Coast to Mevagissey

This stretch of coast is one of the least visited in the county, partly due to the scarcity of good, sandy beaches but also due to the difficulty of getting here and the relative absence of places to stay. There are few sites of special interest, but some good coastal walking and the bonus of relative peace and quiet. There are also some nice villages and places to stay.

Place

Directly opposite St Mawes, on the south side of the river, is Place, a tiny hamlet of no more than a few cottages, church and manor house. From the river, the manor house dominates the view and largely conceals the church located directly behind. The house has a beautiful setting, dates from 1840 and is a symmetrical, neo-Gothic composition, showing some signs of French influence.

The *Church of St Anthony-in-Roseland* is set within its largely overgrown churchyard. It dates from C12 and C13 although it was much restored in the C19 - all the glass, furnishings, floors and roof were replaced at this time. However, despite this rather heavy handed approach, the church still represents one of the best examples of how an early medieval Cornish church would have looked. The church plan is undisturbed. It retains the single nave with north and south transepts and a tower over the crossing point of nave and transepts. This is exactly how it would have looked in the C12 or C13 and is a rare survival of an intact medieval cruciform plan. The south door is the principal decorative feature and boasts superb Norman decoration. It is a grand Romanesque design in Caen stone, brought from Normandy – a feat quite practical due to the waterside location. The doorway has an outer zig zag decoration with carved heads at the base, while the middle order is cusped with each cusp carved with a leaf. The inner order is a plain arch with wedge shaped voussoirs. One is carved in relief with the Agnus Dei, the Lamb of God. There are several monuments to the Spry family, owners of the adjacent house, which were brought together in the north transept at the time of restoration. The floor incorporates some good Minton tiles, another product of the Victorian restoration.

Place marks the resumption of the coast path after Falmouth and the first part is a very pleasant short walk to St Anthony Head. There are superb views over the entrance to Falmouth harbour and across to Pendennis Castle and Falmouth itself. Where the path crosses a concrete dam, there are two superb, sandy coves. They are covered at high tide but otherwise provide a marvellous secluded spot for bathing and picnics. St Anthony Head has been a major part of the defences of Falmouth since the early C19. This role continued right up to the 1950s. The area is now owned by the National Trust who have preserved many of the defensive structures and associated buildings. Some of them have been converted into holiday homes. There is a small car park. The lighthouse itself was built in 1834 and was intended to warn ships of the dreaded Manacles reef to the south as well as mark the entrance to Falmouth harbour. It is possible to climb to the top when the lighthouse is open.

St Anthony Head

The coast path from here follows the top of the cliffs to Portscatho. It is a pleasant walk and generally quiet. The rather tortuous road access to this part of the coast means that large numbers of visitors are unusual and the beaches and walks are rarely crowded. *Zone Point* just beyond St Anthony Head is one of the best places in the area for watching sea birds and there is a bird hide on the National Trust land at St Anthony overlooking the Point. Seals are also often seen along this stretch of the coast. Porthbeor Beach is a lovely, sandy cove backed by high cliffs. There is a steep path down to the beach and a path to the road just inland, although there is no car park as such. From here, one could follow the road to the left and return to the ferry at Place and back to St Mawes. The whole circular walk would take no more than a couple of hours and would allow plenty of time for a picnic and bathing along the way. Towan Beach is a long, sandy stretch backed by low cliffs. There is a car park and toilets located just inland and easy footpath access. At the southern end of the beach can be seen a black and white striped pole with climbing steps. It is a wreck post, a relic of the days when the breeches buoy was used by the coastguard services in ship rescues. The pole simulated the mast of a ship in training exercises. Another circular walk can be taken from the car park here. Proceed northwards behind Towan Cottage to a footbridge over a stream which leads to a lovely creekside path. This continues for about two miles to Place, where the ferry can be taken back to St Mawes or you can continue on to St Anthony's Head and back to the car park via the coast path. Allow 3–4 hours for the entire walk.

Porthbeor Beach

Towan Beach

Portscatho   Portscatho is a pleasant enough village with many Regency and Victorian houses located around its tiny breakwater and steep and equally tiny slipway. At the top of the slipway is a small boatmen's shelter. Many of the houses in the village are available for holiday lets and out of high season the village can have a curious, empty feel. *The New Gallery* (**01872 580445**) is only open Thurs–Sat, but has an excellent range of high quality paintings from a small co-operative of artists. The **Plume of Feathers** is an attractive, old pub with real ales and serves food, lunchtimes and evenings. **The Boathouse** at no.11 The Square (**01872 580326**) is open for lunches, teas and evening meals. Closed Sunday and Monday. Fresh fish is normally on the menu. If you wish to stay, **Hillside House** in The Square (**01872 580526**) *B*, located behind the pub, is a lovely Georgian house and offers good value accommodation. It is newly renovated and a cafe/restaurant is planned as well. The beach in the village is only exposed at low tide and nothing special. However, just 10 minutes walk to the north is Porthcurnik Beach, a beautiful sand beach backed by cliffs. The water is crystal clear and turquoise blue, an excellent beach for swimming and sunbathing. A small car park is located just inland.

The coastline to the north of here is dotted with sandy coves amongst the cliffs and offshore rocks. The only access is by the coast path and it is a pleasant walk **Pendower** around to Pendower Beach with the bulk of Nare Head looming on the far side of **Beach** the bay. Pendower Beach is a fine sand beach about a mile long, one of the few large expanses of sand in the area. There are no less than three car parks serving the beach and all the usual facilities are available. As such, it is one of the most popular beaches in the area and can get busy at times, although the beach is normally big enough to prevent it getting unpleasantly crowded. The **Pendower Beach House Hotel** (**01872 501241**) *E* is the large pink building located at the southern end of the beach. The oldest part dates back to the C16 but most of the character has been lost by subsequent alterations and extensions. The beach front location is wonderful, however, and it makes a nice, if somewhat expensive, place to stay. As an alternative, Veryan is just one mile inland with several, reasonably-priced places to stay.

Veryan   Veryan is an attractive village of granite houses scattered over a hilly, valley site. The village is famous for its five round houses, tiny, thatched and with gothic windows, they were built in the early C19 by a local builder. The explanation for the design being that the round plan allowed no corners for the devil to hide in. Four of them are arranged in pairs like sentries on the entry to the village, the other is found in the centre of the village.

The church is beautiful and most unusual and set within a lovely wooded churchyard with crows nesting in the high trees. The church is big with a nave and aisle eight bays long. The tower is located at the end of the south transept rather than off the main body of the church. The doorway to the west porch has the oddest of capitals with six heads in a row above the top of the scallops. Inside there is an unusual roof of open timbers which is particularly complex where the nave meets the south transept. The font is also a remarkable design, probably a C15 copy of a Norman design, but done with bold, crisp carving that lifts it above others of the same period.

The churchyard is large and slopes steeply up the hill to the south. From the top of the churchyard, one is above the top of the tower. There is a fine view looking back to the church in its wooded valley. The large grave here is to the German crew of the *Hera*, wrecked on Gull Rock in 1914. The building by the churchyard is *Homeyard Homes*, built in 1956 and a modern interpretation of the village almshouse. It is an excellent design picking up on the local vernacular with its overhanging, swept slate roofs and "round house" references.

If you wish to stay, there are several places. **Treverbyn House** (01872 501201) *B* is a nice, period house in the centre of the village. All rooms are en-suite and it is good value. **The New Inn** (01872 501362) *B* is a pleasant pub, with comfortable accommodation, and serving very good food. **Elerky House** (01872 501261) *B*, opposite has five rooms, all en-suite. The *Veryan Gallery* (01872 501469) is on the outskirts of the village and has a selection of work, principally by Cornish artists. Veryan is located just off the coast path and would be a perfectly viable detour or overnight stop for anyone walking the path. There is a regular bus service to St Mawes and Truro (not Sunday).

Heading west from Veryan and Pendower Beach, the coast path climbs to the rocky outcrop of Nare Head through increasingly lush vegetation. There is a National Trust car park inland of Nare Head with a footpath for those not wanting to use the coast path. Kiberick Cove on the east side of the Head is served by the **Kiberick Cove** same car park. It is a small beach of sand and rock with no facilities and quite difficult to reach. Consequently, it is likely that you may well have it to yourself if you make the effort. At high tide, it is largely covered. Just before Portloe, the path climbs high up the cliff to an isolated house with stupendous views out to sea. This is **Broom Parc** (01872 501803) *B–C*, owned by the National Trust and run as guest house accommodation. It was used for the Cornish location in the BBC film, *The Camomile Lawn*. It makes a wonderful place to stay and prices are reasonable. However, no children are allowed. So mild is the climate here, that the owners promise to refund your money if an inch of snow falls on the lawn during your stay.

Portloe is one of the most unspoilt fishing villages in Cornwall. There is no **Portloe** beach and little in the way of other attractions. This, linked with its relatively remote location, means that it has been almost untouched by change. It is rarely busy. The village is basically one street leading up the valley away from the small slipway, which is still used by the fleet of five boats that are based here. The treed slopes of the valley protect the village from the worst of the weather. There are several good places to stay and a nice pub making it a good base for exploring this part of the coast.

The Ship Inn (01872 501356) *B* is located a few minutes walk up the valley from the harbour. It is a pleasant and friendly pub serving real ales and bar food. There is a beer garden on the opposite side of the road which steps down to the stream at the bottom of the valley. They also provide good value accommodation. Nearby is **Rose Cottage** (01872 501128) *C*, which has one bedroom with its own sitting room located on the ground floor of this cosy cottage. **The Lugger Hotel** (01872 501322) *E* is nicely located by the slipway and has views out to sea. The hotel has recently been completely refurbished as a stylish, upmarket retreat. The restaurant has views out to sea and is reputed to be very good. Expensive.

From Portloe, the coast path continues along the top of low cliffs to West

Portholland   and East Portholland each standing at the head of a valley. At low tide, a sand beach joins the two settlements but at other times it is necessary to walk along the cliff top. The villages are tiny and have only a small shop and post office. There is no accommodation. A mile further along the coast is *Caerhays Castle*, built in 1808 by *John Nash* who later designed the Brighton Pavilion. It is a picturesque, castellated mansion in the neo-Gothic style and is prominently located in landscaped grounds overlooking the coast. It is in private ownership and not open to the public. The *Church of St Michael Caerhays* is found about half a mile inland on the edge of the castle grounds. The north transept of the original cruciform church still remains while the C15 south aisle is extremely short, consisting of only two bays. There is a good Norman font with a decoration of large leaves in flat relief. However, the main interest is the reredos and unusual commandment tablets on either side. The reredos has an almost Byzantine quality with three panels of tiled mosaics with the Lamb of God depicted in the centre panel. To either side are the two commandment tablets which are unusual in being of glazed tiles dating from the C19. *Porthluney Cove*, opposite the castle, is a wide stretch of sand with safe bathing in most conditions. There is a large car park, a shop, beach cafe and toilets. It is very popular with families and can get busy at times.

The coast path climbs steeply out of Porthluney Cove and up on to the high cliffs beyond. There are good views across the bay and towards Dodman Point. *Hemmick Beach* is soon reached, small and sandy and just one lovely granite cottage. There is plenty of room for picnics on the grassy slopes at the back of the beach but no facilities of any kind. If driving, it is best to park in the car park at Penare, a 10 minute walk away. There is no room for cars at the back of the beach and the approach lanes are narrow and very steep. Half a mile inland at the secluded hamlet of Boswinger is a **Youth Hostel (0870 7705712) A** located in a former farm house. It is a useful stop over for anyone walking the coast path but is otherwise only practical for those with their own transport.

Dodman Point   Dodman Point is one of the most impressive headlands on the south coast. Over the years it has seen countless wrecks, the large granite cross was built in 1896 as a seamark, but failed to stop the destroyers *Thrasher* and *Lynx* from hitting the rocks on the south west side the following year. More recently, the pleasure boat *Darwin* sank with all its passengers in 1966. There are spectacular coastal views, on a clear day you can see from the Lizard to the west to Rame Head in the east. The Dodman is also the largest cliff castle in the South West defended by the massive Bulwark, a bank and ditch, some six metres high and 600 metres long. It is still clearly evident across the neck of the promontory. Just inland from the cross and almost concealed by the surrounding scrub, is a well preserved C18 watch house. It is a rare survivor of the chain of signal stations set up by the Admiralty during the Napoleonic Wars. The area around is rich in flowers with orchids, bluebells, violets and heathers. Many nesting birds and seabirds also frequent the area. Cars can be left at the National Trust car park in Penare from where it is a pleasant 15 minute walk to the Point.

Vault Beach on the east side of Dodman Point is a beautiful crescent of fine shingle backed by cliffs. It is very quiet and there are no facilities. It can only be approached by foot, the nearest car park being at Lamedra on the edge of Gorran Haven. Gorran Haven itself was a one time fishing village gathered around two small, sandy coves. It has now grown with modern housing developments forming the bulk of the town. The two beaches are nice but there is little else to detain the visitor. Just half a mile inland is *Gorran Churchtown* and the surprisingly big *Church of St Gorran* with its tower of 90 feet and south aisle of eight bays. The church is largely C15 and C16. The piers of the arcade are of creamy Pentewan stone, finely carved. The last three piers and capitals were built at a later stage in the much harder granite and the cruder carving is a result of the difficulty of the material. There is an excellent Norman font, with five supports, corner faces and unusual carved decoration. On the south wall, by the chancel, is an early memorial brass to an unknown kneeling woman dating from around 1510.

From Gorran Haven, the coast path leads you to the low promontory of *Turbot Point* where a small piece of cliff known as *Bodrugan's Leap* testifies to the story that Sir Henry Trenowth of nearby Bodrugan, pursued by his enemy Sir Richard Edgcumbe of Cothele, leapt into the sea and a waiting boat to escape to France during the reign of Henry VII. Chapel Point, just beyond, is notable for the three distinctive houses built by *John A. Campbell* between 1933 and 1938. The adjacent, sandy cove is very attractive and rarely busy. You may find cows on the beach which have wandered from the neighbouring fields.

Mevagissey

The largest settlement on the coast between St Austell and Falmouth, Mevagissey was once an important centre for pilchard fishing and since the Middle Ages has supplied the Royal Navy with salted pilchards or "Mevagissey Ducks." Some 30 pilchard seines were registered in the harbour in the early C19. The first, stone built pier was built in the C15, but the present inner harbour pier was constructed towards the end of the C18. Exposed as it was to south east gales, the pier suffered continual damage until the outer harbour piers were constructed in the 1880's. It is still very much a working harbour and the town as a whole has a business-like bustle that is absent from many of the other coastal villages. The narrow streets are lined with C18 and C19 buildings, many now converted to restaurants, galleries and businesses. The harbour is particularly picturesque with its many working fishing boats and houses clinging to the surrounding hills. Mevagissey is now an established tourist centre and at peak times it can be very busy. The narrow streets can become very congested and parking difficult.

On the East Quay is the *Mevagissey Museum* (**01726 843568**). It has many artefacts and exhibits of the town's fishing legacy and recounts how it was the first town to have electric street lighting fuelled by pilchard oil – an imaginative use of a local by-product. The nearest beaches are at Port Mellon to the south and Polstreath to the north – both a rather strenuous 20 minute walk. Shark fishing trips are available from the *Mevagissey Shark Angling Centre* on West Quay (**01726 843430**). The town has several art galleries concentrated in the narrow streets just back from the harbour.

Goran Haven

Open Easter-Sept, Mon-Sat, 11am-5pm, Sat & Sun opening phone 01726 843105. Admission £1.00, children £0.50

David Weston Gallery 1 St Georges Square (**01726 842754**), watercolours and local scenes.

Mevagissey Fine Art 4 St Georges Square (**01726 844488**), specializes in original paintings and antiquarian prints with keen prices.

High Tide Gallery 21 Church Street (**01726 844598**) good selection of paintings, ceramics and glass. Open every day.

Accommodation

Mevagissey is a popular tourist destination in its own right and also a very convenient base for visiting Heligan and the Eden Project. While there are a good number of places to stay, you would be well advised to reserve rooms in advance.

Ship Inn Fore Street (**01726 843324**) *B*, old, granite inn in the main street. The street and bar can be noisy. Four rooms, three en-suite.

Fountain Inn (**01726 842320**) *A*, located in a narrow alley between Fore Street and the harbour. Superb, atmospheric inn with many exposed timbers. Three rooms and good value.

Sharksfin Hotel The Quay (**01726 843241**) *C*, the large white painted granite building on the quay side. There are fine views over the harbour.

The Wheelhouse West Quay (**01726 843404**) *B–C*, near the above. Four rooms, all with harbour views. However, bookings are only accepted for a minimum of two nights.

Buckingham House 17 Tregoney Hill (**01726 843375**) *B*, four storey grade II listed building on the edge of the town centre.

Mill House 9 Tregoney Hill (**01726 844224**) *B*, nice guest house in an historic building right by the town centre.

Trevalsa Court Hotel Polstreath Hill (**01726 842468**) *E*, on the cliff top just outside the town, this comfortable hotel has 15 en-suite bedrooms with superb sea views and its own landscaped gardens. There is also car parking.

Restaurants and cafes

There are plenty of places to eat in Mevagissey and several of them are very good indeed. As you would expect, fish and seafood feature heavily on the menu. Prices on the whole are reasonable as there is plenty of competition and Mevagissey is not an upmarket resort. If you just want a snack there are plenty of tea shops and bakeries in the town, along the main street and around the harbour.

Salamander 4-6 Tregony Hill (**01726 842254**) *M*, probably the best restaurant in town. Comfortable, with lovely, bright decor. Excellent menu featuring fresh fish dishes as well as imaginative meat and vegetarian dishes. Booking recommended.

Mr Bistro East Quay (**01726 842432**) *M* seafood and fresh fish restaurant with views over the harbour.

The Wheelhouse West Quay (**01726 843404**) *M*, the restaurant is upstairs above a cheaper ground floor cafe. The decor is unimpressive but the food is good, especially the fish dishes, and good value. The wine list is very reasonably priced too. There are a few tables by the window which look out over the harbour.

Sharksfin Restaurant The Quay (**01726 843241**) *M*, located right on the harbour.

Alvorada Fore Street (**01726 842055**) *M*, rather dusty and traditional interior, but Mevagissey's only Portuguese restaurant. Many of the dishes make full use of the local fresh fish.

Fountain Inn off Fore Street (**01726 842320**) *I*, the best of the many pubs serving food. There is a separate dining room and it is very popular.

There is little to do in Mevagissey in the evening other than sit by the harbour, eat at one of the restaurants or have a drink in one of the many pubs. The best and most atmospheric bar is probably the 500 year old **Fountain Inn** with its slate floors and timber beams. **The Ship Inn** and the **Kings Arms** in the main street are also good choices. They all serve real ales and the first two also provide food in the evenings.

Practicalities

The Tourist Information Centre is in St George's Square (**01726 844857**). Mevagissey is well connected by bus to St Austell, which is also the nearest railway station, with regular departures throughout the day. Onward connections can be made from St Austell which is something of a transport hub for the area. By car, Mevagissey is found on the B3273 from St Austell. The streets in the centre of town are very narrow and can be congested at peak times. There are several car parks dotted around but these can fill up quickly at peak times. Between June and October, there is a regular ferry service across the bay to Fowey which is an excellent way of linking a trip to these two very different coastal villages. There are between three and six sailings per day each way and the journey takes around 35 minutes. Return fares are £9.00, children £6.00, family £25.00. Telephone **07977 203394** for details of sailing times.

Tourist Information Centre

Heligan

Open all year, every day except Christmas Eve and Day, 10am–6pm (5pm winter).
Admission, £7.50, children £4.00, family £20.00

Just a mile to the north west of Mevagissey is one of the major tourist sites of Cornwall, *The Lost Gardens of Heligan* (**01726 845100**). There is a tea room and restaurant, plant sales, gift shop and free car parking. The site is signposted from the Mevagissey to St Austell road. Bus no.26 from St Austell to Gorran Haven, via Mevagissey, stops at the entrance. However, there are only five buses a day and less at weekends. Check the times by telephoning **01209 719988** or the local Tourist Information Centres. From Mevagissey, it is an easy hour's walk. Follow the main B3273 out of the village, then take the track and footpath on the left just past the cemetery. After a short while, the footpath meets another track which should be followed through woods until you reach the main entrance. The gardens are sizeable and at least a half day should be allowed for them to be properly appreciated.

The story of the discovery and restoration of the gardens of Heligan is one of the most unusual inspiration and dedication. When Tim Smit and two friends visited the site in February 1990 the gardens were completely overgrown and they had to use machetes to clear a way through the otherwise impenetrable undergrowth. Despite years of neglect, they realised that enough of the garden remained for it to be rescued. The task they faced was enormous and the results achieved in the following 10 years quite remarkable. The story has been told in a television documentary and best selling book, copies of both are on sale at the garden shop.

The manor of Heligan is first known of in the C12 but the current estate did not start to take shape until the Tremayne family bought the estate in the late C16. The current house dates from 1603, although most of the surviving structure today dates from 1692 with further extensions in the early C19. In 1970, the house was sold as flats and it is not open to the public.

The house was surrounded by an estate of 1000 acres and in its heyday was completely self-sufficient. It was during the early C19 that the gardens began to take shape. *Henry Hawkins Tremayne* had a plan of the gardens drawn up which shows the gardens almost as they are today. It is known that this plan dates from at least before 1810. Having established the general shape of the garden, it was left to the subsequent generations to establish the plant collections. By 1914, the gardens contained some of the most elaborate and exotic plants in the country with palms, tree ferns and bamboo as well as many ornamental trees and shrubs. The outbreak of the war in 1914 was to shatter the way of life of master and servants and start the rapid demise of the garden. More than half the staff were killed on the Western Front and in 1916 the house was taken over by the War Department as a convalescent home for officers. After the war, the house was tenanted out and they were unable to maintain the extensive grounds. In the Second World War, the house was again used to billet American officers who were rehearsing for the D Day landings. Rapid decay now set in and the house was subsequently sold in 1970. During this period, the gardens became overgrown. Consequently, no major alterations have been carried out this century and all the garden buildings remained untouched. This in a sense is the importance of Heligan as it represents a rare time capsule of how a major C19 garden would have looked – in effect a living museum of C19 horticulture.

The gardens divide neatly into two areas, the *Northern Gardens* and the Jungle and Lost Valley further to the south. The Northern Gardens contain the more formal planting along with the productive gardens for the house. From the entrance, proceed to the left of the kiosk and then along the path to the south. Off to the left is *The Ravine*, a man-made rockery over 100 yards long and completed just before the Great War. The rustic stone path is uneven to contribute to the impression of a Himalayan mountain pass. At the bottom of the ravine you arrive at an area with walled gardens to either side. To the north, the *Italian Garden* contains one of the first kiwi fruit plants brought to England – look for the fibrous strands in the trees above the summer house. The adjacent *Melon Yard* was an area for intensive cultivation of exotic fruits and has been restored in accordance with the principles of C19 horticulture. The pineapple pits have been reconstructed – pineapple growing being something of a horticultural sport between 1770 and 1850 – and the first Heligan pineapple for 150 years was harvested in 1997. The melon house is similarly productive and the warm, south wall is once again planted with fruit trees trained in the traditional ways. To the south of the Melon Yard, there is a fine collection of bee boles, vaulted chambers for containing bees and the precursors of the hives of today. They date from about 1820–40. The *Flower Garden* to the south is another walled garden used for growing cut flowers but also the more tender vegetables, herbs and fruit. The great brick wall was built in the late C18 with bricks imported from the Low Countries – brick being a rare commodity in Cornwall. There are a number of beautifully restored Victorian glass houses dating from the middle of the C19. To the north of here, is an area known as *New Zealand* which has a fine collection of tree ferns. Just by here is the *Crystal Grotto*, a typical grotto of the late C18, but in this case containing crystals set within the roof. Candles would have been brought out here on summer nights and the light would have reflected off the crystals giving the grotto a magical air. A short walk north is the *Northern Summerhouse*, the oldest building in the garden dating from at least 1770. The 1.8 acre vegetable garden opposite is the productive heart of the garden and it is being cultivated with varieties that would have been popular during the mid C19.

The *Jungle* and *Lost Valley* are to the south of the formal gardens, separated by the private grounds of the house. They can be reached by taking the path east from the flower garden or from the ticket office by taking the path to the right or south. The Jungle was created in the mid C19 as an area for experimenting with the new passion for sub-tropical plants. It is a steep sided valley with four ponds, one above the other. The lush vegetation contains the largest collection of tree ferns in Europe as well as great swathes of bamboo, palm and giant rhubarb. On a warm, wet day the steamy, moist air fully justifies its name. To the west of the Jungle Walk is a path to the Lost Valley. It has now been established that there has been an unbroken use of this site going back to at least medieval times with charcoal burning platforms, leats and a mill pond as evidence of its early history. Overlaying this working landscape is a series of avenues of oak, beech and chestnut – the main rides through the woods to Mevagisssey. The area has a wilder, more natural and indigenous feel than the Jungle. To return to the Northern Gardens and the exit you can follow any of the footpaths that leave the Lost Valley to the left (north).

The Coast to St Austell

Pentewan

To the east of Heligan and a short but strenuous walk along the coast path north of Mevagissey is Pentewan, once a major port for the clay and minerals trade. It opened in 1826 but continuing silting problems led to it losing its clay traffic by 1919. The last cargo ships to use the harbour were in the 1940s. However, the dock remains intact, with water in the basin, and there are a number of surviving dockside buildings. Pentewan is also known for its local stone, a hard, fine grained stone, much used in the local buildings, particularly the churches and wharves. There is a wide, sandy beach somewhat dominated by the large caravan park immediately adjacent. The village itself is pleasant enough. On the hill just to the north is *The Terrace*, a handsome row of cottages dating from the C18 and C19 with a continuous slate-roofed veranda to the front. The church attached to the end of the terrace is a tiny, classical design. The **Ship Inn** is a lovely old inn with a nice beer garden serving real ales and food, lunchtimes and evenings. The **Cove Eating House**, in the square, is a licensed restaurant that also serves cream teas and morning coffee. If you wish to stay, **Pisky Cove** (**01726 843781**) *C* is a centrally-situated B&B. *Pentewan Valley Cycle Hire* (**01726 844242**) is located on the edge of the village and hires cycles from £10.00 per day, £7.50 per half day. The Pentewan Valley has several miles of traffic free cycle track through the wetland and woodland alongside the White River. Heligan is also within easy reach and Charleston just a bit further.

Porthpean

The coast path from here to Porthpean is a strenuous and unpleasant walk. Hemmed in between a barbed wire fence and the cliff top, the path is narrow, overgrown and often muddy with a series of climbs and descents. At The Vans, the path descends to a lush wooded coombe with an isolated house by the small beach. Black Head is the promontory just beyond and was a one time Iron Age cliff castle. Porthpean has a nice, sandy beach in a small cove. There is a sailing club and beach cafe and car parking and toilets are nearby.

Charlestown

Charlestown is a surprisingly complete and unaltered late C18 maritime port. It was developed by *Charles Rashleigh*, a local landowner and mining entrepreneur with construction starting in 1791 and being completed by 1801 to the design of John Smeaton. Originally designed to transport copper, it soon became the major port for the transhipment of china clay. Around the harbour, Rashleigh established other industries including lime burning, shipbuilding, brickmaking, a rope walk and pilchard cellars. The population grew from 9 in 1790 to 281 by 1801. By the mid C19 the community numbered some 3000. The harbour itself is an impressive construction but there are also many period buildings that help to maintain the essence of a working C18 port. Indeed, the harbour is regularly used by film crews so unaltered is its appearance. There are often tall masted sailing ships in the harbour, some of which can be boarded for a small fee.

The **Shipwreck, Rescue and Heritage Centre** (01726 69897) is located in an old china clay building and has a number of artefacts relating to the port of Charlestown as well as shipwreck salvage and other curios. The **Pier House Hotel** (01726 67955) *C* and the **Rashleigh Arms** (01726 73635) *C* are both historic buildings located near the harbour. They serve real ales and food, lunchtime and evenings. If you wish to stay, and Charlestown certainly makes for an unusual and atmospheric overnight stop, they both have en-suite rooms while the Pier House has the best harbour views. Alternatively, try **T'Gallants B&B** (01726 70203) *B* for good value accommodation in this large period house overlooking the harbour. There is also a tea room with garden on the ground floor.

Open, Mar–Nov, 10am–5pm. Admission, £4.95, children over 10, £2.50, under 10 free

A number of historic buildings have been sensitively converted to new use, including the **Harbourside Inn**, serving real ale and food, and **Revival** (01726 879053) *M–E*, a smart cafe/restaurant/bar with a terrace overlooking the harbour.

The coast from here to Par is dominated by the adjacent railway line, housing estates and the large china clay works. The beach at Carlyon Bay is big and sandy, but overshadowed by the gruesome Coliseum entertainment complex and the large car parks next to it. The **Carlyon Bay Hotel** (01726 812304) *E* on the cliff top is considered one of the finest in Cornwall. Facilities include its own golf course, indoor and outdoor swimming pools and all the other facilities you would expect.

St Austell and Inland

St Austell, one of the biggest towns in Cornwall, has little interest for the visitor but is a transport hub for the local area. Its growth is almost entirely down to the discovery of china clay deposits by *William Cookworthy* in 1748 at Carloggas, just to the west. Today, the industry dominates the town and surrounding area – the spoil heaps creating a fascinating man-made landscape, often referred to as "The Cornish Alps." In St Austell itself, the church is worth a visit. The tower is one of the most distinctive in Cornwall with all four faces being enriched by sculpted figures in niches. The tower dates from the late C15 and is faced with local Pentewan stone. Inside, the old wagon roofs are original and there is a particularly fine Norman font with much carved decoration. Elsewhere, the town has the feel of a busy market town with a number of old buildings in among the more modern development. Just to the north, on the B3274, is the **Wheal Martyn China Clay Museum** (01726 850362) where a C19 clay works has been restored to house a display on the history of the china clay industry in the area.

Open daily, Easter–Oct, 10am–6pm, Nov–Easter, Wed–Sun, 10am–4pm. Admission £5.75, children £3.50, family £15.00

Eden Project

Open every day 10am–6pm (last entry 5pm). Between November and March, it closes at 4.30pm (last entry 3pm). Admission, £12.00, children £5.00, seniors £9.00, family £30.00. Telephone **01726 811911**

Located just two miles north-east of St Austell, the Eden Project is one of the most ambitious projects of the late C20. It is certainly one that has caught the public imagination and its extraordinary success is helping to transform the surrounding area, one of the most deprived in the country. Designed for 750,000 visitors per annum, the first year saw over 2 million people cram onto the site. After the initial enthusiasm, the number of visitors has dropped slightly, but 2003 still saw 1.8 million. Despite the fact that the site is linked to the National Cycle Network and there are regular buses from St Austell, Newquay, Helston, Falmouth and Truro, the great majority of people arrive by car. There are 3000 car parking spaces at Eden and on a busy day they are full by mid morning. The resulting queues can block the narrow lanes surrounding the site for the rest of the day. At peak times the advice is to plan your visit carefully – the best times to arrive being early (9am) or late in the afternoon. Pre-booking tickets can also help. If you do arrive by bike or foot, you can beat any queues by going to the Fastrack desk and get £3.00 off the adult entry charge. Children under 15 on bikes accompanied by an adult are free – a good deal.

The main attraction are the two huge biomes that have been created in the bottom of a disused quarry – quite simply the biggest greenhouses in the world. One recreates a tropical rainforest while the other, the climate and vegetation of California, South Africa and the Mediterranean. Some 200,000 trees and up to 4000 different species of plants have been installed. Many of the plants need to be further established before they can be said to "fill" the biomes which, at the moment, tend to overwhelm the plants themselves. Indeed, many people visit the site to see the biomes as much as the plants and there is no doubt that they are hugely impressive structures with their ETFE foil skin letting UV light through to the plants within. The range of plant species is impressive and the keen gardener and horticulturalist will find it fascinating. However, it is well to remember that this is very much a plant collection rather than a landscaped garden and there is little attempt to create a visual landscape within the site. The project is heavily geared towards education and research and there is also an Education Resource Centre and a Research Foundation.

Although the biomes draw the people, the majority of the site is open to the elements with extensive planting throughout the rest of the site. There is also a visitor centre, cafe, restaurant and a well-stocked bookshop. The site also hosts events throughout the year with its open air stage and arena being used for concerts, theatre and dance performances, many by leading artists. Look out for leaflets on-site or from local Tourist Information Centres or telephone for details.

St Blazey Gate

St Blazey Gate, just to the south, is notable for two things – *George Street*'s first church design and one of Cornwall's best art galleries. The Church of St Mary stands back from the main road and is an extraordinarily accomplished design for an architect's first church commission. The steeple is clearly modelled on that at Lostwithiel but if anything is more satisfactorily proportioned and accomplished.

The rest of the church is plainly but comfortably proportioned. Adjacent to the church is the *Mid Cornwall Galleries* (**01726 812131**), open Mon–Sat, 10am–5pm. It is located in a large converted school and contains an excellent range of paintings, prints, ceramics, sculptures and jewellery.

To the north of St Austell, is the heart of the china clay workings and a trip through this extraordinary landscape of spoil heaps and abandoned quarries can be rewarding. The extent of the waste tips is explained by the fact that only one ninth of the excavated soil is used for china clay production with the rest being discarded as waste. Treverbyn is found off the main A391 and has Street's second **Treverbyn** church design. The church is only normally open between 11.00am and 12 noon. It has a simple plan form and large barn-like roof with massive slates. The use of different levels is particularly clever and helps to give greater prominence to the altar than otherwise may be the case. Roche Rock to the north is a granite tor with **Roche Rock** the ruined chapel of St Michael on top. The chapel can be accessed by ladders that are fixed to the rock walls. One of the best views of the china clay country is from the church at St Dennis, some 700 feet high. The church lies inside an Iron **St Dennis** Age hillfort, the churchyard wall now following the line of one of the ramparts.

Astride the River Fal, Tregony was an active port in the C14 before silt from tin **Tregony** streaming blocked the river. The town now has a wide main street, an attractive church with a low, two storey tower and most unusual carved decoration to the porch. The almshouses at the west end of the village date from 1696 and have a wooden gallery supported on six, heavy granite piers. The *Tregony Gallery*, 58 Fore Street (**01872 530505**) has a good range of pictures and sculpture. They have another gallery at nearby Trewithen. Down a narrow lane to the north east of Tregony (take the first right turn past the bridge, going north) is the isolated *Church of St Cornelius*. The church is small, just a nave and an extraordinary, tiny tower, the bottom part of which is slate and C13 with a small lancet window. The north side is also C13 with another lancet window while the south side has had Perpendicular windows and a south porch added. It provides a rare example of how a C13 Cornish parish church must have looked.

Probus is a large village just north of the A390 Truro to St Austell Road. There is **Probus** an attractive village square with a number of shops, but the most important sight is the early C16 *Church of St Probus and St Grace*. The tower is the tallest in Cornwall at 123 feet and is decorated in a lavish manner, but wholly more restrained and more successful than that at Launceston. The tower has a decorated plinth with another strip of ornament above. There are niches for statuary on the north and south sides. The second stage of the tower has windows with elaborately decorated sound holes and the stage above more windows similarly decorated. The battlements are also decorated and there are pinnacles holding the corners with further little pinnacles surrounding them. The whole is marvellously accomplished and extraordinary for such a relatively small community in remote Cornwall. The church itself has two aisles of identical design and a tall, bright interior. It is one of the many churches in this part of the County restored by *Street* in the C19. In the churchyard is a grand monument to the Hawkins family with four kneeling Cavaliers at the corners and the surprisingly modern date of 1914. The nearby **Hawkins Arms** (**01726 882208**) *B* is a charming old building serving real ales and bar food. They also have good value accommodation should you wish to stay. The **Lamplighter Restaurant** (**01726 882453**) **E** is nearby and has an imaginative menu.

Ladock   Two miles north of here is Ladock, notable for its church with the only *William Morris* glass in the county other than St Germans. The church is C13 with a C15 south aisle. There is a most unusual, primitive stone face set within a box over the south door. Its date and origin are unknown. Next door, there is a picturesque granite schoolhouse of 1867.

Trewithen

House open, April–July, Mon & Tues only, 2pm–4pm. Admission £5.00, children under 15 free. Gardens open, Mar–Sept, Mon–Sat, 10am–4.30pm. It is also open on Sundays in April and May. Admission £4.25, children under 15 free. A combined ticket for house and garden is £8.00. Telephone 01726 883647

Just to the east of Probus is the country estate of the Hawkins Family, Trewithen, one of the finest C18 houses in Cornwall and also one of the finest woodland gardens. The house is a formal, classical composition with two detached, brick pavilions for stables on the north side around a carriage drive and lawn. The house dates largely from 1715–40 and is attributed to *Thomas Edwards* of Greenwich. It is a marvellous study in understatement with classical proportions but almost no detailing or ornament. Perhaps only Antony can rival its classical restraint in Cornwall. The stone to the south, garden elevation is plain ashlar with a pinky hue imbued by lichen growth. The east front is a quite different stone and constructed slightly later around 1750. The interiors display some good stucco work and there is a glazed dome over the stairwell.

The gardens were created by *George Johnstone* in the first 50 years of the C20 and are considered to be some of the best woodland gardens in the country. They cover an area of some 30 acres and have a particularly good collection of camellias, rhododendrons and magnolias set amongst the many mature woodland trees. The gardens are surrounded by a traditional landscaped parkland. There is a small tea shop which serves lunches and refreshments.

East Cornwall, Par to Plymouth Sound

Introduction

Stretching some 25 miles along the south coast between St Austell and Plymouth, this area has long been one of the most accessible parts of Cornwall. As such, it has been more open to outside influences than elsewhere in the county and the influence of Celtic traditions correspondingly less. It is an area of gently rolling hills, largely put to agriculture, with the river valleys of the Tamar, Looe and Fowey cutting north-south through the landscape forging their own distinct identities. The coast and beaches are not among Cornwall's best with Whitsand Bay and the stretch between Fowey and Looe being notable exceptions.

On the whole, the area is not much visited by tourists, though there are the major tourist destinations of Fowey, Looe and Polperro. One of Cornwall's more charming, small country towns is found at Lostwithiel and the nearby castle of Restormel is considered by many to be one of the most beautifully-sited and romantic in the country. There are also a number of sites of exceptional historic interest including the first cathedral of Cornwall at St Germans and the great country houses of Cothele and Antony. The recent opening of the Eden Project near St Austell has greatly increased visitors to the western part of this area and accommodation can be hard to find at certain times. Pre-booking is recommended.

The Gribbin

Just two miles east of St Austell, Par is a non-descript town dominated by the large china clay works and docks which date from 1840 when silting of the nearby Luxulyan River made a new port essential. The dry dock, the only one between Falmouth and Plymouth, was in use until 1957. There is a nice sandy beach but it is completely dominated by the adjacent works. Heading south, you approach the more agreeable landscape of the Gribbin peninsula. Polkerris

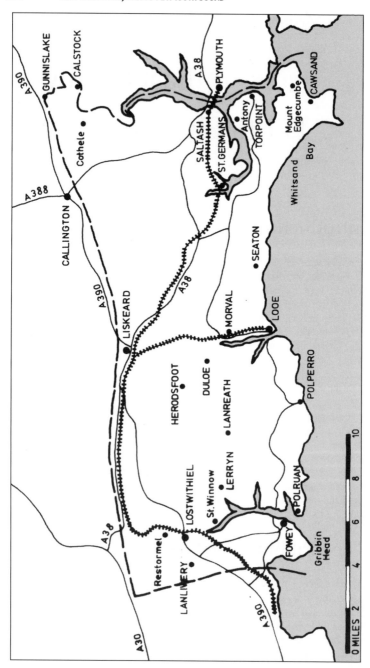

is a largely unspoilt fishing village, the derelict pilchard cellars and protecting pier are all that remain. It is now a popular, sheltered beach with plenty of sand at low tide. The old lifeboat house has been converted to a seasonal café and shop. The **Rashleigh Arms** is right on the sea front and serves real ales and good food, lunchtimes and evenings. There are tables outside overlooking the beach and live music at weekends. The public car park is a 10 minute walk from the beach accessed down the narrow lane that leads to Polkerris. Alternatively, it is a pleasant 30 minute walk along the coast path from Par.

Polkerris

Gribbin Head affords good views across St Austell Bay to Mevagissey and beyond. The red and white daymark was built in 1832 to help sailors distinguish the Gribbin from the many other south coast headlands and mark the narrow entrance to Fowey harbour. William Rashleigh granted the land for the daymark and contributed stone from a local quarry on the understanding that "the beacon would be an ornament to my grounds." The resulting square tower of handsome proportions with its corbelled top seems to fit the bill handsomely. Unusually for Cornwall, the headland is quite heavily wooded, planted by the Rashleighs purely to enhance the view from their house. The eastern wood was planted in the late C18 and is a rare example of a coastal elm wood. Just inland is **Menabilly**, ancestral home of the Rashleighs and the home of Daphne du Maurier from 1943 onwards. The house was the setting for "Manderley" in her famous novel *Rebecca*. It is privately owned and not open to the public. There is a car park at nearby Menabilly Barton from where it is a 20 minute walk to Poldrimouth Cove and a further 20 minutes to Gribbin Head. Poldrimouth Cove is a rather ordinary beach of sand and shingle but with fine views out to sea and inland over the parkland of Menabilly. Just to the west of the beach is the substantial wreckage of the coaster *Romanie*, wrecked here in 1930. From here the coast path leads round to Combe Hawne and Fowey. The Gribbin is around an hours walk from Fowey and makes a pleasant excursion and fine picnic spot.

Gribbin Head

Poldrimouth Cove

Fowey

Fowey, pronounced Foy, has long been an important port with its sheltered deep water and easily defended harbour. It is one of the most attractive places on this stretch of the coast with a marvellous riverside position, many good walks, plenty of places to stay and eat and a good selection of shops and galleries. The opening of the nearby Eden Project has only increased the attractiveness of Fowey as a holiday destination and it is now exceptionally busy throughout the year. It is recommended to pre-book accommodation if at all possible.

Historic development

Fowey was a port from pre-Roman times when tin was shipped out from its

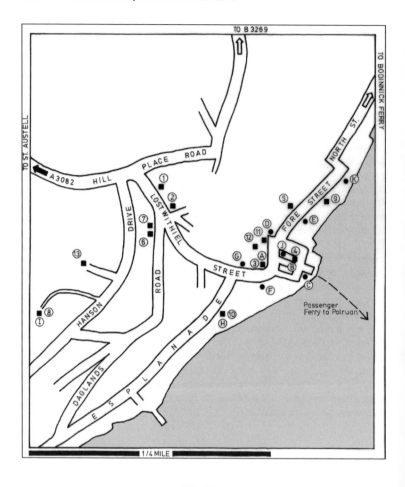

FOWEY

ACCOMMODATION

1   Trevanion
2   Safe Harbour Hotel
3   Ship Inn
4   King of Prussia
5   Globe Posting House
6   Daglands
7   St. Keverne
8   Fowey Hall Hotel
9   Old Quay House Hotel
10 Marina Hotel

ESSENTIALS

11 Tourist Office
12 Church
13 Main car park

RESTAURANTS AND BARS

A   The Ship
B   King of Prussia
C   Food for Thought
D   Taipan

E   Sams
F   The Toll Bar
G   Maxwell's
H   Waterside
I   Fowey Hall

GALLERIES

J   Cry of the Gull
K   Fowey River Gallery

sheltered harbour. It was the southern end of the overland route from Padstow whereby gold from Ireland was supposedly traded with the Continent. The massive *Fowey Ingot*, which was raised from the harbour and is now in the Royal Cornwall Museum in Truro, is evidence of this trade. The sailors of Fowey were always an independent and unruly bunch that considered piracy their natural right. This led them into frequent conflict with other seafaring nations. In 1380 the town was raided by the Spanish and in 1457 the French burnt the town. In response, two blockhouses were built at the harbour entrance, one on the Polruan side and the other on the Fowey side. A chain was strung between them to protect the harbour at times of danger. Behind their new defences, the sailors of Fowey became increasingly belligerent, attacking all shipping that took their fancy, including English ships of the East Coast fleet. Edward IV eventually felt obliged to bring his subjects to heel, confiscating their harbour chain and handing it to Dartmouth in Devon. With the threat of foreign invasion, the defences were further strengthened in 1540 with the construction of St Catherine's Castle, part of Henry VIII's **St Catherine's Castle** string of coastal forts. The remains of the castle can still be seen just to the south of the town. Fowey maintained its maritime history and many local men sailed with John Rashleigh in his famous ship *Frances of Fowey* on voyages with his cousins, Drake and Raleigh. In 1578, the ship sailed with Frobisher to discover Baffin Island and later fought with Drake against the Spanish Armada.

In the Civil War, the town was strongly Royalist, like most of Cornwall. At one point, the Parliamentarian Army of Lord Fairfax was trapped by Royalist forces on the nearby Gribben peninsula and largely wiped out, Fairfax and his cavalry escaping at the last minute. However, the town fell to the Parliamentarians in 1644. One of the last sea battles in Fowey was in 1666 when a Dutch squadron cornered the Virginia fleet in the harbour and a long battle ensued. The harbour was an important base for naval ships during the Napoleonic Wars and an increasing trade developed exporting the products of the china clay industry around St Austell that continues to this day and accounts for the many large ships that can be seen in the river.

The Town

The town has a spectacular setting on a steep hill overlooking the narrow harbour entrance and the wooded slopes of the Fowey valley. The centre of the town is along the shoreline where there are a number of fine old buildings from the C15 onwards. One of the oldest is *Noah's Ark* in Fore Street, a merchant's house reputed to date from before the fire of 1457. The *Ship Inn* was built in 1570 by John Rashleigh and named after his ship *Frances of Fowey*. Although greatly altered, it still retains much charm as well as one upstairs room with ornamental ceiling, oak panelling and C16 fireplace. Right opposite the small quay in the town centre is *The King of Prussia*, rebuilt in 1886 on the site of a much earlier building but retaining the old market place below with its granite columns. The town hall was built in 1792 around an older building and is now occupied by the town museum which has a collection of old photographs and memorabilia but little of real interest. It is open Monday to Friday, 10am–5pm. Admission £1.00, children under 14 free. The nearby *Aquarium* (**01726 816188**) occupies the town's old salt cellar and contains locally-caught specimens. To the south of the centre on the Esplanade there is a large house, *The Haven*, which was once the home of the author *Sir Arthur Quiller-Couch*.

Open daily
11am –5pm.
Admission
£1.50
children
£1.00

The two most important buildings in Fowey are located next to each other in the very centre of the town. The *Church of St Nicholas* dates largely from the early C14 and is big and spacious as befitting the powerful and influential town of the time. The west tower is lavishly decorated with stone carving at the base and at each stage and with battlements and pinnacles atop – again a bold statement of wealth and power. The two storey porch is a prominent feature of the exterior with good carving to the capitals. It is one of the few Cornish churches with clerestory windows, that is an additional row of windows above the main aisle windows and is another reflection of the status of the town and its church. Inside, there is an exceptionally fine carved wagon roof, an interesting Norman font and an Elizabethan pulpit with intricate carving. There are a number of monuments to the Rashleigh family including that to John Rashleigh of around 1610, depicting him lying down with ruff and beret. In a side chapel is the tomb and memorial slab to Thomas Treffrey (1633) and an incised stone slab with archaic figure that is late C16.

Immediately beside the church and forming a very pleasing composition is the manor house of Place, the seat of the Treffrey family. A fortified mansion was first built here in 1260 and was substantial enough to resist the French attack of 1456. The current building dates from the early C19, the work of *J.T.Treffrey* and is an exuberant display of Victorian Gothic. The only substantial remnant of the early house is a C16 bay window to the courtyard that is heavily carved and decorated in the manner of Launceston church. The C19 building is less extravagant but still of fine quality. The house is not open to the public although there are good views of it from the river where it is seen in the context of the waterfront buildings and the nearby church tower – one of the most distinctive and romantic vistas in Cornwall.

Place

A walk through the town, particularly Fore Street, reveals any number of interesting period buildings clustered around the narrow lanes. There are some interesting shops in Fowey including several galleries and book shops. *Bookends* at the church end of Fore Street has an excellent range of second hand books. The *Cry of the Gull*, 2 Webb Street (**01726 833838**) has a good collection of contemporary crafts and painting as well as classical music, while the *Fowey River Gallery*, 38 Fore Street (**01726 833828**), specializes in Cornish contemporary art with a good range of paintings, ceramics, glassware and jewellery. The *Millstream Pottery* is at no.19 North Street on the way to the Bodinnick ferry and slightly further along the same road is *Fowey Pottery*.

St German's Church

Antony

Cinema at Padstow

Hayle Sands

Beaches and walks

There are no beaches in Fowey itself but several pleasant coves on the Gribbin peninsula to the east. The nearest is a small strip of sand, Whitehouse Beach, along the Esplanade south of the town centre. The first real beach is Readymoney Cove, a twenty minute walk from the town centre and just before you reach St Catherine's Castle. It is sheltered, south facing and backed by low, wooded cliffs. However, the sands are mostly covered at high tide. There is a car park about five minutes walk inland. Near the castle is the *Rashleigh Mausoleum*, built for William Rashleigh in 1867 and an elaborate design with four springing stone arches supporting a cross over the tomb itself. It was built on the site of St Catherine's Chapel, licensed in 1390, and one of many small seaside chapels that served as landmarks and rudimentary lighthouses as well as places of worship.

Whitehouse Beach

Readymoney Cove

Following the coast path beyond St Catherine's Point is the small cove of Coombe Hawne with its stony beach backed by a profusion of reeds and

Coombe Hawne

FOWEY'S LITERARY HERITAGE

Fowey has a significant place in Cornwall's literary heritage with two of the county's most celebrated authors living here for the better part of their lives. *Sir Arthur Quiller Couch*, known as Q, moved here in 1892, having first seen the town as a schoolboy. He continued to live at Fowey until his death in 1944, contributing fully to the life of the town becoming a magistrate, Chairman of the Harbour Commissioners and Commodore of the Fowey Yacht Club. He wrote of Fowey in his second novel *The Astonishing History of Troy Town*. He became friends with Kenneth Grahame when the latter was recovering from pneumonia at the Fowey Hotel in 1899. Grahame subsequently married at Fowey church. His frequent boat trips with Q on the Fowey river are said to have influenced his writing of *The Wind in the Willows*, his most famous book. It certainly seems that Sea Rat is describing Fowey when he talks of "the little grey sea town......that clings along one steep side of the harbour." A stone memorial to Q was erected in 1948 on the Hall Walk opposite Fowey.

Daphne du Maurier is perhaps the writer most closely identified with Cornwall – it was the one enduring influence on her life and work. Her family moved to Cornwall in 1926 buying Ferryside at Bodinnick, on the east bank of the river. Here she wrote her most famous novels, *Jamaica Inn, Rebecca* and *Frenchman's Creek* – all set in Cornwall and inspired by its history and landscape. She was married in Lanteglos Church having arrived by boat from Ferryside. In 1943, she moved to Menabilly, the house and estate just to the west of Fowey.

A slightly more obscure literary association is with *Mary Bryant*, a Fowey girl transported to Australia for seven years for stealing a cloak. She sailed on the first fleet in 1787. Once in Botany Bay, she escaped with fellow convicts and sailed 3250 miles to Dutch Timor, one of the longest voyages ever undertaken in an open boat. They passed themselves off as shipwrecked sailors, but eventually, the truth was discovered and they were returned to England and imprisoned again. However, news of her epic voyage earned her respect and support, particularly from James Boswell, who petitioned for her pardon, which was granted in 1793 whereupon she returned to Cornwall. She is depicted as one of the main characters in *Timberlake Wertenbaker*'s celebrated play *Our Country's Good* and there is also a book about her which is on sale in the bookshops in the town.

The **Fowey Literary Centre** at 5, South Street (**01726 833619**) is open every day from May to mid-September, 10am–5.30pm. Admission is free and there is a small exhibition on authors associated with the town.

vegetation. It was a well-known smugglers cove with a hidden entrance and an isolated farmhouse, **Coombe Farm** (**01726 833123**) *B*, at the head of the valley. There is a path up to the farm where there is a small car park. The farmhouse has an C18 facade although the building underneath is probably older and for most of its life was a Rashleigh dower house, lived in by the widows of the family. Between two of its rooms is a large cavity, reputedly used for contraband brought up from the cove. Now it is a working farm, which also provides overnight accommodation. Cream teas are served in the walled garden in fine weather.

Fowey is a good starting point for many walks in the immediate area. The walk down to Gribbin Head takes in fine coastal scenery, seductive coves and the magnificent vista from the head itself. There is also a fine circular walk across the river and around to Polruan returning by the ferry. From the centre of Fowey, proceed up Fore Street and follow the road to Caffa Mill where the

Bodinnick ferry crosses the river to Bodinnick. Just north of here is the Fowey Docks where ECC export some 1.8 million tonnes of china clay, making it the ninth busiest port in the country in terms of cargo value. As you cross on the ferry, the large house with the projecting gables on the river front opposite is Ferryside, onetime home of Daphne du Maurier. Bodinnick is a small village with no facilities other than a church and pub, **The Old Ferry Inn** (**01726 870237**) *B*, which serves real ales and food, lunchtimes and evenings. Accommodation is also available if required. A path leads from above the inn

Hall Walk to Hall Walk which provides striking views over the river towards Fowey. At Penleath Point is the Q memorial, a stone monument to the author, Sir Arthur Quiller Couch. The path now turns east and follows high above Pont Pill, an

Pont arm of the Fowey, until it crosses the creek on a footbridge. Pont Pill is one of those silent creeks where there are few boats and even fewer people. Pont, itself, is a tiny quayside hamlet which until recently was an important river quay servicing the farms and communities of the area. It is now owned by the National Trust and they have a number of self catering properties to let. From here a diversion can be taken up the hill to *Lanteglos Church*, a big church in an isolated location, where Daphne du Maurier was married. Return by the same footpath and then take the path off to the west along the hills to the south of Pont Pill. This path continues around to Polruan with exceptional views across the river to Fowey and beyond. From Polruan the passenger ferry can be taken back to Fowey. Allow 3–4 hours for the walk.

 ## Accommodation

There are a large number of places to stay in Fowey in all price ranges and many of them in interesting historic buildings. Booking ahead is strongly recommended as, in addition to its own charms, Fowey is also a convenient and popular base for visiting the nearby Eden Project.

Trevanion Guest House 70 Lostwithiel Street (**01726 832602**) *A*, comfortable rooms in a C16 house located just two minutes walk from the centre of town and close to the main car park. There is also limited parking on-site, something of a rarity in Fowey.

Safe Harbour Hotel Lostwithiel Street (**01726 833379**) *B*, near the above, early C19 inn that provides accommodation.

The Ship Inn Trafalgar Square (**01726 832230**) *B*, right in the centre of town next to the church, this is one of the oldest buildings in Fowey, the family home of the Rashleigh family. Rooms lack any real historic character, but good value.

King of Prussia Town Quay (**01726 832450**) *C*, opposite the ferry and with marvellous views over the river from the front rooms. All the rooms are en-suite.

Globe Posting House 19 Fore Street (**01726 833322**) *A*, located right in the middle of town and one of the cheapest places to stay.

Dagland's 6 Daglands Road (**01726 833128**) *B*, small guest house in a Victorian building with good views over the town and estuary.

St Keverne 4 Daglands Road (**01726 833164**) *B*, next door to and similar to Dagland's.

The Old Quay House Hotel 28 Fore Street (**01726 833302**) *E*, elegant hotel, located in the centre of town and with fine views over the river.

Marina Hotel Esplanade (**01726 833315**) *E*, smart hotel in early C19 building with views over the river.

Fowey Hall Hotel Hanson Drive (**01726 833866**) *E*, set within five acres of gardens and with superb views over the estuary this is the best hotel in Fowey. There is an indoor swimming pool, games room , comfortable lounges and a magnificent terrace overlooking the harbour. It is regarded as one of the best 'family hotels' in the country.

Restaurants and cafes

Fowey is a major tourist destination and there is a good range of places to eat and the quality is generally high.

The Ship Trafalgar Square (**01726 832230**) *I*, serves good pub food in its atmospheric bar and there is a separate restaurant.

King of Prussia Town Quay (**01726 832450**) *I*, excellent bar food and a separate dining room too.

Food for Thought Town Quay (**01726 832221**) *E*, superb location right on the riverside. This elegant restaurant has a fine reputation.

Taipan Fore Street (**01726 833899**) *M*, excellent Asian inspired cuisine with the emphasis on fish and seafood. Reservations recommended.

Sams Fore Street (**01726 832273**) *M*, small bistro-style restaurant with cosy decor. Serves burgers, pizzas, steaks and fish. Very popular with locals and good value.

The Toll Bar 1 Lostwithiel Street (**01726 833001**) *I*, cafe/restaurant with pleasant, airy interior and an outside terrace with river views. Open all day, serving breakfasts, coffee, teas and lunch. The food has a Mediterranean influence with pasta, moussaka and risottos.

Maxwell's Lostwiltiel Street (**01726 832023**) *M*, fish restaurant with an imaginative menu. Good value.

Waterside Restaurant The Esplanade (**01726 833315**) *E*, situated in the Marina Hotel. Good views over the river from the dining room and highly rated food.

Fowey Hall Hotel Hanson Drive (**01726 833866**) *E*, elegant dining in this converted country house. The food has an excellent reputation. The hotel is also open for light lunches, coffee and teas which provide the opportunity to enjoy the facilities without the expense of dinner.

ⓘ   Practicalities

Tourist Information Centre

The Tourist Information Centre (**01726 833616**) is located at 5 South Street, by the church. They are very helpful and can provide all sorts of information about Fowey and the surrounding area. The passenger ferry to Polruan runs all year, every 15 minutes and one of the best views of Fowey is from the ferry.

Ferries

The fare is £0.80, children £0.50. The Bodinnick ferry also runs all year with the last sailing at 8.45pm or dusk whichever is earlier. Fares: car £2.00, motorbike/cycle £1.00, passenger £0.80, children £0.30. If you want to explore the river more fully, canoe expeditions are run by the *Fowey Gallery*, 17 Passage

Canoe expeditions

Street (**01726 833627**). The day trips take about five hours and are well-managed with a safety boat in attendance at all times. All equipment is provided. Advance reservations are essential and departure times are dictated by the tides. Prices are a very reasonable £20 per person. In the summer, there are

River cruises

also river and coastal cruises, subject to tides and demand – telephone **01726 870775** or **833192** or the TIC for further information. Between May and September, there is a regular ferry service across the bay to Mevagissey. There are between three and six sailings per day and the journey takes around 35 minutes. Return fares are £9.00, children £6.00, family £25.00. Telephone **07977 203394** for details of sailing times. The *Daphne du Maurier Festival of Arts and Literature* is held annually, normally in May, and attracts many well-known names from the world of literature. Booking for the more popular events is essential. Further information is available from the TIC.

Fowey is easily approached by car and is signposted off the main St Austell to Liskeard road. Alternatively, it can be approached from the east via the Bodinnick ferry. On-street parking is strictly limited but there are a number of car parks dotted around the edge of the town centre. There is a regular bus service from Fowey to St Austell, which also calls at Par main line railway station, the nearest to Fowey. The coast path passes through Fowey and then over the Estuary to Polruan, making Fowey an attractive overnight stop for anyone walking along the coast. The Saints Way is a fairly ordinary long distance path that has been cobbled together from a combination of public footpaths and quiet lanes and runs between Fowey and Padstow on the north coast. There is no evidence that this was an ancient route, although it is known that there was considerable overland traffic between the north and south coasts hereabouts from prehistory onwards. The use of long stretches of road detract from the attraction of the route and the scenery is often relatively uninspiring. The Saints Way Guide provides detailed route information and describes many of the sites that can be visited along the route. It can be purchased from *Cornwall Countryside Access* (**01208 73441**) or from TICs along the route.

Saints Way

The Fowey Valley

Golant, a couple of miles upriver from Fowey is a an attractive village of pretty cottages stepping up the steep hill from the river. The quayside is particularly busy as this is a major yachting centre and boat building, repair, chandlery and engine maintenance all lend it a busy workmanlike air. The railway between Lostwithiel and Fowey Docks (freight only) runs along the shoreline further adding to this sense of industry. The church is located outside the village in a raised position with marvellous views over the river. It has a low tower, aisle and nave, all in lichen-covered granite. The church is unusual in having been little altered since it was first built in 1509. The roofs to the nave and aisle are particularly noteworthy and the pulpit utilizes some fine carved bench ends. There is a large Royal Coat of Arms and some C15 glass in the window to the north of the altar. In the churchyard, by the porch, there is a small holy well. The **Fishermans Arms** is a lovely pub, which serves real ales and food at lunchtimes and evenings. The **Cormorant Hotel** (**01726 833426**) *E* is a small upmarket hotel with river views. In the summer, rooms are only let on a half board basis. To the north of the village is the **Youth Hostel** (**0870 770 5832**) *A* at Penquite House, a Georgian country house in its own grounds. The site is isolated and there is no public transport to the hostel. Golant is a pleasant hour's walk from Fowey, taking the B3269 from the ferry then turning right up the lane signed for the Saints Way and following the signs across the Downs, through woods and finally along the river to Golant. By car, the access is down narrow lanes from the B3269. In summer, there are occasional ferries from Fowey, check at the TIC in Fowey.

Golant

Just by the junction of the B3269 and the Golant road is *Castle Dore*, a well-preserved hillfort consisting of two substantial ramparts, still standing to about 7 feet high and reputed to be the castle of the Celtic, King Mark. During the Civil War battle of Lostwithiel (1644) the fort was used as a temporary refuge by the besieged Parliamentarian army. To get to the fort, park on the road just past the junction and take the footpath on the right. The fort is over the gate on your right. There is no car park or signs.

Lanlivery

Lanlivery, just west of Lostwithiel, is located on one of the more interesting parts of the Saints Way. From here, the path goes north west up onto the high land of Crift Downs and towards Helman Tor with fine views all the way across to Bodmin Moor. Lanlivery itself is a tiny village with a big church, its tower nearly 100 feet tall. The south aisle and porch have particularly fine carved roofs, while the floor is paved with large flags of the local slate. The **Crown Inn** (**01208 872707**) **C** directly opposite the church is a magnificent C12 inn serving real ales and excellent bar food. There are also two en-suite bedrooms with their own private garden and patio.

Lostwithiel

Located on the lowest bridging point of the Fowey, Lostwithiel had an early strategic significance. It was a major port up to the mid C14 when the river silted up with the debris from tin workings. However, it remained important as an administrative centre and was the location for the Stannary Court – the centre of royal authority over tin mining. Unusually for Cornwall, the town was planned and laid out with a central grid of streets in the medieval manner. This historic plan is still in evidence today. Lostwithiel played a significant part in the Civil war when a Parliamentary army was besieged in the town for a month in 1644 before finally surrendering at Castle Dore to the south. A number of buildings were badly damaged during the siege. It continued to be a prosperous town and there are many good C17 and C18 buildings around the town. As mining ceased to be an economic force in the area, the town transformed itself into a centre for the farming community and now has the air of a quiet country town, largely undisturbed by recent developments.

 ## The Town

Lostwithiel is a pleasant place to spend an hour or so walking around the network of narrow streets in the centre. It is now a local centre for antiques and the many shops provide an interesting diversion. *Gallery 8* in Fore Street (**01208 873063**) has an excellent range of paintings and sculpture. To the south of the centre is the C14 *Tudor Bridge* over the River Fowey, one of the best such bridges in Cornwall. The parapet was added in 1676, the original bridge being open to the sides. The *Duchy Palace*, built to regulate the tin industry, was built about the same time and covered a two acre site. The only remaining building is the *Coinage Hall* on the corner of Quay Street and Fore

Street and now used as the Freemasons Hall. The nearby buildings show traces of masonry from the Palace that have been absorbed into later buildings.

The *Church of St Bartholomew* is largely C14 and is one of the most distinctive in Cornwall. It sits in the heart of the town, its small churchyard hemmed in by buildings on all sides. Its outstanding feature is its spire. The tower is standard C13 with its lancet windows while the spire was added in the C14 and shows clear Breton influences. It displays an extraordinarily accomplished and flamboyant transition from the square plan of the tower to the octagon of the spire. The spire is broached and has dormer windows on four of its sides while around its foot is an elaborate octagonal screen with on each side double lights, tracery and a surmounting gable. A public way passed through the ground floor of the tower until 1878 when an unfortunate extension blocked the route. The main body of the church is C14 too and similar to nearby Fowey with its range of clerestory windows above the spandrels of the windows below. The great east window is one of the finest in Cornwall, the glass is Victorian but good nevertheless. The interior of the church is relatively uninteresting compared to the flourishes of the exterior. However, the early C14 font is a remarkable piece of carving with carved figures, beasts and heads adorning the bowl. In the churchyard is a medieval lantern cross. The church interior is open between 11am and 3pm, Tuesday, Thursday and Friday.

Elsewhere in the town, there are some good C17 and C18 buildings, particularly in Fore Street where *Edgcumbe House* and the adjacent *Dower House* date from the mid C18 and are solid granite but with the classical proportions of the period. The Guildhall opposite dates from the same period, the ground floor originally having been an open corn market. The building is now occupied by the *Town Museum*, which contains local items of interest and photographs of old Lostwithiel. On the main road is the remains of the old Grammar School erected in 1781 – only the front elevation remains. *Tapprel House*, off North Street, is now the public library and thought to date from at least the C16. The interior amply demonstrates the simple nature of many of these early Cornish manor houses. On the corner of Malthouse Lane is the leasestone for a former property, dated 1652 and to last for 3000 years!

Open Easter to mid–Sep daily except Sundays, 10am– 12.30pm & 2.30–4.30pm

There is little need to stay in Lostwithiel as its attractions can be seen in a few hours but it makes a pleasant base for this part of Cornwall and is quieter and less visited than Fowey. It also makes a very convenient base for visiting the Eden Project, only a few miles to the west. Like elsewhere in this area, advance booking is recommended. If you do wish to stay, the nicest place is probably the **Royal Oak**, Duke Street (**01208 872552**) *C*, a C13 inn with real ales and good food. The **Globe Inn**, 3 North Street (**01208 872501**) *C*, is another C13 pub in the town centre and serves a good range of real ales as well as good pub food. There is a small beer garden and accommodation, which is being refurbished for the 2003 season. The **Kings Arms**, Fore Street (**01208 872383**) *A* is a large pub which also has accommodation. If these are all full, the R**estormel Lodge Hotel** (01208 872223) *D* on the main road is likely to have room, but it is a grim-looking place and overpriced, although it does have a swimming pool.

The public houses listed above all serve food, lunchtimes and evenings, the Royal Oak and the Globe being particularly good. The **Trewithen Restaurant** (01208 872373) *E* in Fore Street is one of the few restaurants in the town centre and has a good reputation. **The River Brasserie** (01208 872774) *M* is at the end of Fore Street and is another good option. The **Duchy Coffee Shop** in Fore Street, opposite the church, provides teas and lunches in an old building with exposed timbers.

Tourist Information Centre

The Tourist Information Centre (01208 872207) is located in the community centre on the main road. Lostwithiel is on the main west coast railway line and the station is a short walk from the town centre on the other side of the river. There are frequent bus services to St Austell and Liskeard. For those travelling by car, there is a large car park to the north of the town centre accessed off the main road by the community centre. The Saints Way long distance path passes just to the west and Lostwithiel would make a pleasant diversion for anybody walking the route.

Restormel Castle

English Heritage: April to October, July and August, 10am–6pm (April–June and Sept, 10am–5pm, October 10am–4pm). Admission, £2.20, children £1.10

The site is signposted and is approached along a narrow lane through beautiful countryside. It is an easy drive or alternatively a pleasant half hour walk from Lostwithiel. Located just a mile upriver, the castle pre-dates the town itself. It originally commanded a crossing point of the river and its strategic importance was diminished with the building of the bridge in Lostwithiel. However, it continued to be an important residence and administrative centre. The castle is one of the finest examples of military architecture in the county and also one of the most romantic with its geometrically-perfect shell keep sitting atop its hill and marvellous views over the upper Fowey valley.

Normans

The site's early history is unknown but it is likely that the first castle was built around 1100 by the Normans as part of their occupation of England and in particular the troublesome Celts of the west. The site overlooks what was then the major crossing point of the river and from its elevated position there are commanding views over the surrounding countryside. The earliest castle was an earthwork with most likely a wooden keep and surrounding wooden palisade. Around 1270, the estate passed to Richard, Earl of Cornwall who was succeeded by his son Edmund in 1272. On his death in 1299, the Earldom of Cornwall reverted to the Crown and since then Restormel has belonged to the Duchy of Cornwall. It was probably Edmund who moved the administrative centre for the area from Launceston to Lostwithiel at the end of the C13, thereby significantly increasing the status of Restormel, which may also have become Edmund's residence. The stone castle dates from this time and the large rooms with big windows, the prominent chapel and the quality of stonework and finishes suggest a residential use as much as a military one. On Edmund's death in 1299, there were no further resident Earls and the building was probably occupied by stewards. In 1337, the castle passed to the first Duke of Cornwall, the Black Prince, who is known to have visited the castle in 1354 and 1365. After his death, the castle was rarely used other than by stewards of the Duchy. By the time of the Civil War, the castle was in a virtually ruinous state when it was patched up and garrisoned by the Parliamentary Army of Lord Essex. Their headquarters were at Lostwithiel and Restormel acted as a lookout post and gun platform. However, its defences proved ineffective and it was easily captured by Sir Richard Grenville on 21 August 1644. Thereafter, the building remained a romantic ruin until restoration earlier this century.

As you approach the stone keep across the high saddle of land from the car park, you are walking on the outer bailey now disappeared. The defences here would probably have been earth and timber even after the stone keep was built. The keep is one of the most perfectly preserved shell keeps in the country with its perfect circle of stone, 125 feet in diameter, sitting within its moat and mound. The keep is largely constructed of local shillet, a kind of slate, and there is evidence of plastering both internally and externally. The finer architectural features of the castle, door surrounds and window details for instance, were carved from higher quality Pentewan stone. Most of this has now been lost, but their existence along with the plastering indicates a high status for the castle.

The keep is surmounted by a *wall walk* and battlemented parapet which is well preserved. Around the internal walls of the keep were a series of rooms with storerooms and kitchens on the ground floor and the principal rooms on the first floor. A good view of the internal layout can be had from the wall walk along with magnificent views over the surrounding countryside. It is not difficult from here to understand the strategic significance of the castle. The *great hall* would have been the most important public room of the castle and the large windows here denote its status as a prestigious home rather than military fortification. The solar, or lord's private rooms, are adjacent and off these the ante chapel and chapel, which forms the only break in the otherwise perfectly circular curtain wall. It was added in the C13 and a wide archway was cut through the outer wall to accommodate it. There is some evidence to show that this was adapted as a gun platform during the Civil War.

The East Bank of the Fowey

Some two miles south of Lostwithiel, and approached down narrow lanes, is the church of St Winnow, one of the many Cornish churches in isolated and beautiful riverside settings. Its design is typical Cornish and the setting picturesque enough for it to have featured in the Poldark films. There are a number of interesting features to the interior including a good carved roof and elaborate C16 bench ends. There is an exceptionally fine carved pulpit and rood screen, with the screen extending across both nave and aisle. The east window in the south

St Winnow

aisle is a good example of C15/early C16 stained glass and a rarity in Cornwall. There are some good slate memorials including one in the porch dated 1722.

From the church, a path follows the rivers edge southwards with good views. After about 15 minutes, it enters *Great Wood* and climbs onto higher ground before turning back north along *Lerryn Creek*, a tidal branch of the Fowey. The path follows the creek until it turns due north towards St Winnow Mill, a working mill until the 1940s, now a picturesque ruin. There has been a mill on this spot since at least 1331. To return, follow the mill road and then take the footpath on the left back to St Winnow Church.

Ethy Wood
Taking the path over the stream at the Mill would bring you to Ethy Wood, owned by the National Trust and now criss-crossed with tracks and paths among the steep, wooded slopes. The stretch between the Mill and Ethy Quay is ancient woodland, mostly old oak coppice which has not been cut since before World War I. It can be a place of exceptional peace and quiet and is **Ethy Quay** considered to be one of the best woodlands in Cornwall. Ethy Quay, on the tip of Ethy Creek where it meets Lerryn Creek, would once have been busy serving the manor house, mills and farms of the area. Remains of the quay walls and a small dock can still be seen. Just downstream is the ruin of Ethy boathouse and a good spot for a picnic. Lerryn Creek is a haven for birds with heron, kingfisher, redshank, cormorant and curlew all in evidence.

Lerryn
The path continues along the north side of the creek to Lerryn, a small village with shops, a pub and a car park. There is a very limited bus service to Lostwithiel and Liskeard. The footpath continues from here along the southern shore of the creek through Lerryn Wood and with wonderful views over the river. South of here, there is only very limited access to the river and the road stays inland, past the isolated church at *St Veep* to the tiny hamlet of **Penpol** Penpol at the head of Penpol Creek. The narrow lanes cross the high ground before dipping down again to Bodinnick for the ferry to Fowey and the path along the east bank to Polruan.

The South Coast, Polruan to Looe

Polruan
Polruan has much in common with Fowey on the opposite bank, steep, narrow lanes tightly packed with old cottages leading down to a small, busy quay, but it has none of the grandeur of Fowey nor the number of tourists. As such, it is a pleasant trip from Fowey on the passenger ferry, although there are few sites of any real interest. The only building of any note is the C15 blockhouse on the river's edge directly opposite that of Fowey and between which a great chain was hung to defend the harbour. Another good reason for coming is the marvellous **Lugger Inn** (**01726 833435**) **A**, an unspoilt C16 granite building right on the quayside. They serve real ales and excellent food including locally caught fish and seafood and also have accommodation on a room only basis. The **Russell Inn** in nearby West Street also serves real ales and food.

The coast from Polruan to Polperro is one of the finest stretches between Falmouth and Plymouth. The coast path follows the top of high cliffs with several steep descents and climbs. There are excellent views all the way and no roads or settlements to disturb the sense of isolation. The walk is quite strenuous and takes about four hours. As you leave Polruan, there are fine views of the Gribbin to the west. Soon the secluded, sandy coves of *Lantic Bay* appear. They can also be approached from a car park located some 10 minutes walk inland. The path down to the beach is very steep. Care should be taken when swimming as there is often an undertow here. *Pencarrow Head*, at the west end of Lantic Bay, affords magnificent coastal views from its 400 foot high cliffs. Lantivet Bay stretches away into the distance with a suc- **Lantivet Bay** cession of sandy coves divided by rocks and with a more gentle path giving access. There is a car park some 15 minutes walk inland. At the west end of the bay, where the footpath from Lansallos meets the coast path, is *West Combe*, a beautiful, unspoilt inlet. There is a small car park in the village of Lansallos from where it is a short walk down a lovely footpath to the Combe. The coast path continues along the cliff top to Polperro. The mournful tolling that may be heard is the bell-buoy on the Udder Rock out to sea.

Polperro is one of the most picturesque villages in Cornwall with its cot- **Polperro** tages, inns and shops clustered tightly around the harbour and leading back up the steep valley. It is also one of the most visited and at peak times the number of visitors can be a serious disincentive. However, when the crowds have gone, it is a magical, watery place hemmed in by woods on either side of its steep-sided valley. Crows and gulls compete for the skies and their cries resonate between the buildings. It is well worth trying to stay the night as most visitors are day trippers and the evenings are quieter and have a quality of their own. There are plenty of places to stay and some excellent places to eat and drink, including one of the finest pubs on the south coast.

There are no real sights in Polperro, although there is a small *Museum of* **Open 10.00–** *Fishing and Smuggling* (**01503 272423**). The museum is located in an old **6pm daily,** pilchard factory overlooking the harbour and explains the importance of both **admission** fishing and smuggling to the small community. At low tide, a small sandy **£1.60, chil-** beach is revealed but the real attraction of Polperro is the place itself and the **dren £0.50** best thing to do is to wander the narrow lanes and soak up the atmosphere.

If you want to stay, there are many places to stay in the village itself, with sev-eral guest houses on the road between the village and the car park. They are much the same, but you could try **Natal House** (**01503 272491**) *B* or **Fernhill** (**01503 272491**) *A*. The **Cottage Restaurant** (**01503 272217**) *B*, in the same road, also has pleasant en-suite accommodation. Perhaps, one of the nicest places to stay is the **Old Mill House Hotel**, Mill Hill (**01503 272362**) *B*, located in the heart of the village. There are eight en-suite rooms and they also have their own car park nearby. The **Crumplehorn Inn** (**01503 272348**) *B* is locat-ed on the edge of the village near the main car park and provides comfortable accommodation. **Chyavallon**, Landaviddy Lane (**01503 272788**) *B* is a short walk from the harbour and provides comfortable accommodation.

There are plenty of places to eat in Polperro. The **Old Mill House** and **Crumplehorn Inn** both have their own restaurants as well as providing bar food. The **Nelson Restaurant** (**01503 272366**) *M*, in the centre of the village, provides good food, including fresh fish, in an interesting ambience. There is a bar and brasserie downstairs which is cheaper. **Couch's Brasserie** (**01503 272554**) *M*, almost opposite, serves fish and pizza. **Noughts and Crosses** is a handsome old building in the centre of the village, backing onto the river. They have a small but interesting bar menu.

The only nightlife in Polperro is provided by the restaurants and pubs, so it is fortunate that, in the **Blue Peter**, they have one of the finest and most atmospheric pubs on the south coast. Located in an old granite building by the harbour entrance, it is warm, friendly and all a pub should be. The floor is wood, the bar is wood, the ceiling is wood and the walls are the colour of nicotine. Log fires burn in the grates on chill evenings and a good selection of real ales are served, but no food. There is occasional live music at weekends. If you are in Polperro do not miss it. The **Three Pilchards** is also a nice old building and serves real ale and food. The name comes from the Italian traders who used to room here and take the pilchards for breakfast before buying shipments for export to their homeland. The **Old Mill House** and **Crumplehorn Inn** also serve real ales and have nice, atmospheric bars.

Cars are not allowed in the centre of the village and there is a large car park on the edge from where horse drawn or electric vehicles ferry people down to the harbour. If you want to walk it is an easy and pleasant 15 minute walk. There are regular buses to Looe which is also the nearest railway station.

From Polperro, it is a further two hours on the coast path to Looe. The walk is easier than that from Polruan with the high slate cliffs now more rounded, as they have slipped towards the eroding sea. There are numerous rock ledges out to sea and masses of pungent, wild garlic line the path. After

Talland Bay

about half an hour, the beaches at Talland Bay are reached. There is a car park, a seasonal cafe and rock pools and ledges dotted around the sands. A short 10 minute walk inland will bring you to *Talland Church* which is known for its unusual detached tower, linked by a later porch to the main church. There are also an unusually large number of elaborately carved C15 and C16 pews. Beyond Talland Bay, the offshore Looe Island comes into view with Rame Head in the far distance.

If you have your own transport, there is an interesting inland circuit to Looe that takes in a number of historic sites and pleasant villages as well as some good woodland scenery. From Polperro, take the main A387 for Looe but turn left onto the B3359 after two miles. Two more miles brings you to

Pelynt

Pelynt where the church is largely C15 but is unusual for its stately arcade of classical granite columns erected in 1680 to replace the medieval piers. There are also a number of slate memorial tablets of exceptional quality from the C16 to the present day. There are two fantastic examples on either side of the main altar, that to the south wall of the chancel to William Achym, engraved in 1589, the year after the Armada. It shows him in armour and puffed breeches with his ruff, dagger and sword. It is superbly carved in deep relief, an indication of the early date of the memorial, later ones tending to be in shallow relief, easier and less prone to flaking. The Buller tomb on the north wall of the chancel consists of a tomb chest with an elaborate back plate and dates from 1615. Francis Buller is shown with his wife and eight daughters and four sons, all deeply and superbly carved. The chest itself is also deeply carved and coloured with coats of arms on the side panels. The Trelawney memorial of 1630 displays some exquisite lettering with the wry inscription "Here lies an honest lawyer, wot ye what. A thing for all the world to wonder at." There are several other monuments including a modern C20 slate in memory to the 6 sons of William Grigson, all killed in the First or Second World Wars and the seventh son, Geoffrey Grigson, the poet. In the churchyard, the headstone for William Grigson was carved in 1931 by Eric Gill, the famous sculptor. The **Jubilee Inn** (**01503 220312**) *C* is an attractive inn with a reputation for good food. Accommodation is also available in en-suite rooms.

Two miles further north and signposted to the west off the B3359 is Lanreath, an attractive village with a picturesque group of cottages beside the church. The **Punch Bowl Inn** (**01503 220218**) *B* provides food and real ale in what was once a court house, coaching inn and smugglers haunt. There are log fires in winter and plenty of atmosphere. They also have accommodation. The church provides a remarkably complete picture of a C16 church, having been repaired in the C19 rather than restored like so many churches in Cornwall. The church is standard Cornish Perpendicular but the main interest in the church is its furnishings. There is a good Norman font with exceptional carving and on the window cill of the Lady Chapel is a small Norman altar stone showing how small these were before the large altars we know today became commonplace in the Middle Ages. The rood screen extends across both nave and aisle with ten traceried bays, superbly carved. The most notable survival, however, is the fragments of painted decoration of the saints on the bottom panels from the early C16. Although only partial, they give a good idea of how highly decorated many medieval churches would have been. There is also a painted wagon roof in the aisle with carved bosses to the nave, aisle and porch. There are also well carved C16 benches, seats and a pulpit with excellent figure sculptures on the chancel stalls. There is an elaborate monument to Charles Grylls and wife of 1623, unusually carved in wood but in imitation of contemporary stone memorials.

Continue up the B3359 for a further two miles, then take the narrow lane to the east for Herodsfoot and Deerpark Forest, a largely coniferous forest which is managed for its timber but also provides a number of interesting walks and a haven for wildlife. It is possible to stay in timber chalets set within the woods by a large pond. *Forest Holidays* (**0131 314 6100**) can provide further details. Herodsfoot itself is a tiny community around a bridging point of the West Looe River with the steep sides of the wooded valley crowding around. From here, a walk following quiet lanes and footpaths can be followed alongside the river all the way to Looe some five miles to the south. The steep sides of the valley, the woods and the river itself combine to make it a very pleasant walk. You should allow three hours to complete the whole walk although there are plenty of places where the route can be terminated before Looe. The only problem is transport as there is virtually no public transport to Herodsfoot. The nearest connection is to take the train or bus from Looe to

Lanreath

Herodsfoot

St Keyne but this would put an extra two or three miles on the walk.

Duloe

To continue the tour by car, take the steep narrow lane out of Herodsfoot to the east and follow the signs to Duloe, two miles to the south. On the southern edge of the village is the *Duloe Stone Circle*, the smallest in Cornwall and consisting of only eight stones. It is signposted and approached up a public footpath between buildings. Just to the south and outside the village proper is the *Church of St Cuby and St Leonard*. It has an unusual plan form with the tower apart from the main body of the church and attached by the south transept. It dates from the C13 and is exceptionally well preserved. The pyramid roof dates from restoration work in the C19 but is similar to what would have been there originally. The chancel aisle was built as the family chapel by the Colshull family in the C15 and is clearly expressed from the outside by the buttresses, battlements and pinnacles which are not found elsewhere on the building. Internally, the chapel is notable for its elaborate carved bays with flowers, leaves and grapes and the eastern arch resting on an angel corbel. The chapel was built for Sir John Colshull (died 1483) and his monument still survives – a tomb chest with decoration around the base and a rather crudely carved figure on top. There are also two good slate memorials in the chapel dating from 1592 and 1601. The font was originally located in the nearby Holy Well and was first used as a font in the C6, although it may well be older. Certainly, the style of the carvings of griffins and snakes on the side are familiar from the Roman period.

Morval

Continuing towards Looe, the road meets the A387 and you need to turn left and then take the narrow lane signposted for Morval after about one mile. The house and church are located right next to each other. There are glimpses of the house from the footpath beyond the church. It is one of the best in Cornwall and dates from the C16. It is in private ownership and not open to the public. The church is small and low and beautifully located in a lush landscape of trees and rhododendrons. There is an interesting slate memorial of 1637 to Walter Coode with kneeling parents and the children represented as fruits growing out of branches issuing from the parents. The skulls above some of the fruits indicate the death of the child before the parents. From Morval, the A387 is followed for the three miles to Looe.

Looe

Looe is the biggest town on the coast between St Austell and Plymouth and one of the major tourist centres of the area. Part of its attraction is its accessibility, as there are good public transport connections, particularly by train, making it a convenient day trip from Plymouth. The town has outgrown its historic core and now straggles along the river and up onto the hills behind.

Historic development

Looe has been a busy port since medieval times. Its natural, sheltered harbour made it an important fishing and trading port and, like Fowey, its sailors had a reputation for fierceness and independence that led to the inevitable temptation of piracy. The roll of Edward III's fleet before Calais shows Looe providing 20 ships and 315 sailors, only five ships fewer than London. Later, smuggling was to become an important part of the local economy, but it was the discovery of minerals on Bodmin Moor and the subsequent construction of the Liskeard to Looe canal that were to sustain the importance of the port into the C19. The railway arrived in the 1860s making the canal largely redundant and at the same time opening Looe up to the mass tourism that was to follow in the C20. The port is still a busy fishing harbour and many boats can be seen pulled up along the quayside.

The Town

The towns of East and West Looe are built on opposite sides of a deep river valley – a setting which gives the town much of its character. They are largely contemporary but most of the interest is now concentrated in East Looe. They are connected by a handsome C19 bridge that replaced a bridge of 13 arches that dated from 1411–18. Just to the north of the bridge in West Looe is the **South East Cornwall Discovery Centre**, providing information on the history, flora and fauna of the area. There is a large car park adjacent. The *Church of St Nicholas*, by the quay, dates from the C13 but was largely restored in the C19. A good number of ships' timbers were used in the rebuilding, including some from ships captured during the Napoleonic Wars.

East Looe is now the far bigger of the two and contains most of the accommodation, restaurants, bars and sites of interest. The historic centre is to the south, set back just behind the beach. It is a tight grid of narrow streets packed with fishermen's cottages, many now turned into restaurants, cafes and guest houses. There are few real sights but it is a pleasant place to wander and there are some nice period buildings dotted around. The *Guildhall*, in Higher Market Street, dates from the C15 and has a distinctive first floor gabled porch. High up under the roof is the pillory, one of the few examples remaining in the country. Here criminals would be confined in full view of the townspeople as a warning to all. It is now **The Old Guildhall Museum**, which has a number of exhibits relating to Looe's history and development, but also allows you to view the old gaol and court. Outside the old centre, the town has been largely overrun by the demands of tourism and there is a profusion of cafes, take-aways and gift shops. The quay provides plenty of opportunities for boat-watching as the harbour is still a busy fishing port. The Banjo Pier, so named because of its distinctive shape, provides a good vantage point. Looe is the headquarters of the Shark Fishing Club of Great Britain and fishing trips depart from the quayside. There are also coastal cruises that depart on a regular basis in the summer months, including trips to Looe Island, a privately-owned bird sanctuary, a mile offshore. The large mill pool where the West Looe River joins the main estuary is now a children's boating pool.

Open 11.30am– 4.30pm (closed Sat), admission £1.50, children £0.50

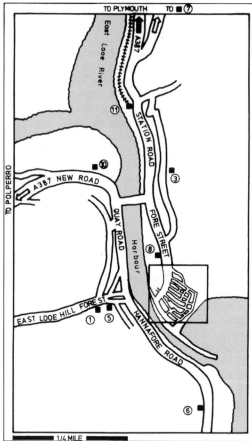

LOOE

ACCOMMODATION

1   Old Malt House
2   Sea Breeze
3   Silver Birch
4   The Ship
5   Tidal Court
6   St. Aubyns
7   Barclay House

ESSENTIALS

8   Tourist Office
9   Museum
10   Discovery Centre
11   Railway Station

RESTAURANTS AND BARS

A   Smuggler's Cottage
B   Papa Nino's
C   Liaisons Bistro
D   Fournier's
E   The Water Rail
F   Trawlers
G   Old Sail Loft
H   Capers
I   Pepes
J   Fishermans Arms
K   Old Salutation Inn
L   Bullers Arms
M   The Ship
N   Admiral Boscawen

Beaches

The main beach is in East Looe and is a pleasant enough crescent of sand with generally safe bathing. All the facilities of the town are close by and while this is convenient, it does mean that the beach is constantly overlooked and can get very crowded at peak times. At the eastern end of the beach there are concrete sea defences that provide plenty of space for sunbathing when the tide is high. A 15 minute walk to the east along the coast path will bring you to Plaidy Beach, a small and more secluded shingle beach with a seasonal cafe. Millendreath Beach, a little further on is bigger and sandier, especially at low tide, but is totally dominated by the nearby holiday camps and can be unpleasantly crowded. West Looe has no beaches as such, but at the southern end of the town, opposite Looe Island, is Hannafore Point, a spectacular rocky outcrop that reveals strips of sand and shingle separated by numerous rock pools and outcrops at low tide. Parking is limited but it is only a 20 minute walk from the centre of town.

Plaidy Beach

Milendreath Beach

Hannafore Point

Walks and river trips

The waters of the Looe estuaries are some of the most sheltered in Cornwall and are surrounded by the steep wooded sides of the valley providing an extremely attractive environment rich with wildlife and woodland fauna. Kilminorth Woods, on the south bank of the West Looe River and immediately adjacent to the town are open to the public and there are a number of prepared trails. A free leaflet is available from the Discovery Centre in West Looe and the walks start from the adjacent Millpool car park. The woods are primarily oak with beech and hazel and rich in wildlife. The adjacent river is tidal and the expansive mud flats at low tide provide fertile feeding grounds for many breeds of bird and the area is popular with bird watchers. The *Giant's Hedge* is an early defensive fortification probably dating from the C6 and still clearly evident today. It runs along the southern boundary of the wood alongside a clearly marked trail. For those with the energy, the course of the West Looe river can be followed by a series of paths and quiet lanes all the way to Herodsfoot and beyond. The route is about five miles and takes around three hours. There is some spectacular scenery with the steep sides of the valley crowding in ever closer to the river as you head north and you are unlikely to meet many others on the route. Take sturdy shoes, food and water. Trenant Wood on the opposite bank of the West Looe River also has forest trails and provides good views over the estuary to Looe. However, it is difficult to reach from Looe, the only access by road being from the north bank.

Kilminorth Woods

Trenant Wood

The calm and shallow waters of the Looe estuaries provide an excellent and safe opportunity for canoe trips which allow you to experience the river from a different perspective. *Floating Leaf Canoes* (**01503 240566**) provide guided canoe trips costing £15 per person. Trips start two hours before high tide and depart from the Mill Pool opposite the Discovery Centre and Millpool Car Park.

Canoe trips

Accommodation

A   –£44
B   £45–£64
C   £65–£80
D   £81–£100
E   £100+

The price coding system that is used throughout this guide is on a scale of A to E and indicates the cost of the lowest priced double room in that establishment during the peak summer period. This is clearly marked by the telephone number of the listing for each establishment. It should be borne in mind that single rooms are likely to be considerably more than half the price of a double. In the off peak months, many establishments reduce their rates considerably and even where they do not you may be able to negotiate a discount.

Looe is a major tourist centre and there will be no problem finding accommodation other than at the very peak season. Much of the accommodation is reasonably priced due to the general oversupply and prices can be even cheaper out of peak season.

The Old Malt House Fore Street, West Looe (**01503 264976**) **B**, C17 period house near the harbour with en-suite rooms and car parking.

Sea Breeze Lower Chapel Street, East Looe (**01503 263131**) **A**, located in the old part of town near the beach and other facilities. Some limited parking.

Silver Birch Guest House Shutta Road, East Looe (**01503 262918**) **B**, spectacular views over the river and a nice patio to the front. Approached up a very steep lane from the town centre. No car parking.

The Ship Fore Street (**01503 263124**) **B**, centrally located pub with rooms. Could be noisy at night.

Tidal Court 3 Church Street, West Looe (**01503 263695**) **A**, en-suite rooms in a small guest house set just back from the river. Good value.

St Aubyn's Marine Drive, West Looe (**01503 264351**) **C**, an attractive, large Victorian house situated on the edge of the town at Hannafore with fine sea views. En-suite rooms.

Barclay House St Martins Road, East Looe (**01503 262929**) **D**, a large Victorian, family house in six acres of grounds. Located just outside the town, it has extensive views over the river estuary and surrounding countryside. There is also a nice swimming pool and terrace.

Restaurants and cafes

There are plenty of good places to eat in Looe, many of them specializing in fish and seafood dishes. Most are concentrated in East Looe, particularly along the quayside and in the narrow lanes behind. All the suggestions below are in East Looe and centrally located.

Smugglers Cottage Restaurant Middle Market Street (**01503 262397**) **M**, located in a C15 building this atmospheric restaurant on two levels serves good food including fresh fish dishes and seafood. Reservations are recommended.

Papa Nino Spaghetti House Higher Market Street (**01503 264231**) *M–E*, Italian restaurant, but also serving fresh fish and seafood.

Liaisons Bistro Higher Market Street (**01503 265568**) *M–E*, a nice bistro atmosphere and a menu including meat and fish dishes.

Fournier's Lower Chapel Street (**01503 262674**) *M*, open in the evenings only. Small menu of meat and fish dishes in this tiny restaurant in the centre of the town.

The Water Rail Lower Market Street (**01503 262314**) *M*, located in a beautiful C14 building in the heart of the old town.

Trawlers Buller Quay (**01503 263593**) *E*, located on the quay where the fishing boats tie up. Specializes in fish and seafood.

The Old Sail Loft Restaurant Buller Quay (**01503 262131**) *M*, next door to the above. Serves fresh fish as well as a selection of meat dishes in one of the oldest buildings in Looe.

Capers Higher Market Street (**01503 265437**) *M*, fresh fish a speciality with good value "Early Bird Specials" before 7.30pm.

Pepes Buller Street (**01503 262057**) *I*, for a change from fish, try the Tex/Mex food in this cheap and cheerful restaurant.

Bars and nightlife

Looe can be quite a lively spot due to the number of tourists and daytrippers and there are many pubs located in the old part of East Looe. There is really no need to leave East Looe as this is where most of the night-time activity is concentrated. All the suggestions below are located in the old town of East Looe.

Fisherman's Arms Higher Market Street, reputedly C16 and the oldest pub in Looe. There is a garden for fine weather and they serve real ales and food at lunchtimes. There is a regular programme of live music.

Old Salutation Inn Fore Street, there is a welcoming atmosphere in this 400 year old building with its timber beams and open fires. Serves real ales and food, lunchtimes and evenings.

Buller's Arms Buller Street, a more basic locals pub but welcoming enough for the visitor to enjoy too. Real ale and food, lunchtimes and evenings.

The Ship Fore Street, a big pub with a large ground floor drinking area. Tends to attract a younger crowd and can get very busy at weekends.

Occasional live music. Real ales and food, lunchtimes and evenings.

Admiral Boscawen located right next to the beach. Big, characterless pub, but Looe's only nightclub if you are desperate for a late night.

ⓘ   ## Practicalities

Looe is well served by public transport routes. Regular buses connect to Liskeard, Plymouth and Polperro. The town has its own branch railway line connecting to the West Coast main line at Liskeard. It is one of the most scenic routes in Cornwall and follows the winding East Looe River with good river views along its length. By car, Looe is easily located on the A387. Car parking in East Looe can be very difficult with only a few small car parks that fill up quickly. However, there is a large pay and display car park just over the bridge in West Looe by the millpool and it is normally always possible to find space here. Driving around the centre of East Looe is not recommended. The

Tourist Information Centre Tourist Information Centre (**01503 262072**) is at the Guildhall, Fore Street, East Looe.

South Coast – Looe to Plymouth

This part of the coast is not well endowed with beaches with the notable exception of Whitsand Bay. It is an area of low cliffs and some rather ordinary coastal villages, although the twin villages of Cawsand and Kingsand are among the most picturesque in Cornwall.

Some two miles to the east of Looe you may be surprised to find the

Open from the week before Easter to Sept, Sun–Thurs, 11am – 4.30pm. Admission, £5.00, children £3.00, under 5 free *Monkey Sanctuary* (**01503 262532**) signposted down narrow lanes from the B3253 or from Seaton. It was established in 1964 to provide a stable setting in which South American woolly monkeys, that had been rescued from poor conditions of captivity, could live in as natural an environment as possible. In the intervening years, the Sanctuary has become an established breeding colony and is now open to the public on a regular basis for people to view these handsome animals.

Seaton sits at the foot of a wooded valley and has a rather unattractive beach of grey sand and pebbles. *Downderry* and *Portwrinkle* are to the east but have little to attract the visitor. Somewhat surprisingly, the highest points on the south coast of Cornwall are to either side of Downderry. A high point of 503 feet to the west, just north of the Monkey sanctuary and Battern Cliffs to the east at 458 feet. Past Portwrinkle, the magnificent four mile sweep of

Whitsand Bay Whitsand Bay comes into view. The beach is the finest sand and is backed by 250 foot high cliffs. Much of the beach is covered at high tide, but at any other time the sands are perfect for sunbathing, walking and beach games. Swimming is dangerous though due to strong offshore currents and is not recommended under any circumstance. There are a number of car parks along the cliff top road although it is a stiff descent down to the beach. At the eastern end of the bay is a cafe sited on the cliff top with superb views. The cliffs themselves are dotted with innumerable small chalets dating from the 1930s. Due to its proximity to Plymouth, the beach can be very popular on summer weekends, but overcrowding is rarely a problem due to the sheer size of the beach.

Rame Head dominates the eastern end of the bay and provides expansive views up and down the coast. On a clear day, the Eddystone lighthouse can be seen some nine miles out to sea. The tiny stone chapel dates from the C14 and it is from here that the arrival of the Spanish armada was signalled to the English fleet in Plymouth Sound in 1588. There is a car park at the Head, accessed down narrow lanes. The *Church of St German* at Rame, just inland, has one of the few broached spires in the county. From Rame Head, there is a pleasant walk east along the coast path towards Penlee Point from where there is a view across to Plymouth and Devon. The path then enters the *Earls Drive*, part of the landscaped grounds of Mount Edgcumbe House. The cottages that you pass just before reaching Cawsand were built for the coastguard in the 1820s to try to curb smuggling in the area.

Rame Head

Penlee Point

Cawsand and Kingsand are now to all intents and purposes one village, but until 1844 they were in different counties – the boundary between Devon and Cornwall being marked on the wall of a house in Garrett Street. Cawsand Bay offers a safe anchorage and is sheltered from all but south-east winds. It has long been an important fishing harbour and pilot boats for the Port of Plymouth were also stationed here. It was also an important centre for smuggling, out of sight of Plymouth, and yet near enough to allow for the easy transfer of contraband into the city. Today, it is a quiet backwater for most of the week, but at weekends the close proximity of Plymouth means that the number of day-trippers can add to the crowds considerably. The village is a maze of narrow streets, lined with brightly painted cottages, many of them built directly onto the seafront. There are two small sandy beaches which have generally safe bathing and are also popular for windsurfing and sailing. There are several good pubs serving excellent food and some attractive places to stay. As such, it is probably one of the nicest places in the area, either as a base for exploring the surrounding area or as a quiet beach resort.

Cawsand Kingsand

The **Halfway House Inn** in Fore Street (**01752 822279**) *B* is one of the best places to stay in the village. All rooms are en-suite and the whole place has been pleasantly refurbished and decorated. The **Cross Keys** (**01752 822309**) *B* by the square in Cawsand has good value en-suite rooms. **Clarendon** (**01752 823460**) *B* is a nice guest house with good value accommodation in Garrett Street overlooking the sea. The **Cawsand Bay Hotel** (**01752 822425**) *C* is right on the beach and has good value en-suite rooms, although the building has little character.

The **Halfway House Inn** and the **Devonport Inn** are both warm, friendly and atmospheric pubs serving real ales and good pub food – the Halfway house has a particularly good reputation for food, while **The Devonport** has good views over the bay. The **Cross Keys** is in Cawsand's attractive square and serves food at lunchtime and in the evening. The **Cleave Tea Rooms** overlooking the beach near the Devonport Inn serves teas, snacks and coffees.

There is a regular bus service to Plymouth and to Cremyll from where the passenger ferry can be taken to Plymouth. In the summer, there is a ferry service between Cawsand beach and Plymouth. However, sailings tend to be irregular and depend on the weather conditions. Parking in the village can be a problem. There is a car park in the centre of Kingsand, but it can fill up in busy times and the narrow lanes are difficult to negotiate. There is a bigger car park on the edge of Cawsand from where it is only a short walk into the centre. There is a pleasant walk from Kingsand to Mount Edgcumbe House and its country park and gardens. From the centre, go up Market Street, right into Heavitree Road and then follow the signs.

Mount Edgcumbe House and Country Park

House and Earl's Garden (**01752 822236**) Open April–September, Closed Friday and Saturday, 11am–4.30pm. Admission, £4.50, children £2.25, family £10.00. Country Park and Gardens, open every day. Entry free

Mount Edgcumbe Country Park covers over 800 acres and includes Rame Head and the coastline along Whitsand Bay. The main interest of the park however is around Mount Edgumbe House. There are many walks around the park with fine views over The Sound to Plymouth and beyond. Various buildings are scattered through the park, either garden pavilions and follys or the more purposeful forts and batteries guarding Plymouth Sound. *Maker Church* on the high ground above the house commands the most panoramic of views. There are three car parks, the one beside the church is free, the one by the house and Cremyll car park by the ferry and formal gardens are pay and display. Most visitors arrive by ferry from Plymouth which lands at the northern end of the park. The journey takes just seven minutes and costs £1, children £0.50. Ferries are every half hour. The **Edgcumbe Arms** (**01752 822294**) *B* is directly opposite the ferry landing and they serve real ales and bar food. They also have accommodation in en-suite rooms if required.

The *Formal Gardens* (free entry) are located just inside the entrance from Cremyll and the ferry. They were created between the mid C18 and the early C19, although in recent years an American and New Zealand garden have also been planted. The first garden you come to on entering is the *Italian Garden* dating from the late C18. The orangery of 1760 was built to shelter orange trees brought from Constantinople and is now a restaurant and tea garden (open April to October). To the north is the newly planted *New Zealand Garden* in recognition of the family's connections with that country. The *English Garden* dates from around 1770 and was designed to look like a miniature English landscape, but not necessarily to contain English plants. The garden house dates from 1729 and would have originally been in a clearing in the C17 wilderness garden. The new garden of the 1770s was designed to use the building as a focal point. It was used as a pleasure house for the family for picnics and music and was extended in 1820 with the two wings and a room with a sunken marble bath. To the east of here is the *French Garden* from the early C19, with its formal geometric plan and low box hedges. Further towards the shore is a bowling green dating from around 1670 and a C16 blockhouse that was one of the early defensive fortifications of Plymouth Sound. It was superceded with the building of the much bigger batteries on the shoreline in 1747 and 1863.

Mount Edgcumbe House was in its day one of the most advanced house designs and considerably more 'modern' than the family's then house at Cotehele. The house was designed by *Sir Richard Edgcumbe* and built in 1547–53 to his plans by *Roger Palmer*, a Devon contractor. It has been much remodelled since, but originally its tall central hall had round battlemented towers on each corner and looked outwards across Plymouth Sound. This contrasts with the typical mid C16 manor houses which still loooked inwards to central courtyards. The house was highly regarded in its day and it is said that the Admiral leading the Spanish Armada gazed upon Edgumbe and vowed to have it for himself when England was conquered. Later alterations were made to the house, including the replacement of the round towers with octagonal ones in 1749. Disaster struck in the Second World War when the house was gutted by incendiary bombs leaving little more than the standing walls. The house was rebuilt in the 1960s and the interiors modernised yet furnished in a traditional style. The *Earls Garden* was created beside the house in the C18 and formed the private gardens for the house. The house is open to the public but there is little genuine interest in the interior which is modern reproduction.

Tamar Valley – Edgcumbe to Cothele

The lower Tamar valley is dominated by the nearby presence of Plymouth and is as near as Cornwall gets to an edge of metropolis feel. As one moves further north, the valley closes in, the river narrows and the rural landscape begins to dominate. The area is notable for its historic buildings, for this was the most accessible part of Cornwall until the railways arrived in the mid C19. Antony is perhaps the finest C18 house in Cornwall, St Germans' possesses the finest Norman work and Cothele, the finest medieval house. In these, the area has much interest, although there is little else to detain the visitor.

Antony House

National Trust (01752 812191) April to May and September to October,
Tuesday to Thursday and Bank Holiday Mondays, 1.30pm-5.30pm. June to
August, open on Sunday also. Woodland garden open March to October, daily
except Monday and Friday (open Bank Holiday Mondays), 11am-5.30pm .
Admission, £5.00, children £2.50, family £12.50, garden only £2.60, wood-
land garden £4.00

The Carews, one of the most influential families in English history, have lived
at Antony since the early C15. Nothing remains of the house of that period
other than some Tudor panelling in the hall of the present house and some
pictures and furnishings. The Carew fortunes were devastated during the Civil
War when they failed to back the right side at any time in the conflict. The
present house is the creation of one man, Sir William Carew (1689–1744) who
saw his fortunes transformed when he married the only daughter and heir of
the 4th Earl of Coventry. The date 1711 is cast in lead over the central doorway on the north front of Antony but does not relate to the building of the
house but rather to the date on which the Carew fortunes were reinvigorated.
The present house dates from around 1718 to 1724. Its architect is something
of a mystery for it is certainly a very accomplished and restrained design.
Whoever it was, has taken the classical Palladian style of the late C17 and
stripped it down to its very essentials until it is little more than a rectangular
box of two principal storeys, nine bays by five. The building is almost without
decoration. The beauty of Antony is its perfectly judged proportions and its
sensuous, silver grey Pentewan stone facing. It has long been thought that the
architect James Gibbs may have been the designer but there is no evidence to
link him to the design of the house. Gibbs's *Book of Architecture* though
does illustrate a design strikingly similar to Antony but this book was not produced until 1728, after Antony had been completed. The current consensus
seems to be that the main house was put up first by an accomplished, but as
yet unnamed architect. Subsequently, Gibbs proposed enlivening the design
by rusticating the central three bays, adding another storey and the flanking
pavilions and forecourt – the design illustrated in his book. For whatever reason, Carew only added the pavilions and forecourt in brick, a cheaper material
than stone. The result is the house you see today, with the exception of the
clumsy porte-cochere on the south front, added in the C19.

By car, the
house is sign-
posted just off
the A374 to
Plymouth, via
the ferry at
Torpoint.
There are
regular buses
from
Plymouth that
stop on the
main road to
the south.
Alternatively,
it is about a
two mile walk
or cycle ride
from the ferry
at Torpoint

The interior of the house does not quite live up to the expectations raised
by the exterior and there are disappointingly few rooms open to the public.
However, there are some good furnishings and some excellent pictures. The
house is entered via the handsome forecourt with its flanking entrance pavilions, one of which contains the Carew family museum where drawings from
Repton's Red Book improvements to the grounds are on display. They were
only partially completed. The Hall is the first room entered and it is notable
for its wooden panelling and the superb portrait of Richard Carew, painted in
1586 and one of several fine early Englsh paintings in the house. The picture
of Charles I at his Trial by *Edward Bower* (1648) has a certain resonance, for
John Carew was one of the judges at the King's trial and signed his death

warrant. At the restoration of the monarchy in 1660 he was convicted of regicide at the Old Bailey and hung, drawn and quartered at Charing Cross. In the Inner Hall there is an excellent C16 court cupboard said to have come from the original house at Antony. There is a fine staircase leading off the hall which still has the original bubble globes for candles. In the library is a damaged picture of Sir Alexander Carew by an unknown English artist (c1630) of very fine quality. Royalist members of the family slashed the painting from its frame, in anger, when the subject raised the Cornish militia for the Parliamentarians during the Civil War. He was subsequently executed by the Parliamentarians for attempting to defect to the King when he considered the fortunes of war were deserting Parliament. The picture was thereupon restored to its frame. On the upper floor there are a number of small bedrooms which give a good idea of how the C18 gentry would have lived. In the corridor, there is an excellent portait by the celebrated Victorian painter James Sant and a good C17 English picture of Sir Amyas Bampfylde.

The gardens, today, are very much in the tradition of the English parkland landscape. The more formal gardens to the north of the house were removed by *Repton* at the end of the C18 who replaced them with lawns sweeping down to the trees in the distance. There are substantial woods through which vistas were cut to open up views to the surrounding rivers. The round dovecote beside the north lawn is contemporary with the main house and is a fine example of early C18 brickwork. The woodland garden adjoins the National Trust garden but is in separate ownership. Within the garden, there are over 300 different varieties of camellias. Just to the west of the main walk north from the house, near the river, is the Bath House, built in 1789 and consisting of a plunge bath and panelled changing room. It is only open to viewing by written application to the custodian. The nearby saltpans were used to collect the salt left behind when the tide receded. In the far north east of the garden is the fishful pond, an enclosed estuarial inlet designed by *Richard Carew* and intended to act as a fish trap. There are good views across the estuary here to Saltsash and Brunel's Royal Albert bridge.

The lodge by the entrance was most probably designed by Repton as part of his remodelling of the estate. To the east of the entrance drive is a mid C19 church which has a lively interior of marble columns and red and white arches.

Torpoint has no interest for the visitor other than as a point of entry or exit from Cornwall. The vehicle ferry to Plymouth runs 24 hours a day, every 10–15 minutes (30 minutes at night). The crossing time is 10 minutes. Telephone **01752 812233**. Fares are £1.00 for cars.

The village of Antony is separate and away from the house. The church dates from the C13 and contains a fine, early memorial brass of 1420 – reputed to be one of the finest in Cornwall. On the road to St Germans, Sheviock possesses a church of some interest. It has a big, slim tower and spire, similar to

Antony

Sheviock

nearby Rame. The tower is C13 and much of the church C14 which means that it is earlier than many of the churches elsewhere in Cornwall. The south side in its exterior and interior is all C14, while the north transept was removed in the C15 and replaced with the north aisle you see today. The difference between the windows is clearly evident and a good example of the change of architectural style. In the south transept are two badly defaced stone tombs to a knight and lady, dating from around 1375. The font is plain C13 and there are many C15 carved bench ends, which have suffered varying degrees of restoration. The church was well restored by the respected Victorian architect *George Street* in 1850 and he also designed the excellent stained glass in the east window. Opposite the church is **Shevrock Barton** (**01503 230793**) *B*, an excellent bed and breakfast in a 400 year old period property.

St Germans

The church at St Germans is among the finest ecclesiastical architecture in the county and the best surviving example of Norman architecture. The church was the seat of the Saxon bishops of Cornwall and records exist since 931. However, nothing of this building survives and the building you see today dates from the C12 onwards.

The church is located in a tranquil setting just outside the village and below the road so that the tops of the towers appear at eye level as you approach. Due to this, and the fact that once you enter there are further steps down to the floor of the nave, it is only on entering that the true scale of the church is apparent. The original Norman church would have been some 55 feet longer still, the East end having collapsed in 1592. The aisles were originally narrower and with lean to roofs. The south aisle was reconstructed in the C15, while the north was demolished in the early C19. The line of the lean-to roof of the aisle can be clearly seen on the north tower.

The main interest in the church is the west end with its two towers flanking the most magnificent doorway in Cornwall. The earliest part is that between the towers, dating from before 1185. The simplicity and strength of the gable, porch and doorway is typical of early Norman work. The cross above the porch is an unusual feature not often found on Norman churches. The doorway itself consists of seven concentric arch rings with the usual Norman decoration of zig zags, vigorously and deeply carved. The composition is pure Romanesque, a style which would shortly be replaced by the new fashion for English Gothic. Five small round-headed Norman windows punctuate the otherwise blank gable end. The Norman builders seem to have progressed next with the main body of the church before returning to build the flanking towers around 1200. By then, the building style had changed considerably and the Gothic pointed arch had taken the place of the rounded Romanesque. So, the north tower has a Norman base out of which grows an octagonal tower, lit by narrow lancet windows. The tower may once have boasted a spire but there is no clear evidence remaining. The south tower has a quite different history. The base is again Norman but the tower above is much later C15 work in the Perpendicular style. Several C18 engravings show the south tower surmounted by a cupola. The base of the tower retains the only Norman stair in Cornwall. Inside, the ground floors of the towers were open to nave and aisles by arches of the transitional Norman style – simple and pointed. The capitals of the clustered shafts are a particularly good example of Romanesque decoration. Originally, the towers were connected by a gallery as the two doorways indicate but this has long been removed. The five small Norman windows in the otherwise blank west wall provide a dramatic backdrop to the interior.

In the nave, two of the early Norman bays are preserved with their thick, short circular piers and square capitals in contrast to the thinner, more finely decorated later work. On the south wall of the nave can be seen the remains of the Norman clerestorey windows with their rich zig zag decoration. Elsewhere, the interior is slightly disappointing as the proportions, while lofty and impressive, nevertheless fail to inspire. The furnishings are of relatively little interest and only the great east window needs to be picked out for special attention. Thirty feet high and sixteen feet wide, the window was designed by *Edward Burne Jones* and the work carried out by *William Morris*, two of the most influential artists of the Victorian period. The window was dedicated in 1896. The east wall of the chapel, the virtual extension of the south aisle, is probably C14 and has two windows with a decorated niche between. The south aisle of today dates from the mid C15 and replaces the earlier Norman aisle. Under the north tower is a large and elaborate memorial to *Edward Eliot* from 1722, one of the most ambitious C18 monuments in Cornwall. It was made by Rysbrack, the finest memorial artist of his time, and was probably his first commission in England after arriving from Antwerp in 1720.

The Priory buildings to the north of the church have now been lost apart from elements that have been built into the adjacent Port Eliot, the home of the Eliots of St Germans. The house is clearly visible to the north of the church but is in private ownership and not open to the public. Most of what is now visible is the work of *Sir John Soane* and dates from 1802–6. The grounds were laid out by *Repton* who carried out a number of commissions in this immediate area. There is an elaborate gatehouse on the main road. The village is pleasant enough with a number of fine granite buildings. The almshouses are particularly picturesque with their upper balcony and lower floor loggia. **Port Eliot**

Bus services to St Germans are limited, although the village does have its own railway station on the Plymouth – Penzance line. While not all the trains stop here, there are enough to make it a quite feasible way of visiting – between six and ten trains a day during the summer months.

The area between here and Saltash is one of narrow lanes, shallow creeks and isolated buildings. There are few settlements of any size and little of interest for the visitor. Footpaths are strictly limited and it is a difficult area to negotiate with many of the narrow lanes ending abruptly at the edge of a creek. *Trematon Castle*, just to the west of Saltash, is one of the major fortifications in Cornwall with a strategic location perched high on a bluff overlooking the river. However, the castle is in private ownership and there is no **Saltash** access to the site nor any clear views of it from the area around. Saltash is the main gateway to Cornwall for both train and car. The magnificent railway bridge was built by *Brunel* in 1857–9 and in its time was at the forefront of known technology. It is a combined suspension and arched bridge and, while by no means beautiful, the clear expression of is structure and the forces at work give the whole a pleasing solidity. The most dramatic viewpoint is from the riverside in Saltash where the true scale of the massive piers can be appreciated as they tower over the houses of the town. The adjacent road bridge was built only as recently as 1961, the first road crossing of the lower Tamar in history. Located directly under the piers of the railway bridge, the **Union Inn** can hardly be missed with its Union Jack painted front. It was decorated to commemorate the 50th anniversary of the D-Day landings. Since then a local artist has added a mural to one of the side walls showing many historic figures associated with the town, including Sir Francis Drake. There is little else to interest the visitor and most quickly move on to elsewhere in the county.

Cothele

National Trust (01579 351346). House open April to October, daily except Fridays (open Good Friday), 11am–5pm (4.30pm in October). Admission, £7.40, children £3.70, family £18.50. Garden open daily all year, 10.30am to dusk. Mill open as house, but daily in July and August, 1pm–5.30pm (6pm in July and August, 4.30pm in October). Admission to garden and mill, £4.40, children £2.20, family £11.00. The number of visitors to the house is limited to 80 at one time so at busy times a queuing system operates. Also, as there is no electric light, dull days early or late in the season should be avoided if possible

Cothele is located one mile east of Calstock and accessed down narrow lanes signposted off the main A390 and A388. There is ample parking on the site. By public transport, it is easiest to take the train or bus (from Tavistock) to Calstock from where it is a 45 minute walk to the house. The train ride from Plymouth up the Tamar valley is one of the most scenic in Cornwall and highly recommended. Between mid-June and the end of September, a ferry runs from Calstock to Cothele, leaving hourly depending on the state of the tides. Phone 01822 833331 to confirm times of sailings.

Cothele is the most extensive, best preserved and most important Tudor house in Cornwall. It is sited high on a bluff overlooking the River Tamar, far removed from any other development. The present house was built largely between 1485 and 1539 by the Edgcumbe family but there has been a house on the site since at least the late C12. The house is built to an early medieval plan, inward looking and grouped arond three courtyards. The manor was semi-fortified with only small windows and narrow entrances piercing the exterior walls. While this plan had long been dispensed with in other parts of the country, Cornwall was still a relatively lawless place in the C15 and C16 with several rebellions and other minor disturbances. A wise and wealthy landowner would still build with defence in mind.

The extraordinary state of preservation of Cothele is inextricably linked to the fortunes of the Edgcumbe family who owned the estate from 1353 to

1947, when it passed to the National Trust. The present house was begun by *Sir Richard Edgcumbe* after being handsomely rewarded for his loyalty to Henry Tudor at the Battle of Bosworth. His son *Sir Piers* completed the work and further increased the family's wealth by marrying into the Durnford family in 1493. His wife brought with her the lands around Plymouth and it was here in 1533 their son, *Richard Edgcumbe*, began to build the new house at Mount Edgcumbe which was to become the main family residence. Cothele was further improved around 1620 with the addition of the north tower and later in the mid century but otherwise was left undisturbed and unmodernised. By the late C18, there is evidence that Cothele was already being appreciated for its antiquarian qualities and boat parties were brought up from Plymouth to be shown around the house. The east range was remodelled in 1862 for the widow of the third Earl but this was done with great sensitivity which was unusual for the period and suggests a more than academic interest in maintaining the historic authenticity of the house.

As you approach the house you come across the south range which is the south wall of the original house from the late C13 or early C14. Sir Richard Edgcumbe added the castellated gatehouse with its Gothic door. To the left of the south range is the retainer's court or servant's quarters. The chapel of Sir Richard projects into this space with its bellcote and decorative finials. The doorway to the main court here is probably the original entrance. There is a porter's squint to allow those outside to be seen before opening the gate. A video of the history of the house is shown in the building by the south range. The hall court, the first courtyard you come to, is the main space within the house with all the major rooms grouped around it. In the north west corner the big, Perpendicular window of the chapel and the Tudor windows of the solar almost collide, for these are clearly two different periods of building. The chapel by Sir Richard and the solar and hall by his son, Sir Piers.

The hall is entered directly from the courtyard rather than via a screens passage which is a very unusual arrangement. The hall is comparatively small but is nevertheless one of the most impressive and evocative interiors in the county. The present hall is very similar to how it would have looked in the Late Middle Ages with the walls hung with arms and armour ready for use in times of alarm. The roof is relatively old fashioned for its time with massive truncated beams carried on a network of smaller timbers and wind braces giving a complicated interlace of timber across the ceiling. The upper or dais end is lit by the large window with the late C15 heraldic panes of the window emblazoned with the families into which the Edgcumbe's married. Opposite is a large fireplace, so that the Lord of the Manor was well served by light and heat.

The old dining room would have been added in the early C16 as Sir Piers' private parlour. Communal eating in the hall was already in decline by this time. The first of the many tapestries in the house are on display in this room. They are Flemish and date from around 1700. They cover virtually every inch of the walls and have been cut and rejoined to act more as wall coverings than works of art. The chapel leads off this room and is one of the most atmospheric rooms in the house. It dates from the late C15 and is part of Sir

Richard's building. The roof is barrel vaulted with the Tudor rose at the inter-
sections and the carved oak screen is contemporary with the building. The
tracery and cresting are later additions. There are three squints into the
chapel to allow those outside to see in, two on the south side and one from
the upper room on the north side. The stained glass in the south window is
from the early C16. The floor retains some of its medieval tiles, the green and
white tiles are C19. The clock in the south west corner is of exceptional interest and was installed by Sir Richard when he built the chapel between 1485
and 1489. It is the earliest domestic clock in England, unaltered and in its original position. The clock has no face but tolls a striking bell on the hour. It is
still in working order and in use when the house is open.

The punch room, again lined with tapestries, leads through to the base of the
tower which was added in 1620. The white room, so named after its furnishings
is the only one in the house to have a decorative ceiling, added some time after
the tower was built. On the lower landing is an excellent late C16 cabinet with
intricate carving. The red room and the adjoining south room were originally
one space with an arched roof similar to that in the hall. It is now concealed
behind a later ceiling. It falls into the familiar pattern of West Country houses
with large chambers on their upper floors, such as at Lanhydrock and Trerice.
This would have been the private quarters of Sir Piers with its views down into
the hall and chapel and its big, south facing window. The old drawing room on
the middle floor of the tower has a solid oak door sporting Tudor roses. Inside,
there is a particularly fine and intricately carved cabinet in walnut veneer that
dates from around 1600. On the top floor of the tower are two further bedrooms, one of which is known as King Charles' room, on the belief that Charles
I slept here in September 1644 on his way from Liskeard to Exeter. The small
kitchen courtyard separates the kitchen and larders from the hall and living
quarters. The kitchen is notable for its height which was designed to allow
smells and smoke to exit via louvred vents, now gone. The oven and hearth are
of the size necessary to cook for a household of this size. In a room off the
lobby are displayed pictures of the house executed in 1839 by *Nicholas Coody*,
a Plymouth artist. It is interesting to note how little has changed since that time.

The great barn outside the south range was built between 1485–9 with
massive stone walls and simple open truss roof. It is now a tea shop & restaurant. The gardens at Cothele are relatively modest and reflect the secondary
nature of the place as a residence. In their present form they date from the
mid C19 when the formal terraces to the east of the house were established.
There are magnificent views from the terrace towards Calstock and its viaduct.

**Cotehele
Estate**

**Cotehele
Quay**

The 1300 acre Cotehele Estate is also owned and managed by the National
Trust and has a number of sites worth seeing as well as many fine woodland
walks. Cotehele Quay is located at the foot of the driveway to the house. It is
one of many such quays that line the banks of the Tamar for until recently the
river was the only practical way of moving bulky goods. The growth of mining
and market gardening in the C19 led to a boom in activity on the river and the
quays were busy trading ports. There is a small maritime museum (open

11am–5pm) with an excellent introduction to the quay's history and shipping on the Tamar. The ruined limekiln behind the museum is one of many in the valley that burned lime, imported from Plymouth, for use as fertilizer on the acid rich soils around about. The Tamar sailing barge *Shamrock* built in 1899 is often moored at the quay and is typical of the boats used to haul cargoes up and down the river. The **Edgcumbe Arms** (open 11am–5pm) serves teas and lunches and the *Cotehele Quay Gallery* (open 12–5pm) occupy converted buildings on the quayside. There is a large car park and toilet facilities.

Cotehele Mill (open 1pm–5.30pm) is approached along a footpath from the bridge by the quay. There has been a mill on the estate since early medieval times and this building dates from the C18. The mill has been extensively restored and is open to visitors. If you walk beyond the mill you will enter Elbow Wood which has a series of paths along the side of the valley. To the north of the quay is Cotehele Wood, a mature woodland on the steep slope above the River Tamar. In spring, the floor is carpeted with daffodils, primroses, bluebells and other early flowers. Just to the east of the house you will see the *chapel in the wood*, a simple stone chapel supposedly from the late C15 but subsequently restored in the C17 and C18. It is meant to mark the spot where Sir Richard Edgcumbe outwitted his pursuer, Sir Henry Trenowth of Bodrugan, and his men by casting his hat into the river weighted with a stone while he hid nearby. His pursuers thinking him drowned left Cotehele.The postscript to this tale, and a good indication of how fortunes could change in those times is that once Henry VII came to the throne he rewarded Edgcumbe for his support by giving him all Trenowth's estates and ordered the arrest of Trenowth himself. Edgcumbe pursued Trenowth to the cliffs near Mevagissey where he himself was ouwitted by Trenowth jumping off the cliff to a waiting boat. The site of this escapade is now known as Bodrugan's Leap. Just beyond here, there is a viewpoint with marvellous views of the river and Calsock viaduct. From here the path either heads back to Calstock or heads up the secluded Danescombe Valley. The valley was a major mining centre during the C19 when it was the richest copper and arsenic producing centre in England. Many of the ruined mine buildings can still be seen in the valley. The valley was also a major centre for fruit and flower growing which surprisingly co-existed with the mining operations for some time. There is still some market gardening carried on and the remains of the old terraces and walls can be seen amongst the trees.

Calstock, just to the north, is a small town and now something of a backwater, but convenient as a base for visiting Cothele. The area has a long history of habitation and it was the fertile and sheltered nature of the Tamar valley along with the surrounding mineral wealth that led to the development of the area. Mining in the area had existed before Roman times but it only really became a major force in the 1790s with the extraction of copper, tin, arsenic, tungsten and silver. The river became the means of transport for the ore and for supplies to service the mines and their labour force. By the 1860s more than 7000 people were employed in the mines of the Tamar valley. The chimneys and ruined engine houses still dot the landscape. As the mining

Cotehele Mill

Elbow Wood
Cotehele Wood

Danescombe Valley

Calstock

waned, horticulture came to the fore and many early season crops were grown here in the sheltered valleys and sent by rail to London and the Midlands. The magnificent viaduct, built in 1907, was part of the Tamar valley railway line. It has 12 sixty foot span arches and towers nearly 120 feet above the water. It was an early example of building with concrete blocks and still dominates the town and its river frontage. There are good views of it from the quay and riverside. Elsewhere, the village is of narrow lanes and pretty cottages.

There are a number of shops and the **Tamar Inn** has an excellent selection of real ales and serves food, lunchtimes and evenings. **The Riverside** is a pleasant cafe with a terrace overlooking the river and the viaduct. If you need to stay overnight, and you might if you are to spend any time at Cothele, then accommodation is available at **Homepark** in Eric Road (**01822 832523**) **B**. There is a regular bus service to Tavistock and Callington, but far better still is the Tamar valley railway line, one of the most scenic branch lines in the country. There are regular trains throughout the day and the 14 mile route skirts the edge of the beautiful Tamar valley from Plymouth through Calstock and terminates at Gunnislake just to the north. On summer Sundays, special bus links allow visits to Cothele and other sites of interest in the valley. Telephone **01392 382800** (Monday to Friday) for further information. If you decide not to take the bus, it is an easy and attractive walk to Cothele, simply follow the road along the river in a westerly direction and then follow the footpath until you see the signs for the house. It is about a 45 minute walk. There is also a passenger ferry from Calstock Quay to Cothele Quay in the summer months – see above for details. If driving, there is a public car park in the centre of the village by the quay. Parking elsewhere is limited.

Gunnislake

Gunnislake is dramatically sited on steep cliffs over the Tamar river. Like Calstock, it was a major mining centre in the C19. The *New Bridge* was built in 1520 and is the best of all Cornish medieval bridges. Until the 1960s, this was the lowest land crossing point on the Tamar. The bridge and the surrounding scene was captured by *Turner* in his painting *Crossing the Brook* which he painted in 1815 when visiting Cornwall. The railway station, the terminus of the branch line, is inconveniently located some 20 minutes walk from the village centre. There are shops and a number of pubs including the **Tavistock Hotel** (**01822 832217**) **B** and the **Cornish Inn** (**01822 834040**) **B** which also both provide accommodation if required.

Liskeard

Some miles to the west and just south of Bodmin Moor is Liskeard, one of the larger towns in the area and something of a public transport hub. There are regular buses to Launceston, Tavistock, Plymouth, Bodmin and St Austell. The main line railway station is on the southern edge of the town with a separate station nearby for the branch line to Looe. The town has a good range of shops catering for most needs, and there is some pleasant Regency and Victorian architecture around the tightly packed town centre. The church is the second largest in Cornwall but has little of interest, having been badly restored during the C19. All in all, there is little to detain the visitor as there are few sites of any merit and nor is it that conveniently located for the surrounding area which has many better and more attractive places to stay.

Index